LABOR AND THE LEFT

LABOR AND THE LEFT
A Study of Socialist and Radical Influences in the American Labor Movement, 1881–1924

JOHN H. M. LASLETT

BASIC BOOKS, Inc., Publishers • New York • London

FOR MY MOTHER
AND IN MEMORY OF
MY FATHER

©1970 by Basic Books, Inc.

Library of Congress Catalog Card Number: 78–110774

SBN 465–03742–9

Manufactured in the United States of America

PREFACE

For help at various stages during the preparation of this manuscript I should like to thank the George W. Ochs-Oakes Senior Scholarship Fund, the Department of History at Northwestern University, the British Association for American Studies, and the Provost and Fellows of The Queen's College, Oxford, without whose financial support the study would not have been written. I am also grateful for the advice of my research supervisor, Dr. Henry Pelling, now of Cambridge University, and for a Willett Award from the College of the University of Chicago in 1965.

Numerous trade-unions, research libraries, and other institutions gave me their help during the course of my research. I should like to acknowledge, in particular, the facilities extended to me by the Wisconsin State Historical Society, the Midwest Inter-Library Center, the AFL-CIO, the Tamiment Institute, the Library of Congress, the New York Public Library, the Illinois State Historical Society, and the U.S. Department of Labor. Manuscript collections and labor newspapers were also consulted at Duke University, Wayne State University, the University of Michigan, the University of Louisville, the University of Colorado, the University of Illinois Historical Survey, and the Catholic University of America. In addition, my thanks go to the International Ladies Garment Workers Union, the Boot and Shoe Workers Union, the International Association of Machinists, and the United Mine Workers of America for permitting me to make use of their libraries and archives.

v

Various friends and colleagues at the University of Chicago and elsewhere read portions of the manuscript and gave me the benefit of their advice. Among them were Joel Seidman, Herbert Gutman, Melvyn Dubofsky, Henry Bedford, Mark Perlman, Nuala McGann Drescher, Lee Cary, Grant McConnell, David Greenstone, Arthur Mann, and Fred Jaher.

My greatest debt is to my wife, whose patience during the writing of this manuscript was greater than I deserved.

It should be added that the manuscript was completed in the summer of 1968 but could not be published until 1970.

JOHN H. M. LASLETT

CONTENTS

LABOR AND THE LEFT

1

Introduction

I

In recent years a number of detailed studies have been written about American socialism and trade-unionism, considered as separate entities. But less attention, except in very general terms, has been paid to the relationship between them. This is despite the acknowledged importance of a successful socialist, trade-union alliance in the formation of mass, revolutionary political parties.

Where historians have examined the role of socialists in the American labor movement, moreover, they have confined themselves very largely to the mutual antagonism which developed between the national leadership of the AFL, on the one hand, and the leaders of the Socialist Labor party, the Socialist party, and the various Farmer-Labor parties, on the other. For example, they have concentrated their attention on the failure of the Socialist Labor party to secure indirect representation in the AFL convention of 1890, which was denied on the ground that no political party could legitimately be part of a national labor federation. They have described the defeat of Thomas J. Morgan's Political Program of 1894, which came near to success and included, in its celebrated Plank Ten, a declaration for collective ownership of the means of production and distribution. This defeat embittered many socialists and was largely responsible for the growth of dual unionist tendencies under the leadership of Daniel DeLeon and for the establishment of the Socialist Trades and Labor Alliance as a rival to the AFL in 1895. They have examined the bitter antagonism which the socialists displayed toward the National Civic Federation, which was established in 1900 by representatives of both business and labor in an attempt to diminish the frequency of industrial disputes. Or they have described the mutual hostility which developed between the AFL and the IWW after its founding in 1905; the 1912 defeat of Max Hayes as socialist candidate for the AFL presidency; and the failure of the post-World War I labor-party movement in 1919.[1]

Alternatively, labor historians have analyzed the institutional role and ideological outlook of the national labor leaders themselves, as a way of explaining the relative weakness of socialism in the American labor movement. On the trade-union side, they have concentrated particular attention on the personality of Samuel Gompers, who was president of the AFL almost uninterruptedly between 1886 and 1924 and opposed both socialism and third-party politics in the labor movement almost from the first. Among the socialists, they have examined the dogmatic Marxism of De-Leon, who led the Socialist Labor party between 1891 and 1914; the conservative opportunism of Victor Berger, who was leader of the socialist movement in Wisconsin; and the cautious parliamentarianism of Morris Hillquit, the most important socialist leader in New York. Save for a few outstanding exceptions such as Eugene Debs, they have argued, most of the socialist leaders were immigrants from continental Europe who brought over with them an unwanted ideology and were unable to operate effectively in the pluralistic framework of American politics.[2]

Virtually all previous analysis of radicalism and third-party politics in the American labor movement has been of this type. It is true, for example, of Philip Taft's double-volume history of the AFL, of David Shannon's *Socialist Party of America,* of Marc Karson's *American Labor Unions and Politics, 1900–1918,* of Philip Foner's multivolume history of the labor movement, and of Gerald N. Grob's *Workers and Utopia, A Study of Ideological Conflict in the American Labor Movement, 1865–1900.* It is also true of more general works such as Selig Perlman's *A Theory of the Labor Movement,* published in 1928, and of Daniel Bell's essay *Marxian Socialism in the United States,* which was republished in book form in 1967.

II

The views of these national leaders were important, both in themselves and in shaping the opinions of the labor movement as a whole. But they do not provide sufficient evidence on which to base a general theory of the American labor movement, as they have been employed to do. It is the major contention of this book that the primary explanation for the rise and fall of socialist and radical influences in the American labor movement is to be found, not in the ideological character and internal organization of the labor movement, or in the immigrant nature of its leadership, but in a variety of political, technological, and economic factors which affected American society during the period under review. Immigrants played an important role in the attempted radicalization of the labor movement. But indigenous causes, deriving in part from economic and political developments, and in part from the native tradition of American reform, exerted a much greater influence than is usually supposed.

The evidence on which this view is based is drawn from a carefully selected sample of six labor organizations which included a large proportion of the socialists and third-party advocates in the labor movement during the period under review. It includes unions which were both craft and industrial in their structure; immigrant, native-born, or mixed in their ethnic composition; and located in the East, the West, and the Midwest, and also in the South. It therefore reflects the differing ethnic, structural, geographical, and other attributes which characterized the American labor movement at this time.

The first labor organization to be examined is the Brewery Workers Union, a Marxist industrial union composed largely of German immigrants with its center of gravity in Wisconsin, Ohio, and the Midwest. Next comes the Boot and Shoe Workers Union, a New England craft union made up primarily of native-born or second-generation Irish and English workers. This is followed by chapters on the International Ladies Garment Workers Union, a New York based movement composed largely of Russians, Italians, and eastern European Jews; the International Association of Machinists, originally a southern union and dominated by native-born Americans and by immigrants of long standing; and the United Mine Workers of America, a broadly based industrial trade-union composed in part of Slavs and Italians, but controlled either by native-born workers or by immigrants from Great Britain. The final union considered in the sample is the Western Federation of Miners, the metal miners' union of the Mountain West, which remained outside the AFL for much of this period and constituted the major initial source of support for the Industrial Workers of the World.[3]

Not all these labor organizations were controlled nationally by the socialists or disposed in favor of third-party politics throughout the whole period under review. In the United Mine Workers of America, for example, the socialists were influential only in certain districts of the organization, and in the Boot and Shoe Workers only for a short period of time.

But a major part of the interest in studying these unions, as in the case of others, has been to try to explain the reason for the limited degree of control.

Nor does the available evidence permit as detailed an analysis of rank-and-file opinion in the labor movement as had been hoped. With some exceptions, manuscript collections, union publications, and the labor press have devoted themselves to preserving the opinions of the leaders of the labor movement, rather than those of the union rank and file. Moreover, in the cases of the ILGWU and of the Western Federation of Miners, a number of excellent studies of socialist influence have already been written, making it necessary to use previously published accounts, supplemented wherever possible by new materials. But it was important to include these unions in the study, in order to compare the position of the socialists in them with their role in other unions. I believe the sample provides a more reliable basis on which to generalize than the opinions of the national leaders of the AFL and the Socialist party alone.

III

The dates chosen for this study are not intended to be exclusive. There was some degree of socialist influence in the American labor movement before 1881. Similarly there was, of course, a major resurgence of radicalism in the labor movement of the 1930's. In fact, it can be argued that it was only then that the American labor movement acquired both the maturity and the numbers to enable it to sustain an independent political party of its own. Nevertheless, it is also apparent that it was during the period covered by this study that the socialists achieved their greatest degree of penetration in the labor movement, both in the AFL and in American society generally, even though the labor movement was relatively small at this time and dominated by conservative craft unions. It is illuminating to compare this situation with that in Great Britain or in Germany, where mass industrial unionism had already begun to develop in the last decades of the nineteenth century, providing the widespread numerical base which alone could sustain an independent labor party. This development did not occur in the United States until some forty years later, by which time it can be argued that the trade-union movement was so heavily committed to the Democratic party that it was too late to make any significant difference.

Nor is a rigid definition intended in the use of the word "socialist." By this is meant, not Marxism alone, or the more indigenous form of social democracy represented by Eugene Debs and the Socialist Party of America, but a broad range of political ideologies ranging from a Populistic form of evolutionary socialism on the right to DeLeonite impossibilism and Communism on the left. Where relevant, jurisdictional disputes and other internal union matters have also been examined, insofar as they helped substantially to reinforce existing radical opposition to the conservative political and economic policies of the AFL and to increase sympathy and support for more revolutionary forms of trade-unionism, such as the Socialist Trades and Labor Alliance or the Industrial Workers of the World. In addition, an attempt has been made to include the full range of issues on which the socialists and their opponents in the labor movement held differing opinions, including industrial unionism, immigration, welfare legislation, and the Negro question, as well as political action itself.

This broad definition of radicalism also makes it possible to take into account the impact of World War I on the American labor movement and the brief resurgence of third-party activism which took place after it. By this time the Socialist Party of America had been split into mutually antagonistic Communist and socialist factions, and the political effectiveness of the party had virtually been destroyed. Nevertheless, it is clear that many of the same issues which had been the concern of socialists before the war —industrial unionism, labor legislation, antagonism toward trustification and corruption in industry, and a broad range of political and economic reforms—were taken over almost intact by the socialists, Farmer-Labor parties, and progressives who made up the radical coalition supporting the election of Senator Robert La Follette in 1924. That year was also the only Presidential election in American history in which the AFL came out openly for a third-party candidate.

In nearly every election since that time, despite public protestations of nonpartisanship, labor's commitment to the Democratic party has increased. Only in very recent years has it shown any signs of serious dissatisfaction with its Democratic allies. Whether this will lead to the breakup of the coalition on which the Democratic party has been organized since the 1930's remains to be seen. But in whatever direction labor moves, it is highly unlikely to turn again toward third-party political action on a national scale.

Notes

1. For the failure of the SLP to secure representation in the AFL, the defeat of the Morgan Program, and the establishment of the ST & LA, see Gerald N. Grob, *Workers and Utopia, A Study of Ideological Conflict in the American*

Labor Movement, 1865–1900 (Evanston, 1961), 172–186; Philip S. Foner, *History of the Labor Movement in the United States,* 4 vols. (New York, 1947–1965), II, 279–294; David Saposs, *Left Wing Unionism, A Study of Radical Policies and Tactics* (New York, 1926), 21–28; and Philip Taft, *The A.F. of L. in the Time of Gompers* (New York, 1957), 67–74, 149–150. For debates over the National Civic Federation, antagonism between the iww and the afl, and the failure of the postwar labor-party movement, see Marguerite Green, *The National Civic Federation and the American Labor Movement, 1900–1925* (Washington, 1956), 133–189; Paul F. Brissenden, *The IWW, A Study of American Syndicalism* (New York, 1919), 65–66, 83–110; Nathan Fine, *Labor and Farmer Parties in the United States, 1828–1928* (New York, 1961), 248–260; and Harry B. Sell, "The A.F. of L. and the Labor Party Movement of 1918–1920" (M.A. Thesis, University of Chicago, 1922), 95–117.

2. For Gompers, see Taft, *op. cit.,* 38–59, *passim;* Bernard Mandel, "Gompers and Business Unionism, 1873–1890," *Business History Review,* XXVII (September, 1954), 241–269; Louis S. Reed, *The Labor Philosophy of Samuel Gompers* (New York, 1930), 55–73; and Samuel Gompers, *Seventy Years of Life and Labor,* 2 vols. (New York, 1925), I, 69–105, 188–204, 381–427. For Daniel DeLeon, Victor Berger, and Morris Hillquit, see David Herreshoff, *American Disciples of Marx, from the Age of Jackson to the Progressive Era* (Detroit, 1967), 106–172; Howard H. Quint, *The Forging of American Socialism, Origins of the Modern Movement* (New York, 1953), 142–174; Ira Kipnis, *The American Socialist Movement, 1897–1912* (New York, 1952), 117–119, 375–389 ff.; David Shannon, *The Socialist Party of America, A History* (New York, 1955), 10–13, 21–23 ff.; and James Weinstein, *The Decline of Socialism in America, 1912–1925* (New York, 1967), 22, 75, 79 ff. See also Robert W. Iverson, "Morris Hillquit, American Social Democrat" (Ph.D. Thesis, University of Iowa, 1951); and Edward J. Muzik, "Victor Berger, A Biography" (Ph.D. Thesis, Northwestern University, 1960). There are numerous biographies of Debs, the best one being by Ray Ginger, *The Bending Cross: A Biography of Eugene Victor Debs* (New Brunswick, 1949).

3. These unions were not, of course, the only socialist-oriented organizations in the labor movement at this time. But taken together they cast from one-third to one-half of the total socialist and radical vote in afl conventions between 1890 and 1920. See *Proceedings, Tenth Annual Convention of the A.F. of L.* (Detroit, 1890), 24–26; *Proceedings, Fourteenth Annual Convention of the A.F. of L.* (Denver, 1894), 36–42; *Proceedings, Twenty-second Annual Convention of the A.F. of L.* (New Orleans, 1902), 183–184; *Proceedings, Thirty-second Annual Convention of the A.F. of L.* (Rochester, 1912), 374–375; *Proceedings, Fortieth Annual Convention of the A.F. of L.* (Montreal, 1920), 419–420.

2

Marxist Socialism and the German Brewery Workers of the Midwest

Artisans and intellectuals from Germany had more influence than any other immigrant group in the establishment and early growth of the American socialist movement. The theoretical literature of socialism, from the *Communist Manifesto* of 1848 to the outbreak of World War I, was largely written in German, and the German Social Democratic party, founded in 1875, was by far the largest and most influential socialist party in Europe. This gave German radicals a unique position of authority in the American socialist movement—a position which was further enhanced in the period after 1878 when Bismarck's unavailing efforts to crush the Social Democratic party brought a further wave of German political refugees to the United States.

Skilled workers from Germany also provided the backbone of organization in printing, cigar making, and other American trades. In the 1880's, when German immigration reached its peak, there were German labor federations in New York, Philadelphia, and several other cities, and in 1887 plans were made for the establishment of a National Federation of German trade-unions. These did not materialize, but German influence in the AFL was sufficiently strong that it was not until the AFL convention of 1890 that Gompers felt free to refuse a point of order made in the German language.[1]

Many of these German unions, save for minorities, became conservative

9

early in their careers, partly because of the relatively rapid assimilation of German immigrants into the community generally, and partly because of disillusionment with the dual unionist tactics of the Socialist Labor party.[2] But others, such as the Bakers, the Furniture Workers, and the Brewery Workers Union, remained socialist for many years. Of these the National Union of Brewers,[3] organized in Baltimore in 1886, but with its greatest strength in Ohio, Wisconsin, and the Midwest, was one of the largest and most important. Marxist in orientation, it began as a craft union, but was one of the first to adopt industrial methods of organization. In the early years it played a crucial role in the ideological disputes over the relationship between trade-unionism and the American socialist movement, and it was equally important in the debates over industrial unionism in the AFL. The decline of socialism in its ranks provides the most interesting example of the displacement of a European political ideology by pressure-group tactics of a characteristically American kind.

I

Although the Brewery Workers Union was not established until 1886, there had been numerous previous attempts to organize the brewery workmen. The first report of such efforts was in 1850, when an attempt was made to establish an "association," according to the ideas of the German Forty-eighter Wilhelm Weitling, in St. Louis.[4] The first brewery union proper was established in Cincinnati in 1879. But it was in New York, as with so many other labor organizations, that the first real trade-union was born. In 1881 the New York *Volkszeitung,* the German organ of the SLP, drew attention to the bad working conditions in the city breweries, and a union was established embracing the workers in Brooklyn and Newark as well as in New York City itself. In June 1881 a strike took place for the twelve-hour day, supported by both the socialists and the New York Central Labor Union. But the unorganized beer-wagon drivers took the places of the brewery workers, and the strike was lost, its leaders being blacklisted for their pains.[5]

After this, brewery workers in New York and all over the country began to join the Knights of Labor, which was now the dominant national labor federation. They were attracted by the generally more radical program of the Knights, with its declarations for a cooperative system to replace the existing capitalist structure, and also by its efforts to enroll all the elements in the labor force irrespective of their trade, which provided a broader basis for the enforcement of the union's boycotts against non-union beer than did the narrower constituency of the AFL. This was an important matter, since beer was largely a workingman's drink, and boycotts against saloons which sold nonunion beer were the union's most powerful weapon. In 1884 many New York breweries were organized under the auspices of the Knights, and for a period in the 1890's the Brewery Workers Union, like the United Mine Workers of America, had a national affiliation with both the AFL and the Knights of Labor, as National Trade District 35.

But this arrangement did not last long. Much of the AFL was hostile to the Knights of Labor, and the 1894 AFL convention refused to endorse the Brewery Workers' label as long as it remained affiliated to the Knights. The Brewery Workers themselves were also put off by the utopian character of the Knights' radicalism, which was non-Marxist and Populistic in its appeal, and by its willingness to support reform and Democratic candidates in elections. In addition, it did not consider the class solidarity of the Knights to be sufficiently thoroughgoing. In a strike of coal shovelers in the New York area, for instance, Brewery Workers Local No. 1 (the largest local in the union) left the Knights of Labor because its District Assembly 49 refused to order the engineers and firemen, who worked with the coal shovelers, out on strike also. Finally, the rapid decline of the Knights after 1886 diminished its ability to support the union's activities, and the Brewery Workers disapproved strongly of the support which Grand Master Powderly and other elements of the Knights gave to the temperance movement. Thus, when the 1896 AFL convention urged the Brewery Workers Union to leave the Knights or lose its AFL charter, the union agreed to do so.[6]

This break did not appear to hurt the Brewery Workers Union. It was now growing rapidly, and by 1903, after a further long struggle for recognition in New York, it was firmly established on a national basis, with headquarters in Cincinnati, and over 30,000 members in New York, St. Louis, Milwaukee, Philadelphia, Chicago, and other major beer-brewing centers. The Germans were good trade-union organizers, and the union was, for the most part, a well-knit and disciplined organization. By this date its contracts with the brewery owners had already succeeded in reducing hours and raising wage levels in many breweries.[7]

It is possible to discern some of the sources, and part of the character, of the Brewery Workers' socialism in this brief account of the union's early career. The attempt in 1850 to establish an "association" under the influence of Weitling indicates that there was cooperation between the German socialists and the brewery unions even from pre-Civil War days. The interest in the Knights of Labor and the attempt to secure the broadest possible support for the union's boycotts indicate a predisposition in favor of industrial rather than craft unionism. And in the AFL's threat to withdraw the Brewery Workers' charter in 1896 may be found the seeds of a conflict which was to make the union one of the leaders of dissent against the AFL's leadership, on both industrial and political grounds.

Each of these elements will be explored further. But first it should be noticed that low wages, excessively long hours, and brutal treatment were independent causes of radicalism in the early years. Germans dominated the industry, among both the brewery owners and the employees. But this did not appear to make the owners solicitous of their employees' welfare, any more—as we shall see later—than it did among the Jewish contractors in the garment industry of New York. Down to 1880 a working day of fourteen to eighteen hours was not uncommon, with six to eight hours on Sunday. Beatings of employees were frequent, and the techniques of brewing and fermentation meant that much of the work was done at night. As late as 1886 a report from St. Louis said that working hours were "from two or three o'clock in the morning until seven or eight o'clock at night, and sometimes even longer." The consequent exhaustion led to the heavy drinking of beer, which was sometimes given to the workers as part of their wages or as an inducement to work for less in cash. In addition, when the breweries were small many employees boarded with the employers, often sleeping all together in one large room. Sometimes the workers were so tired that they simply threw themselves down on the hop sacks in the brewery for the few hours before work began again. Consumption, heavy drinking, and hard work meant that many employees died before they were fifty.[8]

In the 1860's wages were as low as $20 to $25 a month, which was considerably less than the average manufacturing wage at this time. With the rapid growth of the industry and the replacement of small breweries by large, steam-driven establishments, wages rose to $40 or $55 a month. But many brewery workers now lived in boardinghouses, under the control of brewery foremen, and a considerable amount of their wages was deducted for living expenses, leaving an average cash wage of between $5 and $10 a week. Moreover, the development of large-scale breweries made it more difficult for the worker to become a brewery owner himself, as a number had done in the early days, and the increasing use of machinery displaced many of the more experienced workers and led to a dilution of skill. In his presidential address to the convention of the United States Brewers Association in 1885, for example, H. B. Scharmann asserted that members of the association were "particularly solicitous of the welfare of the men who work for us, as we worked for others then, twenty or thirty years before." This suggests a considerable degree of economic mobility in the industry in the period immediately after the Civil War. But the introduction of refrigeration, homogenization, and other expensive technical processes greatly increased the capital outlay required to become an independent brewer and made it more difficult for the individual worker to aspire to ownership.[9]

It is instructive to compare these conditions with those of the brewery workers in Germany. Wages were appreciably higher in the United States, but there were complaints that the exploitation of labor was no less, because many brewery owners came from the more backward areas of southern Germany where hours and conditions were at their worst. One immigrant brewer, reminiscing in 1901, complained that "in the social life the American brewery was just as much, if not more, depressed and disregarded as in South Germany." [10]

Industrial unionism, characterized by a desire to organize all the workers in the industry into a single union on ideological as well as pragmatic grounds, was a second major source of radicalism among the Brewery Workers. In fact, it has been called "the oldest of the true industrial unions within the A.F. of L." When first organized in 1886 the Brewery Workers Union included only those who actually mixed the malt and hops and attended to the fermentation process. But these men were a minority in the industry. The others performed tasks which could well have enrolled them in some other labor organization. Thus the Brewery Workers Union was more of an artificial creation than most other unions, and it depended for its very survival on the organization of groups of workers (coopers, engineers, firemen, and teamsters) who were not brewery workers as such, but were integral to the work of the brewery.

This encouraged the growth of class rather than job consciousness as the basis for organized action, and it made the Brewery Workers more tenacious in their advocacy of industrial methods of organization than almost any other trade-union body. "If the [beer] drivers, the coopers, the engineers, the firemen, the maltsters, had helped us," said the national secretary in 1887, reporting on a recent strike, "our victory would have been assured within twenty-four hours. . . . Not only are the brewers dependent upon these branches; no, each one is dependent upon the others. Solidarity, man for man from roof to cellar, all for each and each for all—this alone can secure our future." As a result, at the convention of that year the name of the organization was changed to National Union of United Brewery Workmen of the United States (instead of National Union of Brewers), and the organization was extended to include beer drivers, brewery engineers, firemen, and maltsters.[11]

The industrial structure of the Brewery Workers Union did not mean that there was no concern for skill among the members. The mechanization of the industry, like that of many traditional crafts, made it vulnerable to the introduction of unskilled labor, and there was sometimes a conflict between a desire to protect the position of the trained brewery workers (as opposed to the beer drivers and the like) and the equalitarian element in the union's socialist philosophy which required it to organize all elements in the trade, including the unskilled, on equal terms.[12] The union adopted a policy of seeking uniform wages for all those working in the brewery, on the ground that wage differentials were "reactionary" and that they created in the trained brewers an unwarranted sense of superiority over the bottlers, or washhouse men. But on several occasions concern was expressed about the need to improve the apprenticeship system so as to protect the trained brewers, while attempting to avoid the invidious distinctions on grounds of skill which this seemed to imply. "Although we harbor no craft pride," the national secretaries reported to the 1906 convention, "still we must call your attention to the danger accompanying the filling of these positions [vacancies in the large-scale breweries] with men that do not know the ABC of the brewing industry." [13] This was to be a perennial problem for socialists in an achievement-oriented society, and it may have been one of the important reasons why the Socialist party generally failed to make any significant inroads into the skilled sections of the American working class.

But the German connection was the principal source of socialism in the Brewery Workers Union. Most German immigrants to the United States, even those that had come for reasons of religious or political persecution, were fairly rapidly absorbed into the existing body politic, and many of the employers in the brewing industry, a number of whom had been Forty-eighters themselves, disapproved strongly of the socialism of their employees. Nevertheless, ex-Forty-eighters and other socialists of German origin (notably victims of Bismarck's Anti-Socialist Laws), dominated both the leadership and the rank-and-file membership of the Brewery Workers Union throughout the entire period under review. Louis Herbrand, the first national secretary, was a socialist immigrant who returned to Germany in 1888. Ernest Kurzenknabe and Charles Bechtold, national secretaries between 1888 and 1899, were both German socialists. And so were Julius Zorn, editor of the *Brauer-Zeitung* for many years until his death in 1926, Joseph Proebstle, a national secretary between 1903 and 1922 (there were three secretaries between these dates), and Adam Hübner, national secretary from 1904 to 1924. In fact, one of the few national leaders in this period who was not from Germany was Louis Kemper, born in New York City and secretary between 1902 and 1914. But he was the son of a Forty-eighter and a committed socialist also. Besides this, Germans dominated the International Executive Board for many years.[14]

In addition to German control of the union leadership, the Brewery Workers Union had agreements with the brewery workers' organizations in

Germany, Austria, and Switzerland which permitted immigrant members from these organizations to join the American union without paying an initiation fee. Thus, workers from these three countries continued to reinforce the immigrant and socialist character of much of the rank and file. As late as 1912, for example, well after the decline of major German immigration to the United States, it was reported that seventy-two "comrades" from the German Brewery Workers Union and seventeen from the Austrian organization had joined the union in the previous year. The union constitution included a clause requiring every member to become an American citizen "in order to assist in the social and political reform of our adopted fatherland"; and it was made clear from the first that the purpose of this was to encourage members to vote socialist * in state and federal elections. Some locals fined their members for failure to become citizens, and in 1898, when the member of a St. Louis local union protested at being fined for this reason, the *Brauer-Zeitung* commended the local's action, adding that locals "must insist that their members secure their nationalization papers and fulfill their duties as class conscious soldiers of the grand army of the . . . Social Democratic labor movement." [15]

Although Germans provided the leadership in the Brewery Workers Union and dominated most of its locals until after World War I—a breakdown of local officers by nationality in 1919 shows that of 381 locals, 227 had German secretaries [16]—they were not the only ethnic group in the industry. Germans controlled the lager beer industry, but among the ale and porter workers and later throughout the union as a whole, Irish and native-born members constituted a strong and increasing minority. Predictably, the Irish were much more skeptical about the socialist orientation of the union than the German members were. A number of delegates from Irish locals, particularly from Massachusetts and elsewhere in New England where the English-speaking brewery workers were in a majority, were later to vote against endorsing socialism at union conventions. But the German-Irish differentiation was not wholly a socialist-nonsocialist one. In 1901 and 1904 a number of Irish delegates voted for socialist resolutions at union conventions, and a number of Germans against; and at least some of the Irish were as radical as the Germans, although for somewhat different reasons. For example, Edmund F. Ward, of Boston, a member of the International Executive Board, returning in 1905 from a visit to his native Dublin, reported that the Irish battle for freedom against the absentee English landlords was as fierce as ever, and called it part of the international struggle against capitalism.[17]

* The word is not capitalized generally in this book because (as here) the distinction between philosophical concept and political party is not always clear cut.

II

Bad conditions and low wages, the decline of the brewery workers' craft, industrial unionism, and the German character of much of the labor force were thus the main determinants of the Brewery Workers' socialism. Its chief characteristic, within the broad ideological spectrum of American socialism as a whole, was a commitment to the fundamental principles of Marxism. The Preamble to the union's constitution, which was retained in the same form as late as 1926, contained a classical analysis of capitalism on Marxist lines. Society was divided into two antagonistic classes, the Preamble asserted, on the one side the "possessing class" and on the other the workers, "who possessed nothing but their mental and physical labor power." The position of the working class, made increasingly large by the emasculation of the petite bourgeoisie, was becoming steadily worse. "Its consuming power becomes less and less, it is able to buy a smaller part of the goods produced, the stock accumulates, production is restricted and partly stopped. The crisis is here." Faced with this revolutionary prospect, it was the workers' duty to organize themselves "locally, nationally, and internationally" into trade-unions and to undertake independent working-class political action. "The emancipation of the working class," the Preamble concluded, "can take place only when the economic and political movement go hand in hand." [18]

These principles were frequently commended to the union membership for study and reflection and were taken much more seriously than they were in most other socialist labor organizations. In addition, the international aspects of Marxism were clearly attractive to a union which had such strong ties with Europe. In fact, the Brewery Workers Union took a more intense interest in developments in the European labor movement than almost any other American union. It sent delegates to international socialist congresses and received European trade-union leaders in return.[19] The columns of the *Brauer-Zeitung* were filled with news of the activities of German socialist leaders, such as Liebknecht, Bebel, and Kautsky, and they provided detailed and admiring accounts of the rapid increase in the number of Social Democrats in the German Reichstag. There was news of other European countries, too, ranging from historical reminiscences of the Paris Commune to fervent support for the Russian revolution of 1905—for which several union locals collected money. There was even an advertisement in the union journal for Robert Blatchford's *Merrie England* (a popular English pamphlet on socialism) in German translation! Throughout, the purpose was not simply to maintain ethnic ties: it was also to exhort American workers to follow the European example. "Among our Comrades in Germany great enthusiasm prevails," the union journal commented on the Reichstag elections of 1898, which should bring heart to progressive wage workers in America. "The time will come when similar victories of Socialism can be reported from the American continent." [20]

Concern for working-class solidarity was also expressed in other ways. The Brewery Workers Union exchanged greetings with other American socialist and progressive organizations, and in 1905 it sent a considerable contribution to the Moyer-Haywood-Pettibone Defense Fund. In 1906 Secretaries Kemper and Proebstle supported a Socialist party request to the AFL for a mass meeting of all labor organizations to protest the denial of habeas corpus to these three men and expressed their irritation to President Gompers when the request was turned down.[21]

The equalitarian ideology of the union was also manifested by a determination, on the part of the leadership at least, to organize the Negro brewery workers, of which there were quite a number among the beer drivers, and by opposition to AFL support for restriction of immigration. In January 1901 the union administration thanked Negroes in Virginia for their help in boycotting a nonunion brewery in Alexandria, expressing the hope that this would induce more narrow-minded trade-unionists "as adherents of the broad trades union movement, still more as socialists, to stop . . . debarring the Negroes from membership." And later, discussing the "yellow peril," the union journal held that it was inconsistent with socialist principles to restrict Asiatic immigration, still less that from Europe. Restriction laws were in any event ineffective, the journal argued, since businessmen found means to evade them. The solution was not to restrict oriental immigration, but to educate and organize the Asiatics, making them into allies against capitalism. "Race prejudice should cut no figure in the endeavor to uplift the oriental proletarian." On both the Negro and the immigration issues the Brewery Workers Union showed greater ideological consistency than the Socialist party itself.[22]

The emphasis laid by Marx on the educational role of trade-unions was also upheld by the Brewery Workers Union. The union regarded itself, and was regarded by others, as a leading disseminator of socialist propaganda in the AFL. It considered one of its major responsibilities to be to educate the ignorant, apathetic American proletariat into a true understanding of the nature of capitalism, which could be secured only by reading socialist literature and the socialist press. In 1903 William E. Trautmann, editor of the *Brauer-Zeitung* and later to become a leader of the IWW, urged the Irish- and English-speaking members of the union to purchase "the best socialist works from which to secure more knowledge on the theories of socialism," and successive editors repeatedly stressed the educational value of the union journal. At the 1912 convention there was a complaint from more conservative members that the *Brauer-Zeitung* gave too much attention to "political and sociological" problems and too little to trade-union activities. But the editor defended the journal's editorial policy, saying that the journal "must first of all consider the requirements of the advanced members, those we have to depend upon for further progress." [23]

Finally, there was a recognizably Marxist element in the anti-Catholic attitudes which were often expressed in the *Brauer-Zeitung*. In Germany the dominant free or socialist trade-unions (Gewerkschaften) were separated from and in some respects antagonistic to the Christian or largely Catholic unions (Christliche Gewerkvereine). The American Brewery Workers Union naturally identified itself with the free socialist trade-unions, and the German freethinking and anticlerical tradition was reproduced in the political outlook of the organization. The journal editor frequently criticized the Catholic church in America for its hostility toward socialism. He attacked Catholic workingmen's organizations such as the Militia of Christ, saying that they should have "no place in the progressive labor movement." And despite the large Irish element in the union, he informed his numerous Roman Catholic readers that the chief end of religion was "to perpetuate the hell upon earth which capitalism has brought into existence." [24]

In its more specifically political policies, the Brewery Workers Union began by shunning all reform movements which were not wholly socialist. It called Populism a "capitalist middle class fake reform." Instead, in the early 1890's it gave its full and undivided support to the Socialist Labor party. The union's leaders were intimately involved with the work of the party,[25] and each of the early conventions of the union, up to and including that of 1896, endorsed the organization.[26] In fact, for as long as orthodox Marxists were in control of the SLP, there seemed no reason why the alliance between the union and the party should not continue. But once DeLeon became powerful and began to move the SLP away from its earlier position of support for existing trade-unions, the Brewery Workers became increasingly uneasy. Finally, after considerable heart-searching, it broke with the SLP and endorsed the Social Democrats and then the Socialist Party of America instead. In fact, as the largest and most influential union directly committed to the SLP in the 1890's, the Brewery Workers played an important role in the revolt against DeLeonism and in the return of the socialist movement to a position of general support for the existing trade-union movement and the AFL.

The disaffection of the Brewery Workers Union from the SLP began with a variety of complex party and trade-union maneuvers in New York. The Brewery Workers' locals there had been among the founding members of the socialist Central Labor Federation of New York. But the union leadership in St. Louis was skeptical of the Central Labor Federation's attempt to secure indirect representation for the SLP at the 1890 AFL convention (although the union's delegate did vote in favor of the proposal); [27] and the union in general was sympathetic toward the establishment of a third central trade-union body, the New York Federation of Labor, which was set up in August 1891 by socialist unions which had left the Central Labor Federation because of its increasingly hostile attitude toward the AFL. By this time, however, DeLeon was firmly in control of the Central Labor Federation, and in November 1891 Brewers' Local I (the largest in the union) was expelled from it because of the local's sympathetic attitudes toward the AFL. What was worse, the Central Labor Federation organized a dual brewery workers' union in New York, attracting into it several Brewery Workers Union locals, and in December 1891 the Central Labor Federation discontinued support for the union's boycott against the non-union breweries of the New York Brewers Pool. National Secretary Kurzenknabe was even expelled from the SLP because of his refusal to follow DeLeon's lead. [28]

In view of this, it was perhaps surprising that the Brewery Workers Union should have remained such a consistent supporter of the SLP for so long. But in Germany, from which so many of the union members came, socialist traditions of party loyalty were strong, and the union leadership, from its vantage point in the Midwest where the orthodox Marxist element in the SLP was in control, believed that DeLeonism was only a passing phase. Nevertheless, when DeLeon stepped up his attacks on the union, alleging in the party organ *The People* that Kurzenknabe and other union leaders were "sodden with alcoholism" and denouncing the organization as a "pure and simple" trade-union because of its efforts to avoid strikes and its substantial financial reserves, the administration became increasingly concerned. In England, and even in Germany, conservative trade-union economic policy was not considered to be inconsistent with revolutionary trade-unionism. So in the February 1896 issue of the *Brauer-Zeitung* National Secretaries Bechtold and Kurzenknabe issued a statement rebuking DeLeon as an "upstart intellectual" who had no business instructing the party membership in matters of socialist theory. The Brewery Workers Union, they said, had always been committed to socialism, while at the same time maintaining friendly relations with other unions and with the Knights of Labor, which were not yet "as far advanced in their ideas as the leading members of our organization and the Socialist movement at large." Attempts by trade-unions to secure limited gains by means of strikes and boycotts, upon which DeLeon poured such scorn, were necessary and could not be forgone. They well knew the limits of such action, the secretaries concluded, but it was essential, as Marx had himself acknowledged, "to prevent the further degradation of the working people even under the capitalist system." [29]

The establishment of the Socialist Trades and Labor Alliance in December 1895 was the last straw for the Brewery Workers Union. In January 1896 the ST & LA set out to organize the brewery workers into rival trade-unions, despite the protests of socialists in New York and elsewhere who well knew the importance to the socialist cause of the union's support. Several locals, notably Local 69 in Brooklyn and Local 2 in Newark, as well as locals in New York and in other cities, were induced to join the ST & LA for a time. Under the leadership of Ernest Boehm (who had earlier been a member of the union), the ST & LA repudiated the union's boycott against New York Pool Beer. As a result the International Executive Board denounced the ST & LA and threatened to expel any local unions which joined it. It also took an active part in supporting midwestern opposition to DeLeon. Local 6 was influential in the anti-DeLeonite wing of the St. Louis section of the SLP, and the union in general praised G. A. Hoehn, one of the leading figures in the anti-DeLeon insurgency, for resigning from the party and for coordinating the opposition of the German socialists. The September 1896 convention of the Brewery Workers Union adopted a resolution condemning the "policy of destruction" followed by the ST & LA and demanded that the SLP put a stop to it. [30]

But this appeal had no effect, and relations between the Brewery Workers and the SLP continued to deteriorate. In January 1897 Bechtold deplored the serious effects which the establishment of the ST & LA had had on the position of the socialists at the 1896 convention of the AFL, urging socialists to act independently of the SLP instead of allowing "incapable party leaders to mislead them." The ST & LA responded at its own convention, held in July 1897, by reaffirming its determination to organize dual brewery workers' locals. So at its tenth convention, held in Boston in September 1897, the Brewery Workers formally withdrew its support of the SLP and endorsed Debs' Social Democracy of America instead. [31]

It was a measure of the ideological fervor of the Brewery Workers Union, at this stage in its career, that it should have transferred allegiance so readily from the SLP to the Social Democracy of America, even though the Social Democracy was in many respects less congenial to it than the SLP and was even less significant on the national political scene. The *Brauer-Zeitung* was skeptical about the reform and Populist elements which joined the Social Democracy of America and highly critical of its plans to establish a cooperative colony. For the Brewery Workers this represented a reversion to the unscientific utopian socialism of pre-Civil War days, which was, in Marxist terms, a deplorable anachronism. [32] But the union was heartened by an article of Debs in the *New Times* early in

1897 relegating the colonization scheme to a subsidiary role in the Social Democracy, and it was even more encouraged by the rapid accretion to the new organization of ex-SLP affiliates from New York and the Midwest, including the group of German socialists under Victor Berger and G. A. Hoehn. With these additions, the union hoped that the Social Democracy would become "the organization that the Socialist Labor Party should have developed into," namely, "a true Social Democratic Labor party." [33]

The Brewery Workers Union certainly did its best to make it so. It fully supported the trade-union element which sought to turn the Social Democracy into a regular political party, and it welcomed unreservedly the split which occurred at the convention of June 1898, when the ex-SLP element broke with the colonizers and established the Social Democratic party. After this the brewery workers did their best to reestablish unity in the socialist movement, and while publicly supporting the Social Democratic party they used their influence behind the scenes to work for a single, united party which would adopt a more positive attitude to the trade-unions than the SLP had done. They wholeheartedly endorsed the joint Debs-Harriman presidential ticket in 1900, both with money and with a considerable number of votes, in Milwaukee, New York, St. Louis, and elsewhere; and when the Socialist Party of America was finally established in 1901 the union was jubilant. "Comrades," the *Brauer-Zeitung* said, "cheer with us the new united party, become recruits and enlist others." The 1901 convention endorsed the Socialist party platform, with only a small minority of delegates voting against, and for the next decade or more the union became one of the Socialist party's most loyal and enthusiastic supporters.[34]

Throughout the 1890's, the Brewery Workers Union had made it clear that it was unwilling to support the establishment of a revolutionary trade-union organization which would be a rival of the existing trade-union movement, despite the political and economic conservatism of the AFL. This was an important reason for the failure of the DeLeonites generally, who looked to the Germans for support. And it was important also for the socialists who remained in the AFL, who counted on the brewery workers in their efforts to promote socialism within the federation. This did not mean that the union was an uncritical supporter of the AFL. It expressed strong disappointment at the rejection of Thomas J. Morgan's Political Program in 1894, and later on it was highly critical of the AFL's support for the National Civic Federation.[35]

But at the turn of the century a major jurisdictional dispute arose between the Brewery Workers Union on the one hand and the Coopers, Firemen, Engineers, and Teamsters unions on the other, which led to the revocation of the union's charter for a brief period in 1907 and 1908 and tempted some of its members to seek an alliance with revolutionary and

syndicalist elements outside of the AFL. This was a matter of great importance for the future of the radical element in the labor movement in general, for the Brewery Workers Union was one of the largest and most powerful socialist unions in the AFL, and had it left the AFL and joined the IWW
or some comparable organization it might well have tempted other
organizations to do so, a development which would have had a significant
impact on the distribution of forces in the labor movement as a whole.[36]

The dispute with the Firemen and Engineers unions, which claimed jurisdiction over the firemen and engineers organized by the Brewery Workers Union, was the most serious, and for a time it appeared as though it
might be settled by compromise. The 1900 AFL convention adopted a resolution stating that engineers and firemen working in the breweries were
normally to be organized by the Engineers and Firemen unions, but that
those wishing to remain in the Brewery Workers Union might do so. However, this did not satisfy the Brewery Workers, who were determined to retain control over all the workers who were employed in the breweries,
whatever their particular skill. In April 1902 the Executive Council of the
AFL requested the Brewery Workers to revoke all charters issued to locals
of engineers and firemen, asserting that all of these workers must now join
their respective craft organizations.[37] This decision was denounced as
"infamous" by the national secretaries of the Brewery Workers Union,
who accused the AFL of discriminating against the union simply because it
was socialist and because it was organized on industrial lines. A special
union convention was called in February 1903 to consider the matter, and
it was decided that the engineers and firemen should be given up only if all
the other AFL unions which included these categories of workers also relinquished theirs. The question of whether the Brewery Workers should
be forced to acquiesce soon became one of the touchstones of the socialist
versus conservative debate throughout the labor movement as a whole. The
United Mine Workers took the part of the Brewery Workers against the
AFL administration. So did much of the socialist press, and so also did the
radical western labor federation, the American Labor Union.[38]

The support of the American Labor Union was a matter of considerable
importance, for it was this organization, along with the Western Federation of Miners and the ST & LA, which was to form the nucleus of the IWW
in 1905. Although it disapproved of dual unionism, the Brewery Workers
had allowed a number of its locals in Colorado, Nebraska, Washington,
and Montana to affiliate with the American Labor Union, both because it
sympathized with the socialist and industrial orientation of this organization and because the influence of the AFL west of the Mississippi was at this
time quite small. Thus in June 1902, when Gompers wrote to the union asking it to withdraw its locals from the American Labor Union because of the

ALU's hostility toward the AFL, the Brewery Workers Union refused to comply and William E. Trautmann, editor of the *Brauer-Zeitung,* launched a sharp attack on the AFL over a whole range of issues. He denounced it for its political conservatism, for its support for the National Civic Federation, and for its hostility toward industrial unionism, as well as for its attempts to coerce the union in its jurisdictional dispute with the Engineers and Firemen.[39]

Events now moved forward to a crisis. The November 1903 AFL convention reiterated the demand that the Brewery Workers Union give up its engineers and firemen, this time threatening expulsion if the union failed to do so. As a result, numerous Socialist party members and industrial unionists throughout the country urged the Brewery Workers to join hands with the western labor movement and leave the AFL altogether.

For a brief time the leaders of the Brewery Workers appeared to hesitate. Representatives of the American Labor Union appeared at both the 1903 and 1904 conventions of the Brewery Workers Union, urging it to join the revolutionary organization, and when the AFL failed to discipline the United Mine Workers for refusing to give up *its* engineers and firemen, the belief intensified that the AFL was deliberately trying to destroy the Brewery Workers Union because of its known socialist proclivities. In June 1904 Joseph Proebstle, usually a moderate, denounced the AFL with almost DeLeonite ferocity, urging the membership not to heed the "attacks from the East," but to stand firm in their solidarity with their "western brothers."

In fact, however, there was never any strong likelihood that the Brewery Workers would join the American Labor Union, if only because the ALU was too small and ineffective to become a plausible alternative to the AFL. In April 1904 the International Executive Board issued a statement deploring the continued hostility of the AFL toward the Brewery Workers, asserting that a thoroughgoing reorganization of the AFL was necessary on socialist lines, but stating that there was no question of the union's voluntarily leaving the federation. It also requested Trautmann, as editor of the *Brauer-Zeitung,* to moderate his attacks on the federation.[40]

The establishment of the IWW in June 1905 was a different matter, however. The IWW was much larger than the American Labor Union, with a much broader basis of support, and although the International Executive Board of the Brewery Workers Union refused an invitation to send an official representative to the founding convention, Milwaukee Local 9, one of the largest and most influential locals in the organization, did send one. William E. Trautmann, moreover, angered by the attempt which had been made by the Executive to discipline him, had taken the lead in calling the secret conference in Chicago on January 2, 1905, which laid the groundwork for the IWW. He argued that the attempts of the socialists to "bore from within" the AFL had proved futile and that they should be "supplanted by other methods." [41]

For this Trautmann was dismissed as editor of the *Brauer-Zeitung* by the International Executive Board. But his opinions were evidently popular among the union's membership, for in a referendum vote appealing against the decision of the Board he received 10,801 votes to 11,960 in favor of the decision. Trautmann argued that the vote against him was rigged, that it was the result of AFL pressure, and that it did not truly represent the wishes of the rank and file. Nevertheless the expulsion stood, and thereafter Trautmann devoted his energies to building up the IWW.[42]

This did not solve the jurisdictional crisis in the Brewery Workers Union, however. Throughout 1905 and 1906 the AFL made further attempts to mediate the dispute, and after these failed it repeated its threat to expel the Brewery Workers if it would not give up its engineers and firemen. A referendum vote of the membership refused point-blank to do so, a few even welcoming the prospect of expulsion on the ground that the AFL charter was not worth having if the union had to face "uncalled-for interference from the Civic-Federation-Carnegie element, and see treason committed constantly." So at the end of May 1907, the union's charter was revoked (despite Gompers' personal opposition),[43] and its locals were automatically expelled from the AFL's central bodies all over the country.[44]

It might seem that now would be the time when the greatest pressure would be exerted on the Brewery Workers Union to join the IWW, and efforts along these lines were certainly made. Resolutions from locals in Denver and in Butte, Montana, had been presented to the 1906 convention urging the union to disaffiliate from the AFL and join the IWW, and Max Hayes, writing in the *International Socialist Review,* said that "the rank and file [of the Brewery Workers] in many parts of the country are clamoring to cut loose from the Federation and join the Industrialists." [45] But by now the moment had passed. The Brewery Workers were unwilling to cooperate with the DeLeonite ST & LA (which had now entered the IWW), and the splitting of the IWW and the withdrawal of the Western Federation of Miners in 1907 meant that it lacked any substantial element of trade-union support. Moreover, the partially syndicalist and antipolitical character of the IWW was repugnant to the Marxist philosophy of the Brewery Workers membership. The *Brauer-Zeitung* frequently carried articles and excerpts from the socialist press criticizing sabotage and syndicalism as "retrogressive." [46]

But perhaps the most important reason for the refusal of the Brewery Workers Union to leave the AFL and help in the establishment of a new, revolutionary trade-union federation was the fact that it simply could not afford the all-out conflict with the AFL which joining the IWW would have entailed. The union was heavily dependent on the support which organized workingmen gave to its union label and to the boycotts which it attempted to enforce against nonunion beer. Had it left the AFL for the IWW, the Brewery Workers Union would have forfeited organized labor's support in both of these areas, besides risking the establishment of a new union by the AFL, which would have received its official support. Moreover, the union needed the cooperation of the Firemen, Engineers, Teamsters, and other AFL unions in order to maintain its bargaining position vis-à-vis the employers, and only if these unions had come over en masse to the IWW, which they showed no sign of doing, would membership in the IWW have brought any meaningful advantages.

Thus the Brewery Workers Union decisively rejected the IWW's efforts to secure its allegiance, and it refused to cooperate with the Western Federation of Miners in an attempt to resuscitate the organization late in 1907. This was a not insignificant factor in the decline of the IWW throughout the labor movement as a whole. Instead, the Union devoted its efforts to gaining readmittance to the AFL, which it succeeded in doing in principle at the November 1907 convention of the federation. The IWW not unnaturally opposed these moves, alleging that the sole motive of the Brewery Workers in rejoining the AFL was to preserve its own jurisdiction intact and that it intended to abandon the cause of revolutionary trade-unionism altogether. The union ignored these attacks, and after long and complicated negotiations a compromise jurisdictional settlement was reached with both the Engineers and Firemen unions and ultimately with the Teamsters Union also.[47]

The restoration of the Brewery Workers Union charter by the AFL in 1908 did not mean that the organization had abandoned its general commitment to socialist ideology. It was still regarded, and with reason, as one of the leaders of socialism in the AFL. "We are convinced," wrote a midwestern socialist newspaper soon after the union's return to the AFL, "that . . . hundreds and thousands of trade unionists . . . are ready to accept your policy in the economic and political class struggle." But it now contented itself, like most other socialist trade-unions, with efforts to reform the AFL from within. At the 1914 convention a resolution was presented urging the Brewery Workers Union to leave the AFL and join the IWW "in consideration [of the fact] that the American Federation of Labor is not the organization which intercedes fully and entirely for the emancipation of the proletariat." It was heavily defeated.[48]

Nevertheless, the union remained highly criticial of the AFL's association with the National Civic Federation, and it praised the United Mine Workers for their repudiation of it in 1908. It also strongly opposed the AFL's nonpartisan political tactics. Like other radical elements in the labor movement, it initially welcomed the March 1906 AFL Bill of Grievances (the series of legislative demands which Gompers and the Executive Council sent to President Theodore Roosevelt and to both houses of Congress) in the hope that it would lead the AFL into supporting an independent labor party. It should be remembered, the *Brauer-Zeitung* commented in August 1906 (dissociating itself from the more "extreme comrades" in the Socialist party, who saw no significance in the move), that the German Social Democratic party and the English Labor party had grown out of similar humble origins. But the journal was soon disillusioned by the "reward your friends, punish your enemies" tactics which the AFL pursued in the 1906 fall elections, accusing it of hypocrisy for having kept politics out of the unions for so long because they created dissension, and then opening the unions up to "political swindlers" of both the major parties. And it was even more critical when the AFL sent delegations to the 1908 Republican and Democratic conventions, claiming after the 1908 presidential election that these pressure-group tactics had been wholly unsuccessful, and reproaching Gompers in particular for his allegations that Debs' "Red Special" campaign train had been financed by business interests.[49]

From the point of view of general working-class solidarity, however, the Brewery Workers professed to find encouragement in some, at least, of the other developments in the AFL. It had regarded the Scranton Declaration of 1901, which had enabled the United Mine Workers to organize all the workers in the mines, irrespective of their craft, as having very little significance, asserting that both industrial unionists and the "strict trade autonomy party" could place their own interpretations on it. But it welcomed the establishment of the Building Trades and other AFL industrial departments in 1908 and 1909 as a step toward genuine industrial unionism. Secretary Proebstle regretted the fact that the main purpose of these departments was to coordinate the activities of the separate craft unions rather than to amalgamate them into larger industrial units. But he believed that "by forming these departments the principle of consolidation and concentration of power is being recognized, which will finally lead to full realization of the necessity of industrial organization." Here, as in many other areas, the union was influenced in its views by the example of European trade-unions. The Brewery Workers in Switzerland (with which the American union had strong ties) had recently been organized into the Swiss Culinary Trades Organization. Similar efforts were being made in Germany, and in January 1908 Proebstle suggested the establishment of a new industrial department in the AFL along the same lines, to include brewery workers, farmers, restaurant and saloon keepers, butchers, bakers, and all other workers concerned in the production of food and drink. Nothing came of the suggestion, however.[50]

In addition, the union took a strong interest in the prolonged negotiations which took place for amalgamation between the Western Federation of Miners and the United Mine Workers, which also had considerable significance for the socialists in the AFL. In fact, because of the United Mine Workers' large size and the radical character of much of its membership, the Brewery Workers' leaders regarded this as one of the best prospects for a radical transformation of the AFL and used it as a means of placating the small radical element on the extreme left of their own union, which still regretted the fact that the Brewery Workers had rejoined the AFL, rather than allying itself with the IWW. Welcoming the Western Federation of Miners into the AFL in May 1911, the *Brauer-Zeitung* wholeheartedly endorsed a declaration in the *Miners' Magazine* that the Western Federation of Miners could do more for the cause of socialism inside the AFL than out. "The subdivision of the A.F. of L. with departments controlling all crafts in certain industry," the journal added, "is all that any true industrial unionist can desire at present." [51]

Outside of the AFL, the Brewery Workers continued their official commitment to the principles of socialism and Socialist Party of America. Examples of cooperation between the party and the union were manifold. In 1902 Leon Greenbaum, national secretary of the Socialist party, had issued a circular to all party members urging them to support the union's boycotts, and in return nearly all the union conventions from 1903 through 1914 endorsed the socialist platform, or even the party itself. Considerable sums were donated to the party's funds. At the convention of 1912, for example, $1,000 was given for Debs' campaign fund, and the three national secretaries of the union urged the membership to vote socialist in a formula which, in one way or another, had been used at most of the union conventions ever since the 1880's. "Support the candidate of the party that represents the working class, regardless of his chance of being elected," Proebstle, Kemper, and Hübner urged. "Do it as a matter of protest against the existing wrongs perpetrated in favor of a small minority . . . against the majority of the people. Let the workingmen of this country awaken to the point of class-consciousness, and both old capitalistic parties will fall over each other to make concessions to the working class, which all the begging and lobbying in Washington will not bring in a thousand years." [52]

At the local level, unions all over the country gave money to socialist campaigns. Party speakers were invited to local meetings, and union members attended socialist rallies, picnics, and lectures and ran for office on the Socialist party ticket. Close relations were maintained in New York, Philadelphia, and other cities, but they continued to be exceptionally strong in the Midwest, notably in Ohio, Missouri, and Wisconsin. Julius Zorn attended the 1904 Socialist party convention as a state delegate from Ohio, and members of Local 77 in Indianapolis, Locals 66 and 187 in St. Louis (especially in the Tenth Congressional District, where most of the brewery workers lived), Local 175 in Cincinnati (especially in the Nineteenth Ward), and locals in Columbus and other midwestern cities gave strong support to the party. However, it was in Milwaukee, famous for its German beer and its socialism alike, that the Brewery Workers played their most important role. The local executive board in that city required members to subscribe to either the German *Vorwaerts* or the *Social Democratic Herald,* and it did much to help make Milwaukee the first major American city to go socialist. In 1904 two of the nine socialist aldermen elected were members of the union, and brewery workers helped elect Emil Seidel mayor in 1910. They were also behind the election of Victor Berger as the first socialist congressman in that same year. The *Brauer-Zeitung* hailed Berger as the "congressman-at-large for the entire American working class," and his subsequent career in Congress was followed with interest and pride.[53]

III

All of this confirms the fact that in the period before World War I the leaders of the Brewery Workers Union, and much of the membership also, gave strong political support to the Socialist party, especially in the radical enclaves of the great midwestern beer-brewing cities where the socialists had a strong hold over the union and where the large size of the German-speaking communities slowed down the processes of Americanization.[54] But this support was by no means universal throughout the union, and even before 1917 there were indications that despite the rising socialist vote, rank-and-file opposition from various quarters to the socialist policies of the leadership had begun to grow.

In part this opposition arose out of increasing irritation at the constant pressure which the administration exerted on the membership to vote for the Socialist party. Traditional German respect for authority, expressed in the assumption that all members should live up to the socialist principles enunciated in the Preamble to the union's constitution, conflicted with the view held by most American trade-unionists that the disposition of one's vote, like one's religious beliefs, was a private matter over which the union as such should have no control. There was another aspect to this question of compulsion also. The successful use of the boycott against nonunion beer often enabled the union to require brewery owners to establish a union shop as a condition of signing a contract. This forced many brewery workers into the union on a compulsory rather than a voluntary basis, and some of these workers objected to the socialist policies of a union which they had had no part in formulating. It is also likely, although there is little documentary evidence on this point, that some of the new groups of workers who joined the union as its jurisdiction expanded—yeast workers, vinegar, alcohol, wine, cider, and mineral water workers—were different both in their ethnic origins and in their political outlook from the original German element which had founded the union in 1886. It was probably toward this group of workers that a resolution was directed (although not passed) at the convention of 1914, urging that lecture courses be established in the winter months for those members who paid insufficient attention to the "political question." [55]

Another important factor was the opposition which came from the growing Irish element in the union. Although technically Germans dominated the leadership, both local and national, until well after World War I, the number of Germans and other continental brewery workers who emigrated to the United States fell off rapidly after 1900, as conditions in Europe improved. This diminished the number of German immigrants among the union rank and file and increased the proportion of Irish and other members. The Irish had less experience in trade-unionism than the industrious and well-organized Germans, but by this time they were a powerful factor in other areas of the labor movement, and in the Brewery Workers Union they resented the prolonged German control. At the 1912 union convention, for example, C. M. McCarthy, an Irish delegate from St. Paul, Minnesota, urged that the German-sponsored constitutional provision requiring members to take out their citizenship papers be repealed and that the convention pass a resolution specifying that members should vote "according to the dictates of your own conscience." This resolution was rejected, but it engendered a considerable amount of heat, with Isidor Rathgeber, of Detroit, accusing McCarthy, and indeed all the Irish in the union, of anti-German prejudice and of wanting union members to vote Democratic instead of socialist simply out of party loyalty, without giving thought to the importance of issues in politics at all.[56]

Some of the native-born members of the union, of which there were now an increasing number, also expressed disapproval of the union's commitment to the Socialist party. In November 1911 a Missouri member complained at the frequent articles on socialism which appeared in the *Brauer-Zeitung.* He had, he said, like all the other members of his local, been born and raised in America. He voted Democratic and would continue to do so, whatever the journal might say. Socialism might be all right "for the lower classes . . . but not for us that are above the common herd. If there is a socialist at our local he must be among the laborers." The editor took public issue with this letter, and so did a number of German rank-and-file members, deprecating the sense of class differentiation which it appeared to betray and asserting that the union's successes on the economic field had lulled the Missouri member into a false sense of security.[57]

This latter point was important. After it finally overcame the opposition of the New York Brewers Pool in the early 1900's, the Brewery Workers Union made rapid progress in reducing hours, securing wage increases, and improving conditions of work; and there is evidence to suggest that this began to undermine the political radicalism of at least some of the members at quite an early date. By 1901, for example, the nine-hour day had been established in many breweries (a dramatic reduction from the twelve hours and more of the 1880's), and in November of that year the union journal warned members not to be misled into believing that there was no longer any need for revolutionary political change. This was of particular importance in the case of German immigrant brewery workers, who had earlier provided the basic support for the union's socialist policies. Conditions were improving in the German breweries in the early years of the new century, but they were improving even more rapidly in America than they were in Germany, and by 1910 recently arrived immigrant brewery workers, in particular, were finding a marked increase in their standard of living.[58]

In the prewar period none of these influences—German-Irish antipathies, differences between the immigrant leadership and the native-born members, or rising wages—were strong enough to overcome the deeply entrenched socialist traditions of the union; and at the December 1917 convention of the union, more than six months after the Socialist party had declared its opposition to the war, the Brewery Workers reaffirmed their support for the principles of the party. But, taken together, these changes had slowly begun to erode the revolutionary fervor of the membership; in fact, they were already sufficiently noticeable in 1911 (the twenty-fifth anniversary of the union's founding) to elicit the regrets of old Julius Zorn, who had been active in brewery workers' organizations since 1879. The present strong economic position of the union, Zorn wrote in an anniversary article, had brought about "a certain indifference" on the part of the younger generation of members, who did not remember the hard struggles of the union in its early days and tended to rest on the laurels won for them by the older leaders. Such of the older generation as were still in the union, Zorn said, "must agitate among the younger element, must keep alive the memory of hardships and struggle of times gone by, and in this way teach the younger generation that if they want to keep what they have and want to achieve further success, they must fight on until the final aim of the working class, emancipation from wage slavery, is obtained." [59] Although Zorn's remarks reflected nostalgia and the generation gap which had developed between the older leadership and the new members, as well as other factors, it is legitimate to see in them suggestions of concern for a declining interest in the ideals of socialism also.

Two further developments began to affect the political outlook of the Brewery Workers Union in the years before World War I. One was increasing cooperation between organized labor and the Democratic party, which affected the Brewery Workers just as it did the AFL as a whole. The other was the growth of the Prohibition movement. The union leadership had opposed the support which many of the Irish ale and porter workers had given to the Democrats in the days of the Knights of Labor; but although this cannot be documented with any high degree of accuracy, it seems clear that in the years after 1900 the administration failed to persuade more than a small minority of the Irish members to abandon their traditional support for the Democratic party. As the proportion of Irish and other elements in the union increased, it reduced the number of rank-and-file members who could be relied on to vote socialist.

After 1908 the increasingly favorable attitude of the organized labor movement toward the Democratic party generally began to put the socialists in the Brewery Workers Union into an even more difficult quandary. In the 1912 election the union journal acknowledged that the Democratic platform seemed to offer much to the labor movement. But it expressed doubts as to whether the Democratic party, as a capitalist political party, would actually translate it into legislation; and it was equally skeptical about Woodrow Wilson, whom it described as a "pedant" who had only recently been converted to Progressivism and had on several occasions shown hostility toward organized labor. At the 1914 convention the national secretaries asserted that there was no reason for the union to change its support for the Socialist party simply because of the reforming legislation which had been enacted in the previous two years. But in 1916, when faced with the record of the first Wilson administration as a whole, the *Brauer-Zeitung* admitted that many workingmen were likely to vote Democratic, including members of its own union.

The problem was exacerbated for the Brewery Workers by the fact that Charles Evans Hughes, the Republican candidate, openly favored women's suffrage, a development to which many Germans (like other immigrant groups) were opposed, giving them an additional reason for voting Democratic. Nevertheless, in 1916 the *Brauer-Zeitung* still urged the membership to vote the socialist ticket, saying that the labor reforms of the Democratic administration were either sops thrown out to secure the labor vote or the result of President Wilson's personal intervention. The Democratic party as a whole, it argued, should not be trusted by the labor movement.[60]

The growth of Prohibition presented a still more serious threat to the Brewery Workers' commitment to working-class solidarity and socialist politics. The labor movement generally was divided over the Prohibition issue, but the Brewery Workers Union, predictably, was strongly opposed to Prohibition in all its forms, since it directly affected the livelihood of all its members. As we saw earlier, it had opposed the temperance element in the philosophy of the Knights of Labor in the 1880's, and it kept a watchful and increasingly anxious eye on the growth of the Prohibition movement in the years which followed. The union journal was filled with long and detailed refutations of all the standard arguments in support of Prohibition and even produced a socialist critique of the Prohibitionists' case against drinking, asserting that drunkenness was a result of poverty, not a cause of it, and that intemperance in all its forms would be ended only when the impoverishment of the masses by the capitalist economic system had been done away with. There was also a characteristically anti-clerical element in the journal's anti-Prohibition campaign, although this time it was directed against the Methodist and other Protestant churches instead of against the Catholics, most of whom opposed Prohibition.[61]

The difficulty was, however, that on this issue the Socialist party was neither large enough nor powerful enough to provide the Brewery Workers Union with sufficient political leverage to halt the rising temperance tide. Nor was it a reliable political ally. In the large cities and in states where German and other anti-Prohibition elements were influential in the party, socialists fully supported the anti-Prohibition campaign. But in other parts of the country, particularly in rural areas of the South and the Midwest, many local branches of the Socialist party were either indifferent to the Prohibition movement or actively in support of it. The 1912 convention of the Socialist party adopted a resolution asserting that the evils of alcoholism could not be overcome by the intervention of the state. But the party as a whole refused to throw such influence as it had into the anti-Prohibition struggle, and the union became increasingly irritated by its unhelpful attitude. "It is high time," the union journal declared in July 1915, "for the party . . . to put a stop to some great prohibition lights who use their party membership more to make propaganda for prohibition than to work for socialism." [62]

In fact, as time went on it became increasingly clear that on this issue, which became the overriding concern of the union as Prohibition spread and a growing number of its members were thrown out of work, the "reward your friends, punish your enemies" tactics of the AFL were much more likely to be effective than nationwide political support for the Socialist party. Both of the major parties, as well as the Socialist party, were divided over the Prohibition issue. But—although again this cannot be documented precisely—it may safely be assumed that the Irish element in the union (who were as much concerned about the imminent disappearance of whisky as the Germans were about the drying up of beer) were confirmed in their allegiance to the Democratic wets in the northern cities, and it is likely that many German members changed their political allegiance in favor of the Democrats on this issue also. At all events, side by side with notices of Socialist party meetings, editorials began to appear in the *Brauer-Zeitung* after 1910 urging members to lobby their state and federal representatives to oppose Prohibition measures and, what was more important, to vote for political candidates who opposed Prohibition irrespective of their political party.

Equally important was the fact that in order to fight Prohibition effectively the Brewery Workers Union found it necessary to cooperate with the brewery owners in devising anti-Prohibition measures, a development which ran directly counter to the class-conflict doctrines which the union leadership had sought so assiduously to preserve. In 1913, after eight states had adopted state-wide Prohibition and the situation was becoming increasingly serious, a committee of the International Executive Board attended the United States Brewers Association convention in Chicago, offering the union's full support in the anti-Prohibition struggle. At the 1914 convention of the union an Anti-Prohibition Department was established, with a new national secretary at its head, and a dollar a year was levied on each member to be spent in helping the industry as a whole cooperate with the United States Brewers Association, the German-American Alliance, Irish-American groups, and other favorably disposed labor elements in bringing pressure to bear on both the major political parties to ward off the calamity of total national Prohibition.[63]

In New York, an anti-Prohibition publicity bureau was operated jointly by the union and the United States Brewers Association, and in 1916 in Boston the union cooperated with the Master Brewers Association in an attempt to defeat candidates of both the major parties who voted for Prohibition in the state legislature. Further cooperation with the beer manufacturers was indicated by the willingness of Denver brewery owners to keep union members employed in the production of nonintoxicating beverages, even when contracts between the union and the employers for the production of beer itself had to be abrogated because of lack of business. Measures of this kind were duplicated in other cities as well.[64]

These decisions were not taken without careful thought, or without opposition from the more militant socialists in the union, who were deeply suspicious of cooperating with the employers on this issue, and rightly recognized in this development a threat to the long-standing commitment of the Brewery Workers Union to the Socialist party. At the 1914 convention objections were raised to working with the United States Brewers Association (which, although its relations with the union were now quite good, had earlier bitterly resisted unionization), on the ground that this represented class collaboration. And Hermann Schlüter, the official historian of the union, who was also a socialist, tried hard to suggest that the proper course for the union was not to cooperate with the employers, who were simply out for material gain, but to convert the Socialist party as a whole to the anti-Prohibition cause, arguing that the only real solution to the evils of intemperance was the nationalization of the brewing industry.

But the future of the union was at stake, and the brewery workers could not afford the luxury of ignoring their natural allies. At the 1914 convention the administration defended its cooperation with the brewery owners by saying that only if the union could be preserved could it continue its fight against capitalism, and that for this the halting of Prohibition was essential. The national secretaries declared:

> In the fight against prohibition, brewery capital and brewery workers have some common interests. But this community of interest goes only so far as the preservation of the brewing industry is involved. Beyond that our organization has had . . . enough differences with the employers during the last two years . . . that it can readily be seen that even the brewery proprietors do not believe in identity of interests of capital and labor.

This may have been true, but the mutual support which the brewery owners and brewery workers gave to each other in the political fight against Prohibition made the class struggle seem increasingly less of a reality when compared with the struggle to preserve the brewing industry as a viable economic entity.[65]

IV

By the time America entered World War I in April 1917 the Brewery Workers Union had changed considerably from what it had been in the early years of the century. Then, it was a rising and militant organization, still struggling for recognition in many cities, at odds with the AFL over its jurisdiction, and, politically speaking, fully committed to the Socialist Party of America. Now, much of the older German leadership was passing from the scene—Louis Kemper, national secretary since 1902, died in October 1914, and Gustav Mostler, editor of the *Brauer-Zeitung* since 1906, died in April 1917—and a new generation of members was rising which lacked the socialist traditions of the old. Most of the union's differences with the AFL had been composed, and it was grateful to it for the distillery, soft drink, and other categories of workers which were added to its jurisdiction in an effort to mitigate the developing effects of Prohibition. Statewide Prohibition had already reduced the membership from its peak figure of 67,561 in 1914, and it had taken a particularly heavy toll of the trained brewery workers who actually brewed the beer, many of whom were the original German radicals. In September 1917 an office was established in Washington to lobby both of the major parties against the imminent passage of the Eighteenth Amendment to the Constitution establishing Prohibition on a national scale—indicating a further departure from the union's previous political commitment to the Socialist party. The old socialist tradition was still there, but it seemed increasingly hard to reconcile it with the practical demands of pressure-group politics.

There were other signs of increasing caution and conservatism. The administration frequently urged the membership not to undertake strikes where they could possibly be avoided, so as to husband the union's resources for the fight against Prohibition, and despite what had been said at the 1914 convention about continuing class differences between the union and the employers, there was evidence of further cooperation between them. During the war, for example, voluntary wage increases were awarded by some brewery owners because of the increasing cost of living, and earlier a plan had been drawn up by the International Executive Board and the United States Brewers Association for an accident compensation and pension fund to be financed and administered jointly by both sides. This was a somewhat novel proposal in these days since most unions, if they had such schemes, operated them for themselves; and the militants in the union opposed the plan as a stratagem designed to undermine the independence of the organization and make it subservient to the employers, particularly since it had first been suggested by Louis B. Schramm, chairman of the Labor Committee of the United States Brewers Association and head of the Workmen's Compensation Committee of the National Civic Federation in New York.[66] "A true socialist," declared one union member from Wilmington, Delaware, "demands the full value of his toil from capital and not charity." In any event, he went on, pointing to the situation in Germany, it was the responsibility of the state to provide social insurance, not that of the trade-unions, and he urged that additional working-class representatives, like Victor Berger, be sent to Congress to secure pensions and employers' compensation by means of legislation.

The question of whether social insurance should be secured by political action or by the unions themselves had been one of the major issues between the socialists and their opponents in the AFL generally, and in defending the plan drawn up with the employers, the administration indicated that, on this issue, as on others, it had now moved considerably nearer to the AFL point of view. It would take years to secure nationwide legislation providing for old-age pensions, Secretary Proebstle argued; and although he agreed that this should be the ultimate aim, he delivered a mild reproof to those socialists who "still believed that the cooperative commonwealth with all its dreamed-of accomplishments may be established at the ballot box overnight." "We are of the opinion," Proebstle said, "that if the members of our organization are able to get some of the dreams of the future realized now, we are entitled and in duty bound to accept them."

This represented a major concession to the pragmatic outlook which dominated the American labor movement as a whole, and Secretary Hübner, in his defense of the plan, indicated how deep were the inroads which the conformist and conservative values of the American labor movement generally had made on some of the older German leaders of the union. As an enthusiastic young socialist in the 1880's, Hübner said in March 1912, he had naïvely believed that socialism could be brought to the United States within a generation. Now he was far less sanguine. "Under the present conditions and the conditions to be expected in the near future none of the American workingmen . . . will be able to achieve more than we can [hope for] under the [insurance] proposition." However, cooperation with employees over the insurance plan was defeated when it was put to a referendum vote.[67]

Thus it is apparent that even some of the deeply held socialist convictions of the brewery workers had begun to wane before the advent of World War I, just as radicalism did throughout the AFL as a whole. The war itself undermined the socialist philosophy of the union still further, and served to draw the German-speaking brewery owners and their employees —both equally affected by the anti-German propaganda which swept the country—still closer together. Ethnic ties, which in the United States have traditionally been stronger than those of class, were now invoked to silence the suspicions of those who were unwilling to cooperate with the employers on Prohibition, and both sides submerged themselves in the common effort to defend their industry, their ethnic interests, and their cultural identity.

Like the Socialist party, the Brewery Workers Union began, in 1917, by being firmly antiwar. It had applauded the antiwar stand of much of the European labor movement in the years before 1914, and it shared the hope of many European socialists that international action by the working class would be able to prevent the outbreak of war. "A socialist's patriotism," the *Brauer-Zeitung* declared loftily as the war clouds gathered early in 1914, "is naturally above the narrow-minded national pride and idolatry of the unthinking and bigoted army. . . . The ethics of his teaching demand the recognition of the brotherhood of man, and thus for the socialist to be patriotic in the sense of the common conception of the term would be inconsistent and ridiculous."

These hopes were rudely shattered by the virtually universal support which was given to the war by European trade-unionists. In fact, the first and most serious casualty of World War I, from the point of view of the socialists in the union, was the destruction of their faith in the international solidarity of the working class, which had been held to with all the more fervor because so many of them were European in origin themselves. The Brewery Workers found themselves forced to accept, perhaps a little shamefacedly, the explanation sent by Karl Legien, President of the German Federation of Trade Unions, to German-American trade-unionists that the German trade-unions had supported the war on the ground that they would be unable to contribute effectively to the international labor movement if Germany were defeated. The union also sought comfort in the hope that the strains and conflicts which the war provoked might result in the destruction of the capitalist system as a whole. This hope was partially sustained by the Russian Revolution, but it proved unavailing in the case of Germany itself, with the failure of the 1918 revolution there. The Brewery Workers enthusiastically welcomed the overthrow of the Kaiser and the establishment of a German republic in 1919, but it was saddened and disillusioned by the failure to follow this up with a successful socialist regime.[68]

Of more immediate importance was the dilemma which was created, as American participation on the side of the Allies drew nearer, by the Brewery Workers' natural sympathies for the German cause. Many members still had relatives in Germany and strong feelings of attachment to it, and they naturally did not want to see Germany defeated. For example, late in 1914 Martin Etzel, President of the German Brewery Workers Union, reassured the German-American members of the union that Germany's prospects of winning the war seemed good and comforted them with news of recent German victories over the Russians in East Prussia. But the union administration soon realized the dangers of appearing to be pro-German, and in the middle of 1915 the publication of this kind of news in the union journal abruptly stopped. Nevertheless, it was these national ties, strengthened by the anti-English sentiments of the Irish members, as well as by the characteristically socialist opinion that the war was a conflict between European ruling classes in which America should have no part, that led the Brewery Workers Union, initially at least, to oppose American intervention more strenuously than almost any other labor organization.

In addition it must be remembered that the German Social Democratic party, like other European socialist parties, had a long and deeply held tradition of hostility to militarism and war, and this undoubtedly affected the attitude of many, at least, of the older German members of the organization. Thus, along with the German community as a whole, the union opposed President Wilson's preparedness campaign, gave its support to groups like the Friends of Peace (which was organized by the German-American Peace Society, the United Irish-American Society, and some labor elements), and came out fully behind the Socialist party's early declarations on the war.[69]

These views were tolerated in 1914 and 1915, when both the Democratic administration and the labor movement generally upheld American neutrality. But they became increasingly difficult to hold onto when the AFL came out for preparedness and war fever began to mount. When April 1917 came, the Brewery Workers commended the Socialist party for its courageous stand against the war. But it also publicly endorsed the AFL's declaration of support for President Wilson's position, despite the opposition of a minority in the union. Thereafter, the union gave reluctant but increasing support to the war. In April 1918 the International Executive Board purchased fifty thousand dollars' worth of Liberty Loan Bonds, for which it received Gompers' personal congratulations; and in other ways it drew further away from the Socialist party's antiwar position and nearer to that of the AFL. It commended Gompers' statement of labor's loyalty at the 1918 AFL convention, and its attitudes were softened still more by the gains union labor made as a result of the liberal trade-union policies followed by the National War Labor Board.

However, this did not save the union from being condemned as pro-German. Its objections to conscription were denounced by a variety of sources, including elements within the labor movement itself, although these objections were made on grounds of hostility to compulsion, rather than because of opposition to the war as such. The editor of the *Brauer-Zeitung* came near to being arrested for his criticism of the conduct of the war, and although the journal was very careful about what it allowed itself to print, there were demands from several English-speaking locals for the removal of German-language materials from the journal altogether. The position of the German leaders of the union was made increasingly difficult, and on at least one occasion the International Executive Board had to appeal publicly to the non-German members of the union to cease their attacks against those of German descent. It was perhaps precisely because they were so suspect that by mid-1918 these union leaders were protesting their patriotism even more vehemently than many native American trade-unionists. "As Americans," the German-born editor of the union journal wrote on August 31, 1918, "we stand united as one man behind the prosecution of this war." [70]

After the Russian Revolution had taken place, to be considered socialist, a "red," was second only in gravity to being considered pro-German. But on this issue, at least, the union remained loyal to its socialist convictions. The journal gave a warm and enthusiastic welcome to both the March and the October 1917 revolutions, congratulating the Russian people on their "great work of liberation" and expressing the hope "that their example will be followed by the oppressed and enslaved peoples of other countries." It showed no particular qualms at the authoritarian measures of the Bolsheviks, as the AFL in general did, and it defended the Soviet regime from what it regarded, with considerable justice, to be the hostile reporting of the American press. While the war was on, the *Brauer-Zeitung* alleged in February 1919, the American press had been quite willing to encourage Germans and others to revolt against their authoritarian governments. But now that the Russian Revolution had actually taken place, it was terrified lest the same developments might occur in the United States.[71]

Important as these issues of war and revolution were to the Brewery Workers Union, the threat of nationwide Prohibition overshadowed everything else. The union, working now in full cooperation with the United States Brewers Association and other anti-Prohibition elements, tried desperately to prevent the enactment of the Eighteenth Amendment to the U.S. Constitution, requiring its locals to join the Trade Union Liberty Leagues which had been established in many states to fight it, and seeking anti-Prohibition sentiment wherever it could be found. The 1919 AFL convention for the first time passed a resolution openly critical of Prohibition, and Gompers in particular was opposed to it. But it was all to no avail. During the war, Congress prohibited the manufacture or sale of all intoxicants, supposedly for reasons of efficiency and economy. While this ruling was still in effect, the Eighteenth Amendment, adopted by Congress in December 1917, was ratified by the states and proclaimed in effect in January 1920. In addition the Volstead Act, passed over President Wilson's veto in October 1919, defined intoxicating liquor as any beverage containing over one-half of 1 per cent of alcohol and provided stringent regulations for the enforcement of Prohibition as a whole.

Thus the beer-brewing and liquor-producing industry was doomed to inactivity for more than a decade, and many breweries, except those producing "near beer" (beer with no more than the statutory amount of alcohol), were forced to shut down. Large numbers of brewery workers were thrown out of work, local unions were disbanded, and many workers were forced to take other jobs. In addition, due partly to the general postwar reaction, and partly to the desperate condition of the industry, a number of employers embarked on a campaign for the open shop and went back on their contracts with the Brewery Workers Union, even in its main areas of strength. The union journal complained bitterly at this changed attitude on the part of the owners, who, it said, "ought to appreciate our cooperation" in the fight against Prohibition. Nevertheless, the consequences for the union were severe. By 1917 the membership figure had fallen from the 67,561 of 1914 to about 40,000, and in January 1921 it had fallen still further, to approximately 30,000. Some benefit was derived from the new members brought in by the expansion of jurisdiction, but the union's income had been considerably reduced, and it found it difficult to organize new workers in the depression of the immediate postwar years. It was not until the 1930's that it regained something like its former position.[72]

The effect of these various developments on the Brewery Workers' ideological outlook was to accelerate still further the abandonment of its radical political position. In areas which did not affect the immediate interests of the union, such as the international labor movement, an interest in left-wing causes was still maintained. The union continued, for instance, to defend the Russian Revolution. The 1920 union convention deplored the aid given by the United States to the "imperialistic and counter-revolutionary war" then being urged by the Allies against the Bolshevik regime, and the union supported efforts to prevail on the federal government to grant it diplomatic recognition. Similarly, Irish members looked with increasing interest and concern upon the culmination of Ireland's long struggle for independence from Great Britain, condemning as "barbarous and inhuman" the repressive activities of British troops in Ireland in 1920 and 1921, and urging support for efforts by Eamon de Valera to secure United States recognition for the Irish republican regime. And, naturally, interest was maintained in Germany. Friendly relations were reestablished after the war with both German and Austrian brewery workers' unions, the German organization being described by its new president after the war as deriving a renewed radical impulse from the German revolution of 1918.[73]

But the situation was far different for the American Brewery Workers Union. On certain domestic issues it continued to take a liberal stand. For instance, it strongly, and courageously, opposed the threat to civil liberties posed by the more excessive manifestations of the Red Scare. It condemned the refusal of the House of Representatives to seat Victor Berger after his reelection to Congress in 1918, and it condemned also the wholesale deportment of alien radicals. John Sullivan, a member of the International Executive Board, was treasurer of the Central Labor Conference working for the granting of amnesties for all political prisoners. And the union journal continued to report developments in the socialist and radical movements at length, expressing deep regret and concern at the internecine feuds within the Socialist party and at the Communist-socialist split.

But these were relatively abstract issues, removed from the union's immediate sphere of interest, and for an organization with such a strong tradition of socialism, the Brewery Workers played remarkably little part in the postwar revival of radicalism and third-party movements, although it did approve in general of the move to nationalize the mines and the railroads, and of the new militancy shown in the major industrial strikes. This detachment was partly because of the pressures and disillusionments which resulted from the war, partly because of concern with the brewery proprietors' open-shop campaign, and partly because the reformist and Progressivist character of the postwar radical movements was alien to the union's Marxist traditions. The old socialists in the union, for example, were lukewarm toward the idea of establishing a broadly based labor party, just as they had been toward Populism. The declining influence of the German element in the union, which was further reduced by the experiences of the war, was also an important factor.

But the major fact was that the Brewery Workers Union was so preoccupied with Prohibition and with the struggle to preserve the brewing industry that it had neither the money nor the time to devote itself to general radical causes; and on matters of immediate interest, including politics, it now acted in a strictly conservative and pragmatic manner. For example, it continued in general to uphold the cause of industrial unionism in the AFL. But in 1919, when a number of Canadian locals were threatened by the One Big Union movement, a circular was sent out condemning this and similar dual union movements, bringing a riposte from the Detroit IWW that ever since the Brewery Workers had "crawled back into the AFL" in 1908 they had "lost the little radicalism they once had and become as arch reactionary as the rest of the Gompers' machine." This, coming from the IWW, was somewhat unfair, but a circular issued by the union administration to the membership just before the 1918 congressional elections read very much like a nonpartisan directive of the AFL: "Under no conditions should we cast our ballot for any candidate whose record is not clear on the prohibition question," the circular said, ". . . no matter on what party ticket their names may appear." [74]

In fact, there was now a wide gap between the socialist rhetoric that was still to be found in the *Brauer-Zeitung,* and occasionally at union conventions, and the actual practice of the organization. This had always been to some extent present, in view of the avowedly educational character of the journal, which had earlier acknowledged itself to be more militant than the rank and file. But after World War I the gap between rhetoric and reality became increasingly apparent. In 1918 Julius Zorn, who continued as editor until his death in 1926, again urged the younger members not to forget the socialist traditions of the organization and to vote socialist whenever they could. But there was increasing impatience with the old German leadership, and at the 1920 convention an attempt was made, unsuccessfully as it turned out, to modify the union's constitution so that the national officers need no longer be required to speak the German language, on the ground that this was an injustice to the thousands of newer members who had been brought in as a result of the union's expanded jurisdiction, but who could not speak German.

At this same convention the contrast between the earlier socialist sympathies of the union and its new-found pragmatism was brought into even sharper relief. At all previous conventions, including that of 1917, the union membership had been urged, in one way or another, to vote socialist. But at the 1920 convention a resolution urging endorsement of Debs and the Socialist party was withdrawn, and the national secretaries completely abandoned their prewar socialist line, acknowledging for the first time that the union contained, and always had contained, a variety of political views. "The membership of our organization," they said in their report, "has like all other bodies of men always been divided in the various political parties. Some are ardent Republicans, others just as sincere Democrats, and others are just as loyal Socialists." They indicated that they personally (all three national secretaries) still held socialist convictions. But they showed clearly that the union's impatience with the failure of the Socialist party to actively oppose Prohibition, allied to the whole circumstance of its decline since the war, had now reached a point where support for the party had been virtually abandoned. Socialists and other "so-called labor representatives," when asked by the union to oppose Prohibition, the secretaries reported, were "as much put out . . . as the average dry Republican from the North, or dry Democrat from the South." [75]

Hence, the secretaries concluded, the union had now, to all intents and purposes, fully adopted the "reward your friends, punish your enemies" political policy of the AFL. The members of the union, they said, "should learn to dissociate themselves from party domination" and instead should choose "discriminating [ly] from the candidates of all parties, voting for men who will pledge themselves to carry out what they promise to their constituency." In particular, members should vote only for political candidates who were specifically pledged to repeal the Volstead Act and work for the repeal of national Prohibition. "You will finally get results," the secretaries concluded, "when you show that every man who betrays our trust will lose our support." [76]

These recommendations were overwhelmingly adopted by the 1920 convention, as also by the conventions of 1923 and 1926, and they henceforth became the guidelines for the Brewery Workers' political policies as a whole. And in March 1922 Julius Zorn, faced with a fall in the circulation of the union journal, and aware that the views expressed in it seemed less and less relevant to the union rank and file, finally brought the *Brauer-Zeitung* into line with the administration's new political policy, thus demonstrating the final collapse of the old German socialist tradition, save in individual pockets among the union membership in Wisconsin and elsewhere. Acknowledging reluctantly that experience had shown most American workers unwilling to "be content with the hope of a coming millennium, but rather that they are intent on improving their conditions as much as they can under the present order of things," he advised members to vote on a nonpartisan basis and indeed to devote more attention to the economic than to the political movement.

Thus, as already indicated, the main political consideration throughout the union as a whole was now the effort to secure the repeal or amendment of the Volstead Act, so that breweries could produce something more akin to full-strength beer, and to bring pressure to bear on public opinion so as to bring about the ultimate repeal of national Prohibition. It was this attitude which dictated the union's policy toward the Conference for Progressive Political Action. The CPPA itself did not take a clear stand on the Prohibition issue, any more than the Socialist party had done, but there were indications that it, perhaps even more than the Socialist party, contained a considerable proportion of reformers who favored the dry position. At all events, the union supported the candidacy of CPPA-backed Senator Robert La Follette for the Presidency in 1924, but it did so more because he personally opposed Prohibition than out of any strong enthusiasm for the CPPA. In fact, it took far less interest in the election campaign than most other radical trade-unions, and was much more concerned with the question of how many wets were elected to Congress, and in state and local elections, than it was with the presidential contest. Pressure-group politics, for the Brewery Workers Union, were now the order of the day.[77]

V

The rise and fall of socialism in the Brewery Workers Union does not correspond exactly to the period covered by this book. Active organization of the brewery workers by German socialists was begun well before 1881, and the decline of socialist influence in the union was under way long before 1924. Yet in general it may be said that the official commitment of the brewery workers to socialist politics and principles ran from the founding of the union in 1886 to World War I and just after.

For just how long this official commitment represented the actual views of a majority of the union membership, however, is open to question. Complaints about the excessive ideological fervor of the union journal, exhortations from the union leaders to vote socialist, and the revealing statement made by the national secretaries at the 1920 convention that the union "always had contained" a variety of political views indicate that the German socialist leadership, at both the national and the local levels, was considerably more radical than part, at least, of the union rank and file. Many locals, probably most, were composed of socialists in the early years, and although national union elections were contested infrequently, there is little evidence to suggest that the socialist leaders were not elected fairly and democratically.

Nevertheless, it seems clear that from an organization which at its founding was the exclusive preserve of German socialists, many of whom had some previous experience in the socialist movement in Germany, the Brewery Workers Union came to incorporate many elements which were either indifferent to socialism or actively opposed to it. In part these were the Irish members, who had earlier joined the Knights of Labor and who joined the union when that organization declined, and in part they were other English-speaking and native-born workers who entered the union later, particularly from areas in the beverage-producing industry which did not form part of the union's jurisdiction in the early days. The German element retained its leading position until after World War I, partly because of its continuing numerical strength and partly because it was able, until the advent of Prohibition, to provide genuinely successful union leadership. But it seems clear that as time went on the socialist policies of the leadership had an increasingly narrower base of popular support and that the older generation of German leaders were impelled by increasing prosperity, by the influence of the AFL (upon whom the union came to depend heavily when Prohibition brought hard times), by the exigencies of the Prohibition movement, and by the shattering experience of World War I to abandon their socialist position and to adopt instead the dominant political and economic policies of the American labor movement as a whole.

The relative weight to be given to the various reasons for the rise and decline of socialist influence in the Brewery Workers Union is hard to assess. Bad conditions, low wages, and the undermining of the trained brewery workers' craft as a result of the development of the industry, coupled with a view of industrial unionism which saw it as a means of promoting working-class solidarity as much as a device to improve the union's bargaining position, were obviously important. But it is difficult to isolate these factors, which were indigenous to the American brewing industry, from the fact that many of those who founded the union were German immigrants who were already socialists before they came to America. The precise relationship between these two sets of factors depended, in part, on how far the immigrants who entered the industry experienced an improvement in their wages and working conditions when they came to America, and how far they did not. Documentary evidence on this point so far is slight; but despite the apparent willingness of many German brewery proprietors to exploit their fellow countrymen, it is clear that from the first wages were considerably higher in the United States than they were in Germany, even though they were often lower than in other areas of industry in the United States at this time.

This would suggest, if we assume that higher wage levels reduce a predisposition in favor of radicalism, that the immigrant brewery workers remained socialist more because of traditional patterns of behavior brought over from Germany than because of conditions peculiar to the American brewing industry. Union sources certainly spoke less of low wages and the displacement of skill as causes of radicalism in the brewing industry (although they may have reinforced it) than comparable sources in the machinists' or the shoemaking trades. Instead, the union administration often tended to assume that the brewery workers were by definition socialists— sometimes unwarrantably, as we have seen—and that they would naturally support the SLP or the Socialist party in much the same way that most trade-unionists in Germany supported the Social Democratic party. It was the realization that this was neither the most successful way of advancing the brewery workers' interests, nor the characteristic American way of conducting the labor movement, that lay at the root of the union's abandonment of socialism.

The view that the Brewery Workers' socialism was in large part ethnically derived also clearly explains the decline of socialist influence in the union. AFL influences, the need to fight Prohibition by pressure-group methods, and other factors already mentioned were obviously important here. But the fact that opposition to the socialist policies of the leadership began to develop during the period between 1900 and 1912, before Prohibition had become a major threat, and the sudden official reversal of the union's political policies between 1917 and 1920, when the German-American community was under tremendous pressure to conform to accepted American values, would appear to indicate that it was the changing behavior of the German element, more than anything else, which accounted for the decline of socialism in the union. It would be going too far to say that socialism developed in the Brewery Workers Union solely because of the presence of radical German immigrants and disappeared when the Germans either lost their dominant position or themselves abandoned their socialist convictions. But an ethnic explanation for the rise and fall of socialism in the Brewery Workers Union, coupled with the effects of Prohibition in turning the membership away from the Socialist party in favor of lobbying inside the two major political parties, as most other AFL trade-unions did, clearly makes more sense than any other.

Notes

1. Morris Hillquit, *History of Socialism in the United States* (New York, 1956), 272; Nathan Fine, *Labor and Farmer Parties in the United States, 1828–1928* (New York, 1961), 89–90; Louis Lorwin, *The American Federation of Labor, History, Policies, and Prospects* (Washington, 1933), 31n. For German socialist and labor movements in America generally, see Hermann Schlüter, *Die Anfänge der Deutschen Arbeiterbewegung in Amerika* (Stuttgart, 1907); A. Sartorius Freiherm von Walterhausen, *Der Moderne Socialismus in den Vereinigten Staaten von Amerika* (Berlin, 1890); Carl Wittke, *Refugees of Revolution, the German Forty-Eighters in America* (Philadelphia, 1952), especially 166–175.

2. Victor Berger and Max Hayes, as newspaper editors, were members of the International Typographical Union, which was in general a conservative organization, and J. Mahlon Barnes was a member of the Cigarmakers International Union, which had a minority of German socialist members.

3. The National Union of Brewers changed its name several times as it acquired additional groups of workers. By 1924 it was called the International Union of United Brewery, Flour, Cereal and Soft Drink Workers of America. It is here called the Brewery Workers Union throughout in order to avoid confusion.

4. A full-length study of Wilhelm Weitling, a German utopian socialist who emigrated to the United States in 1848 and had a considerable impact on the German workingmen's movement in New York, is Carl Wittke, *The Utopian Communist: A Biography of Wilhelm Weitling, Nineteenth Century Reformer* (Baton Rouge, 1950).

5. Hermann Schlüter, *The Brewing Industry and the Brewery Workers' Movement in America* (Cincinnati, 1910), 96, 100, 102–106. All page references to Schlüter hereafter refer to this work.

6. Schlüter, *op. cit.*, 112–119, 212–218; Marion Savage, *Industrial Unionism in America* (New York, 1922), 62–64; Norman J. Ware, *The Labor Movement in the United States, 1860–1895; A Study in Democracy* (New York, 1929), 209, 221–227; *Brauer-Zeitung*, VI (October 31, 1891), 1. See also Terence V. Powderly, *The Path I Trod* (New York, 1940), 292, 344.

7. Schlüter, *op. cit.*, 121–127, 148–166, 188–204.

8. *Ibid.*, 92–94, 123; *Brauer-Zeitung*, XXV (January 29, 1910), 1.

9. *Proceedings, Twenty-fifth Convention of the United States Brewers' Association* (Chicago, 1885), 260. For a further discussion of technological changes in the brewing industry, see Thomas C. Cochran, *The Pabst Brewing Company, The History of an American Business* (New York, 1948), chapter 5.

10. Schlüter, *op. cit.*, 93; *Brauer-Zeitung*, XVI (March 30, 1901), 4; XVIII (February 28, 1903), 1; *Proceedings, Tenth Convention of the Brewery Workers' Union* (Boston, 1897), 5–6.

11. Savage, *op. cit.*, 61, 65–66; Schlüter, *op. cit.*, 135, 219–220.

12. *Ibid.*, 92.

13. *Ibid.*, 134–135; *Brauer-Zeitung*, XXII (February 23, 1907), 1; XXIII (August 1, 1908), 2; XXIII (October 3, 1908), 1; *Proceedings, Sixteenth Convention of the Brewery Workers' Union* (Toronto, 1906), 103.

14. Wittke, *Refugees*, 162, 174, 338–339; Schlüter, *op. cit.*, 158, 164–165, 169; Albert Faust, *The German Element in the United States*, 2 vols. (Boston, 1909), II, 156–198; *Brauer-Zeitung*, XVII (January 11, 1902), 1; XVIII (May 9, 1903), 4; XXI (August 25, 1906), 1; XXIX (October 17, 1914), 1; XXXII (April 14, 1917), 1–2; *Proceedings, Twenty-fourth Convention of the Brewery Workers' Union* (Cincinnati, 1926), 22–23.

15. *Brauer-Zeitung*, XIV (January 28, 1899), 1; *Proceedings, Eighteenth Convention of the Brewery Workers' Union* (Chicago, 1910); *Proceedings, Nineteenth Convention of the Brewery Workers' Union* (Denver, 1912), 150; Maurer, Fleisher *et al.*, *Union with a Heart: International Union of United Brewery, Flour, Cereal, Soft Drink and Distillery Workers of America, Seventy-five Years of a Great Union, 1886–1961* (Cincinnati, 1961), 10, 15.

16. *Brewery, Flour, Cereal and Soft Drink Workers' Journal*, XXXIV (July 5, 1919), 4.

17. *Brauer-Zeitung*, XX (October 21, 1905), 1; *Proceedings, Ninth Convention of the Brewery Workers' Union* (Cincinnati, 1896), 75; *Proceedings, Thirteenth Convention of the Brewery Workers' Union* (Philadelphia, 1901), 69; *Proceedings, Fifteenth Convention of the Brewery Workers' Union* (Indianapolis, 1904), 147.

18. *Constitution*, Brewery Workers Union (1892), 1–2.

19. For example, Charles Bechtold attended the International Socialist and Labor Congress held in London in 1896 on behalf of the union; and Hermann Schlüter did the same thing in 1910. At its 1897 convention H. G. Wiehle, of the German Brewery Workers Union, brought greetings from German, Swiss, and Austrian socialists. See *Brauer-Zeitung*, XII (October 2, 1897), 1; XXV (October 15, 1910), 2; *Proceedings, Ninth Convention of the Brewery Workers' Union* (Cincinnati, 1896), 9–12.

20. *Brauer-Zeitung*, XIII (June 25, 1898), 1; XV (February 24, 1900), 1; XVI (October 5, 1901), 4; XVIII (October 31, 1903), 4; XX (March 11, 1905), 1; XX (April 15, 1905), 1; XXI (January 13, 1906), 1.

21. Gompers to Executive Council, December 21, 1906; Gompers to Louis Kemper, January 19, 1907 (Gompers' Letterbooks, AFL–CIO Collection).

22. Schlüter, *op. cit.*, 248–249; *Brauer-Zeitung*, XVI (January 26, 1901), 4; XX (May 16, 1905), 4; XX (June 30, 1905), 4; XXII (November 2, 1907), 1.

23. *Brauer-Zeitung*, VII (July 11, 1891), 1; VIII (January 7, 1893), 1; *Proceedings, Twelfth Convention of the Brewery Workers' Union* (Detroit, 1900), 9; *Proceedings, Fourteenth Convention of the Brewery Workers' Union* (Cincinnati, 1903), 168; *Proceedings, Fifteenth Convention of the Brewery Workers' Union* (Indianapolis, 1904), 103, 111; *Proceedings, Nineteenth Convention of the Brewery Workers' Union* (Denver, 1912), 188–191.

24. *Brauer-Zeitung*, XVI (February 2, 1901), 4; XVII (May 31, 1902), 4;

XXIII (June 20, 1908), 1; XXVIII (June 7, 1913), 1; *Proceedings, Ninth Convention of the Brewery Workers' Union* (Cincinnati, 1896), 49, 54–56.

25. For example, in 1895 the union administration used its influence, through its joint affiliation with the AFL and the Knights of Labor, to support DeLeon's efforts to get SLP leader Lucian Sanial appointed as editor of the Knights of Labor journal. See Charles Bechtold to Daniel DeLeon, January 21, 1895 (Daniel DeLeon Collection, Wisconsin State Historical Society).

26. *Brauer-Zeitung,* IX (February 3, 1894), 1; IX (October 27, 1894), 1; IX (December 15, 1894), 1; XII (January 9, 1897), 1; *Proceedings, Eighth Convention of the Brewery Workers' Union* (Cincinnati, 1896), 74–75. These endorsements were made on ideological grounds, but they should also be seen in the context of the German labor movement, in which it was customary for the free trade-unions to support the Social Democratic party almost as a matter of form. See Carl Landauer, *European Socialism, A History of Ideas and Movements,* 2 vols. (Berkeley, 1959), I, 311, 314.

27. See *Proceedings, Tenth Annual Convention of the A.F. of L.* (Detroit, 1890), 26.

28. Schlüter, *op. cit.,* 188–192; *Brauer-Zeitung,* X (December 7, 1895), 1; XI (February 1, 1896), 1; *The Socialist Labor Party in New York,* pamphlet issued by anti-DeLeonite members of the SLP, New York, 1892 (Socialist Labor Party Collection, Wisconsin State Historical Society).

29. *The People,* V (October 13, 1895), 1; *Brauer-Zeitung,* VIII (October 21, 1893), 1; IX (May 12, 1894), 1; XI (February 22, 1896), 1; XVI (November 16, 1901), 1; XVII (January 4, 1902), 1.

30. Newspaper clipping, February 1, 1896, paper unknown (Socialist Labor Party Collection, Wisconsin State Historical Society); Arthur Keep to Daniel DeLeon, January 25, 1895 (Daniel DeLeon Collection, Wisconsin State Historical Society); *Brauer-Zeitung,* X (October 19, 1895), 1; XI (February 1, 1896), 1; XI (May 9, 1896), 1; XI (June 13, 1896), 1; XI (July 25, 1896), 1; XI (August 8, 1896), 1; XI (November 7, 1896), 1; *Proceedings, Ninth Convention of the Brewery Workers' Union* (Cincinnati, 1896), 19, 21–22, 67–68.

31. *Brauer-Zeitung,* XII (January 9, 1897), 1; *Proceedings, Second Annual Convention of the Socialist Trades and Labor Alliance* (Boston, 1897), 8, 10.

32. Behind this lay the profound ideological conflict in European socialism between the eighteenth- and early nineteenth-century utopian socialists, originating largely in France, who held that a socialist society could be evolved out of a series of communitarian experiments, and the Marxists, originating in Germany, who repudiated utopianism as misconceived and nonrevolutionary. It was natural that the Brewery Workers Union, with its German background, should have sided with the Marxists.

33. *Social Democracy Red Book* (Terre Haute, 1900), 130–131; *Brauer-Zeitung,* XII (August 14, 1897), 1; XII (August 28, 1897), 1.

34. *Brauer-Zeitung,* XIII (June 11, 1898), 1; XIII (June 18, 1898), 1; XIII (June 25, 1898), 1; XIV (April 22, 1899), 1; XV (March 31, 1900), 1; XV (May 26, 1900), 4; XV (November 17, 1900), 1; XVI (May 25, 1901), 4; *Proceedings, Thirteenth Convention of the Brewery Workers' Union* (Philadelphia, 1901), 69.

35. *Brauer-Zeitung,* IX (December 4, 1894), 1; XV (November 17, 1900), 1; XV (December 1, 1900), 4.

36. Schlüter, *op. cit.*, 220–221; Philip Taft, *The A.F. of L. in the Time of Gompers* (New York, 1957), 187. For a general discussion of the jurisdictional conflict, see Benjamin C. Roberts, "Jurisdiction Disputes between the Brewery Workers and Other A.F. of L. Affiliates" (M.A. Thesis, University of Chicago, 1936).

37. Savage, *op. cit.*, 67–68; *Brauer-Zeitung*, XV (December 22, 1900), 1; XVI (January 26, 1901), 1; XVI (October 26, 1901), 4; XVII (April 26, 1902), 1; XIX (January 23, 1904), 1.

38. *The Worker*, XV (June 24, 1905), 2; Cleveland *Citizen*, XVII (June 10, 1907), 2; *American Labor Union Journal*, I (February 19, 1903), 5; I (September 3, 1903), 15–16; Savage, *op. cit.*, 68; *Brauer-Zeitung*, XVIII (February 7, 1903), 1; XVIII (February 28, 1903), 1; XIX (January 23, 1904), 1.

39. *Brauer-Zeitung*, XIV (July 8, 1899), 1; XIV (September 30, 1899), 1; XVII (June 7, 1902), 1; XVII (June 14, 1902), 1; XVII (June 28, 1902), 1; XVII (July 5, 1902), 1.

40. *Ibid.*, XVII (November 1, 1902), 1; XVIII (March 7, 1903), 1; XVIII (May 9, 1903), 4; XVIII (August 1, 1903), 4; XVIII (November 28, 1903), 1; XIX (April 30, 1904), 4; XIX (July 23, 1904), 1; *Proceedings, Fourteenth Convention of the Brewery Workers' Union* (Cincinnati, 1903), 77–79; *Proceedings, Fifteenth Convention of the Brewery Workers' Union* (Indianapolis, 1904), 134, 152–153; *International Socialist Review*, IV (January 1904), 434. Clarence Smith, secretary of the American Labor Union, exaggerated considerably when he told the founding convention of the IWW in June 1905 that the Brewery Workers were ready to join the American Labor Union in September 1904. See Paul F. Brissenden, *The IWW, A Study of American Syndicalism* (New York, 1957), 58–59.

41. In a report to the AFL Executive Council on January 12, 1905, Gompers noted that Trautmann "took a very active part [in the January 2 meeting], claiming that he went and saw Mr. Debs, to get him to sign a call for the meeting, but found him sick with nervous prostration, and unable to read or write." In any event, Debs did sign the letter, although he did not attend the January 2 meeting. Gompers to Executive Council, January 12, 1905 (John Mitchell Papers, Catholic University of America). See also Brissenden, *op. cit.*, 60n; Ray Ginger, *The Bending Cross: A Biography of Eugene Victor Debs* (New Brunswick, 1949), 237.

42. Brissenden, *op. cit.*, 57–62, 68–72; Ira Kipnis, *The American Socialist Movement, 1897–1912* (New York, 1952), 195; *Brauer-Zeitung*, XIX (April 30, 1904), 4; XIX (May 7, 1904), 2; XX (February 4, 1905), 1; XX (April 22, 1905), 1; XX (April 29, 1905), 4.

43. Gompers' role in the affair was interesting. With his known antipathy toward both socialism and industrial unionism, it might have been supposed that he would favor the expulsion of the Brewery Workers Union from the AFL. In fact, however, he counseled patience and caution, partly because he realized the need to carry the bulk of trade-union opinion along with him, and partly because he feared that the Brewery Workers, and other unions too, might leave the AFL for the IWW voluntarily if they believed that gross injustice had been done. He believed that it was particularly important to retain the confidence of the United Mine Workers of America, in view of its large size and its own strong feelings on the subject of industry-wide organization. See J.

C. Shannesy to Gompers, October 4, 1905; Gompers to J. C. Shannesy, December 2, 1905 (A.F. of L. Collection, Wisconsin State Historical Society).

44. *Brauer-Zeitung*, XIX (April 16, 1904), 1; XIX (May 14, 1904), 1; XIX (May 28, 1904), 1; XIX (June 18, 1904), 1; Savage, *op. cit.,* 68; Taft, *op. cit.,* 191.

45. *Proceedings, Sixteenth Convention of the Brewery Workers' Union* (Toronto, 1906), 125–128, 144; *International Socialist Review,* VI (January, 1906), 435.

46. *Brauer-Zeitung*, XXIII (November 28, 1908), 1; XXIV (February 6, 1909), 1; XXV (October 15, 1910), 1; XXV (November 19, 1910), 1.

47. Vernon H. Jensen, *Heritage of Conflict, Labor Relations in the Nonferrous Metals Industry up to 1930* (Ithaca, 1950), 190; *Miners' Magazine,* VIII (October 31, 1907), 1; *Brauer-Zeitung,* XXII (November 30, 1907), 1. For the attitude of the IWW, see *Industrial Union Bulletin,* I (November 30, 1907), 1; I (January 25, 1908), 1–3.

48. *St. Louis Labor and Arbeiter Zeitung,* cited in *Proceedings, Eighteenth Convention of the Brewery Workers' Union* (Chicago, 1910), 142; *Proceedings, Twentieth Convention of the Brewery Workers' Union* (Baltimore, 1914), 147.

49. *Brauer-Zeitung*, XX (April 29, 1905), 1; XX (November 11, 1905), 1; XXI (May 12, 1906), 1; XXI (August 18, 1906), 1; XXIII (June 27, 1908), 1; XXIII (September 12, 1908), 1; XXIII (November 14, 1908), 1; XXV (January 29, 1910), 1; XXVI (February 4, 1911), 1; XXVII (June 29, 1912), 1.

50. *Ibid.,* XVI (December 21, 1901), 1; XXIII (January 4, 1908), 1; XXIII (January 11, 1908), 2; XXIII (January 18, 1908), 2; XXIII (March 14, 1908), 1.

51. Savage, *op. cit.,* 40; *Brauer-Zeitung,* XXIV (February 6, 1908), 1–2; XXIV (July 31, 1909), 1; XXV (January 29, 1910), 1; XXV (March 19, 1910), 1; XXVI (May 20, 1911), 1. For a further discussion of the relationship between the Western Federation of Miners and the United Mine Workers, and its significance for socialism in the labor movement, see, pp. 215–217, 260–262, 269–272.

52. *Proceedings, Fourteenth Convention of the Brewery Workers' Union* (Cincinnati, 1903), 111; *Proceedings, Eighteenth Convention of the Brewery Workers' Union* (Chicago, 1910), 167–168; *Proceedings, Nineteenth Convention of the Brewery Workers' Union* (Denver, 1912), 167–168, 233–234; *Brauer-Zeitung,* XVII (July 19, 1902), 4.

53. In the Tenth Congressional District of St. Louis, Socialist party candidates received between 15 per cent and 33 per cent of the vote in congressional elections between 1906 and 1912. A breakdown of Milwaukee wards where brewery workers were known to reside also shows a high correlation with the socialist vote. See *Official Manual of the State of Missouri, 1911–1912* (Jefferson City, 1913), 481–489; *Wisconsin Blue Book* (Madison, 1910), pp. 551–553; 1912, pp. 581–584. See also Marvin Wachman, *History of the Social Democratic Party of Milwaukee, 1897–1910* (Urbana, 1945), 22–23 ff.; Frederick I. Olsen, "The Socialist Party and the Unions in Milwaukee, 1900–1912," *Wisconsin Magazine of History,* XLIV (Winter, 1960–1961), 110–116; *Brauer-Zeitung,* XV (November 17, 1900), 1; XVI (March 2, 1901), 1; XVII (November 1, 1902), 1; XIX (April 16, 1904), 1; XIX (October 22, 1904), 1; XXV (April 16, 1910), 1; XXV (November 19, 1910), 1; XXVII (August 24, 1912), 1.

54. The pace of assimilation depended, of course, on a variety of factors, including the rate of social and economic mobility among the immigrants, the strength of Old World bonds, and the attitude of the surrounding community. But it is generally clear that the larger the size of the immigrant population in any given city, the longer its immigrant traditions endured. For a general discussion of the assimilation of German immigrants in Milwaukee, see Gerd Korman, *Industrialization, Immigrants, and Americanizers* (Madison, 1967), especially chapters 6 and 7.

55. Schlüter, *op. cit.*, 274–277; *Brauer-Zeitung*, XX (November 4, 1905), 1; *Proceedings, Twentieth Convention of the Brewery Workers' Union* (Baltimore, 1914), 149.

56. *Proceedings, Sixteenth Convention of the Brewery Workers' Union* (Toronto, 1906), 103–107; *Proceedings, Eighteenth Convention of the Brewery Workers' Union* (Chicago, 1910), 160, 168; *Brauerei Arbeiter Zeitung*, XXV (November 5, 1910), 2; XXVII (August 31, 1912), 2; XXVII (September 7, 1912), 2.

57. *Ibid.*, XXVI (May 4, 1911), 2; XXVI (November 18, 1911), 1; XXVI (December 2, 1911), 2; XXVI (December 9, 1911), 2; XXVI (December 23, 1911), 1.

58. *Brauer-Zeitung*, XVI (May 25, 1901), 4; *Proceedings, Thirteenth Convention of the Brewery Workers' Union* (Philadelphia, 1901), 44; *Proceedings, Eighteenth Convention of the Brewery Workers' Union* (Chicago, 1910), 160.

59. *Brauerei Arbeiter Zeitung*, XXVI (April 1, 1911), 1; *Proceedings, Twenty-first Convention of the Brewery Workers' Union* (Houston, 1917), 60, 144.

60. *Proceedings, Twentieth Convention of the Brewery Workers' Union* (Baltimore, 1914), 140; *Brauerei Arbeiter Zeitung*, XXVI (July 1, 1911), 1; XXVII (July 20, 1912), 1; XXVII (June 14, 1913), 1–2; XXXI (October 14, 1916), 2.

61. Andrew Sinclair, *Prohibition, the Era of Excess* (Boston, 1962), 104–105; *Brauer-Zeitung*, XIX (March 19, 1904), 2; XXI (March 17, 1906), 1; XXII (August 31, 1907), 1; XXV (April 23, 1910), 1; XXV (October 15, 1910) 1.

62. *Proceedings, National Convention of the Socialist Party* (Indianapolis, 1912), 168; *Brauer-Zeitung*, XXIII (January 25, 1908), 1; XXIII (April 11, 1908), 2; XXIX (March 14, 1914), 1; XXX (July 10, 1915), 2. See also Kipnis, *op. cit.*, 76; David Shannon, *The Socialist Party of America, A History* (New York, 1955), 103, 172–173, 198, 217–218.

63. *Proceedings, Twentieth Convention of the Brewery Workers' Union* (Baltimore, 1914), 131–134; *Brauer-Zeitung*, XXIII (November 21, 1908), 1; XXV (August 13, 1910), 2; XXV (September 17, 1910), 2; XXV (October 22, 1910), 1; XXVII (November 9, 1912), 1; XXIX (May 16, 1914), 1; XXIX (September 12, 1914), 1; XXIX (September 26, 1914), 2; XXIX (October 17, 1914), 2. See also Clifton Childs, *The German-Americans in Politics, 1914–1917* (Madison, 1939), 10–20. For cooperation with the United States Brewers Association, see *Brewers' Journal* (official journal of the Association), XXXIX (December 1914), 71–74.

64. Savage, *op. cit.*, 73; Schlüter, *op. cit.*, 303–310, 314; *Proceedings, Twentieth Convention of the Brewery Workers' Union* (Baltimore, 1914), 142; *Brewer and Maltster*, XXXV (February 1916), 157; *American Brewer*, LXI

(August 1918), 320; "Brewing and Liquor Interests and German and Bolshevik Propaganda," Senate Document 61, Subcommittee on the Judiciary (Washington, 1918), 315–317.

65. *Proceedings, Twenty-first Convention of the Brewery Workers' Union* (Houston, 1917), 13, 40–51, 60; Savage, *op. cit.*, 75.

66. For the role of Louis B. Schramm, see Marguerite Green, *The National Civic Federation and the American Labor Movement, 1900–1925* (Washington, 1956), 253n, 257.

67. *Brauerei Arbeiter Zeitung,* XXVII (January 20, 1912), 1; XXVII (February 3, 1912), 1; XXVII (February 17, 1912), 2; XXVII (February 24, 1912), 2; XXVII (March 9, 1912), 1–2; XXVII (March 16, 1912), 1.

68. *Brauer-Zeitung,* XXII (October 26, 1907), 2; XXV (October 15, 1910), 2; XXIX (January 4, 1914), 1; XXIX (August 8, 1914), 2; XXX (April 3, 1915), 1; XXXIV (March 22, 1919), 1.

69. *Brauerei Arbeiter Zeitung,* XXIX (October 10, 1914), 2; XXX (August 7, 1915), 1–2; XXX (August 14, 1915), 1–2; XXXI (January 1, 1916), 1; XXXII (February 17, 1917), 1. For a general discussion of the position of the German-American community in the war, see Childs, *op. cit.*, especially 64–135; and Carl Wittke, *German-Americans and the World War (With Special Emphasis on Ohio's German Language Press)*, (Columbus, 1936).

70. *Brauerei Arbeiter Zeitung,* XXXII (March 24, 1917), 1; XXXII (April 21, 1917), 2; XXXII (April 28, 1917), 1; XXXII (June 2, 1917), 1; XXXII (July 14, 1917), 2; XXXII (November 10, 1917), 1; XXXIII (April 27, 1918), 1; XXXIII (June 22, 1918), 2; XXXIII (August 24, 1918), 2; XXXIII (August 31, 1918), 1; XXXIII (September 28, 1918), 1; *Proceedings, Twenty-second Convention of the Brewery Workers' Union* (Milwaukee, 1920), 64.

71. *Brewery, Flour, Cereal and Soft Drink Workers' Journal,* XXXIII (March 2, 1918), 2; XXXIII (March 16, 1918), 1; XXXIV (February 1, 1919), 2.

72. *Brauerei Arbeiter Zeitung,* XXXII (August 11, 1917), 1; XXXIV (June 21, 1919), 1; XXXIV (August 30, 1919), 1; XXXIX (January 25, 1924), 1; Savage, *op. cit.*, 75–77; Sinclair, *op. cit.*, 161, 165, 337, 345–346; Samuel Morison and Henry Commager, *The Growth of the American Republic,* 2 vols. (New York, 1950), II, 378, 528–529. For a general discussion of Prohibition and the labor movement, see Nuala McGann Drescher, "Organized Labor and the Eighteenth Amendment," *Labor History,* VIII (Fall, 1967), 280–299.

73. *Brewery, Flour, Cereal and Soft Drink Workers' Journal,* XXXIV (October 4, 1919), 1; XXXV (February 7, 1920), 1; *Proceedings, Twenty-second Convention of the Brewery Workers' Union* (Milwaukee, 1920), 5–6, 80–82.

74. *Industrial Union News,* January 22, 1921, cited in Savage, *op. cit.*, 75; *Proceedings, Twenty-second Convention of the Brewery Workers' Union* (Milwaukee, 1920), 190–210; *Brewery, Flour, Cereal and Soft Drink Workers' Journal,* XXXIII (October 26, 1918), 1; XXXIV (June 21, 1919), 2; XXXIV (October 4, 1919), 1; XXXIV (November 15, 1919), 2; XXXIV (December 13, 1919), 1.

75. *Ibid.,* XXXIII (March 2, 1918), 1; *Proceedings, Twenty-second Convention of the Brewery Workers' Union* (Milwaukee, 1920), 59–60, 108.

76. *Ibid.,* 60.

77. *Brewery, Flour, Cereal and Soft Drink Workers' Journal,* XXXVII

(March 18, 1922), 1; XXXVII (July 8, 1922), 2; XXXVII (November 25, 1922), 1; XXXIX (October 11, 1924), 1; *Proceedings, Twenty-third Convention of the Brewery Workers' Union* (Philadelphia, 1923), 58–59, 86; *Proceedings, Twenty-fourth Convention of the Brewery Workers' Union* (Cincinnati, 1926), 49–54.

3

DeLeonite Socialism and the
Irish Shoe Workers of New England

The Irish are not usually thought to have made any significant contribution to American radicalism. Indeed, the evidence so far seems to confirm the view that most of them were either indifferent to it or actively opposed. Unlike the Germans, most Irish immigrants were poor peasants with no experience in the urban labor movement. They began by forming a shifting, pick-and-shovel caste in mining, construction, and elsewhere. Later, when they did become powerful in building and in other skilled trades, they exercised a largely conservative influence among the craft unions of the AFL. Politically, most Irish trade-unionists were considered to be Democrats, and such radical tendencies as they had to be held in check by the powerful influence of the Roman Catholic church.[1]

However, this pattern was not universal. A number of the early protest movements of American labor, such as the Mollie Maguires, were led by the Irish, and the Knights of Labor, in which they were influential, was in many respects more radical than the AFL. We have already noticed that a few of the second-generation Irish in the Brewery Workers Union were prepared to support a more formal type of socialism. This will be seen again among the machinists, the metal miners, and elsewhere. But the most interesting example of radical influence among the Irish was to be found among the shoe workers of New England, particularly in Massachusetts, which was the home of shoemaking in much the same way that Wiscon-

54

sin and other midwestern states were the home of the brewing trade. In the small shoe towns of this state, traditionally divided between Yankee Republicans and Irish Democrats, the socialists succeeded at the end of the nineteenth century in building up a considerable socialist movement, which was supported for a time by the Boot and Shoe Workers Union, a largely Irish organization founded in Boston in 1895.[2]

This support did not last for very long. After the turn of the century most of the radicals split off, forming rival shoe workers' unions instead, and the Boot and Shoe Workers Union reverted to the characteristic conservative pattern of the AFL. But during its socialist period it was strongly influenced by the DeLeonites in the Socialist Labor party. Indeed, it was one of the few national unions to try to make the DeLeonite philosophy of trade-unionism work. It is in this fact, coupled with the sudden change to AFL orthodoxy and the results which this produced, that the major interest of this chapter lies.

I

Shoemaking was the first American industry to be organized on any scale. A local union of shoe workers in Philadelphia dates back to 1792, and spasmodic organization took place in several other cities in the years before the Civil War. In 1867 a national organization was founded, the Knights of St. Crispin, which reached a membership of about 50,000 and upheld a variety of social and economic objectives besides those traditionally upheld by a trade-union. In fact, the Knights of St. Crispin were for a time more successful than any previous labor organization in America. Since women were also employed in the shoe industry, a comparable organization for them, the Daughters of St. Crispin, also existed for some years. In later years women continued to play an important role in the national unions of the trade.

The depression of 1873 virtually destroyed the Knights of St. Crispin, although an unsuccessful attempt to revive it was made in 1875.[3] After this the lasters, who were the most highly skilled and best organized element in the shoe industry, formed their own organization, the Lasters Protective Union of America, in 1879. But most other shoe workers joined the Knights of Labor, and in Massachusetts they became the largest group within it. Charles Litchman, grand scribe of the Crispins, was made grand secretary of the Knights, and several of its other leaders were also shoe workers. However, as time went on and the number of shoe workers in the Knights of Labor grew, so did their wish to establish a trade organization of their own. In 1887, under Henry J. Skeffington, who was the foremost leader of the shoe workers at this time, the shoe workers in the Knights established National Trade Assembly 216. The national leaders of the K of L objected to this, as they did in other trades, so in 1889 most members of Assembly 216 left the Knights and established the Boot and Shoe Workers International Union.[4]

Thus in 1889 there were three separate organizations in the shoe trade: the Lasters Protective Union, the Boot and Shoe Workers International Union (both of which affiliated with the AFL), and the remnants of National Trade Assembly 216, in the Knights of Labor. This situation persisted for the next six years. Each union did what it could to improve the lot of the shoe workers in its own organization, but none of them, save to some extent the Lasters, was able to make much progress on its own. Not surprisingly, therefore, demands soon arose for the consolidation of all three unions into one united organization. In June 1894 committees from all three met and agreed on a common union label, and plans were drawn up for amalgamation. These were endorsed by referendum vote late in 1894. As a result, a combined convention—comprising 136 delegates from thirty-five towns and cities,[5] the great bulk of them from Massachusetts—met in Boston in April 1895, and the Boot and Shoe Workers Union was formed. John F. Tobin, of Rochester, New York, a well-known local labor leader and an established member of the Socialist Labor party, was elected general president, and Horace M. Eaton, of Lynn, Massachusetts, who was also a socialist, was elected general secretary. Under their administration, the Boot and Shoe Workers Union was to be committed to socialist ideas and policies for the next several years.[6]

By no means all the delegates to the 1895 founding convention were socialists. The assembly included, according to one account, "all shades of political opinion, from socialist laborite to republican," and the balance of opinion throughout the delegates as a whole was probably left of center. Several of the convention's leaders, such as James F. Carey, of Haverhill (who presided), were ex-Populists who had only just come over to socialism, and the militancy of several of the others was due more to the loss of a bitterly fought strike in Haverhill, and to the economic hardship induced by the prevailing industrial depression, than it was to any specific commitment to socialist ideology. The socialist element failed—although only by a small majority—in their attempt to secure the adoption of a constitutional preamble committing the new organization to the abolition of the "competitive wage system." And when Tobin was elected general president he found it necessary to reassure those who had opposed him in the balloting that whatever his party affiliation, the union would be run "in the interests of the entire membership."

Nevertheless, socialists played a major role at all levels of the proceedings. Fred Carter, an official of the Lynn Lasters Union, an ex-Populist, and a DeLeonite member of the SLP, was a member of the constitution committee. Fred G. R. Gordon, of Manchester, New Hampshire, another ex-Populist socialist, was elected secretary of the assembly. Michael Berry, also a Socialist Laborite, sat on a committee that considered "secret work." So did Carlton Beals, whom the first socialist mayor of Brockton was later to appoint city marshal. An addition to this, besides Tobin and Eaton three of the seven members of the General Executive Board were members of the SLP, and although the third general officer, General Treasurer Alvin C. Howes, was not a socialist, his office was soon afterward merged with that of the secretary. Thus Tobin and Eaton, subject only in some respects to the General Executive Board, were left in virtually complete control. As if to demonstrate that the show of strength at the 1895 convention was not simply a flash in the pan, a new SLP local was founded in Haverhill soon after the assembly adjourned, and the state-wide vote of the party in Massachusetts, which came primarily from the shoe towns, jumped from 4,744 in 1895 to 8,108 in 1897.[7]

Why should this have been so? Why should a growing number of New England shoe workers, many of them native-born Americans or second-generation Irish Catholics, residing in a state where the poor had traditionally sought to better themselves by seeking control of the Democratic party, vote not Democratic but socialist and elect militant socialists to the major offices of their union? It does not, of course, follow because they elected Tobin to the presidency of the BSWU in 1895 that all, or even most, of the rank-and-file members of the union were political socialists. There were a variety of political opinions among the membership, as already indicated, and it may well be that Tobin was initially elected because of his local prominence or because of his talents as a trade-union leader, rather than because he was a member of the SLP. But the fact that the same socialist administration was repeatedly elected to office throughout the 1890's and beyond, even when the union was going through difficult times, indicates that something besides personal influence and electoral good fortune was involved.

There was no obvious ethnic or immigrant explanation for this, as there was in the case of the Brewery Workers Union. Although Dublin had a labor movement in the early part of the nineteenth century, there was no organized socialist party or socialist movement in Ireland until 1896, well after the major Irish immigration to the United States was over, and almost nothing of the relatively sophisticated urban labor movement which had been developing in Germany since the 1870's. It is true that in the 1840's and 1850's some of the Irish, like some of the Germans, fled to America for reasons of political repression, and they often suffered as much from nativist hostility as the continental immigrants did, despite the absence of a language barrier. But most of the Irish came to America simply out of poverty and in the hope of a better life, and although a few did become socialists out of intellectual conviction, Irish Marxists were few and far between.[8]

It is also possible to exaggerate the role of the Irish in the Massachusetts shoe industry. A considerable number of the early shoe workers, especially in the Knights of St. Crispin, were either native-born Americans or of English descent.[9] Moreover, since large-scale Irish immigration to Massachusetts, as to other states, had largely ceased when the BSWU was established in 1895, many of the Irish workers in the trade were of the second generation rather than of the first. For example, Henry J. Skeffington, although of Irish origin, was born in California in 1858 and spent most of his life in Philadelphia. Edward L. Daley, general secretary of the Lasters Protective Union, was born and bred in Danvers, Massachusetts. And Tobin himself, who was to remain general president of the BSWU from 1895 to his death in 1919, was born in Guelph, Ontario, in 1855, of Irish Catholic parents.[10]

However, statistical evidence shows clearly the large and growing role of first-generation Irish in the Massachusetts shoe industry during the period under review. Of the 39,245 workers employed in the industry in 1878, by far the largest immigrant group, numbering 6,056, came from southern Ireland. A considerable proportion of the group were located in the three major shoe towns of Haverhill, Brockton, and Lynn, which were the main centers of factory production in the industry. By 1903 the proportion of Irish had grown still larger. Out of a total number of 72,479 workers employed in the industry in that year, 20,665 (or more than 28 per cent) were Irish-born. The next largest immigrant group were the Canadians, many of whom had also come originally from Ireland. In addition, it is reasonable to assume that quite a number of those who were listed as having been born in Massachusetts itself (19,827, or 27 per cent of the total) were also of Irish origin.

It is also significant that the Irish were even more prominent in the Boot and Shoe Workers Union than they were in the labor force of the industry as a whole. At the 1895 convention, for example, more than 80 of the 123 delegates had Irish names, the remainder being largely English in their nomenclature. Only two were identifiably German or eastern European. In 1897, over half of the delegates were of Irish origin, and in 1904 the proportion was even higher. These estimates can only be considered approximate, because of the difficulty of separating Scottish or Scots-Irish names from Irish names as such. The important point, however, is that the radical period in the history of the BSWU coincides with rising Irish influence in the union, and that some, at least, of the Irish immigrants among the shoe workers seemed no less willing to embrace socialism as an ideology, or at least to follow socialist leaders, than were the English or native-born Americans among them. Although the opposition of Catholic leaders toward socialism did later help to prevent its further growth, the fact that some of the Massachusetts shoe workers were willing to embrace it in the early period suggests that Marc Karson's hypothesis—that the opposition of the Catholic church precluded virtually all socialist influence among Irish workingmen—is somewhat oversimplified.[11]

At all events, it is apparent that the origins of socialism among the shoe workers are to be found in indigenous or native American sources, and not in the immigrant tradition of socialism brought over from continental Europe. It should be pointed out, also, that the Boot and Shoe Workers Union was not an industrial union, as the Brewery Workers Union was, but a craft union, like the majority of trade-unions in the AFL. Thus its radicalism cannot be attributed to a sense of class solidarity derived from the effects of industrial methods of organization. Although the union did seek to enroll cutters, lasters, stitchers, and all the other separate elements in the trade, it organized them into separate craft locals. It made no effort, as the Brewery Workers Union did in its organizing policy, to enroll those who played a part in the industry, but were not involved in the process of shoemaking as such.[12]

Socialist influences in the shoe industry appear to have stemmed, in fact, from two main sources: the radical, humanitarian, and cooperative traditions to be found in both the Knights of St. Crispin and the Knights of Labor; and, more particularly, from the severe effects of mechanization and the introduction of the factory system on the shoe worker and his craft. There was some evidence of an interest in cooperation as an alternative to the wage system even before the Knights of St. Crispin was set up in 1867. In the early 1800's the journeymen cordwainers of Philadelphia opened a boot and shoe workers' cooperative in the hope of securing "permanent self employment." And in 1862 Thomas Phillips, an ex-Chartist shoemaker from Yorkshire who joined the Crispins and later became president of the Boot and Shoe Workers International Union, established another cooperative store in Philadelphia, on Rochdale principles.[13]

But it was the Knights of St. Crispin who first took up cooperation among the shoe workers with any widespread or serious intent. "We believe," the Preamble to the Knights' constitution declared, "in cooperation as a proper and efficient remedy for many of the evils of the present iniquitous system of wages that concede to the laborer only so much of his own productions as shall make a comfortable living a bare possibility, and places education and social position beyond his reach." Each grand lodge had a special committee on cooperation, and in February 1869 cooperative manufacture of shoes was begun by fifteen Crispins in St. John's, New Brunswick. The New York Crispins started a factory in 1870, and there were similar ventures in Newark, Philadelphia, Baltimore, and elsewhere.[14]

This interest was continued under the Knights of Labor, although with less evidence of practical attempts at implementation. Charles Litchman, A. A. Carlton, and other leaders of the Massachusetts District Assembly were all ex-shoemakers who were committed in one way or another to the cooperative ideal, and this time they acted within the broader context of the general Massachusetts movement for utopian socialism and radical reform. Ira Steward, the Boston machinist who originated the eight-hour-day philosophy, was a member of the district assembly, and its leader was George E. McNeill, a contemporary of Albert Brisbane, Wendell Phillips, and other early utopians, and at that time the most celebrated labor leader in the state.[15]

Essentially, however, the shoe workers turned toward cooperation in an attempt to restore the means of self-employment which the introduction of the factory system into the shoe industry had destroyed. In the brewing industry, specialization of function and the development of large-scale breweries indicated that by the middle of the nineteenth century the typical brewery worker was an employee whose prospects for self-employment were relatively slight. In the shoe industry, however, a single skilled journeyman continued to manufacture the entire product until the Civil War and even beyond. Then centuries of self-employment were quite suddenly disrupted by the effects of factory organization and technological change. Since the shoe trade was one of the first to feel these effects on a large scale, the consequent disorientation and disruption were all the more unexpected and severe.

Before 1850 the expansion of the market and the displacement of custom shoe shops (in which a father and son worked together, with perhaps one apprentice or journeyman) by larger, competing retail or wholesale order shops had already begun to alter the traditional pattern of economic relationships in the industry and had undermined, to some extent, the independence of the individual artisan. But the possibility of attaining ownership and control over one of these larger shops was by no means remote, and the hand craft of the shoemaker was still mainly intact. Indeed, some of the new inventions of the 1850's, such as the stripper, the sole cutter, and the adjustable last, were aids to the journeyman rather than substitutes for his skill. But the pegging machine, introduced in 1857, the McKay sole-sewing machine, first used in 1862, and the Goodyear welt machine, introduced in 1875, were quite different. Instead of supplementing the journeyman's skill, they replaced it. The McKay sole-sewing machine, for instance, stitched as many soles together in one hour as a journeyman did in eighty, and it virtually obviated the need for trained hand stitchers, except on the highest class of shoe. One of the main objects of the Knights of St. Crispin was to prevent the employment of "green hands" or unskilled workers on the new machines, but as time went on this became an increasingly difficult task.

In addition, these new machines could be belted up to steam; and the factory system, with hundreds or even thousands of shoe workers gathered under one roof, came rapidly into being, spurred on by enormous government orders for boots and shoes during the Civil War. By 1880 it had already assumed much of its modern form, and the journeyman or small master was increasingly forced to abandon his separate business and find employment in one of the new factories in Lynn, Haverhill, Brockton, or elsewhere. The expanding industry was also going through an intensely competitive stage, so that the shoe worker's factory wages, initially, at least, were often considerably lower than earnings in the industry had previously been. In 1881, for example, in ten out of the fourteen major occupations associated with the industry in Massachusetts, the average weekly wages had all fallen to a level appreciably below what they had been in 1872, some by as much as 25 per cent. By 1897 (at the conclusion of a major economic recession), they had recovered somewhat, but in eight out of the fourteen occupations wages were still appreciably lower than they had been twenty-five years before. Those employed on the new machines suffered most: average weekly wages among the McKay sole operators, for example, which had been $22.22 in 1872, fell to $15.29 in 1898, a drop of almost one-third.[16] Both of these, it should be added, were prosperous years.

The shoe manufacturers were themselves aware of the difficulties created for these employees by the introduction of the new machinery, and some of the more humane among them regarded it as a cause for regret. One midwestern employer, writing in 1899 to the St. Louis *Shoe and Leather Gazette,* reported that "the invention of this machinery has revolutionized the production of these goods, and made it possible for manufacturers to get their work done much better, quicker and more cheaply than by the old hand methods. . . . It is to be regretted that the employment of machinery creates a surplus of shoe factory help," he added, "but it seems to be inevitable." [17] In addition, the piecework system was also rapidly introduced, bringing with it one of the first severe instances of "speeding up." Work in the shoe industry was seasonal, like that in the garment trades, depending on changes in style from winter to summer, as well as on seasonal fluctuations in demand, and one of the first effects of the factory system was to shorten the work season, bringing with it longer periods of unemployment. As if all this were not enough, the shoe workers also had to compete with cheap, imported Chinese labor, with prison-made shoes, and with migratory seasonal labor that came down from Canada to New England.[18]

It seems highly likely that it was these industrial changes, with the loss of skill, of status, and of earning power which they entailed, which were primarily responsible for the growth of socialist sentiment among the shoe workers. Frank Sieverman, a young shoe worker who became prominent in both the SLP and the Socialist party, ascribed his socialist beliefs to the "disappointed aspirations and shattered ideals" which, he said, he experienced upon entering a shoe factory at the age of seventeen. Thomas Phillips, soon after moving from Philadelphia to Massachusetts in 1889, reaffirmed his commitment to cooperative methods as an alternative to the capitalist system, declaring that he was "putting in more work than ever for less wage." And J. W. Sherman, the unsuccessful socialist candidate for mayor of Boston in 1899, attributed a significant proportion of the increased socialist vote throughout Massachusetts in that year to the discontented shoe worker, who today,

> in a great shoe factory, . . . produces fully 20 times what he could do 40 years ago. Nobody thinks for an instant that he is getting 20 times as much in comfort from his labor as he did then. Looked at fairly it is at once seen that his present condition . . . grows from the fact that he is producing for somebody else, who takes for the service of furnishing him a machine to work with and a "job," the slight toil of four-fifths of the product.[19]

This latter point, that the workers received a declining share of the wealth which had been made possible by the technological advances, was taken up again by F. G. R. Gordon in the following year. Citing statistics drawn from the federal census of 1890, he reported that the shoe workers of Haverhill had produced $16,137,350 worth of shoes during the course of that year. But they had received only $3,849,129 in money wages. "How generous we are!" Gordon added. "Under socialism the workers would receive what they produced. Under the present system they receive only about one-fifth." But it was Horace M. Eaton, the socialist general secretary of the BSWU, who summed up the difficulties of the shoe workers in perhaps the most dramatic way. "So long as we allow the employer to traffic in human flesh," he said in his report to the 1897 shoe workers' convention, "and to reduce wages simply on the grounds that he must 'meet competition,' so long as we submit to these brutal conditions without declaring and working for the abolition of such a brutal system of industry, so long have we, in greater or less degree, to endure the evils of which we now complain." [20]

The discontents engendered by these changes showed themselves politically from quite an early date. In 1869, when the Knights of St. Crispin were at their peak, an independent workingman's party was established in Massachusetts which was credited with helping to elect twenty-one representatives and a senator to the Massachusetts legislature. This party disappeared in 1872, but interest in political action, either on an independent basis or within one of the major parties, reappeared from time to time and revived in 1886 when McNeill ran for mayor of Boston on the United Labor party ticket.

The objectives of this early political movement were mainly currency reform, eight hours, and other panacea proposals then fashionable throughout the labor movement as a whole, and this reformist tradition continued to affect the shoe workers for some time. Neither Edward Bellamy's Nationalist clubs, nor the Christian socialist movement of the Rev. W. P. D. Bliss, both of which originated in Massachusetts, attracted many trade-unionists. But the more radical elements in the Massachusetts People's party did manage to secure some support among the shoe workers in the early 1890's. James F. Carey, a young shoe worker who was later to become the leading light of Massachusetts socialism, led the Haverhill branch of the Populists between 1891 and 1894, and other shoe workers who later became socialists, such as John C. Chase and Louis M. Scates, were also Populists at this time. The state-wide Populist vote was minuscule compared with that of the major parties, but it rose from 3,045 in 1891 to 8,306 in 1894.

By April 1895, however, when the founding convention of the Boot and Shoe Workers Union was held, the influence of revolutionary socialism in the Massachusetts movement was growing, and that of reformism and utopianism, as elsewhere in the American socialist movement, was in decline. As we have seen, Carey, who was elected chairman of the 1895 convention, had by this time come over to socialism from Populism, and in addition to Tobin, Eaton, and members of the General Executive Board, several rank-and-file delegates were also members of the SLP. Besides this, two of the organizations contributing delegates, the Lasters Protective Union and the Boot and Shoe Workers International Union, had endorsed Thomas J. Morgan's Political Program of 1894.[21]

Unlike the Brewery Workers Union, therefore, indigenous traditions of cooperation and reform played a major role in the development of socialism among the shoe workers, supplemented only later by the rise of Marxism and the SLP. But whatever form the radicalism took, the essential fact appeared to be, that the deep discontents engendered by rapid industrialization and by the destruction of the shoemakers' craft were strong enough, for a time, to override the individualistic tendencies and Catholic loyalties even of the Irish element among the shoe workers, and to bring the socialists to power in the trade.

II

Despite his promise to the 1895 convention that his connection with the SLP would not interfere with the administration of the Boot and Shoe Workers Union, it soon appeared that John F. Tobin, in the first few years of his presidency, was not simply a militant socialist but a convinced DeLeonite who was one of the very few trade-union leaders to try to make the economic policies of the Socialist Labor party work. Although the BSWU was officially affiliated with the AFL, Tobin caustically denounced its policies on a whole range of issues in a speech at the Cooper Union in New York City when attending the AFL convention of December 1895. In addition, the BSWU at first deliberately refrained from extending its jurisdiction into the New York area, leaving the organization of shoe workers there to the General Council of Shoe Workers, which was dominated by the DeLeon-controlled Socialist Trades and Labor Alliance. In its internal conduct of the BSWU, moreover, the union administration at first belittled the traditional economic weapons of trade-unionism, and sought to develop it as a militant, revolutionary organization without the high dues and benefit systems which were characteristic of most of the other craft unions in the AFL. Thus dues were set very low, so as to enable even the lowest-paid workers in the industry to join; no strike or other union benefits were paid; and local unions had almost complete sovereignty in the handling of their own affairs, especially in control over strikes.[22]

Secretary Eaton was almost equally militant in his opinions, although as the union officer most directly responsible for its financial affairs, he expressed greater concern about the financial stability of the organization. He told the BSWU membership in April 1896:

> It goes without saying that the most successful labor organizations of the future will be the ones standing on platforms best calculated to meet the ever changing conditions of industrial production, and whose members best understand the true relations of labor and capital; . . . provided, always, that the financial plans of such organizations are equal to those of the organizations that may be less progressive in thought.

At first, however, little attempt was made to enforce the union's constitution or to discipline locals who failed to pay their dues.[23]

This method of approach was attractive to many of the shoe workers if only because it made few demands on them and necessitated little change in the tactics which they had previously pursued. Local autonomy had been one of the characteristics of shoe workers' organizations since the days of the Knights of St. Crispin, and in the period immediately preceding 1895, especially since the beginning of the depression, they had taken up an increasingly belligerent attitude toward the employers. The result was a large number of strikes against attempted wage reductions, ending mostly in failure because they soon exhausted the new union's meager financial resources. Instead of deploring these losses, however, Tobin at first appeared actively to welcome them as a means of increasing the militancy and revolutionary fervor of the working class. The lost strikes, he told the June 1896 convention of the BSWU, would serve to

> teach our people that while the strike and boycott are very good, as far as they go, and must be used as a protest against any further encroachment upon our wages, still they fall far short of a solution of the problem. When we learn not to pin all our faith to the strike and boycott, we are not disappointed or discouraged by failures on these lines; we will not surrender our union and give up all hope but keep right on gaining recruits and new strength with each succeeding failure of the old weapons.

Tobin seemed also convinced, as this excerpt from his presidential report implies, that these defeats would actually serve to consolidate the position of the union among the shoe workers as a whole. "We have," he told the convention,

> a large portion of our membership who, together with a still greater number who are not with us, . . . are convinced that an organization with no other aim than a desire to gain a few more cents per day, and having only the strike and boycott as weapons with which to obtain these ends, is doomed to failure, and they are earnestly waiting for us to take a forward move before giving us their active support.[24]

What this "forward move" was to be was not perfectly clear. It might appear that it was a suggestion that the union give up its economic activities altogether and devote itself wholly to politics instead. But this was an extreme position which Tobin did not, in fact, uphold. During the presidential campaign of 1896 he was careful not to go too far in supporting the SLP for fear of dividing the union membership. And at the June 1897 union convention he was reluctant to give his wholehearted support to a resolution openly endorsing the SLP, although he made it clear that this was because he did not wish to compromise his position with the nonsocialist element in the union, rather than because he opposed endorsement of the party as such. "It was not necessary," he said, "for someone to draw a picture of a horse and label it 'This is a horse' to point the way out to the abolition of competition."

After considerable debate, union endorsement of the SLP at the 1897 convention was defeated by 59 votes to 17, despite the fact that Tobin, Eaton, and several other members of the General Executive Board somewhat unwillingly gave it their support. However, the socialists in the convention retaliated by refusing to adopt administration proposals for increasing the union's dues and tightening up control over strikes, which Eaton in particular had recommended. They also succeeded in securing the adoption of a radical preamble to the union's constitution, much like the one which had been defeated in 1895. Without specifically endorsing any political party, the new Preamble (which remained attached to the constitution until 1913) endorsed the central element in Marxism by declaring for "the collective ownership by the people of all means of production, distribution, communication and exchange." This time Tobin and Eaton fully agreed with the proposal, and it was adopted by a majority of three. The "purely economic form of organization," Tobin said in welcoming the result of the vote, had clearly demonstrated its inadequacy to meet the real needs of the shoe workers. "The trades union that does not, and will not change with ever changing industrial conditions is not worthy of the name of a trades union and as such will not survive." [25]

Despite the narrow margin of victory for the new Preamble, the June 1897 convention probably represented the peak of socialist sentiment in the BSWU. In the months which followed, reports continued to come in of widespread radical discontent in the field. The Lynn locals, for example, reported "widespread . . . toleration of the views and plans of the Socialists, and education along those lines increasing fast. Jobs hard. Small wages. More money in chopping cord wood." Rochester similarly reported "actual destitution and want among our membership," despite the lessening of the economic depression. "May their bitter experience teach them," the Rochester secretary added, "that active membership in . . . the Socialist Labor Party must go hand in hand with their union affiliation, if they would enjoy the full fruits of their labor." In his monthly report for October 1897, Horace M. Eaton, who hitherto had been more moderate than most of the other socialists in the union, declared that it was the "first duty of the trade union" to seek government ownership of industry, which could "only be obtained at the ballot box." [26]

However, by this time severe strains had already begun to appear in the relations between the BSWU and the Socialist Labor party—strains which were shortly to transform their initially cordial relationship into one of mutual recrimination and distrust and were to provide a classic example of the serious consequences which DeLeonite control over the SLP was to have on relations between the socialists and the trade-union movement as a whole. The immediate cause of the estrangement, as in other trade-unions, was the dual union activities of the Socialist Trades and Labor Alliance. Although he had given indirect endorsement to the ST & LA when it first appeared in December 1895, Tobin (like other socialists in the labor movement) at first assumed that its major purpose would be to organize the vast numbers of unskilled and semiskilled workers who had not yet been enrolled into the AFL. But he was very soon disconcerted by the widespread and undiscriminating attacks which the ST & LA launched against virtually all the trade-unions associated with the AFL. In fact, he later claimed that he had been "deliberately buncoed" into attending the December 13, 1895, Cooper Union meeting at which the ST & LA had been announced, claiming that the "evident purpose [of the meeting] had been to discredit me in the Federation." On the very next day, December 14, 1895, Gompers indirectly criticized Tobin for having spoken at the Cooper Union meeting, before all the assembled delegates of the AFL; and the attraction of the ST & LA for the BSWU was further reduced by the official endorsement which the AFL gave to the Boot and Shoe Workers Union label as the only legitimate shoe label in the industry. This helped to improve the bargaining position of the union in its relations with the employers and was much more effective than any comparable endorsement from the ST & LA would have been.

The generally divisive consequences of the ST & LA dual union tactics were also a matter of concern. In 1895 Vice-President Howes of the BSWU, who was a conservative, went out of his way to reproach the New York Shoe workers for continually "dividing . . . into factions" and "roasting each other" over matters of socialist and trade-union ideology. But the more radical Eaton also expressed concern over the dissension which had been created at the 1896 convention of the union by a prolonged discussion of socialist political action. "In no local Union," he wrote in his monthly report for May 1896, should "discussions of a political nature be allowed to absorb the entire attention of the members to such an extent as to cause any of the interests of our organization as a trade union to be neglected." [27]

Up to this point the ST & LA had refrained from attacking the BSWU as such, and it had done little more than to elicit mild expressions of disapproval. DeLeon's *The People* went on praising the BSWU as a "progressive trade organization," and relations between the union and the Socialist Labor party continued to remain good. But this situation did not persist for long. Frank Sieverman, general secretary of the influential Boot and Shoe Workers local in Rochester, New York, was one of the socialists who strongly opposed the endorsement of the ST & LA by the Socialist Labor party convention which met in New York in July 1896. For this he was denounced by DeLeon as a traitor to the working class; and shortly afterward there appeared the first signs of an open jurisdictional conflict between the ST & LA and the BSWU. In the fall of 1896 the Rochester local of the union refused to accept the transfer cards of New York members of the General Council of Shoe Workers (the ST & LA affiliate) who wished to find work in that city, and in Buffalo the ST & LA organized a rival shoe workers' union of its own. Some Massachusetts locals (for instance, in Haverhill) continued to accept ST & LA transfer cards for some time. But the union's resentment at the ST & LA encroachments on its jurisdiction was demonstrated at the June 1897 Boot and Shoe Workers Union convention, which decided not to recognize the transfer cards of "any organization embracing shoe workers that is not attached to this union," save in the case of immigrants coming from abroad. The convention also refused to adopt a resolution urging the union to withdraw from the AFL and to transform itself instead into the National Socialist Alliance of the Boot and Shoe Workers of the United States and Canada; that is, into a ST & LA branch. This time Tobin, Eaton, Sieverman, and nearly all the other leading socialists in the organization voted against the resolution.[28]

This show of defiance was too much for the DeLeonites; and at the annual convention of the ST & LA which took place in Boston in July 1897, one month after the BSWU convention had adjourned in the same city, they registered their disapproval in no uncertain way. In his report Ernest Boehm, general secretary of the ST & LA, acknowledged that much had been expected of the Boot and Shoe Workers Union when it had first been established in 1895. But Tobin's failure to commit it to the SLP had shown that it was, at bottom, "a reactionary body." A resolution was adopted condemning the union (unfairly) for adhering to a policy of "organizing the craft on the basis of economic action only"; and it was decided that the ST & LA should now try to organize the shoe workers for itself "in every and all towns where shoe workers are employed." [29]

A jurisdictional war now followed between the two organizations, with the Socialist Trades and Labor Alliance establishing local assemblies in New York, Chicago, and St. Louis, as well as in Haverhill and Marlboro, in Massachusetts. However, it was unable to attract more than a small number of Boot and Shoe Workers locals into its camp, and the conflict simply served to increase antagonism on both sides. In December 1897 Tobin visited New York and established two BSWU locals in the area, openly breaking the two-year truce which had existed between the two organizations there. One, Local 60 in Brooklyn, enrolled 80 members within a few weeks. Local 155, in New York City, had an initial membership of 175. Tobin justified his action on the ground that the General Council of Shoe Workers had done little to organize the New York members of the craft and that wages in the city were so low as to undermine still further the position of the shoe workers in New England. In practice, however, this decision marked the end of any pretense at cooperation between the two organizations. DeLeonites from the General Council in New York stirred up trouble at BSWU meetings; each side accused the other of organizing scabs; and both vied for control of shoe factories in the New York metropolitan area.

A climax was reached on April 24, 1898, when a public debate was held at Teutonia Hall in New York City between Tobin and Sieverman, representing the Boot and Shoe Workers Union, and Daniel DeLeon and William L. Brower, head of the General Council of Shoe Workers, representing the Socialist Trades and Labor Alliance. DeLeon and Brower accused the BSWU of playing politics with the two old parties, of associating with the most reactionary elements in the AFL, and of reneging on its socialist principles. In response, Tobin defended the ideological consistency of the BSWU by citing its 1897 socialist preamble. But it was Frank Sieverman who expressed perhaps best the most important reason why most socialists in the trade-union movement, when faced with a choice between the American Federation of Labor and Socialist Trades and Labor Alliance, found it necessary to remain in the AFL. "It is my humble opinion," Sieverman said, pointing to the failure of the ST & LA to organize more than a few thousand workingmen, "that the present form of trades unions will for a long time be with us. I consider it our duty to organize in them, get the benefits and advantages that result from large numerical strength, and that cannot be had outside of the American Federation of Labor." This argument was not, of course, acceptable to Brower and DeLeon, and it simply served to alienate them still further from the BSWU. Further mutual recriminations and accusations followed, and in the May issue of the *Monthly Report* [30] Tobin signaled his own final and personal break with the De-Leonites. "For years," he wrote, he had considered DeLeon "an able exponent of the doctrine of Socialism, and while not always agreeing as to his methods of expounding the theory, still I did not oppose him, considering that his training, perhaps, better fitted him to judge as to the proper cause to pursue." Above all, Tobin had "unbounded faith in his honesty of purpose." But the use which DeLeon had made of the ST & LA, and his deliberate efforts to undermine the BSWU, had destroyed that faith. DeLeon was, Tobin said, nothing more than an "unscrupulous falsifier." [31]

The conflict between the Boot and Shoe Workers Union and the ST & LA was further exacerbated by the support which the Socialist Trades and Labor Alliance gave to those members of the union, particularly the lasters, who were critical of the organization's official policy of accepting the introduction of new machinery into the trade. As already indicated, the lasters had earlier been among the most highly skilled and best paid of the shoe workers, and they had suffered perhaps more than any other group from the effects of mechanization.[32] As a result, they were also among the most militant radicals in the trade. The union administration, while sympathetic toward the lasters' problems, had decided from the beginning that there was no future in opposing the introduction of lasting machines. Hence they accepted them in principle, while at the same time trying to get the best wages possible for those who worked on them, irrespective of their background and skill. This policy was, however, strongly opposed by the lasters' leaders, who charged the union administration with disregarding their interests and even with selling them out financially to the manufacturers of the new machines. F. S. Carter, of Lynn Lasters Local 32, claimed that the "deplorable condition" of the hand lasters was due to the failure of the union to protect them against competition from those who worked at the new machines; and early in 1898 he threatened to withdraw his local from the Boot and Shoe Workers Union unless a change in policy was made.

This was a serious matter for the union administration, for the Lynn lasters were supported by other Massachusetts shoe workers in Stoneham, Haverhill, and Marblehead. Moreover, they received direct encouragement from the DeLeonites in New York. *The People* commended Carter for his stand, and Brower and his supporters made every effort to persuade the lasters to transfer their allegiance to the Socialist Trades and Labor Alliance. In May 1898, Carter issued a circular to all the lasters in Massachusetts repeating his threat to secede, and at the same time he enumerated the virtues, as he saw them, of the Alliance. The BSWU stood firm, replying that any attempt to oppose the introduction of lasting machinery would be "short-sighted, unscientific, [and] old-fashioned." But this argument proved unavailing. On July 26, 1898, Lynn Lasters Local 32 formally seceded from the union, to be followed shortly afterward by several other lasters' locals. In September 1898 the Lasters Protective Union of America was reconstituted, and it was not until after the turn of the century that most of the seceding locals could be persuaded to return to the BSWU.[33]

The DeLeonites did not, even then, succeed in enlisting many of the lasters into their ranks, although Local 32 was for a time a member of the ST & LA. But the secession served to weaken the BSWU at a critical period of its history, and the whole episode added still further to the personal feelings of antipathy which Tobin and his colleagues felt for DeLeon and the Socialist Trades and Labor Alliance. It also highlighted a further reason for the rift between the two organizations; namely, the difficulties which the BSWU had encountered in its attempt to implement the economic philosophy of the SLP. In 1895, as we have seen, the union had adopted the DeLeonite system of low dues, no union benefits, and limited central control, partly because the shoe workers were accustomed to such methods, but partly also in order to create a broadly based, revolutionary organization which could avoid the business union methods of the AFL.

As time went on, however, it became increasingly clear that these methods had not worked. In 1897 Tobin had expressed a certain amount of concern at the increasing economic difficulties with which the union was faced and at its failure to make any significant membership gains. Then, he had used these difficulties simply as an illustration of the DeLeonite philosophy which he wished to expound. But by June 1899, when the next BSWU convention was held, despite a further (and this time much more extensive) recovery in business, the condition of the union was still worse. A considerable proportion of its strikes had again been lost, most notably one in Marlboro, Massachusetts, where a major wage reduction had been forced. Moreover, membership, instead of rising, had continued to decline. In 1897 it had been 12,229. By 1898 it had fallen to 9,727 and since then had fallen again to 8,966. Financially, the organization could no longer cover its expenses. In 1898 it had run into debt, with obligations which had grown over the previous year, and there was a considerable danger, which Eaton recognized in his financial report, that unless the union reformed its economic policies, it might disintegrate altogether. "This union," Eaton asserted, "must now choose once and forever whether it will speedily go out of existence or whether it will raise the dues for the purpose of binding its members together with benefits, assist them in time of strike, and extend and increase the union by liberal expenditures in the interest of the union stamp." [34]

Still more striking were the views of John F. Tobin himself. In his presidential report on the first day of the 1899 convention he showed that in addition to other reasons for estrangement from the SLP he had completely abandoned his belief in the economic basis of DeLeonism and had accepted the need for strong craft unions, complete with high dues, a benefit system, and large financial reserves. In the interim since the 1897 convention, Tobin said, he had become convinced "that an economic organization based upon high dues and the payment of sick, death, and strike assistance would produce much better results for its members than a union whose only source of solidarity is the class conscious sympathy of its workers one for another."

Tobin was well aware that his views no longer accorded with those of DeLeon or of the dwindling number of his supporters in the BSWU. So he went on to justify his changed position at some length, indicating as he did so some of the most important reasons why DeLeonism had proved unacceptable to the American labor movement as a whole. It was held by some, he admitted, that to build up the financial reserves and economic strength of a trade-union was futile, since the employers were invariably wealthier than their employees and could always call upon greater capital resources in a trial of strength. Tobin acknowledged the strength of this argument, but was now no longer prepared to accept it:

> Those who proceed upon the principle that because an employer . . . can defeat a trade union in an economic battle, that it is useless to build up an economic organization upon a financial or beneficial basis, are, in my opinion, setting up the proposition that because an opposing army is equipped with all the modern implements of war, then, the best kind of army to engage them in battle is one having the very poorest . . . implements of war, or in other words the weaker your defense against the strong army the more mercy they will have upon you.

A reorganized and strengthened union, Tobin argued, equipped with adequate financial reserves and with the ability to provide its members with proper protection in their jobs, would be in a much better position to play its part in the political battle against capitalism than one which was small and weak. A "thorough understanding of the class struggle," he concluded, "supplemented by the implements of war," was the best way to carry the workers to victory.[35]

The next day, Tobin and Eaton together proposed an entirely new constitution to the 1899 convention, providing for higher dues, a strike assistance fund, sick and death benefits, and more centralized control, particularly in the matter of strikes. The new benefits were accepted without much difficulty, but there was considerable opposition to the plans for giving the national administration more power. The real fight, however, came over the proposed increase in union dues. This was considerable, from ten cents per week to twenty-five. But the increase was finally agreed to, and the new constitution as a whole was approved. Along with it went a decision to use the union label, or stamp, rather than the strike as the main instrument of union policy. Contracts were to be signed with employers, known as Union Stamp Contracts, which permitted manufacturers to stamp their shoes union-made in return for recognition of the union, an agreement to submit disputes to arbitration, and other concessions. Promotion of the Union Stamp Contract was now to become the union's major concern.[36]

The new constitution of 1899 proved to be the turning point in the history of the Boot and Shoe Workers Union. Membership recovered to 10,-018 in 1901, and a year later it had more than doubled: at 22,341, it was higher than ever before. The main strength of the union remained in Massachusetts, as it had always done, but now the organization began to flourish in other states. More locals were organized in New York, New Jersey,

Pennsylvania, and Illinois and in other shoe centers such as St. Louis and Cincinnati. The financial position of the union was also transformed. By 1901 its debts had been paid off and it had a considerable surplus. The union's income for 1902 alone was over $160,000, and by January 1904 the membership figure had reached as many as 69,290.

The 1899 reforms were not, of course, the only reason for this change. The years between 1898 and 1903 were in general prosperous, and AFL unions as a whole expanded rapidly during this time. Nevertheless, Tobin and Eaton took much of the credit for these successes and attributed them frequently to the new constitution which they had together introduced. "Before 1899," Tobin wrote in the union journal for January 1904, "the Boot and Shoe Workers was a 'strike organization' with no true understanding of unionism. But the changes which were introduced have shown us the proper course, and since then it has prospered." [37]

III

By 1899, it was clear that the Massachusetts shoe workers had abandoned their DeLeonite socialist philosophy and had adopted the more traditional economic policies of most of the other trade-unions of the AFL. But so far there was no necessary reason to suppose that this would lead them to give up their interest in socialist politics or in the ideology of socialism as such. Other socialist unions were repudiating DeLeonism at this time while still remaining radical in other respects, and during the 1899 convention Tobin went out of his way to insist that although he was no longer a DeLeonite, he still remained a socialist. He told the convention:

> While endeavoring to convince you of the necessity for building an organization upon high dues and one that will take care of the sick and wounded of capitalism, instead of leaving our members to the tender mercies of the enemy, I do not for one moment forget that something more is necessary before the emancipation of the working class is possible, namely . . . [the need to] educate the workers to the point that they will use their ballot for the total abolition of the capitalist system.[38]

It was clear also, as in the case of the Brewery Workers Union, that many of those in the Boot and Shoe Workers Union who had objected to DeLeon's policies in the Socialist Labor party were now transferring their support to the Social Democrats and later to the Socialist Party of America, when it was founded in 1901. The ex-shoe worker James F. Carey, of Haverhill, became the most prominent Massachusetts leader of the Social Democratic party when it was founded in July 1898. But members of the Boot and Shoe Workers Union itself were also directly involved. Stevens, the leader of the Shoe Cutter Union in Lynn, played a leading role in the Social Democratic party in that city; and so did numerous other shoe workers in Brockton, Haverhill, and elsewhere. In Rochester Frank Sieverman led the anti-DeLeonite forces in the SLP,[39] and in the fall of 1898 Tobin himself appeared on campaign platforms alongside of Debs on behalf of the Social Democrats. At a meeting in Haverhill in November 1898 he pleaded for combined political and economic action through the Social Democratic party and the trade unions. And in June 1899, in the BSWU *Monthly Report,* Secretary-Treasurer Eaton came near to endorsing the Social Democrats on behalf of the union as a whole. He was willing to give his wholehearted support to the party, Eaton stated, "as aside from its political principles it is understood to believe in trade unions." [40]

For a time it appeared as though these general statements of approval would be translated into extensive electoral support. In December 1897 Carey had been elected as a socialist to the Haverhill Common Council, largely on shoe workers' votes, and for the next several years the Social Democratic vote was higher in Massachusetts than in almost any other state. In 1898 John C. Chase, another former shoe worker, was elected socialist mayor of Haverhill, and Carey and Louis Scates were voted into the state legislature. Between 1899 and 1902 they were reelected a number of times and introduced a variety of new labor measures—several of which, according to one report, might well have been passed had it not been for combined Republican-Democratic opposition. In the fall of 1899 E. W. Timson, a member of the Lynn Lasters Union, ran for mayor of that city on the Social Democratic ticket. He received quite a respectable vote, thanks partly to the efforts of F. G. R. Gordon, who spoke at shoe factory gates during the noon and evening hours. Brockton, Lynn, Haverhill, and various other Massachusetts towns continued to register a sizable Social Democratic vote in state and municipal elections for the next several years, and although Carey was defeated in his bid for reelection to the state legislature in 1903, a significant socialist movement continued to exist for some time.

The climax appeared to come at the opening of the new Central Labor Union building in Haverhill in October 1900. The Stitchers and several other Boot and Shoe Workers locals had their headquarters in the new building, which also housed the branch offices of the Haverhill Social Democratic party. A parade, headed by the "Social Democratic band," made its way from the Haverhill railroad station, where a special train from Salem and Lynn had brought several hundred shoe workers to take part in the celebrations. Mayor Chase of Haverhill and Representative Carey both spoke, and so did F. G. R. Gordon and William Mailly, editor of the Haverhill *Social Democrat.* Reflecting on the occasion in his paper the following day, Mailly confidently asserted that there was "little difference between a Socialist and a workingman in this part of the country. The workingmen of Massachusetts are learning fast that one cannot be a true union man and not vote a union ticket." [41]

As far as the Boot and Shoe Workers Union was concerned, however, Mailly's confidence turned out to be misplaced. The general attitude of the union administration, as it was reflected in the editorials of the union journal, had by this time begun to show an increasing tendency toward conservatism, not simply on matters of economic policy but also on political issues as well. The union's periodical warned against the impracticality of dreamy reformers who "in ten minutes . . . can prove to you that the world is upside down and that they know the only way to put it right side up." Such enthusiasts were "altogether unfitted" for any responsible executive position, as the wreck of scores of unions "plainly demonstrated." More important, the *Union Boot and Shoe Worker* refused to endorse the Debs-Harriman presidential ticket in 1900, on the ground that it did not "feel qualified to do all the thinking for all the people on all subjects"; and in 1901 it decided to eschew politics altogether. "This journal has a distinct economic mission," the editor wrote, "and . . . will not sacrifice this purpose to any other."

Within a remarkably short space of time, in fact, it became clear that in 1899 most of the shoe workers had not simply repudiated DeLeonism but also abandoned much of their more general socialist orientation as well. This was all the more remarkable because it was precisely in this period, between 1898 and 1903, that the socialist movement in Massachusetts reached its peak. One reason for the sudden change was undoubtedly the legacy of bitterness left by the union's conflict with DeLeon, which led Tobin to characterize all socialists, unfairly, as "radicals who are opposed to contracts of any kind." Another was the rapid assimilation by the union of the values of the AFL. The Boot and Shoe Workers Union, like the Brewery Workers Union, was particularly dependent on the support of workers generally for the success of its union label campaigns, and as its local unions affiliated with AFL city and state bodies throughout the country, they rapidly acquired much of the AFL's antiradical rhetoric as well. Tobin frequently attributed the new-found stability of the union to its adoption of the high dues–high benefits measures of the other craft unions, and this also served to bring the organization closer to the outlook of Gompers and of the other leaders of the AFL. The reelection of Gompers to the AFL presidency, wrote the *Shoe Workers' Journal* in December 1904, was "a fitting and deserved tribute to the man than whom no greater champion of labor's rights and interests has ever lived." [42]

Equally important was the increasing hostility of the Catholic hierarchy in Massachusetts to the socialist proclivities which had developed among its flock. Before 1900 the Catholic church generally had taken little notice of radical tendencies in the labor movement, and the Irish priests in the shoe towns were not initially so hostile toward socialism as they subsequently became. The pastor in Haverhill, for example, was known to be opposed to socialism, but his counterpart in Brockton was neutral, if not benign. When socialist ideas became more widespread after the turn of the century, however, this attitude abruptly changed. Catholic spokesmen throughout the country condemned the socialists for their alleged atheism, and for their attacks on the divinely sanctioned principles of private property. They were supported in Massachusetts by Bishop William Stang, of Fall River, and by William Cardinal O'Connell, of Boston. In 1903 Mrs. Martha Moore Avery and David Goldstein, two of the state's leading socialists, repudiated socialism and later joined the church; and in 1905 their example was followed by Peter Collins, a former president of the Boston Central Labor Union, who became one of the most prolific antisocialist pamphleteers in the Catholic Militia of Christ.

The precise effect of this development on the shoe workers in the BSWU is hard to estimate, but on the Irish and French-Canadian Catholics among them it was likely to be great. Catholic propaganda was first used against the socialists in Haverhill in the municipal elections of December 1899, when the combined Republican-Democratic opposition tried to prevail upon the shoe workers in the Irish wards to vote against the incumbent socialist mayor, John C. Chase. This attempt failed, but in the following year it had more effect. In the municipal elections of December 1900 the socialist vote declined considerably, leading Mailly to complain in the Haverhill *Social Democrat* against the use of "rumsellers [and] churches" by the two major parties. In an effort to avoid the stigma which being a socialist now brought upon Catholics, the Massachusetts socialists imported Father Thomas McGrady, a radical priest from Bellevue, Kentucky, to argue their case. Father McGrady went on an extensive speaking tour of the shoe towns, arguing that socialism was not inconsistent with the Catholic faith. But even this backfired. McGrady found himself forced increasingly on the defensive in his public speeches, and in 1902 he was compelled by the church to give up his pastorate.[43]

But the fundamental reason for the change in the shoe workers' outlook appears to have been the sudden and unprecedented economic success of the Boot and Shoe Workers Union and the improvement in wages and conditions which took place throughout the New England shoe industry as a whole. Prevailing prosperity after 1900 had pushed up wage levels throughout the industry generally, and in Massachusetts, in particular, after long years of depression, they at last began to show a marked and persistent rise. By 1903 wages in ten out of the fourteen major shoe-making operations had increased to a point beyond their predepression levels, and in 1906 they had risen to an all-time high. Save for certain of the machine operators, average wages in the industry were more than $25 per week.[44]

These increased wages were not due solely to the efforts of the BSWU. The shoe industry was still intensely competitive, and the union administration found it difficult to press for general wage increases, without at the same time endangering the competitive position of the manufacturers with whom they had to deal. However, official recognition of the union by an increasing number of employers considerably reduced the number of strikes in the shoe factories controlled by the union, while at the same time bringing the union's leaders face to face for the first time with the realities of collective bargaining. This reinforced still further the conservative tendencies of the administration. Demands for a general wage increase, Tobin said to the 1904 Boot and Shoe Workers convention, "should be avoided under all circumstances." "The employer gains an opportunity to adjust tc a gradual change in wages," he continued, "while propositions for a general advance . . . [have] resulted in failure." [45] This approach did not satisfy all the union membership. From the point of view of the leadership, however, it appears that once the BSWU had been firmly established, and at least a minority of the shoe workers had achieved some degree of security by virtue of their contracts with employers, much of the rationale for their earlier radicalism had departed. In the absence of strong traditions of socialism, such as characterized the Germans in the Brewery Workers Union, the characteristic opportunism and conservatism of the Irish in the industry reasserted themselves and began to dominate the outlook of the organization as a whole.

This opportunism also manifested itself in another way. As the BSWU became more successful, a number of its officers were promoted by the shoe companies to become shop foremen or overseers, or else left the industry altogether to go into business or to fill other managerial posts of other kinds. For example, Horace M. Eaton, the former socialist general secretary-treasurer of the union, left Boston in 1902 to become a shoe company representative in St. Louis. To some extent this simply reflected a characteristic type of economic mobility, which did not appear to be greater in the shoe industry than it was elsewhere. But, perhaps because of the prevailing antisocialist climate of public opinion in Massachusetts, when they left office several of these former members of the BSWU also chose to repudiate their previous socialist opinions in a particularly overt way. A good example of this was F. G. R. Gordon, who had been one of the leading socialists in Brockton in the early days. Soon after 1900 he went to work for the U.S. Department of Commerce. Not only did he abandon his earlier socialism; he went out of his way to denounce his former socialist comrades. Together with Martha Avery and David Goldstein, two other renegades, Gordon contributed articles to the *Million,* a free antiradical weekly published in Haverhill; and in June 1904 he conducted a correspondence with President John Mitchell of the United Mine Workers of America, warning him against the budding influence of the socialists in that organization.[46]

Whatever the reasons for this change of front, however, there is plenty of evidence to show that it did occur. After 1900 the reports of the union officers made little reference to the need for independent political action or to the class struggle. Instead, they were devoted almost solely to the internal problems of the union, to the number of contracts signed with employers, and to the economic progress of the union in general. Throughout 1901 and 1902, when the BSWU was emerging as a conservative craft organization, an occasional item or turn of phrase in the *Shoe Workers' Journal* betrayed the socialist heritage. In December 1901 it reminded its readers of the principles of "the solidarity of labor"; and in 1902 it called for municipal ownership as "the cure for municipal poverty." But during 1903 the incidence of socialist terminology dropped, or the words began to be used for exclusively trade-union ends. For example, the Union Stamp Contract, which was now being signed by an increasing number of employers, was described as "the only remedy guaranteeing a cure" for capitalism's ills. Only the conservative trade-unionist, who understood that labor must not interfere "with the legitimate interests of . . . business," could help the oppressed to find a solution to their problems. And in May 1903 the editor sounded a veritable tocsin for the American virtues of individualism and self-help. "We believe the world is getting better," he wrote. "Try to be somebody and you will succeed." [47]

Tobin himself could not publicly abandon his socialist position straightway, particularly since the socialists in the union had helped him to power. Moreover, his radical rhetoric had been an asset among the shoe workers of Brockton and Haverhill in the years when he desperately needed their support. But by 1902 the climate of opinion was turning against the socialists in Massachusetts generally, and the rapid growth of the union meant that he was no longer dependent on them for support. "He had been a socialist for many years," Tobin told the Detroit BSWU convention in June 1902, "but that which was of the most vital importance was the concentration of thought and activity along lines calculated to get the workers organized in the greatest possible numbers under the trade union banner." By 1904 he was even more emphatic. "The Boot and Shoe Workers Union is a trades union pure and simple," he wrote in the *Shoe Workers' Journal.* "It claims absolutely no other purpose for existing than the protection and advancement of the shoe workers' economic interests. It differs from other trades unions in the detailed manner of accomplishing its purpose. There is not a more conservatively conducted labor organization in the country." [48]

But perhaps the clearest indication of the changed attitude of the Tobin administration was to be found in the policy which it adopted toward the National Civic Federation, hostility toward which was in many ways the touchstone of radical sentiment throughout the labor movement as a whole. As early as December 1900 Tobin had attended a conference of the National Civic Federation while on an organizing tour in the Midwest, and the 1902 convention of the union adopted a resolution commending the efforts of the organization to improve industrial relations. Then in March 1904 the union journal went out of its way to defend the NCF against the attacks of "certain [socialist] unionists and labor journal writers" who considered the AFL's cooperation with it as treachery to labor's cause. The National Civic Federation, the editor wrote, "advocates just what the combined intelligence and experience of its members conceive to be the true foundation of industrial peace . . . namely the application of the principles of conciliation, and the friendly coming together of both employer and employee." [49]

IV

The sudden conversion of the Boot and Shoe Workers Union from revolutionary socialism to conservative craft unionism did not bring an end to radical activity throughout the industry as a whole. There had been, as we have seen, considerable rank-and-file opposition to the adoption of the new constitution at the convention of 1899, and within months of that convention a number of locals in Haverhill had broken away to form another independent organization, the Shoe Workers Protective Union.[50] This opposition did not consist solely of socialists, and it concerned issues of union militancy and democracy as much as the ideology of socialism as such. Nevertheless, the 1899 reforms led to a further withdrawal of radicals between 1907 and 1909 which became a *cause célèbre* between the socialists and their opponents throughout the labor movement in general.

Politically, some rank-and-file shoe workers continued to give their support to the Socialist party in Massachusetts, at least for a time. For example, in the municipal elections held in Brockton in December 1902, all three of the socialist aldermen elected to office were members of the Boot and Shoe Workers Union; and of the eight socialist councilmen elected, at least two were shoe workers. Although the socialist vote throughout the state began to decline markedly soon after that date, it continued to include at least a number of shoe workers until about 1912. This rank-and-file loyalty contrasted sharply with the political practices of the BSWU leadership, which had now—save for the continued socialist opinions of one member of the General Executive Board, Gad Martindale—officially reverted to the nonpartisan position of the AFL. The union journal commended the prolabor sympathies of liberals in both the major parties, and urged union members to cooperate with the Massachusetts State Federation of Labor in pressing for picketing legislation, an overtime bill, and other measures "regardless of party affiliations." [51]

But official nonpartisanship, as with other unions in the AFL, now often concealed a predilection for Democratic candidates, particularly in a state where Irish influence in the Democratic party was growing rapidly. In the Massachusetts gubernatorial election of 1904, for example, the union administration gave virtually open support to the Democratic candidate, William L. Douglas, a wealthy shoe manufacturer from Brockton who had a prolabor record in the state legislature and had been the first major employer to sign the Union Stamp Contract. A "flying wedge" of union officials was organized to deliver the labor vote, and when Douglas won—the first Democratic governor to be elected in Massachusetts for twelve years —Tobin sent him a personal telegram of congratulation, and the *Shoe Workers' Journal* noted that "shoe workers throughout the state gave him [a] splendid vote." [52]

This overt support for Douglas, which received national publicity at the November 1904 AFL convention as an example of how labor could elect its "friends," was particularly galling to the socialists, since it brought a drastic decline in the support which their own gubernatorial candidate received, and it was denounced by Debs as "treason to working class interests." But the Tobin administration was by now impervious to such views. In fact, in 1908 it came nearer to endorsing Bryan, the Democratic presidential candidate, than even the AFL had done. It was afraid that the philosophy of the Buck's Stove and Range case (under which Gompers and other AFL officials had been indicted for advertising a union boycott in the *American Federationist*), might be extended to prevent trade-unions from advocating the sale of union-labeled goods as a whole. Such a development would have undermined the whole basis of the organization's Union Stamp Contract. So the *Shoe Workers' Journal* welcomed the inclusion of an anti-injunction plank in the Democratic platform and strongly urged the membership to vote for the Democrats, although without actually naming the party ticket. There was, the union journal acknowledged, a "sincere" element in the union which favored "a minority party," that is, the socialists. But it sought to convince them that a vote for Debs would simply let the Republicans in. "If . . . the members wish to make their votes effective," the editor said, "they will cast their votes for the direct opponents of Taft." This was a classic example of the wasted vote argument, which was consistently used by opponents of the Socialist party—and indeed against all other advocates of third-party political action, whether to the right or left.[53]

At the political level, therefore, there was clearly a conflict between the pragmatic and largely pro-Democratic considerations which now dictated the Boot and Shoe Workers' official policies and the socialist loyalties of part, at least, of the union's rank and file. But it was the conservative economic policies of the administration which provoked the strongest opposition and were primarily responsible for the withdrawal of dissident elements in the trade. The 1899 constitution, with its emphasis on high dues, stronger central control, and the arbitration of disputes with employers, was not, in itself, inconsistent with militant, or even with socialist, trade-unionism. The problem was that the Tobin administration, in the eyes of its opponents, used its new authority primarily to reinforce its own position in the union and in its relations with employers carried caution and restraint to such lengths as to be guilty of open class collaboration, at the expense of the interests of the shoe workers as a whole.

For one thing, the terms of the Union Stamp Contract negotiated with employers were usually determined by direct negotiations between the manufacturer and the national officials, irrespective of local conditions, causing considerable resentment in a trade in which there was a long tradition of local autonomy. For another, there was a widespread feeling, much as there was in the AFL itself, that the union was run by a minority of the membership and that the union conventions, in particular, were controlled by the Tobin administration and its friends.[54] Enforcement of the closed shop under the terms of the Union Stamp Contract also meant changing the old method of voluntary organizing, by soliciting members to join, for a compulsory method which forced them to become members whether they liked it or not. Militants in the union objected to this, partly because they felt that a voluntary membership would take a more active interest in union affairs, and partly because the compulsory method of organizing in effect made the growth of the organization dependent on the willingness of the employer to establish a closed shop.

Equally objectionable to the radicals in the union was the policy of issuing the Union Stamp Contract to manufacturers simply as a means of securing the closed shop, without making it conditional on improvements in wages or conditions of work. The official justification for this was that profit margins in the industry were so small that the employer could not be expected to raise wages straightaway. "The employer should," the union journal argued, "be given a fair opportunity to test the value of the union stamp as a trade maker, before being called upon to consider a new scale of wages." But many rank-and-file members, unable to understand why the union should take the profit margins of the manufacturers into account at all, accused Tobin of caring more for the interests of the manufacturers than he did for the members of the union. The administration was simply trying, complained one delegate to the 1907 convention, "to make the contract . . . palatable to the manufacturer, regardless of the wants of the workers." [55]

In return for the union shop, the administration also agreed not to authorize any strikes while the stamp contract was in effect, but to accept instead the decisions of the Massachusetts State Board of Arbitration, or those of similar bodies in other states, to which all major disputes were to be referred. This voluntary abandonment of the right to strike while an agreement was in effect, which often accompanied contracts drawn up with employers, caused more resentment than almost any other aspect of trade-union policy, and it was openly exploited by the socialists, in the BSWU as in other organizations, as a means of increasing their support. In the case of the shoe workers, the situation was exacerbated by a clause in the Union Stamp Contract specifying that the union would help the manufacturers find replacements for workers who came out on unofficial strike. In 1903, for example, about two hundred cutters came out on strike in Lynn in violation of their contract, and officials of the union brought in cutters from out of town to fill the places of the strikers, despite strong protests from the militants, both in the union and outside.

But it was in St. Louis that the BSWU's bargaining policies created the greatest difficulty. Early in 1903 the La Prelle Shoe Company, a major concern, applied for the union stamp, to which the local Joint Shoe Council agreed, but only on condition that wage scales in the factories were increased first. But the national headquarters in Boston, as was its custom, awarded the Union Stamp Contract without asking for a wage increase, thus overriding the wishes of the local leaders. As a result, a widespread unofficial strike took place. The rebels were locked out of the Union Stamp factories, and their places were filled with the help of the union national office. Several thousand shoe workers lost their jobs as a result, causing widespread resentment among the strikers. But the Tobin administration stuck to its guns and revoked the charters of all the St. Louis locals who had violated the Union Stamp Contract.[56]

In these circumstances it was not surprising that the socialist American Labor Union, and later the IWW, should have tried to exploit the discontents of the shoe workers' rank and file. In February 1903 the *American Labor Union Journal* attacked what it called the "autocratic power" of the BSWU administration, accusing it of strikebreaking and of "collusion with the employers." Later that year several locals of shoe workers were organized by the American Labor Union in Lynn, in Chicago, and elsewhere. Naturally, it tried also to exploit the St. Louis revolt. When the BSWU locals were expelled for going out on unofficial strike, Daniel McDonald, president of the American Labor Union, went to St. Louis and succeeded for a time in establishing six ALU shoe locals there. A separate union label was prepared, and plans were made for the establishment of a Western Federation of Shoe Workers, which was to challenge the Boot and Shoe Workers Union throughout the entire country.[57]

For a time there was a serious conflict between the Boot and Shoe Workers' administration and the American Labor Union shoe workers in St. Louis and elsewhere. Tobin gave his personal assurances of support to Gompers in the general AFL conflict with the ALU, and dispatched Vice-President Collis Lovely and Organizer C. T. McMorrow on a tour of several western states on behalf of the AFL cause.[58] But the Western Federation of Shoe Workers never materialized, and with the decline of the American Labor Union in 1904 the influence of the western radicals among the shoe workers largely lost its hold. Michael T. Berry, a DeLeonite from Haverhill, represented a number of "wandering, disgruntled spirits" from the shoe workers at the IWW founding convention in June 1905; and in his speeches at the convention IWW Secretary William Trautmann singled out the Boot and Shoe Workers Union especially in his indictment of the trade-union methods of the AFL as a whole. But although it organized a shoe workers' local in St. Louis for a time, the IWW was unable to repeat the successes of the ALU.[59]

Despite this, discontent among the radicals in the Boot and Shoe Workers Union continued to grow, and in 1906 they decided to make a final effort to bring about a change. In the October union elections Thomas Hickey, a socialist from Lasters Local 192 of Brockton, and Charles P. Murray, of Lasters Local 32 in Lynn—the center of the socialist insurgency which had led to the reestablishment of the Lasters Protective Union in 1898—ran against Tobin for president and vice-president respectively. When the vote was counted, Hickey and Murray at first appeared to have won by a substantial majority, and their election was confirmed by the majority report of the general inspectors of election. But the Tobin administration chose to accept the inspectors' minority report, which found irregularities in some of the ballots cast for both men. After numerous complications, including a court action, a special convention was held in Toronto in August 1907 which disqualified both Hickey and Murray from holding office in the union for five years.[60]

For the insurgents in the BSWU this was the last straw. Believing themselves to have been cheated out of a legitimate victory, in October 1907 both Hickey and Murray left the union, taking with them the bulk of the membership in their respective locals. They were soon joined by other discontented locals from Salem, Beverly, and Marlboro, in Massachusetts, and by a number of independent locals in Brooklyn and Newark which had formerly been under socialist control. In addition, some of the expelled St. Louis locals gave the insurgents their support.

The IWW made a special effort to secure the rebels' allegiance. In November 1907 Michael J. Tracey, business agent for the Lynn Lasters Machine Operators Union, met with IWW leaders in New York to discuss the possibility of affiliation; and in return J. J. Ettor—to become famous in the 1912 IWW Lawrence textile strike—visited the insurgents' headquarters in Lynn. The *Industrial Union Bulletin* urged them not to start another "crop of independent unions," which would simply renew the jurisdictional conflicts which had occurred between the independent shoe workers unions in the period before 1895. But the rebels were determined to have their own organization, and in September 1909, after prolonged negotiations, the United Shoe Workers of America was established as a rival to the Boot and Shoe Workers Union, with headquarters in Lynn. Arvid Orlando, of Chicago, was its first general organizer,[61] and Michael J. Tracey was the first secretary-treasurer.[62]

It was no coincidence that two lasters' locals, Local 192 of Brockton and Local 32 of Lynn, had led the insurgency which resulted in the establishment of the United Shoe Workers of America. As we have seen, the lasters had once been the most highly skilled and highly paid workers in the trade, and they still suffered from the effects of mechanization on their craft. Although real wages had risen in all branches of the shoe industry since 1900, the semiskilled and unskilled workers who operated the new lasting machines could often earn twice as much as those who lasted shoes in the old-fashioned way, and there was continued resentment at the policy of the BSWU with respect to the introduction of new machines. Thus, although the United Shoe Workers eventually spread to all sectors of the industry, the lasters continued for some years to provide the basic element of support, confirming once again that it was craftsmen who had lost status and skill, and not an immigrant *lumpenproletariat*, which formed the basis for radicalism in the shoe workers' trade.[63]

From the first there was acute rivalry between the Boot and Shoe Workers Union and the United Shoe Workers, which increased rather than diminished with the passage of time. The United Shoe Workers, partly through the Brockton *Searchlight*, an independent local paper, and partly through the statements of its leaders, attacked the BSWU as a reactionary, machine-ridden organization which had reneged on the true interests of the workers. At a public meeting held in Brockton in March 1910, Hickey, Tracey, and Orlando denounced the Boot and Shoe Workers as "not a labor union, but an organization built up by labor people for the assistance of manufacturers"; and in June 1914 the *Searchlight* satirized the remaining socialists in the BSWU who, it said, professed to believe in socialist principles, but could not be "dragged by wild horses to a soap-box to denounce the [Tobin] system of unionism." [64]

The BSWU, for its part, fully reciprocated this hostility. The *Shoe Workers' Journal* denounced the United Shoe Workers of America as a "low dues, strike organization," led by "an undisciplined rabble" which threatened to "menace business prosperity by [its] irresponsible radicalism." It condemned the organization's pretensions to industrial unionism, pointing out that in practice it organized its locals on the basis of craft. It asserted that the leaders of the United Shoe Workers "seem to think that all that is necessary is to get a lot of wage earners together on an empty treasury and then strike." And it attacked its indiscriminate policy of demanding wage increases without regard to the manufacturers selected as shortsighted and irresponsible, since it forced the union employer to increase his prices, putting him at a disadvantage with the nonunion employer and encouraging him to move his factory and equipment out of the Massachusetts shoe centers into nonunion towns.[65]

It is instructive to compare the attitude of the AFL toward the conflict between the Boot and Shoe Workers Union and the United Shoe Workers with that of the Socialist party. The general policy of the AFL was to uphold the jurisdictions of its own affiliates when they were challenged by seceding or independent unions, and in this case it had no hesitation in supporting the BSWU, even though it was aware that many of its policies were extremely unpopular. AFL support for the narrow and rigid jurisdictional outlook of the BSWU was typical of the kind of policy which gave the socialists much of their ammunition in their general attack on the complacency and craft-union orientation of the labor movement as a whole.

In October 1907, when the radical insurgents were in the process of seceding, Gompers wrote to Tobin assuring him of full AFL support for the BSWU. The only organization under which the shoe workers had made "real tangible progress," Gompers wrote, was the Boot and Shoe Workers Union; and he commended Tobin for taking a strong line against the radicals. Two years later, soon after the United Shoe Workers was established, Secretary-Treasurer Tracey wrote to AFL headquarters requesting the AFL to withdraw its charter from the BSWU and to issue it instead to the United Shoe Workers, as the only legitimate representative of the country's shoe workers. "Without your [the AFL's] support," Tracey asserted, "the organization of the Boot and Shoe Workers Union would collapse." Secretary Frank Morrison, on behalf of the AFL, curtly rejected this request, accusing

Tracey and others of having established a dual union, and replying that the AFL was in any event bound to support the organization to which it had already given a charter.[66]

Undismayed by this, the leaders of the United Shoe Workers sent circulars to organized labor throughout the country criticizing the Union Stamp policies of the BSWU and seeking to generate sympathy for its own cause. In November 1909 it succeeded in prevailing upon Frank J. Hayes, a socialist delegate from the powerful United Mine Workers of America, to introduce a resolution into the AFL convention of that year criticizing the BSWU for its strikebreaking activities and urging an investigation into the Boot and Shoe Workers organizing methods, "with a view to determining whether such methods are consistent with the principles of the American Federation of Labor." This resolution was defeated, as were similar efforts made at the 1910 and 1913 AFL conventions to expose what the United Shoe Workers called "the despicable methods used by the officials of the BSWU to induce manufacturers to sign up their stamp agreement." At the 1913 convention, much to Tobin's satisfaction, the AFL adopted a resolution condemning what it called those "malicious falsehoods" and asserting that the Boot and Shoe Workers Union "has always maintained the highest standard of union ethics . . . as well as the highest standard of wages and industrial freedom existing in the shoe trade." [67]

For the Socialist party, on the other hand, whose natural sympathies were on the side of the United Shoe Workers, the conflict between the two unions presented an interesting test of its official policy of neutrality in relation to internal conflicts in the AFL. As early as 1903 the socialist James F. Carey had found it necessary to dissociate himself from the "unpopular B.S. and W.U." in his reelection campaign for the Massachusetts legislature. But he did not openly attack the organization. In 1909, when the United Shoe Workers was established, Max Hayes, who was one of the Socialist party's leading authorities on trade-union affairs, contented himself with observing that it was "dissatisfaction with the . . . administrative policies" of the Boot and Shoe Workers which had led the militants to withdraw. But as the conflict between the two unions became more intense, the socialists found it increasingly difficult to maintain their impartiality, particularly since the United Shoe Workers asked openly for their support.

Finally William Mailly, who had for a time become national secretary of the Socialist party following his prominent role in Massachusetts in earlier years, wrote a letter to the New York *Call* in August 1910 denouncing the Boot and Shoe Workers' label as a "swindle upon the labor movement." Then in 1912 the *International Socialist Review,* which was associated with the left wing of the Socialist party, published two articles by Phillips Russell openly attacking the Boot and Shoe Workers as "perhaps the rottenest and most corrupt" organization in the AFL. "It is owned, body and soul, boot and breeches, by the bosses and a little gang of union officials," Russell wrote, "who . . . make use of the union shoe stamp merely as a thing for barter and sale and as a means of enslaving the workers and tieing them tight to the bosses' machines." Many Socialist party members had thought they were serving the cause of labor by buying BSWU-stamped shoes, Russell continued. But "no person who believes in clear-cut and uncompromising unionism will hereafter buy any shoe having the tainted label of the Boot and Shoe Workers Union." [68]

Tobin was understandably angry at this assault and wrote to the *International Socialist Review* rejecting Russell's allegations as "flagrantly unfair." But in 1914, when the BSWU broke a United Shoe Workers strike in the Hamilton-Brown plant in St. Louis, the *Review* returned to the attack, this time with an official editorial urging the shoe workers to leave the Boot and Shoe Workers Union and join the United Shoe Workers of America. It described in detail the efforts of the Tobin administration to secure scabs for the Hamilton-Brown plant and the effect which this was having on the men and women who had been thrown out of work. "You B. and S. men, don't scab," it urged. "Rather leave the organization which your officials is [*sic*] using as a scabbing agency. . . . The United Shoe Workers of America are organized to help the shoe workers. They have raised wages, shortened hours. Get in the real organization that fights the battles of the workers." [69]

The support which the AFL and the socialist press gave to the Boot and Shoe Workers Union and the United Shoe Workers respectively made little practical difference to the dispute between the two organizations. It continued unabated through World War I, beyond Tobin's death in 1919, and into the 1920's, weakening both organizations and preventing them from turning their full attention to the task of organizing the large number of shoe workers who remained unorganized. But as time went on it became clear that the United Shoe Workers found it increasingly necessary to modify its earlier freewheeling strike-and-wage-demand approach and to adopt more cautious and disciplined policies instead. This did not mean that the United Shoe Workers had necessarily abandoned all of its former militancy. But it did mean that as far as trade-union policy was concerned, notably in the matter of local autonomy, strike policy, and contracts with employers, the former insurgents were now becoming more pragmatic and conservative.

This development was noticeable as early as 1913, when General Secretary Orlando expressed anxiety at the strains which the union's unrestricted strike policy placed on its slender financial resources. Then, in January 1915, the Lynn Joint Council of the United Shoe Workers negotiated the first known contract between the United Shoe Workers and their employers. This provided for a wage increase, but it also incorporated many of the features of the Boot and Shoe Workers Union Stamp Contract: compulsory membership, arbitration, and the submission of disputes to the Massachusetts State Board of Arbitration. Most important of all, it specified that no strikes should take place while the contract was in effect. Finally, the 1919 convention of the United Shoe Workers considered replacing the anarchic system of internal organization in the union by a strong executive and more traditional trade-union methods of leadership and control. Although no action was taken on these proposals, the general drift of the union was clear. The responsibilities of power and the problems of administering what had now become quite a large organization necessitated a higher degree of discipline on the part of the membership, and more effective control on the part of the administration, than had been thought necessary when the union was founded. And the decision to negotiate contracts with the employers, and to accept the results of arbitration in industrial disputes, represented an even more important acceptance of the conventional trade-union methods which the United Shoe Workers had earlier despised.[70]

To some extent these developments simply reflected a process of maturation. Most unions, including socialist ones, came to accept the need for collective bargaining and strike control as they grew larger and more experienced; and it did not follow, of course, simply because a union had adopted these methods, that it had necessarily repudiated socialism as a general working-class ideology. But in the case of the United Shoe Workers of America, where radicalism had by this time come to be defined more in terms of union democracy and militant antagonism toward the employers than in terms of an overt concern with socialist politics, there was undoubtedly a connection between the two.

V

The nature and the extent of socialist influence in the Boot and Shoe Workers Union were quite different from what they were in the Brewery Workers Union. There, socialism represented a set of deeply held intellectual convictions brought over by Marxist immigrants from Germany, supplemented only to a limited extent by the conditions of the American brewing industry. Socialist influence among the shoe workers, by contrast, resulted essentially from the social and economic disruption brought about by the destruction of the shoemakers' traditional craft. It had little, if anything, to do with ethnic considerations.

Technological advances, the introduction of new machinery, and the rise of the factory system in the period immediately following the Civil War all served to undermine the economic independence, the earning capacity, and the status position of the established craftsmen in the industry, irrespective of their ethnic background. This was especially true of the lasters, who were the most highly skilled element in the trade, and it was they, whether they were native-born Americans or of English or more especially of Irish descent, who were primarily responsible for the development of socialism in the industry. Although some of the more recent immigrants, most notably the Italians, established radical connections in the United Shoe Workers and in the IWW after the turn of the century, these groups were not prominent in the BSWU in the 1890's, during its most revolutionary period. In fact, it was probably the status and economic threat to the English-speaking workers represented by the influx of cheap immigrant labor, coming at a time when these workers were vulnerable because of the destruction of their traditional craft, that was the most important cause of radical discontent in the trade.

Of course, similar technological changes affected other American industries in the period, bringing similar results. But in none did they operate with quite the force and rapidity that they did in the shoemakers' trade. Within the space of twenty years, well within the working life of a single artisan, the traditional skills of the shoemaker were rendered largely useless. Instead of being an independent producer employing apprentices of his own, or a semi-independent artisan with the prospect of acquiring an independent shoemaking shop, the typical shoe worker became a factory employee, subject to intense competitive pressures over wages and without the protection—in terms of bargaining power vis-à-vis the employers—that his traditional skills had earlier been able to afford. Coupled with this was the inability of the BSWU, in the early and mid-1890's, to provide the kind of protection which more successful skill-threatened unions (such as the Cigarmakers International Union) were able to provide.

The initial response of the shoe workers to this situation was to take up producers' cooperation, under the Knights of St. Crispin, in an attempt to restore the independent entrepreneurship which the factory system had destroyed. This movement was not successful, any more than most other producers' cooperation schemes were among the socialists, and it was replaced in the 1890's by temporary support for DeLeon and the SLP. It does not follow that because Tobin and other leading members of the BSWU followed DeLeonism for some years, either they or the bulk of the rank and file in the industry had any deep understanding of, or commitment to, the principles of Marxism. Nevertheless, the rhetoric of the class struggle had considerable appeal for the shoe workers in their current deplorable economic position, and the DeLeonite critique of craft unionism offered a convenient vehicle for Tobin and Eaton to explain the failures of the BSWU to make economic progress in terms of wages, hours, and conditions of work.

The union preserved its connections with the socialists for as long as they seemed useful, but once the DeLeonite tactic of increasing revolutionary sentiment by emphasizing class consciousness rather than job security had been tried, without success, the BSWU rapidly reverted to the AFL method of providing economic security through a strong union treasury, high union benefits, and negotiated agreements with the employers. The fact that socialism was repudiated by the Tobin administration just when the Socialist party reached its peak in Massachusetts indicates that it was a temporary phenomenon, to be abandoned once a limited degree of prosperity and job security had been attained. Socialism in the shoe industry lacked ideological roots, and it never acquired the force of a tradition, as it did among the German workers of the brewery trade.

The BSWU did not provide protection for more than a limited number of shoe workers, however, and it did not, in the eyes of the more radical elements in the rank and file, secure even as much for this limited group as it could have done had the freedom to strike and the generally more militant attitude of the pre-1899 period been maintained. It was this, coupled with the continued decline in the position of skilled elements such as the lasters, which led to the establishment of the United Shoe Workers of America in 1909.[71]

How justified the specific accusations of the United Shoe Workers were against the BSWU is hard to determine. Certainly, Tobin's refusal to press for immediate wage increases as a condition of awarding the contract, which caused more dissension than anything else, represented a more realistic assessment of the economics of the shoe industry than his critics were willing to admit. Once the idea of collective bargaining had been accepted, it was inevitable that certain limitations would be placed on the union's freedom of action—limitations which at bottom conflicted with the impossibilist and revolutionary assumptions of the militants in the Socialist party and the United Shoe Workers of America, but which these same militants were forced to accept when they were themselves faced with the responsibilities of power. In unions which experienced a longer period of economic insecurity, or in those in which there was a more profound radical tradition, such as the Brewery Workers Union or the ILGWU (to be considered in the next chapter), this conflict between the revolutionary aspirations of the socialists and the cooperative assumptions of collective bargaining could be muted, if not altogether disguised. But once the principles of collective bargaining were fully accepted on both sides of industry, in the absence of other compelling factors the attractions of job security outweighed those of class unity, and the career of the socialists was usually short-lived.

Fundamentally, as already indicated, DeLeonism and the more moderate socialist movement which both preceded and followed it in the shoe industry were a response to the problems created by the transition from independent artisanship to the factory stage. Once that transition had been accomplished, the socialist impulse died out. This was true, of course, in other industries also. But the relative speed with which the BSWU went back on its radicalism, once the organization had become established, indicates that although it served a purpose for a time, socialism ran counter to the long-term opportunistic and assimilationist tendencies which characterized the Irish in the labor movement as a whole. Once they had achieved a minimum of status and security, as the conservative attitude of the post-1900 Boot and Shoe Workers Union showed, none were more eager to uphold traditional American values.

Notes

1. For a general description of the role of the Irish in the labor movement, see Carl Wittke, *The Irish in America* (New York, 1963), 216–227; Henry Browne, *The Catholic Church and the Knights of Labor* (Washington, 1949); and Wayne G. Broehl, *The Molly Maguires* (Cambridge, 1964).

2. Henry Bedford, *Socialism and the Workers in Massachusetts, 1886–1912* (Amherst, 1966), is devoted wholly to the socialist movement in Massachusetts, as is Leonard Abbott, "The Socialist Movement in Massachusetts," *Outlook*, LXIV (February 17, 1900), 410–412. Massachusetts socialism also receives considerable attention in Howard H. Quint, *The Forging of American Socialism, Origins of the Modern Movement* (New York, 1953), especially 72–141; and in Ira Kipnis, *The American Socialist Movement 1897–1912* (New York, 1952), especially 62–163. For general background, see Arthur Mann, *Yankee Reformers in the Urban Age* (Cambridge, 1954); and Richard Abrams, *Conservatism in a Progressive Era, Massachusetts Politics 1900–1912* (Cambridge, 1964).

3. Augusta E. Galster, *The Labor Movement in the Shoe Industry, with Special Reference to Philadelphia* (New York, 1924), 8–15, 21–30, 36–45; Don D. Lescohier, *The Knights of St. Crispin, 1867–1874, A Study in the Industrial Causes of Unionism*, Economics and Political Science Series, University of Wisconsin, VII (Madison, 1910), 5–11, 56–59. For the role of women in the shoe industry, see Edith Abbott, *Women in Industry, A Study in American Economic History* (New York, 1928), 148–185; Alice Henry, *Women and the Labor Movement* (New York, 1923), 47, 60, 77–78, 97.

4. Galster, *op. cit.*, 48–74; *A.F. of L. Yearbook* (Washington, 1892),

10–13, 17–18; Norman J. Ware, *The Labor Movement in the United States, 1860–1895; A Study in Democracy* (New York, 1929), 20, 200–209.

5. Bedford's statement that it represented over 100,000 shoe workers from seventy-three cities, according to the figures given at the convention itself, appears to be a considerable overexaggeration. See Bedford, *op. cit.*, 30; *Proceedings, Joint Convention of the Boot and Shoe Workers' Union* (Boston, 1895), 26–28, 33–42.

6. Galster, *op. cit.*, 74–75; *Proceedings, Sixth Convention of the Boot and Shoe Workers' Union* (Boston, 1894), 16; *Proceedings, Joint Convention of the Boot and Shoe Workers' Union* (Boston, 1895), 34–39.

7. This compared with more than 150,000 for the Republican state ticket, which was victorious in both years. Bedford, *op. cit.*, 28–31, 289–290; *Proceedings, Joint Convention of the Boot and Shoe Workers' Union* (Boston, 1895), 26–28, 33–42.

8. There were some, however. J. P. McDonnell represented Ireland at The Hague conference of the First International in 1872 and spent the rest of his career as a labor agitator in the United States. P. J. McGuire, of the Carpenters Union, was at first a member of the SLP, as was J. Mahlon Barnes of the Cigarmakers, later national secretary of the Socialist Party of America. See Wittke, *op. cit.*, 216, 218, 226–227; John R. Commons *et al.*, *History of Labor in the United States*, 4 vols. (New York, 1926–1935), II, 222n. For the early period of Irish labor history, see James Connolly, *Labor in Irish History* (New York, 1919), especially last chapter; or P. S. O'Hegarty, *A History of Ireland under the Union, 1801 to 1922* (London, 1952), 291–378.

9. The Anglo-Saxons among them were probably native-born Americans rather than first-generation immigrants from England. Berthoff notes that several thousand English and Scottish shoe workers emigrated to the United States in about 1890, but that many soon returned because of the mechanization of the American craft. Nor is there evidence to suggest that the Irish in the trade were from among those who had earlier been employed in industry in England, as was the case in a number of other industries. See Rowland T. Berthoff; *British Immigrants in Industrial America, 1790–1950* (New York, 1953), 77; Alan Fox, *A History of the National Union of Boot and Shoe Operatives* (Oxford, 1958), 18, 106.

10. Mann, *op. cit.*, 5n, 100; biographical notes on H. J. Skeffington (S.L.P. Collection, Wisconsin State Historical Society); *Souvenir of the Convention of the Lasters' Protective Union of America* (Lynn, 1890), 13–15; *Shoe Workers' Journal*, XIV (June 1913), 4–5; XX (May 1919), 8–16.

11. Wittke, *op. cit.*, 108; *Proceedings, Joint Convention of the Boot and Shoe Workers' Union* (Boston, 1895), 8–14; *Proceedings, Third Convention of the Boot and Shoe Workers' Union* (Boston, 1897), 1–11; *Proceedings, Sixth Convention of the Boot and Shoe Workers' Union* (Cincinnati, 1904), 3–6; *Ninth Annual Report of the Massachusetts Bureau of Statistics of Labor* (Boston, 1878), 183, 221, 225, 241; *Thirty-fourth Annual Report of the Massachusetts Bureau of Statistics of Labor* (Boston, 1903), 6, 88, 117. For Karson's views, see Marc Karson, *American Labor Unions and Politics, 1900–1918* (Carbondale, 1958), 212–285.

12. *Shoe Workers' Journal*, XIV (March 1913), 13–16.

13. Phillips was a nationally known advocate of cooperation and derived

part of his income from delivering public lectures on the subject. The cooperative system, he wrote in 1869, could transform the position of workingmen "from that of dependent journeyman to independent competitive manufacturers." He also called it "the best system yet devised by man for checking the onward march of aggressive capital." Handwritten list of lecture topics; letter to the Philadelphia *Worker,* April 5, 1869 (Thomas Phillips Papers, Wisconsin State Historical Society).

14. Galster, *op. cit.,* 14; Lescohier, *op. cit.,* 49–55; Clifton K. Yearley, *Britons in American Labor: A History of the Influence of the United Kingdom Immigrants in American Labor, 1820–1914* (Baltimore, 1951), 198–208, 224–228. Few, if any, of these cooperatives succeeded, and recent research by John Philip Hall, of the University of Baltimore, has suggested that the Crispins' emphasis on cooperation was "largely in the thinking of the leaders." Even if this were so, cooperation still remained an ideal to which many of the Crispins were attached, even if they were unable to implement it successfully in practice. See John Hall, "The Knights of St. Crispin in Massachusetts, 1869–1878," *Journal of Economic History,* XVIII (1958), 170–171, 174.

15. Mann, *op. cit.,* 175–182; George McNeill (ed.), *The Labor Movement, The Problem of To-day* (Boston, 1887), 197, 205–213.

16. *Twenty-eighth Annual Report of the Massachusetts Bureau of Statistics of Labor* (Boston, 1899), 12–13.

17. Quoted in Haverhill *Social Democrat,* I (October 7, 1899), 4.

18. For the technological changes in the shoe industry, see Galster, *op. cit.,* 3–8, 16–21, 30–37; Lescohier, *op. cit.,* 12–24; John R. Commons, *Labor and Administration* (New York, 1913), 255–256; Blanche Hazard, *The Organization of the Boot and Shoe Industry in Massachusetts before 1875* (Cambridge, 1921), 3–156.

19. *The Comrade,* XI (November 1903), 32–33; Haverhill *Social Democrat,* I (December 23, 1899), 1; Phillips to John C. Mulryan, March 30, 1890 (Thomas Phillips Papers, Wisconsin State Historical Society).

20. Haverhill *Social Democrat,* I (June 16, 1900), 1; *Proceedings, Third Convention of the Boot and Shoe Workers' Union* (June 1897), 38, 42.

21. Commons, *op. cit.,* 11, 138–144; Mann, *op. cit.,* 182; Bedford, *op. cit.,* 11–26, 289; David Saposs, *Left Wing Unionism, A Study of Radical Policies and Tactics* (New York, 1926), 241; *Proceedings, Sixth Convention of the Boot and Shoe Workers' International Union* (Boston, 1894), 30.

22. Quint, *op. cit.,* 161–162; *Constitution,* Boot and Shoe Workers' Union (1896), 5–6, 9, 11; "Transcript of Debate between Tobin, DeLeon and others, April 24, 1898" (Archives of Boot and Shoe Workers' Union), 9.

23. *Monthly Report* of the Boot and Shoe Workers' Union (April 1896), 2.

24. *Proceedings, Second Convention of the Boot and Shoe Workers' Union* (Boston, 1896), 16.

25. Bedford, *op. cit.,* 53–56; *Constitution,* Boot and Shoe Workers' Union (1897), 1; *Proceedings, Third Convention of the Boot and Shoe Workers' Union* (Boston, 1897), 22–28, 30–33, 99–100.

26. *Monthly Report* (October 1897), 19; (January 1898), 5, 7–8.

27. *Ibid.* (December 1898), 2; (May 1896), 2; "Transcript of Debate," 12; *Proceedings, Fifteenth Annual Convention of the A.F. of L.* (New York, 1895), 65.

28. *The People,* VI (May 24, 1896), 4; "Transcript of Debate," 3, 18; *Proceedings, Ninth Annual Convention of the S.L.P.* (New York, 1896), 30–32; *Proceedings, Third Convention of the Boot and Shoe Workers' Union* (Boston, 1897), 99–100.

29. *Proceedings, Second Annual Convention of the Socialist Trades and Labor Alliance* (Boston, 1897), 6, 9, 11.

30. Not June, as Bedford states. See Bedford, *op. cit.,* 78; *Monthly Report* (May 1898), 20–21.

31. *The People,* VII (October 13, 1897), 4; IX (June 25, 1899), 2–3; "Transcript of Debate," 2, 4–5, 7, 9, 11, 15, 22; *Union Boot and Shoe Worker,* I (September 1900), 4–5.

32. Horace Eaton, himself a laster by trade, indicated the effect of mechanization on lasters' wages in testimony which he gave before the Industrial Relations Commission in 1899. "Eleven years ago," he said, "I used to be able to earn myself, lasting shoes, from $18 to $35 a week, according to how hard I wanted to work; that is, in the city of Lynn. Today, on the same class of work, I would not be able, on any job in the city, to make over $15, and probably my wage would be nearer $12." *Report of the Industrial Commission on the Relations and Conditions of Capital and Labor,* 56th Congress, 2nd Session, House Document 495 (Washington, 1907), 359.

33. "Transcript of Debate," 7–8; *Monthly Report* (May 1898), 14–19; (July 1898), 4–9; (October 1898), 16–20; (November 1898–March 1899), 14–17; (July 1899), 13–18.

34. *Monthly Report* (November 1898–March 1899), 14–17; (April–May 1899), 14; *Proceedings, Fourth Convention of the Boot and Shoe Workers' Union* (Rochester, 1899), 7–8.

35. *Ibid.,* 4–6.

36. Galster, *op. cit.,* 78–79, 82, 86–87; *Monthly Report* (July 1899), 1–3; *Proceedings, Fourth Convention of the Boot and Shoe Workers' Union* (Rochester, 1899), 6, 21–23.

37. *Shoe Workers' Journal,* V (January 1904), 10; *Proceedings, Sixth Convention of the Boot and Shoe Workers' Union* (Cincinnati, 1904), 3–6, 23–29.

38. *Proceedings, Fourth Convention of the Boot and Shoe Workers' Union* (Rochester, 1899), 6.

39. Carey in Massachusetts and Sieverman in New York were two of the most important leaders in the "kangaroo" movement which led to the formal splitting of the SLP in July 1899. See *Proceedings, Tenth National Convention of the S.L.P.* (New York, 1900), 44–48, 50–51.

40. This was not quite "an official endorsement" of the party, however, as Bedford suggests. See Bedford, *op. cit.,* 87, 197; Lynn Section, S.L.P. to De-Leon, April 7, 1897 (S.L.P. Collection, Wisconsin State Historical Society); *Monthly Report* (June 1899), 19.

41. Kipnis, *op. cit.,* 75–77; Bedford, *op. cit.,* 61, 87–136, 205–212; Haverhill *Social Democrat,* I (October 7, 1899), 1–3; I (November 4, 1899), 5; II (October 20, 1900), 3; Brockton *Times,* I (November 8, 1899), 3.

42. Bedford, *op. cit.,* 198–199; *Shoe Workers' Journal,* V (December 1904), 4; VI (February 1905), 8.

43. Bedford, *op. cit.,* 184–196; Haverhill *Social Democrat,* I (December 9,

1899), 2–3; 11 (December 8, 1900), 2; Haverhill *Clarion,* V (November 16, 1901), 3; V (November 23, 1901), 2; Karson, *op. cit.,* 269–281; Philip S. Foner, *History of the Labor Movement in the United States,* 4 vols. (New York, 1947–1965), III, 115–116, 121–123.

44. *Labor Bulletin of the Commonwealth of Massachusetts,* Nos. 39–44 (Boston, 1906), 14–15.

45. *Proceedings, Sixth Convention of the Boot and Shoe Workers' Union* (Cincinnati, 1904), 16–17.

46. Bedford, *op. cit.,* 204; F. G. R. Gordon to John Mitchell, June 5, 1904 (John Mitchell Papers, Catholic University of America).

47. *Shoe Workers' Journal,* II (December 1901), 8; III, 1 (September 1902), 8; IV (February 1903), 7, 11; IV (May 1903), 12.

48. *Proceedings, Fifth Convention of the Boot and Shoe Workers* (Detroit, 1902), 5–22, 43; *Shoe Workers' Journal,* V (January 1904), 6–7.

49. *Union Boot and Shoe Worker,* I (October 1900), 9–10; *Proceedings, Fifth Convention of the Boot and Shoe Workers' Union* (Detroit, 1902), 33–34; *Shoe Workers' Journal,* V (March 1904), 9–10.

50. Galster, *op. cit.,* 160–161.

51. Brockton *Times,* VI (December 3, 1902), 9; *Shoe Workers' Journal,* IV (January 1903), 1, 4; VI (May 1905), 6–7; VI (November 1905), 19; VII (October 1906), 19; VIII (March 1907), 32–33.

52. Galster, *op. cit.,* 105; Bedford, *op. cit.,* 220–223; *Shoe Workers' Journal,* V (November 1904), 11; V (December 1904), 21; VI (February 1905), 3; Michael Hennessy, *Four Decades of Massachusetts Politics, 1890–1935* (Norwood, 1935), 82–84, 88–92.

53. *Shoe Workers' Journal,* IX (June 1908), 5–8; IX (August 1908), 19–20; *International Socialist Review,* V (January 1905), 436; VI (July 1905), 54–55.

54. Galster, *op. cit.,* 83–85, 115–116; *Shoe Workers' Journal,* VI (July 1905), 18–19.

55. Galster, *op. cit.,* 87–89, 91, 95–98, 110–111, 113–114; *Shoe Workers' Journal,* VII (February 1906), 13.

56. Galster, *op. cit.,* 91, 107–110, 114; *Shoe Workers' Journal,* XI (September 1910), 8; *Proceedings, Sixth Convention of the Boot and Shoe Workers' Union* (Cincinnati, 1904), 10–11.

57. Galster, *op. cit.,* 110; *American Labor Union Journal,* I (February 19, 1903), 5; *Shoe Workers' Journal,* V (February 1904), 10–11; V (March 1904), 36–38; V (May 1904), 32–33; V (June 1904), 31; V (July 1904), 27–28; V (December 1904), 8–12, 15–18; VII (March 1906), 18–19; Tobin to Gompers, December 15, 1903 (Gompers' Correspondence with Affiliates, AFL–CIO Collection).

58. Tobin also considered sending Frank Sieverman on this trip, but decided against it because he was "a social Democrat of the Debs variety," and he was not "fully convinced" that Sieverman was "sound on . . . trades union policy." Tobin to Frank Morrison, June 27, 1902 (Gompers' Correspondence with Affiliates, AFL–CIO Collection).

59. *Proceedings, First Convention of the IWW* (Chicago, 1905), 124–125, 280–281; *Shoe Workers' Journal,* VI (August 1905), 29–31; IX (January 1908), 7–15.

60. Galster, *op. cit.*, 119–130; *Shoe Workers' Journal*, VIII (October 1907) 27–28; IX (January 1908), 7–15; *Proceedings, Seventh Convention of the Boot and Shoe Workers' Union* (June 1906), 43–44, 89, 119.

61. It was no coincidence that the Italian-born Orlando should have been general organizer of the United Shoe Workers. With its repudiation of the Socialist party's political policies the Boot and Shoe Workers Union had also given up the more liberal attitudes which socialists generally held on immigration and race, and resentment at the nativist outlook of the union led Italians and other recent immigrant workers in the shoe industry to join the USWA rather than the BSWU. In July 1903 the *Shoe Workers' Journal* criticized the newer immigrants who were entering the New England shoe factories as "degenerate intruders" who threatened the jobs of BSWU members by working for lower wages and brought "foreign conditions, associations and habits" into the life of American industry. And at the 1913 BSWU convention (which took place not long after the great IWW Lawrence textile strike, in which many Italians were involved), Tobin again attacked the new immigrants as "prone to revolutionary ideas" and implied strongly that he hoped no more would join his own union. "No people," he said, "should be allowed to enter on our shores who are incapable of becoming imbued with American ideals." *Shoe Workers' Journal*, IV (July 1903), 9–10; *Proceedings, Eleventh Convention of the Boot and Shoe Workers' Union* (Montreal, 1913), 47. For Irish attitudes toward more recent immigrant groups in Massachusetts generally, see Geoffrey Blodgett, *The Gentle Reformers: Massachusetts Democrats in the Cleveland Era* (Cambridge, 1966).

62. Galster, *op. cit.*, 138–139; Lynn *News*, IV (December 26, 1907), 1; *Shoe Workers' Journal*, X (September 1909), 30; X (October 1909), 23–26; *Industrial Union Bulletin*, I (August 10, 1907), 1; I (October 5, 1907), 3; I (October 26, 1907), 2; *Proceedings, Second Convention of the United Shoe Workers of America* (St. Louis, 1911), 2–3. In 1910 the IWW made another attempt to organize the shoe workers, this time in Brooklyn, where it succeeded for a time in establishing a largely Italian local in the Wickert and Gardiner factory, composed of striking BSWU members who had been expelled for breaking their contract. But the local dissolved in 1911. See *Solidarity*, II (December 17, 1910), 1, 4; II (December 24, 1910), 1, 4; II (January 4, 1911), 1; Foner, *op. cit.*, IV, 306–307.

63. Galster, *op. cit.*, 101–102; *Shoe Workers' Journal*, XI (September 1909), 30; *Proceedings, Ninth Convention of the Boot and Shoe Workers' Union* (Syracuse, 1909), 30.

64. Brockton *Times*, VI (March 21, 1909), 1; VII (March 4, 1910), 2; Brockton *Enterprise*, III (March 4, 1910), 3; Brockton *Searchlight*, VI (August 5, 1910), 1; X (June 26, 1914), 2.

65. *Shoe Workers' Journal*, XI (December 1909), 31–32; XI (January 1910), 31; XIV (March 1913), 13–16; XVI (January 1915), 13–14.

66. Brockton *Times*, IV (October 5, 1907), 1; Michael J. Tracey to Morrison, October 11, 1909; Morrison to Tracey, October 14, 1909 (Gompers' Correspondence with Affiliates, AFL–CIO Collection).

67. Brockton *Searchlight*, VI (August 5, 1910), 1; *Shoe Workers' Journal*, XI (December 1913), 10–12; *Proceedings, Second General Convention of the United Shoe Workers of America* (St. Louis, 1911), 6–9; *Proceedings, Twenty-*

ninth Annual Convention of the A.F. of L. (Toronto, 1909), 250; *Proceedings, Thirty-third Annual Convention of the A.F. of L.* (Seattle, 1913), 348.

68. Bedford, *op. cit.,* 201, 204–225; *American Labor Union Journal,* I (May 7, 1903), 2; *International Socialist Review,* XII (April 1912), 633–636; XII (June 1912), 845–849.

69. *Ibid.,* XIV (March 1914), 520–521. For the Hamilton-Brown strike in St. Louis, see Galster, *op. cit.,* 141–145; *Shoe Workers' Journal,* XIII (July 1912), 1–4, 8–9; XV (February 1914), 8–16; XV (April 1914), 11–12; XV (May 1914), 8–9; XV (June 1914), 11–13.

70. *Shoe Workers' Journal,* XVI (February 1915), 10–16; *Proceedings, Third Convention of the United Shoe Workers of America* (Rochester, 1913), 6–14; *Proceedings, Fourth Convention of the United Shoe Workers of America* (Chicago, 1919), 44, 108–109.

71. For a further radical critique of the Boot and Shoe Workers Union and its policies, see Horace Davis, *Shoes, The Workers and the Industry* (New York, 1940), 166–175.

4

Jewish Socialism and the Ladies Garment Workers of New York

Jewish immigrants from Russia and from eastern Europe played a role in the immigrant tradition of American socialism second only to that of the Germans. In fact, in the later period they were more important, for as German immigration at the end of the nineteenth century declined, so the number of Jewish and other immigrants from Russia and from eastern Europe increased, bringing with them a significant proportion of radicals and revolutionaries, especially after the abortive Russian revolution of 1905.

The center for this massive influx was the garment industry of New York, partly because large numbers of Jews had worked at tailoring in their native countries, and partly because many of their fellows, accustomed to life in the ghetto and denied entrance to business and the professions, sought temporary employment in the city where they first arrived. Chicago, Philadelphia, and other garment centers also took large numbers of the Jewish immigrants, and some became tradesmen, peddlers, or artisans in other trades. But it was on the lower East Side of Manhattan, the heart of the ready-made clothing industry, that the Jews congregated in the largest numbers; and it was here that they helped to establish most of the garment industry's leading trade-unions.

Nearly all these unions, with the exception of the United Garment Workers of America, were socialist for a considerable part of their his-

tory; and the largest and most famous of them was the International Ladies Garment Workers Union, founded at a convention held in New York
City in June 1900. This union, composed at first primarily of cloakmakers,
became one of the strongest bastions of socialism in the AFL. It developed
a unique combination of militancy and idealism, coupled with practical
trade-unionism, which differed both from the intellectual Marxism of the
Brewery Workers Union and from the transient impossibilism of the Boot
and Shoe Workers Union. It was also one of the very few unions to retain
its radicalism for any length of time after World War I, some of its members
remaining socialists into the 1930's and beyond.[1]

I

Even from this brief introduction it is apparent that the most important
source of radicalism in the ILGWU, as in the other garment unions, was the
influx of revolutionaries from eastern Europe and from czarist Russia. Before 1880, most of the workers in the ladies' garment industry were either
Irish, native-born Americans, or German Jews of an older generation who
had become conservative over the years. Not so the Jewish immigrants from
eastern Europe, who entered the industry in ever-increasing numbers between
1882 and 1914. Unable to find an outlet for their talents in Europe, and
confined geographically within the Pale, the Jews in Russia had faced un-
relenting racial persecution as well as the feudal and repressive authoritar-
ianism of the czarist regime; and it was not surprising that many of them
entered the underground revolutionary movement which had been developing in the European cities of the Russian empire ever since the Decembrist
revolt of 1825. Some Jews, in Poland, joined the Socialist Circle of Aaron
Lieberman, the so-called "father of Jewish socialism." Others, in Russia,
joined the People's Will, a terrorist organization which in 1881 succeeded
in assassinating Czar Alexander I, only to bring a major wave of pogroms
in its wake. But perhaps most were members of the Bund, a Jewish underground organization which formed part of the socialist movement in various
countries of eastern Europe.[2]

It was from this background that the ILGWU's early leaders came. Many
of them were former students and intellectuals who, if they had lived in
western Europe, would probably have found their way into the professions. Benjamin Schlesinger, for example, who later became president of
the ILGWU, was at first a reporter on the Socialist Labor party daily
Abendblatt and came from a rabbinical family in Krakai, Lithuania.
Abraham Baroff, general secretary-treasurer between 1915 and 1929,
was described by a contemporary as "a poetic soul, with a gift for journal-

ism, an enthusiast, an idealist" who had been a Nihilist in Russia before coming to the United States. Julius Woolf, a General Executive Board member from 1908 to 1910, was a military tailor from Grodno, Poland, where he had organized cloakmakers into the Bund, until the threat of deportation to Siberia brought him to America. And Saul Metz, also on the ILGWU General Executive Board, had been a Bund leader whose revolutionary activities, according to one account, had "stamped themselves on his mind and character, consecrating him, so to say, for service in the labor movement." [3]

Almost equally important were a group of socialists who were not actually members of the ILGWU, but played a major role in guiding and supporting it, especially in the early days. Among these were Abraham Cahan from Vilna, in Poland, editor of the celebrated Jewish newspaper the *Jewish Daily Forward;* Meyer London, an attorney for the garment workers who was elected to Congress on the Socialist party ticket in 1914; and Morris Hillquit, perhaps the most influential figure of all, who began his career as a shirtmaker and later represented the union as an attorney on many occasions.[4]

The role of these Jewish intellectuals in the needle trades was in some ways comparable to that of the ideologically oriented German leaders of the Brewery Workers Union. Yet in other respects their position was different. Many of the officers of the Brewery Workers Union had worked in the labor movement before they left Germany, and they were, for the most part, brewery workers themselves. The Jewish intellectuals, by contrast, found themselves in the garment industry as a matter of necessity, not of choice, and despite their earlier experiences in the Russian revolutionary movement they approached the problems of trade-union organizing largely from outside. Moreover, their radical sentiments were not always attractive at first to the mass of Jewish workers in the trade, most of whom were artisans and former tradesmen from small towns in czarist Russia who were conservative in their instincts and deeply committed to their orthodox Jewish faith. In addition, many of the intellectuals at first spoke Russian, not Yiddish, the language of most eastern European Jews.

However, in the secular atmosphere of America the rigid mores of eastern European Jewish life began to loosen, so that orthodox Judaism and socialism no longer appeared as incompatible as they had at first. Also, lacking any other leaders and faced with a new and often hostile world, the Jewish workers turned instinctively to the intellectuals for help and were grateful for the leadership which they were able to provide. As a result, the earlier suspicions were broken down, and the joint experiences of both intellectuals and rank-and-file members in the harsh conditions of the sweatshop created a common bond between the two which was in many ways unique throughout the American labor movement.[5]

Sweatshop conditions in themselves, however, were also a major source of radicalism in the ILGWU, almost as important as the presence of European radicals in the trade. The garment industry was a low-wage industry of semiskilled workers at this time, with conditions far worse than those in most other American trades. Its sweatshops were as notorious as those of London or Manchester earlier in the century, and their effects just as far-reaching. Morris Sigman, who succeeded Benjamin Schlesinger in the presidency in 1923, became a radical in his youth because of his experiences as a presser in a cloakmakers' shop. John A. Dyche, secretary-treasurer of the ILGWU between 1904 and 1914, although later a conservative, was at first a socialist as a result of working in the garment industry in England, where many Jewish immigrants went before migrating to the United States. And Benjamin Schlesinger himself left Lithuania too young to have any fixed political opinions: he became a socialist, according to one account, because of the "endless hours, starvation wages, [and] unspeakable conditions" in the Chicago sweatshops where he was first employed.[6]

Equally important were the effects of sweatshop conditions on the bulk of workers in the trade. In the 1870's and 1880's, the production of ready-made garments, both men's and women's, tended to be in relatively large "inside" shops, where all the different stages in the making of a garment were carried out together. Here, control over wages and hours, either by legislation or by the workers themselves, was not impossible to achieve. But with the development of the cheap sewing machine, which was easily transportable, the manufacturers found that it was more profitable, once the cloth had been cut, to farm out the garments for completion to contractors, many of them former workers themselves, who distributed the work among the tenements where the workers lived instead of establishing large-scale factories of their own.

Under these circumstances regulation of hours, or of conditions of work, was almost impossible to enforce. Measures were passed by the New York State assembly to limit the use of tenement flats as workshops relatively early, but for years they were largely unenforced. "Take the Second Avenue Elevated at Chatham Square," urged Jacob Riis in his celebrated account of the sweatshops, written in 1890,

> and ride up half a mile through the sweaters' district. Every open window of the big tenements, that stand like a continuous brick wall on both sides of the way, gives you a glimpse of one of these shops as the train speeds by. Men and women bending over their machines, or ironing clothes at the window. . . . The road is like a big gangway through an endless work-room

where vast multitudes are forever laboring. Morning, noon, or night, it makes no difference; the scene is always the same.[7]

In addition to this, the garment industry suffered, even more than the shoe industry did, from instability and from seasonal fluctuations in demand. Style changes were much more frequent and subtle in clothes than they were in shoes, necessitating sudden changes in employment, and there were often several months of the year in which there was hardly any work at all. Also, like the shoe industry and other consumer industries where the margin of profit on each item was relatively small, competition in the early years was ruthless and intense. Manufacturers would play contractors off against one another, giving the cut garments to those who would accept the lowest price. The contractors, in turn, passed the reductions on to their workers, and between 1873 and 1900 wages, as in the shoe industry, were either static or actively in decline. In New York City, for instance, where the sweating system grew most rapidly, the rates for certain classes of work fell from $15 a week in 1883 to $6 or $7 a week in 1885. These meager earnings were depleted still further when the garment workers were forced to hire their own sewing machines and to pay petty fines for losing the spools from their machines, for example, or for losing the tickets attached to the garments on which they worked.

The sweatshop workers tried to compensate for this decline in wages by increasing their hours of work. At first a team of workers produced about nine ladies' cloaks a day. But soon this number increased to ten, fourteen, or even twenty, until the daily work load was three or four times what it had been. "The task [is] so adjusted as practically to drive from the shop each employe who is not willing to work to the limit of physical endurance," a Congressional committee reported in 1893, "the hours of work under this system rarely being less than twelve, generally thirteen or fourteen, and frequently from fifteen to eighteen hours in the twenty-four." [8]

But it was the unsanitary conditions of the sweatshops, where illness flourished and tuberculosis became an occupational disease, that were their worst feature. In a typical New York tenement, according to one federal government report, "the workers, all immigrants, lived and worked together in large numbers, in a few small, foul, ill-smelling rooms, without ventilation, water, or near-by toilets. They slept on the unswept floors littered with the work, the work table serving as the dining table as well." In Chicago conditions were, if anything, worse. The Illinois factory inspector's report for 1894, for example, summarized the condition of the garment shop of Peter Darwut, at 549 West Nineteenth Street, as

a home shop, in basement of tenement house, low dark and filthy; dimensions of room were 14 x 14 x 7½ feet; two windows; room contained four machines, stove with fire in it, and four men, three women, working; air was intolerably bad; folding doors were open between this shop and the living-room in which Darwut and wife eat and sleep and cook and keep boarders; the boarders (two) slept in low room off shop, unlighted and unventilated.[9]

The socialism of the ILGWU, therefore, as of the other radical garment unions, was in part ethnically derived, as in the case of the Brewery Workers Union, and in part the result of conditions in the garment industry itself. In the 1880's and 1890's it was the intellectuals who played the leading role, organizing unions, leading strikes, and representing the workers in their dealings with employers. But by 1900, when the ILGWU was founded, a cadre of trade-union leaders had been formed, many of whom had worked in the industry for some time and had risen from the ranks. In the union itself there were several different types: the cloakmakers, many of them Marxist ideologues, who were at first the most influential element; the pressers, men of considerable physical strength (to handle the heavy pressing irons), who constituted in many ways the most proletarian group; the dressmakers—called the "romantic" element in the trade—most of them young Jewish girls who eagerly supported the union and its strikes; and the cutters, a small but highly skilled group who were more conservative than the rest.[10]

Save for the cutters, however—many of whom, being of Irish extraction, supported Tammany Hall—most members of the union had by now come to accept the socialist cause, even if the Socialist party itself was not at first endorsed. At its second convention, held in June 1901, the ILGWU unanimously adopted a resolution urging all locals "to educate their members towards taking part in the independent political labor movement"; and the following year it refused to hear a member of the New York state legislature because of his connections with Tammany, while at the same time barring as a delegate anyone who held office in either of the major parties. Finally, in 1903, the union adopted a resolution commending the Socialist party for its official policy of support for the trade-unions and expressing the hope that this would "speed the progress of converting the workingmen of this country to the grand and noble idea of Social Democracy." [11]

II

In this year, 1903, the ILGWU had over 8,000 members and appeared to be growing steadily both in New York and in the other garment centers as well.[12] However, it was not to be successfully established on a permanent basis for another seven years, until the two great New York strikes of 1910. This was in part because of the general contraction which took place in the labor movement after 1903; in part because of the inherent difficulties of organizing a rapidly expanding labor force, divided up between several thousand tiny tenement shops; and in part—the most important factor from our point of view—because of ideological conflicts in the union itself.

As we have seen, the ILGWU, unlike the Brewery Workers Union, was composed almost entirely of new, inexperienced immigrants who had had almost no experience of trade-union organization in the old country. At the beginning of each season, when work was plentiful and piece rates were established, garmentworkers would readily join the organization, strike for higher wages, and pay their union dues. But at the end of the season, with no work and little money coming in, the union locals would lose members or even disintegrate altogether. This created a problem of seasonal unionism which was more serious than that in the shoe industry and which persisted for years, even after the ILGWU had itself been founded.[13]

Besides this, there were strong ethnic differences in the industry, despite the initial preponderance of eastern Europeans. The English-speaking element, which included many of the cutters, looked down on the Jews, who were "always striking and stirring up trouble when it is not necessary." Both differed greatly from the Italians, who began to enter the industry in large numbers after 1890 and were quite different in both their cultural and religious background. In addition, the Russian revolution of 1905 brought a fresh wave of radicals into the industry, many of whom were openly contemptuous of the conservative and slow-moving character of the American labor movement. The American worker, wrote a leading ILGWU official to Gompers during this period, kept away from the union because he was "too slow, too conservative," while the Russian worker "keeps away because he is too radical, because his mind runs in the direction of revolution and revolutionary changes." [14]

All of this meant that the ILGWU remained small and weak for a number of years and was particularly susceptible to the ideological disputes which affected the labor movement in New York more readily than in any other city. Anarchism, associated with the name of Bakunin and the conspiratorial methods of the Russian revolutionary movement, attracted quite a number of Jewish workers in the 1880's. Then came the DeLeonite movement in the SLP, in which the ladies' garmentworkers were also intimately involved. The Progressive Cloak Makers of New York, for example, which in July 1896 was the only substantial cloakmakers' union in the city, was incorporated into the Socialist Trades and Labor Alliance, to be challenged a few months later by a rival organization, the United Brotherhood of Cloak Makers. In 1897 this organization had supported Meyer London,

Isaac Hourwich, Joseph Barondess, and other Jewish socialists in breaking with DeLeon and joining Debs in the Social Democracy of America. There was also a conflict with the Knights of Labor, which some garment workers joined, although fewer than in many other trades.[15]

By 1900, when the ILGWU was founded, these particular disputes were over, and the socialist resolution adopted by the 1903 convention welcomed, with a sense of relief, the "spirit of justice and tolerance" which characterized the official trade-union declarations of the Socialist Party of America. Nevertheless, the conflicts of the 1890's left a legacy of discord in the young organization which, together with the "abstract and metaphysical" characteristics associated with the Jewish temperament or cast of mind, reflected a continuing interest in the doctrines of the extreme left that reasserted itself whenever the union appeared to be weakened or subject to strong pressure from outside. Thus, in 1904, when the garment manufacturers, taking advantage of an industrial depression, undertook an open-shop campaign which resulted in defeats for the union in Chicago, Cleveland, and elsewhere, and the conservatives defeated Benjamin Schlesinger for reelection to the presidency, there was widespread internal dissatisfaction. James McCauley, the new president, was a cutter who was unpopular with many of the Jewish socialists, and the new administration was unable to prevent the loss of membership in the union, which fell from sixty-six locals in twenty-seven cities in 1904 to forty locals in nineteen cities in 1905. In that year some of the dissatisfied elements even suggested that the union be merged with the much larger United Garment Workers of America, or be wound up altogether.[16] Others, more radical, urged that the union turn to the IWW for the solution to its problems. The weakened state of the ILGWU meant that the IWW was able to present a threat of considerable proportions.

Unlike the Brewery Workers Union, the ILGWU had a semi-industrial rather than a fully industrial structure, with some locals organized by nationality, some by sex (the women's locals), and some on the basis of a single craft; and the IWW seemed attractive to many of the members who were dissatisfied with the conservative administration of James McCauley and Secretary-Treasurer John A. Dyche, and who believed that the union should go beyond its semi-industrial position and attempt to organize all the needle workers into one universal garment union. More specifically, the new IWW appealed to members who, for one reason or another, had stayed in the SLP, which remained stronger in New York than it was elsewhere, and which was, of course, more overtly committed to the IWW than the Socialist party was. It attracted a number of Italians, "imbued with the ideas of Syndicalism which they had brought with them from Italy." And it appealed also to many of the recently arrived 1905 Russian revolutionaries.

In addition, the IWW took advantage of the fact that many ILGWU members knew no English, distributing pamphlets and circulars in both Hebrew and Yiddish, as well as in Italian, and in December 1905 Secretary-Treasurer Dyche was sufficiently concerned at the growth of IWW influence to write urgently to Gompers asking him to send a Yiddish-speaking AFL organizer to New York, since "both the orthodox [Hebrew] and the socialist Jewish press is full of lies and abuse of the Trade Union movement in general and the A.F. of L. in particular." Gompers was unable to comply.[17]

A Tailors and Cloakmakers union from Montreal was among the unions which attended the IWW founding convention in June 1905; and soon afterward Local 31, in Cleveland, which had earlier flirted with the American Labor Union, went over to the new organization. In Philadelphia, Skirt Makers Local 7 joined the IWW because of dissatisfaction with the ILGWU. In Chicago, the IWW succeeded temporarily in establishing an organization to replace ILGWU locals which had become disorganized there; and in Boston and St. Louis there were similar developments.[18] But it was in New York that the IWW took its firmest hold. There, Local 59 of the IWW established branches in several areas of the industry, including Cloakmakers Branch 3, Pressers Branch 6 (in which Morris Sigman was active for a time), White Goods Workers Branch 12, and Ladies Tailors Branch 10. No accurate estimate of the membership of Local 59 can be made, nor of how far it enrolled ILGWU members as opposed to those who had not previously joined a trade-union. But it agitated for "the uniform organization of all branches of the clothing industry into one grand industrial body" and in 1907 carried out a number of quite ambitious strikes.

As with both the Brewery Workers and the Boot and Shoe Workers unions, however, the influence of the IWW in the ILGWU did not last for very long, and by 1908 or 1909 virtually all the IWW locals had reentered the parent organization. This was partly because of the disillusioning effect of the successive splits in the IWW, and partly because of the help which Gompers and other AFL officials had given to the union during its struggle for survival in 1905–1908, which tended to cement it more firmly to the AFL. But it was also due to a change in attitude on the part of the 1905 Russian *émigrés*. For a time this group kept aloof from what it called the "American movement" and joined the various organizations attempting to further the revolutionary cause in Russia. The IWW was not, of course, in any direct sense one of these. But its revolutionary and direct-action tactics seemed more appropriate to the militant traditions of the Russian revolutionary movement than did the moderate and conservative policies of the AFL. By 1908, however, with Russia in the grip of Stolypin, the prospects for further revolutionary activity there had temporarily diminished, and most of the 1905 immigrants gave up their plans for returning to Europe and turned their attention, instead, to the conditions of their fellow workers in the sweatshops. As a result, in 1909 hundreds of them joined the ILGWU for the first time, bringing with them fresh energy and a new, if still highly radical, spirit. Many of them also joined the Socialist party at the same time.[19]

Even if the ILGWU was unwilling to endorse the IWW, however, its internal problems still remained unsolved; and side by side with the controversy over the IWW there arose a debate over how best the position of the union itself could be improved. This also had a bearing on the position of the socialists, as it did in other unions. Probably the majority of rank-and-file members of the ILGWU at this time believed that the union's difficulties derived primarily from the seasonal nature of the garment industry and the fragmentation of the labor force into a multiplicity of small, competing shops, and that little could be done until a larger proportion of the sweatshops had been brought under union control. Thus they laid the major emphasis on organizing more of the actual workers in the trade and paid less attention to the problems of union structure and reform. But Secretary-Treasurer Dyche, together with Abraham Rosenberg, who became president in 1908, believed that much could be done by overhauling the structure of the organization and also by increasing the union's dues. The result was a series of conflicts over the nature and purposes of the union which in many ways recalled the conflicts between impossibilists and conservatives in the Boot and Shoe Workers Union and in many other trade-unions as well.[20]

Dyche and Rosenberg had both originally been radicals, like the majority of ILGWU leaders. But under the impact of the crisis through which the union was passing they became cautious and conservative in their views. Dyche was the more influential of the two. A stocky, combative man, he had already moved away from his earlier socialism while working in England, and in America he acquired the reputation of the "Jewish Gompers." This was partly because he had come to share Gompers' view of the labor movement—in 1908 he told the AFL president privately that his aim was "the freeing of the Jewish unions from the influence of the Socialists"— and partly because he was personally closer to Gompers than most of the other ILGWU leaders. There was, for instance, some suggestion that Gompers helped secure his appointment as secretary-treasurer of the ILGWU in 1904.[21]

At all events, in his first report as secretary-treasurer to the ILGWU convention of 1905, Dyche condemned the "loose character of the affiliation of our locals" and the "ridiculously small Per Capita" of two and a half cents per week which the members paid to the International.[22] He suggested that a national strike fund and a death and disability benefit be established "to bind members to the International" and that the power of locals to declare strikes be limited. This was the same kind of argument which Gompers and other craft-union leaders had used in the 1880's to build up the Cigarmakers International Union—the archetype of conservative craft unionism in the AFL—and at a subsequent convention Dyche repeated similar views. "As long as our locals," he said, "enjoy . . . almost complete local autonomy and our present Per Capita, from which members get no more than 'moral support' in case of need [remain the same], then our International Union, however large its membership may be at any time, will never be more, to put it bluntly and frankly, than a paper organization." However, there was considerable resistance toward these views on the part of the rank and file, and although the 1905 convention did agree to establish a strike fund and a death and disability benefit, and even to limit the locals' power to strike to some extent, these proposals remained largely a dead letter for a number of years, primarily because of the refusal of the union to raise the per capita tax.[23]

In this debate over union reform, which continued for a considerable number of years, it seemed as though a split were developing in the ILGWU between a conservative administration on the one hand and a more radical rank and file on the other, similar to that which occurred in the Boot and Shoe Workers Union at the end of the 1890's. To some extent this was true. But the more conservative element which Dyche and Rosenberg represented in the ILGWU was much smaller than that of John F. Tobin in the BSWU, and the underlying political strength of the socialists on the lower East Side was clearly much greater than it was in the shoe towns of Massachusetts.

By 1904 the socialist vote in New York was beginning to make itself felt. Large numbers of garmentworkers, save for the Tammany Irish and some of the older ethnic groups in the union, supported the Socialist party's candidates at the polls, irrespective of their views on matters of trade-union policy. In 1904 Joseph Barondess, a cloakworkers' leader from the 1890's, received 3,167 votes in a campaign for Congress in the Ninth Congressional District, where many of the garment workers lived. In 1906 Morris Hillquit, running in the district for the first time, did even better, benefiting from the concern which was felt by many Jewish voters at the failure of the revolution in Russia in 1905. "Thousands of families . . . have lost relations in the revolution," ran one account just before the election, "and scores of Socialist orators are making that one of their strong points, and picturing Hillquit as the man who will look after the interests of the Jews." In 1908, campaigning for the congressional election in the same district with the help of Robert Hunter and J. G. Phelps Stokes, Hillquit might well have won altogether had it not been for an electoral alliance between the Tammany Hall candidate and the Voters' Independence League, headed by William Randolph Hearst.[24]

Then, at the end of 1909, came the dramatic general strike of waist and dressmakers in New York City, under the aegis of Local 25, which transformed the entire position of the union and seemed directly to refute Dyche's contention that the ILGWU would never be really successful until it adopted the high dues and extensive benefit system of the conservative craft unions. The strike, which lasted from November 1909 to February 1910 and spread also to Philadelphia, was known popularly as the Uprising of the Twenty Thousand. The strikers, who actually numbered between fifteen and twenty thousand, consisted primarily of young Jewish and Italian girls who rose up suddenly and spontaneously against the low wages and long hours, petty tyrannies, and subcontracting methods of the sweatshop. Although the settlement which the girls received at the end of the strike was a compromise, reducing hours and raising wages in many shops, but failing to secure recognition for the strikers as a whole, the membership of Local 25, which had earlier been about a hundred, rose to over ten thousand. The way was also paved for the even larger cloakmakers' strike which followed between July and September 1910.

This strike, which involved over fifty thousand workers, was better prepared than the dressmakers' strike and consequently more successful. Several hundred of the smaller manufacturers accepted the union's terms almost at once, and Louis D. Brandeis—only one of a number of distinguished public figures to be involved in the negotiations—prevailed upon both sides to accept the preferential union shop (union men to be employed over nonunion men of equal ability), which was regarded as a major victory for the union. Then, on September 2, 1910, the Joint Board of Cloakmakers and the Cloak, Suit and Skirt Manufacturers Protective Association of New York signed the famous agreement which became known as the Protocol of Peace. This raised wages, ended "inside" subcontracting and charges for power, and provided for a fifty-hour work week. It also created a Joint Board of Sanitary Control to supervise conditions in the sweatshops, and established machinery for the conciliation and arbitration of disputes which was more advanced than that in almost any other industry at this time.[25]

Neither of these 1910 strikes, which finally established the ILGWU on a permanent basis, was in any direct sense the result of agitation by the socialists. Both represented a general uprising against the evils of the sweatshop, much as the coal miners' general strikes of 1894 and 1897 represented a general uprising against the conditions in the mines.[26] But the solidarity and fervor of the strikers, and the aid and leadership provided

by the socialists in many different forms, illustrated how close the relationship between the socialists and the ILGWU had now become. Morris Hillquit was attorney for the workers in the first strike, Meyer London in the second; and both sat for the workers on the Board of Arbitration under the
Protocol of Peace. The Workmen's Circle and other radical Jewish organizations raised money for the strikers. The *Jewish Daily Forward* and the
New York *Call* defended the strikers' cause and opened subscription lists
on their behalf—an important matter when much of the press was hostile
and the International had so little money of its own. During the negotiations over the Protocol the *Forward,* in particular, lent its great prestige to
union demands for the closed shop, to which London gave his support.
And numerous branches of the Socialist party, including the Italian
branch of New York City, gave money and organizers to help. In fact, the
national office of the party estimated, when the strikes were over, that
more than $11,000 had been donated by socialists across the country.[27]
But as already indicated, perhaps the most interesting fact, from the point
of view of the debate between radicals and conservatives in the labor
movement generally, was that the strikes in New York and elsewhere were
won, and the Protocol achieved, without the large treasury and strong central administration which most of the craft unionists in the AFL considered
to be essential for success.[28]

As a result of the benefits conferred on the ILGWU by the Protocol of
Peace the organization expanded rapidly. By 1913 the membership figures,
which before 1910 had never risen above 10,000, were as high as 90,000,
and the union had contracts of one kind or another with 1,796 out of a
total of 1,829 garmentworkers' shops in New York.[29] Nevertheless, despite
the advantages of the Protocol, it also involved sacrifices on the part of the
union, as the Union Stamp Contract in the Boot and Shoe Workers Union
had done. As a result it precipitated a further conflict over the structure
and policies of the ILGWU which was even more serious than the first.

The Protocol of Peace, like the Union Stamp Contract in the BSWU, prohibited the use of the strike as a means of settling disputes and insisted
that the decisions of the Board of Arbitration (which consisted of one
manufacturer, one union member, and one representative of the general
public) be accepted as binding on both sides. Moreover, although it could
be terminated by either side, the Protocol was intended as a permanent
agreement, limiting still further the union's freedom of action. Numerous
complaints were made by the more radical members that the scale of
wages laid down by the Protocol were not properly observed and that
workers were discharged for insisting upon it; that in order to avoid payment of wages on legal holidays—often Jewish religious festivals—
manufacturers would deliberately lay off their workers a few days before

the holiday; and that the Board of Arbitration was dilatory and unfair in making its decisions.

Meyer London, who was attorney for Local 25, under the Joint Board of Cloakmakers, expressed some of this dissatisfaction in a letter to Dr. Henry Moskowitz, secretary of the Board of Arbitration, in January 1911. The Manufacturers Association had shown an "utter lack of judgement" in its handling of the agreement, London wrote, and unless it withdrew some of its complaints against the union he would be forced to press counter-charges, "to the great delight of those [in Local 25] who believe that the cloak industry should be governed by the divine principle of 'dog eat dog.' " Nevertheless, tension continued, and the number of illegal strikes against the Protocol, which in 1911 was 70, rose to 160 in 1912.[30]

The issue was further complicated by a dispute in the ILGWU over who was actually responsible for administering the Protocol, raising afresh the question of central versus local control. The Protocol had been signed for the union by representatives of the Joint Board of Cloakmakers of New York, to which most of the cloakmakers' locals there were attached. But President Rosenberg and Secretary Dyche had also signed it on behalf of the International, and as the size and strength of the locals attached to the Joint Board increased—in 1912 they represented over 50,000 members, or more than half of the total membership of the union—its leaders sought to dispense with the International officers' presence on the board and to negotiate with the employers by themselves. In July 1912 the Joint Board dropped President Rosenberg, Secretary Dyche, and Vice-President Polakoff from its Board of Directors and in January 1913 appointed Dr. Isaac A. Hourwich, a brilliant but contentious economist and lawyer, as its chief clerk and negotiator with the employers. Hourwich promptly announced that the International had no authority over the Protocol, straining relations still further between the union administration and the Joint Board.[31]

Neither at this point nor later did this conflict represent a division between socialists and nonsocialists in the ILGWU as such. By now virtually all those connected with the leadership, save Dyche, were socialists of one kind or another, whether they were members of the union administration or the Joint Board. Nevertheless, it did reflect a difference in approach between the younger and more revolutionary members of the locals in the Joint Board, who regarded the right to strike as virtually synonymous with the right to organize, and the broader view taken by the officers of the International, who were more conciliatory in their approach and believed that cooperation with the manufacturers was essential if the garment industry was ever to be stabilized. There were in the union "two different policies that are contending for supremacy," wrote one contemporary observer. "One is the policy of constructive statesmanship, and the other is the policy of constant and continuous warfare with the manufacturers because of the 'war between the classes.' " [32]

The internal conflict in the ILGWU was between a moderate leadership and a militant rank and file, not, as in the Boot and Shoe Workers Union, between a conservative leadership on the one hand and a group of militants on the other. However, in the heat of the controversy this tended to be forgotten, and rank-and-file members who began by suggesting certain modifications in the Protocol ended up, like the DeLeonite impossibilists, by attacking the idea of trade agreements as a whole. In 1913 the *New Press,* the Italian *Loti de Classe,* and the Russian *Nova Potchta,* all connected in one way or another with the Joint Board, treated the International officers who defended the Protocol as though they were allies of the manufacturers, while those who criticized the Protocol were looked upon as the only true radicals.[33] As one study puts it,

> The union leadership was largely composed of Marxists who had been slowly converted to pragmatic unionism by experience. The bulk of the rank and file, however, still believed that the conflict between capital and labor was irreconcilable. It was therefore not surprising that when the more radical Union leaders attacked the Protocol as class collaborationist and demanded more militant action to prevent discharge of active union members, many of the rank and file followed these extremists.[34]

The IWW, despite the failure of its earlier efforts, naturally attempted to exploit these difficulties. In January 1912, William D. Haywood, in a debate with Hillquit held in New York on the attitude of the Socialist party toward the trade-unions, denounced the Protocol of Peace as an example of class collaboration which would "tie the hands of the working class not temporarily, but permanently"; and a number of Italian workers, under the leadership of Nicholas Lauretano, attempted to frustrate the establishment of the Protocol in the New York women's trades. As far as can be ascertained no new ILGWU locals actually joined the IWW in this period, although Ladies Tailors and Dressmakers Local 38 of New York seemed for a time as though it might. But at union conventions there were repeated criticisms of the union leadership for having abandoned the right to strike, both from avowed syndicalists and from delegates who represented the more militant locals; and in August 1912 the *New Post,* the official organ of the Joint Board of Cloakmakers, went so far as to describe the leaders of the union as "reactionaries" and "traitors," who had made themselves "slaves to the Protocol." [35]

To this Dyche replied on behalf of the International that Hoffman, editor of the *New Post,* and the other leaders of the Joint Board were guilty of "ignorance and dogmatism" in their handling of the Protocol and that they approached it "from the point of view of a Russian revolutionary." The success of a trade-union, he went on, "does not consist in the number of strikes it calls, but in the number of strikes it avoids. Its efficiency consists in being able to convince the employer that it is much more to his benefit to acceed [*sic*] to the demands of the union rather than to refuse them." [36] But this did not satisfy the extremists on the Joint Board. In articles in the *New Post* and at mass meetings of union members Isaac Hourwich asserted that the Arbitration Committee met too infrequently, that union demands for higher wages were never met, and that the whole system of mediating industrial disputes was dubious from a socialist point of view. "True enough, the Protocol has no definite terms," he wrote on June 20, 1913. "We may at any time, notify the Association that we want to abrogate the Protocol. That is a fine answer for Revolutionary Socialists, who do not believe in agreements with the bosses. . . . Are we going to put an end to the Protocol?" [37]

The crisis over the Protocol came to a head early in 1914. In December 1913 the manufacturers threatened to withdraw from the Protocol altogether unless Hourwich was replaced as chief clerk of the Joint Board. A committee headed by Gompers urged Hourwich to resign, but instead he was reelected for a further term by referendum vote of all the locals attached to the Joint Board, causing Meyer London, who had throughout played a restraining role, to resign as attorney, declaring bitterly that he had been "driven out." In January 1914, Hourwich was at last prevailed upon to withdraw, but only after intense pressure had been exerted by the union administration. In protest Locals 9 and 11 recalled those of their delegates who had voted against Hourwich from the Joint Board, and there were caustic recriminations at the subsequent ILGWU convention of June 1914. Resolutions were adopted condemning Hourwich for having deliberately provoked "dissension and ill will" between the officers and members of the union and between the union and the Manufacturers Association, while at the same time reproving Rosenberg and Dyche for their handling of the affair. And a further resolution, urging the ILGWU to repudiate the Protocol altogether as an interference with "the historical mission of the working class to do away with capitalism," was only narrowly defeated.

Both President Rosenberg and Secretary Dyche clearly felt themselves to be on trial at the 1914 convention, as indeed in many ways they were. Rosenberg defended himself against the many attacks which had been made on him in the *New Post* and denounced the "so-called radicals" who believed that the workers "must always and everywhere be at liberty to strike, even at the risk of ruining the entire industry." And Secretary Dyche went into his defense of the Protocol at length, arguing that even the revolutionary German Social Democratic party accepted the need for individual and collective agreements with the employers and pointing, interestingly enough, to the many contracts which the Brewery Workers Union had drawn up with the brewery owners. Both men demanded that the convention publicly exonerate them from the charges of treacherous conduct which had been made against them in their handling of the Hourwich affair.[38]

Dyche and Rosenberg were only to receive partial vindication, however. The convention presented them with "engrossed resolutions" of thanks for their service to the union. But it did not specifically absolve them from the charges which had been made against them, and it failed to reelect them to union office, choosing instead a new and more radical administration, headed by Benjamin Schlesinger as president and Morris Sigman as secretary-treasurer. According to some accounts, Dyche and Rosenberg declined to be renominated for office by the convention; but if this was so it was probably more because of anger at the way they had been treated by the radicals in the Joint Board than because they wished to withdraw from the positions they had held. In a private letter to Gompers soon afterward, for example, Dyche left no doubt that he strongly resented his own removal from office. He had, he said, been elected delegate to the next AFL convention by the ILGWU as some sort of compensation for his failure to be reelected secretary-treasurer, but he had refused to serve on the ground that he was unwilling "to identify myself with that crowd," meaning Schlesinger and his supporters, whom he called "a set of irresponsible socialists." [39]

III

With the resignation of Hourwich as chief clerk of the New York Joint Board of Cloakmakers and the election of a new administration at the 1914 convention, the Hourwich affair came officially to an end. The reelection of Schlesinger to the presidency placated much of the dissatisfaction with the administration which had been present among the rank and file, and with the return of prosperity in 1915 the ILGWU made rapid progress. By the end of 1916 it had 80,000 members in its ranks—almost as many as the Brewers and the Boot and Shoe Workers unions combined—and it had become the third largest union in the AFL.[40]

But the election of Schlesinger and Sigman did not mean a victory in the ILGWU for the extreme left. Schlesinger himself was an ardent socialist—he had spent much of the time since leaving the union presidency in 1904 as manager of the *Jewish Daily Forward*—and he deplored the idea that the dissatisfaction which the membership had expressed with the Protocol was mere "kicking," as Dyche and Rosenberg had implied. He called it instead a "healthy and normal discontent" with the evils and injustices which had always characterized the workers' lot. "Our International Union and the membership of which it is composed have this 'divine gift' of discontent in a high degree," he wrote in an editorial in the *Ladies' Garment Worker* (the ILGWU's official journal), "and that is precisely their saving grace." Nevertheless, Schlesinger also recognized the need for upholding the authority of the International if it were not to disintegrate altogether under the influence of the larger locals and the Joint Board in New York, and he also realized the importance of improving the union's relations with the employers if the limited concessions which had been made under the Protocol were to be maintained. Thus, although his election to the presidency did represent a move to the left, it was not followed by any immediate repudiation of the Protocol by the union or by the abandoning of the efforts at maintaining and strengthening the position of the central administration which Dyche and Rosenberg had previously made. In January 1915, when the Board of Arbitration under the Protocol made a minor concession to the union over the hiring and firing of workers in the shops, which had long been a source of contention, Schlesinger urged the membership to "accept it in the spirit in which it was uttered," even though in practice it added very little to the union's actual power; and he repeatedly urged the members to cease holding informal meetings in the streets in order to "sound off" against the employers.

Within the union, Schlesinger continued the campaign for raising the union's dues so that the International could establish a strike fund of its own, partly because of the inherent need for such a fund, but partly also because it would make the locals more dependent on the International for financial aid, thus strengthening its position. He succeeded, despite the opposition of the extreme left-wing element, at the national convention of 1916, when the per capita tax to the International was raised from ten to sixteen cents per month. Sigman, also, as secretary-treasurer, initiated a uniform system of bookkeeping and established an auditing department at International headquarters so as to exercise proper control over the accounts and financial standing of the locals.[41]

Nevertheless, the problems which had originally created dissatisfaction with the Protocol—especially the dilatory operation of the negotiating machinery and the prohibition of the right to strike—still remained unresolved; and despite numerous attempts to improve the negotiating machinery, it was clear by mid-1915 that both sides had lost their confidence in it. In addition, despite its willingness to cooperate with the employers in maintaining the Protocol, the new ILGWU administration also suggested, soon after taking office, that this should only be "until a more practical form of agreement could be devised." Thus in May 1915, when the cloak manufacturers suddenly and unilaterally repudiated the Protocol, the Schlesinger administration was not unduly disturbed. Instead, it worked diligently for the negotiation of a new agreement which would avoid the excessive restrictions of the Protocol while at the same time securing equivalent concessions from the employers. This did not come until August 1916, after a further confrontation with the cloak manufacturers which brought sixty thousand workers out on strike.

The AFL sent Secretary Frank Morrison and Treasurer John B. Lennon to help in this strike, and Gompers himself presided over the negotiations which brought it to an end.[42] Extremists in Local 1 and elsewhere protested strongly over the discharge clause, which restored the right of discharging workers to the employers, and for a time there was a threatened division in the ranks of the union reminiscent of the division over the Protocol, with President Schlesinger and Morris Hillquit this time playing the conciliatory role. Nevertheless, the settlement which followed brought wage increases and a reduction in hours from fifty to forty-nine per week. But the significant thing, from the union's point of view, was that while the employers regained complete control over the hiring and firing of workers, ending, for the time being, any attempt at the formal union shop, the rank and file's two main objections to the Protocol were also overcome: the new agreement was to be for a limited period of time, and it restored to the workers the power to strike.

Soon after this the Protocols which had been established in the New York dress and waist industry, as well as in various other branches of the trade in Boston, Philadelphia, and elsewhere, were also abrogated, to be replaced by similar collective agreements of the conventional type. Internal cohesion was restored, and the ILGWU once more moved ahead. At the 1916 union convention it was hailed by visiting labor leaders as "by far the most advanced and progressive [organization] of any of its standing at the present time" and by socialists as the "stronghold of the American class-conscious socialistic proletariat." [43]

This assessment, if a little exaggerated, was on the whole correct. After the departure of the Rosenberg-Dyche administration the socialists controlled virtually all the union's offices, at both the national and the local levels, and the earlier differences in ideology and outlook between the radical intellectuals and the more conservative shopworkers had largely disappeared. Some of the older cutters in New York's influential Local 10, of Irish and German descent, remained opposed to the socialist policies of the leadership, and a number of them had connections with Tammany Hall. But by now they played a relatively insignificant role in the union as a whole.[44]

This was not the case with the Italians, who increased in numbers after

1910 and who, with their Catholic faith and largely peasant background, might have been expected to act as a conservative influence in union affairs. To some extent this was true. But the leadership among the Italian members, as among the Jews, was often assumed by the more radical elements, and there appear to have been quite a number of active socialists among them. The two largest Italian locals, for example, Cloak Makers Local 48 and the Italian Waist and Dress Makers Union, Local 89, were named in honor of the revolutionary years 1848 and 1789, respectively, and the Italian Branch of the Socialist party in New York City had several members of the ILGWU in its ranks. The openly syndicalist element among the Italian members which we noted earlier had by now largely subsided. But Italian delegates at union conventions were among the most vocal in urging the union to adopt a policy of outright industrial unionism, and in 1912 they did their best to raise money for IWW organizers Ettor and Giovannitti after their arrest in the Lawrence textile strike.[45]

In fact, despite the wage increases and various other benefits which the union had secured from its negotiations with employers, this period saw, if anything, an increase in its socialist zeal. This was all the more noteworthy in view of the accession to power in 1912 of Woodrow Wilson and the Democrats, with all that this implied for labor's relations with the Democratic party. Remarkably little interest was displayed by the ILGWU in the reforming legislation passed by the first Wilson administration, although, of course, in general terms the union approved of it. Most members, at least in New York, associated the Democratic party with Tammany Hall, to which they were strongly opposed, and the 1914 convention adopted a resolution criticizing the AFL for allying itself with "one of the old political parties [that is, the Democratic party], managed and conducted principally in the interests of the employing class."[46] This disapproval of moderate reform politics even extended to the Progressive party of 1912: in 1913 there were expressions of shocked surprise that Dr. Hourwich should have run for office in New York on the Progressive ticket, on the ground that he had lent his support to a "capitalist party."[47]

Instead, the ILGWU reaffirmed and expanded its commitment to the Socialist party. Before 1912 the International as such had resisted any formal endorsement of the socialists on the ground that it was not a "political movement." At the 1912 convention, however, delegates from various parts of the country succeeded in amending the Preamble of the national constitution to include the phrase that "the only way to acquire . . . the full value of our product" was to "organize industrially into a class conscious labor union politically represented in the various legislative bodies by representatives of our own party and class." This still did not constitute a formal endorsement of the Socialist party, such as occurred in the Brewery Workers Union. But it was taken by many as tantamount to such,[48] and there was no doubting the increased enthusiasm and energy with which the ILGWU supported Socialist party candidates in the years which followed. As each election came around—whether municipal, state, or federal—committees were formed in the local unions, money was collected in the shops, and poll-watchers were sent to see that the socialists were not cheated out of their full vote. Especially noteworthy were the activities of the Cloakmakers Committee, formed of representatives of the locals in the Ninth Congressional District and headed several times by Saul Metz, which coordinated the activities of the ILGWU and other garmentworkers' unions in support of the socialist candidates. Besides Debs and other socialists, leading reform and literary figures such as William Dean Howells were brought in to support the campaigns.

There were further disappointments in 1910 and 1912 when Meyer London, who had replaced Hillquit as the Socialist party candidate in the Ninth Congressional District, came second to the Democratic candidate, largely, it was alleged, because the Democrats in Albany deliberately reorganized the district in order to frustrate the growing socialist vote. In 1912 this was despite the fact that Gompers made the rare gesture of endorsing London on behalf of the AFL. But in November 1914 the years of effort were rewarded when London finally defeated the incumbent congressman by 5,969 votes to 4,947, to become the only socialist besides Victor Berger in Milwaukee ever to be elected to Congress. The *Ladies' Garment Worker* expressed pride in the part which ILGWU members had played in the campaign, and there was tremendous excitement when the result was announced in front of the *Jewish Daily Forward*'s offices in Rutgers Square. "The cheering, dancing, singing and speech-making lasted until the dawn," one account recalled. London himself was welcomed like a conquering hero at the union's subsequent conventions. In 1916 he was reelected to Congress with an increased majority, while Hillquit only narrowly lost in the Twentieth Congressional District where there were somewhat fewer Jewish votes.[49]

Besides this, socialist candidates with a background in the garment trades were running for city and state-wide legislative office also. In 1915 A. I. Shiplacoff, of Brownsville, secretary of the United Hebrew Trades, was the first Socialist party candidate to be elected to the New York State assembly, again with ILGWU help; and the 1916 ILGWU convention endorsed Elmer Rosenberg, its own first vice-president, and Jacob Panken, a long-time friend of the union, for election to the assembly, besides donating $1,000 to the Hillquit-London campaign funds. Nor was this political activity confined solely to New York. In 1912 Secretary Dyche was taken to task for having given his support to Baker, the Democratic candi-

date for mayor of Cleveland, instead of supporting Ruthenberg, the Socialist party candidate, as most garmentworkers in the city did, and ILGWU
members worked for socialist candidates in Chicago, Philadelphia, and numerous other places as well.[50]

The large size and increasing success of the ILGWU also brought it considerable influence in the AFL. Relations between the two bodies were in
general better than they were between the AFL and some of the other socialist unions, partly because no serious jurisdictional disputes between the
ILGWU and other unions arose to create tensions and disagreements, as they
did in the case of the Brewery Workers Union, and partly because the AFL
itself gave considerable help and encouragement to the ILGWU in its early
years. Gompers and Herman Robinson, the AFL organizer in New York,
helped to keep the union going in the critical years from 1905 to 1908,
and the AFL was particularly helpful on a number of other occasions also,
notably during the unsuccessful arraignment of several ILGWU officers on
murder charges in 1915. Thus a sense of loyalty toward the AFL was developed, and there were rarely any suggestions that the ILGWU should withdraw from the federation altogether, such as were sometimes made in
other radical trade-unions.[51]

But this did not mean, of course, that the ILGWU accepted the general
trade-union philosophy of the AFL, as the Boot and Shoe Workers Union
did. On the contrary, it used its considerable vote at AFL conventions on
behalf of radical resolutions—on politics, on industrial unionism, and on
other matters—more consistently than almost any other trade-union. For
example, from 1911 on it favored the establishment of a Needle Trades
Department in the AFL on the model of the Railroad and Building Trades
Departments, which finally bore fruit in the Needle Trades Workers Alliance in 1920. Disapproval was also expressed at the negative attitude
which the AFL took up toward welfare legislation, at its support for the
National Civic Federation, and at its "undignified and unfruitful political
lobbying and begging." The election of Meyer London to Congress in
1914, in fact, was used by ILGWU spokesmen as an example of what could
be achieved by collaboration between the AFL and the Socialist party if
only the AFL would cooperate.

However, the ILGWU did not allow its criticisms of the AFL to go too far.
Its delegates to AFL conventions resisted efforts to require them to vote
against Gompers and other conservative officers—although attempts to do
this were quite often made—and the *Ladies' Garment Worker* discouraged
purely negative criticism of the federation. In 1912, for instance—a year
in which there were many socialist attacks on the AFL—the union journal
publicly defended it against the radicals in the IWW and on the left of the
Socialist party. The AFL was, the journal argued, the only American labor

federation to have brought "stability, progress and lasting benefits to the workers of this country." And a similar editorial three years later, in December 1915, cautioned radical members of the union against losing patience with the AFL, reminding them that it was not a secret, underground movement, like the labor movement in Russia, whose policies could be dictated from above. "Socialists are certainly justified," the editor wrote, "in urging a quicker rate of progress. . . . But it is not wise policy to force on the [AFL] conventions ideas which the majority of delegates have not yet assimilated." [52]

These concerns, with industrial unionism, with socialist politics, and with attempts to reform the AFL, were not unique to the ILGWU. What distinguished the ILGWU's socialism and gave it a special character of its own was—paradoxically, perhaps, in view of the large number of intellectuals in its ranks—not so much a preoccupation with the basic elements of Marxist theory, such as could be found among the German socialists of the Brewery Workers Union. It was, rather, a humanitarian, idealistic, and deeply held desire for equality and social justice, which resulted as much from the historic minority position in which the Jews had found themselves in Europe as it did from a specific commitment to Marxist ideology. As a result of their long history of ill-treatment the Jews were more sensitive to oppression in all its forms than any other American ethnic group, and it was this sensitivity, coupled with the continuing influence of the sweatshop, that gave Jewish socialism its unique and characteristic appeal. "With the emotional urgency of a long-persecuted people," as one account has put it, "they envisaged a promised land where differences of race, religion, and nationality would no longer divide mankind, where worldly goods would be apportioned equitably and all energies would be devoted to the cultivation of the arts of peace." [53]

There were numerous general statements in the ILGWU which reflected this concern for the higher aims of the labor movement. At the 1916 convention, for example, Abraham Cahan praised the ILGWU for having "a soul as well as a body" and for concerning itself with more than just "wages and conditions," as the majority of AFL unions did; and at the same convention Robert W. Bruere, a writer and former member of the Cloakmakers' Board of Arbitration, asserted that in its efforts to abolish the sweatshop, end child labor, and elevate the position of women, the ILGWU was playing an important role in the general American movement for social reform. Jane Addams made the same point in a speech to the 1918 convention.[54]

This broad and humanitarian outlook can also be seen in the ILGWU's attitude toward a number of familiar national labor problems. Its policies were usually the same as those of other socialist trade-unions, but there was an element of compassion and social concern in its attitudes which was often lacking elsewhere. On the matter of European immigration, for example, the 1912 union convention opposed the Dillingham Immigration Restriction Bill not only on the Marxist grounds of labor solidarity but also on the ground that restriction "intensifies national and race hatred" and that the bill would, if enacted, "prevent the victims of political, religious and economic oppressions from finding a place of refuge in the United States."

To some extent this reflected a desire to keep the avenues of immigration open for relatives and compatriots of union members themselves, who were still being persecuted as a result of the Russian pogroms. But from the reputation which the union acquired for its liberality and fair-mindedness toward racial and minority groups of all kinds, it seems clear that this policy was also upheld as a matter of moral principle. For instance, the ILGWU welcomed Negroes into its ranks more readily than almost any other trade-union, although the argument of self-interest in this case clearly did not apply. At the 1922 union convention Negro girls, who had been entering the waist and dress trade in appreciable numbers since 1917, were singled out for praise for having "acquitted themselves creditably" in a recent strike, and $300 was donated to the *Messenger,* an early Negro radical paper.[55]

A similar breadth of vision affected the ILGWU's attitude toward the international labor movement. For Jewish socialists, lacking a strong sense of loyalty to any one country, yet being present in so many, the idea of the international solidarity of labor was particularly attractive; and the *Ladies' Garment Worker* displayed a strong interest in the growth of socialism in England, France, Germany, and czarist Russia. In 1913 the ILGWU affiliated with the Tailors International Secretariat, partly to permit the entry of unionized European garment workers into the American union without payment of initiation fee, and partly to "show practical solidarity with the workers abroad." But its attitude toward this organization was also bound up with the general hope of the Jewish community for "Jewish emancipation the world over," to which ILGWU leaders also frequently referred. For some this meant helping the oppressed Jews in Europe; for others it meant emigration to Palestine. But for many the idea of Jewish emancipation also became connected, in a general and romanticized way, with the emancipation to be found in the socialist vision of a cooperative commonwealth. At the 1920 ILGWU convention, for example, a resolution was adopted commending the British Labor party for its electoral successes, while at the same time thanking it for its support for the establishment of "a national homeland on the ancient Jewish soil of Palestine." [56]

The ILGWU's strong stand on female suffrage also reflected its concern with the need for equality and social justice. Women and girls constituted well over half the membership in many locals, particularly in the New York waist and dress industry, and Mollie Lifshitz and Fannia M. Cohn, a vice-president of the International, were prominent members of the Women's Trade Union League. Convention resolutions and journal editorials repeatedly urged members to vote for woman suffrage, and there was much rejoicing when New York State adopted it in a referendum vote in December 1917. Nor was this a question of abstract rights alone. As we have seen, the women in the union were often as militant and class-conscious as the men; and an argument frequently made for female suffrage was that the women would vote socialist as well as their husbands or their fathers. In February 1918, for example, Fannia M. Cohn described the giant, twenty-five-thousand-strong Local 25 as "an inspiration" to the rest of the union because of its "struggle for the freedom of the working class," and expressed the hope that because women in New York State had now been given the vote they would support socialist candidates for office in the fall.[57]

But perhaps the most distinctive contribution of the ILGWU was its various provisions for the health, education, and general welfare of its members, which went far beyond the sick, death, and other benefits provided by most other American trade-unions. In fact, as we have seen, many ILGWU locals had objected to these benefits in the earlier years, like the socialists in the Boot and Shoe Workers Union, on the ground that they were inconsistent with the militant functions of a trade-union. But by 1917 much of this prejudice had been overcome, and the high incidence of tuberculosis in the trade, together with other occupational diseases, showed that something dramatic must be done. Thus in 1919 the union established a Unity Health Center in New York, complete with X-ray equipment, a drug department, and a medical staff of its own, which was the first union medical clinic of its kind in the country. Earlier, Local 25 had rented Pine Hill, the first of a series of vacation lodges where members could escape into the country from the evils of the city slums.

It was on the educational program of the union, however, that the greatest emphasis was laid. Many AFL leaders looked upon the labor movement as an educational medium in one way or another, and a number of individual unions ran courses to educate their members in the virtues of trade-unionism. To a considerable extent this was the purpose of the ILGWU also. The 1914 convention established the General Education Committee, which was to instruct the recently arrived garment workers in the elements of trade-unionism, and also to train leaders for administrative positions. Nevertheless, the ILGWU took a much broader and more radical view of the purposes of trade-union education than did most other labor organizations. As early as 1902, for example, Benjamin Schlesinger had suggested that the union arrange a series of lectures in order to demonstrate that "labor's intellectual power" was the "only effectual weapon in the struggle for emancipation"; and although a deliberate effort was made, when the educational program was first established, to keep separate the function of trade-union education from that of socialist propaganda, in practice the two were intertwined. The fact that many of the courses were arranged in conjunction with the Rand School of Social Science, a socialist institution, and that Local 25, which was one of the most radical locals in the union, was a pioneer in this field, indicates that the educational program was based on the assumption, as one account put it, that "intelligent . . . union men and women" strive "consciously or unconsciously for the reconstruction of society" on the basis of justice, production for use, and general solidarity.

In all its welfare programs, which became celebrated throughout the labor movement as a whole, the ILGWU was in part providing practical help for a downtrodden and ill-treated community. But it was also, as a journal editorial wrote in November 1916, implementing "a burning desire to place the labor movement on the right principles"—the principles of socialism and of the cooperative commonwealth.[58]

IV

By April 1917, therefore, when America declared war on Germany, there seemed little to suggest that the ILGWU had diminished its enthusiasm for socialism or the Socialist party. Like other trade-unions, the ILGWU benefited from the general prosperity of the war and from the liberal trade-union policies followed by the federal government. Factories that normally produced women's garments received government orders for army uniforms, enabling the ILGWU to secure recognition in a number of cities, such as Cleveland, where it had hitherto been unsuccessful, and there were widespread increases in wages. As a result, the forty-four-hour week was secured in a number of places, and with favorable agreements signed with employers in many cities and a membership of nearly 100,000 in 1919, the ILGWU reached a new peak in influence and prestige.

But neither war prosperity nor public hostility toward the socialists appeared to have any immediate effect. The *Ladies' Garment Worker* denounced the war, in Marxist terms, as "a fratricidal conflict brought about by the greed and jealousy of kings and rulers," and the ILGWU was, significantly, one of only four major unions which failed to send representatives to the national trade-union conference called by Gompers to declare labor's support for the war in March 1917. In fact, it openly criticized the AFL for pledging labor to a general no-strike policy for the duration of the conflict, despite the unpopularity of such a step, and it opposed the efforts of the American Alliance for Labor and Democracy to whip up war fever as a means of counteracting the antiwar sentiments of the socialists. Although disconcerted by the breakdown of international working-class solidarity which the war occasioned, the ILGWU did not appear to take this so seriously as the Brewery Workers Union did. The nationalistic fervor which the working classes of Europe had displayed in supporting the war, an editorial in the *Ladies' Garment Worker* ran, was "all the more reason why we in free America should keep the light [of international solidarity] burning." [59]

Predictably, therefore, the ILGWU tried to resist the hyperpatriotic mood which swept over the country and vigorously defended its right to dissent from the prowar stand of the AFL and of public opinion generally. The union criticized the June 1917 Espionage Act, protested the removal of second-class mailing privileges from New York socialist newspapers such as the *Call,* and complained that the AFL did not go far enough in its defense of the civil liberties of radical trade-union members. At a General Executive Board meeting in August 1917 General Secretary-Treasurer Abraham Baroff openly criticized Gompers for attacking the socialists in an *American Federationist* editorial, describing the AFL's tendency to stigmatize "everything and everybody who dares to disagree with them as unpatriotic" as "wrong, unfair, and injurious to the labor movement." Union members raised considerable sums of money for the Liberty Defense Union of New York and other organizations providing legal aid for socialists and IWW members imprisoned during the war, and later, at the 1920 convention, adopted a resolution strongly urging an amnesty for all those who still remained in prison. [60]

All of this appeared to indicate full support for the Socialist party's April 1917 St. Louis declaration against American participation in the war and an equally full determination to uphold it: a move which reached its peak in the fall of 1917 when Morris Hillquit, in the most ambitious undertaking of his career, campaigned for mayor of New York on the Socialist party ticket. Running on a specifically antiwar platform and with the ILGWU's full support, he received 145,332 votes to 313,956 for the successful Democrat (and 155,497 for incumbent Mayor Mitchel), which was more than any previous radical candidate had received since Henry George in 1886, despite a public declaration that he would not buy any Liberty Bonds. Hillquit also made quite a lot of capital out of his support for woman suffrage in the campaign, which was on the ballot as a constitutional amendment, and before the election took place both of the major parties in New York expressed concern at the probable size of the socialist vote. On October 13, writing to his friend Eugen Schoen, Hillquit thought he might even win, calling the election "the greatest test of American Socialism and radicalism" in the history of the labor movement. His vote was swelled by shortages, by wartime inflation, and also by some anti-Allied Irish voters who temporarily deserted Tammany Hall. Despite Hillquit's defeat the socialists elected no less than ten assemblymen to Albany—including First Vice-President Rosenberg of the ILGWU—seven city aldermen, and the union's "faithful and devoted brother" Jacob Panken as a municipal court judge.[61]

At the very time when ILGWU members in New York were going to the polls in support of Hillquit's candidacy, however, news was received of the great October revolution in Russia, which was to have a profound effect both on the union's attitude toward the war and on its general ideological position. The overthrow of the hated czarist regime created tremendous excitement and enthusiasm among the Jewish masses on the lower East Side, and its first effect was to reinforce the radical traditions of the union, not to undermine them. The great object for which many ILGWU members had themselves struggled in their earlier years had been obtained, and a new era seemed to be dawning in eastern Europe. Mass meetings were held to celebrate the event, and the *Ladies' Garment Worker* ran short biographies of prominent union members who had earlier served in the Bund.

Nor did the ILGWU praise the March 1917 revolution in Russia, only to condemn the seizure of power by the Bolsheviks in October, as most AFL trade-unions did. Despite widespread misgivings about Lenin's tactics which were expressed in the New York Jewish press, the 1918 convention of the ILGWU hailed the October 1917 revolution as "the first time in the history of the world [that] the workers showed a determination not to allow themselves to be defrauded of the fruits of their victory by their master classes." And it urged union members to support their Russian brothers "not only because many are linked to them by ties of kinship and sentiment, but also because the fate of the first great working class republic in the world can not be but a matter of prime concern to the organized and progressive workers of the world." [62]

However, the Russian Revolution of October 1917 also made the ILGWU reconsider its opposition to American participation in the war. In the chaos which ensued immediately after the revolution the armies of the Central Powers advanced deep into Russian territory, and it soon became apparent that the new regime might be endangered by military defeat. Hence in early 1918 many in the New York Jewish community in general, and the ILGWU in particular, switched from a position of opposition to American participation in the war to one of support, partly because the continued German advance threatened the safety of many families who had relatives in Europe, but also because it endangered the future prospects of the struggling young Soviet regime. The ILGWU was also influenced in its change of policy by the increasing minority in the Socialist party generally who were coming out for the war and also by the hope, erroneous as it later turned out, that President Wilson would protect the Bolshevik regime from outside attack. Thus when, at the June 1918 convention of the ILGWU, the General Executive Board of the union proposed that it be authorized to purchase $100,000 worth of Liberty Bonds—in direct contradiction to the union's policy the previous year—there was very little dissent. The Board was careful to justify its proposal in terms of the need to destroy the "Junker power" of the Kaiser, in the hope that this would lead to the overthrow of capitalism in Germany in much the same way that the "Junker power" of the Czar had been overthrown by the revolution in Russia. But the fact that the Liberty Loan was authorized at all shows how far union opinion on the war had changed.[63]

Thus the socialism of the ILGWU survived World War I largely intact— indeed, in some ways strengthened—in part because of the strong traditions of radicalism which had been developed in the sweatshop and the ghetto (reinforced by succeeding groups of immigrants which had continued to arrive until 1914), and in part because of the renewed impetus which was provided by the Russian Revolution. This enabled it, when it did come around to supporting the war, to do so on grounds which did not compromise its socialist principles. By the middle of 1918 there was, in addition, an increasing amount of sympathy with President Wilson's war aims, and the ILGWU gave its full support to the President's proposals for the League of Nations.

But any possibility that this might lead the union into a more general rapprochement with the Democrats—except on the issue of the war— was reversed in the general collapse of Wilsonian liberalism at the end of the war. The ILGWU was particularly angered by the President's acquiescence in the red-baiting of Attorney-General Palmer—in October 1920 the *Ladies' Garment Worker* described Wilson as the "apostle for democracy for the rest of the world [who] has destroyed every shred of democracy here in America"—but it was even more bitterly disillusioned by his sending of American troops to oppose the Bolshevik regime in Russia. At the 1920 AFL convention the ILGWU delegation introduced a resolution describing American intervention in Russia as a "most heinous crime against a free sovereign people with whom the American people have always been at peace" and urged strongly the lifting of the Allied blockade, withdrawal of troops, and recognition of the Soviet government. And at the union's own 1920 Chicago convention a leading delegate from New York, appealing for votes on behalf of the Socialist party, expressed the anger and sense of betrayal which many other delegates felt at American intervention, as well as at the general reactionary tendencies of American society at the end of the war:

> We are protesting to-day against the . . . nefarious conduct of officials of Democratic and Republican leaning who are sending shot and shell and bullets to Poland for the purpose of crushing Russia! We are endeavoring to expose the sham hypocrisy of those persons who say we are to have the last war and eternal peace, and yet today are augmenting their navies and building airships with which they hope to bomb those countries and peoples they would hold in subjection!

A standing ovation followed this speech, and the 1920 convention went on to reject a direct appeal from Gompers to support the AFL National Nonpartisan Campaign Committee in the 1920 elections—describing labor's efforts to secure concessions from the Republicans and Democrats as "a monumental failure"—and instead gave its unanimous endorsement to the imprisoned Debs, "the old standard bearer of industrial and political working class emancipation," as well as to the socialist candidates running in New York, regardless of the fact that the Socialist party was now a shadow of its former self.[64]

Despite the renewed zeal for social change generated by the Russian Revolution, however, the ILGWU soon found itself divided, like other radical trade-unions, over the actual tactics and policies of the Communists. This division grew, of course, out of the much larger 1919 socialist-Communist split, in which the ILGWU found itself inevitably involved. A number of its more recently arrived members had joined either the Russian or one of the other eastern European language federations in the Socialist party, and for these members, as well as for many of the older radical stalwarts on the union's left, the Communist party became the legitimate representative of the Russian Revolution, whatever tactics it undertook. For the more moderate members of the union, however, the Communists' surreptitious efforts at "boring from within" the labor movement, and the accusations which they made against the ILGWU leadership of corruption, antidemocratic methods, and class collaboration, particularly in an organization so well known for its progressive and democratic policies, were utterly repugnant. The result was a conflict between Communists and socialists in the ILGWU which, because of the large size of the Communist faction, was more serious than it was in almost any other American trade-union.

There were two aspects to this conflict, which is described here only in summary form, since it lasted into the 1930's and the latter part of it goes beyond the province of this book.[65] One was the increasing concern which members of the ILGWU, like other radicals, felt at the suppression by the

Soviet government of elements hostile to the regime within Russia itself. This was first referred to, half apologetically, in June 1920 by the editor of *Justice* (now the official journal of the union), who expressed concern at the way in which Lenin condemned Kautsky, Bernstein, and other socialist theorists as "traitors, because they do not agree with him." More serious was the imprisonment and exile of socialists and liberals who opposed the Bolshevik regime itself. At the 1924 ILGWU convention an appeal was made for funds on behalf of the Red Cross for Political Prisoners in Russia, by Rose Pesotta, later a garmentworkers' leader in her own right. While the civil war in Russia was still continuing, Miss Pesotta said, most American supporters of the revolution had accepted the need for harsh and disciplinary measures. But now the fact had to be faced that socialists, anarchists, and moderates of all kinds were being imprisoned simply because they disagreed with Bolshevism. A resolution was passed by 222 votes to 25, calling upon the Soviet government to release all its political prisoners immediately. Nevertheless, in the debate which followed, a number of delegates strongly opposed the resolution, delegate Wishnevsky of New York, for example, arguing that it was based on misinformation about the Soviet Union drawn from the anti-Bolshevik American press.[66]

This disagreement was significant, for Wishnevsky was a Communist from New York Dressmakers' Local 22, which had for some time been involved in the second, and more important, aspect of the conflict: the attempt by the Communist party to secure control of the ILGWU on behalf of William Z. Foster and the Trade Union Education League. The origins of this attempt can be found in the shop delegate movement in New York Waist and Dressmakers' Local 25, akin to the shop stewards' movement in England in World War I, the original purpose of which was to make the decisions of elected shop committees the basis for union control, as well as to express rank-and-file grievances against the leadership, much as in the 1913–1914 Hourwich affair. After the establishment of the TUEL in 1920, the Communists exploited the shop delegate movement as a means of securing power in the ILGWU as a whole, using Local 25 as their base of operations. To prevent this the General Executive Board divided Local 25 into two, putting the dressmakers into the newly chartered Local 22, which then became the largest union in the International. The unpopularity of this decision simply served to accelerate the Communist insurgency, however: in April 1921, Local 25 demanded, unsuccessfully, that the ILGWU affiliate with the Third (Communist) Trade Union International.[67]

Thereafter, Communist influence grew rapidly in Locals 25 and 22 and also in Locals 2 and 9 in New York, as well as in locals in Philadelphia, Chicago, and elsewhere. Under the leadership of President Sigman, who replaced the ailing Schlesinger in February 1923, and also of David Dubinsky, who was now a leading figure in the union, the administration fought to retain control of the union, arguing that TUEL members were dual unionists who exploited internal union differences for political ends and were, in any event, acting under the directives of a foreign power. In 1923 the General Executive Board suspended nineteen members of Local 22's executive board and ordered all members of shop leagues to cease their activities or face trial. At the 1924 convention a number of left-wing delegations were refused a seat because of membership in the TUEL, and the International constitution was amended, banning from membership anyone "holding membership or office in a dual union or in any other organization not constituted or functioning within this Constitution." Then, in 1925, the leftists returned to the attack, running Louis Hyman, of Cloak Finishers and Tailors Local 9, against Morris Sigman for the presidency. Hyman got 108 votes to Sigman's 158, a relatively close contest.

The climax in the anti-Communist struggle in the ILGWU came in 1926, when Communist leaders in the New York Cloakmakers Joint Board forced the International into a disastrous general strike against the coat and suit manufacturers, which lasted for six months and brought very few practical gains. Over $3,000,000 was spent, and when the strike finally ended, in January 1927, the terms were probably less advantageous than could have been obtained simply by negotiation. After this the leading left-wing locals were either suspended or removed, and the Communists were to a considerable extent discredited. But although the administration had won, the ILGWU was in a parlous state. Membership had fallen to under 70,000, the organization was saddled with tremendous debts, and control over many garment markets had been lost. It was not until the 1930's that the union fully recovered.[68]

The remarkable thing was, however, that despite its postwar preoccupation with combating the Communists—as well as with the open-shop campaign of the employers, which was pursued just as vigorously in the garment industry as it was elsewhere—the ILGWU did not lose its interest in the Socialist party or in socialism. In many trade-unions the Communist-socialist split of 1919, coming on top of the Red Scare, virtually destroyed whatever interest remained in the Socialist party after World War I. Not so in the ILGWU. The union vigorously supported the postwar revival of the radical movement, upholding, for example, government ownership of the railroads, as well as the idea of union-owned shops and factories in the garment industry as a "first step towards collective ownership."

And, as we have seen, in 1920 it endorsed Debs for the Presidency. This 1920 endorsement appeared to indicate continued support for the Socialist party as a national political organization, especially since the New York locals also worked for other socialist candidates in that campaign with what one observer described as quite the "old time vigor." But despite Debs' excellent showing in the November elections—he received nearly a million votes, although this was a smaller percentage of the popular vote than he got in 1912—most members of the ILGWU were fully aware that the Socialist party's chances of recovery from the effects of the war and the Communist split were small; and as the various new political groupings vied for leadership of the radical movement in the years after the war, a major debate arose in the union over just what its future political policy should be.[69]

There were a considerable number of socialists in the ILGWU who argued that for the union to give its support to the Farmer-Labor party or to the Progressives, or to seek to influence the Socialist party as a whole into allying itself with these groups, would be to compromise the working class and revolutionary traditions of the union and to go back on all it had earlier achieved. Equally, there were those who saw plainly that the Socialist party had been virtually destroyed as an effective political organization and that to ignore the development of other radical and labor-party movements would not only be unrealistic as far as the union itself was concerned: it would also condemn the Socialist party itself to becoming a small, ineffective clique outside the mainstream of American politics, much as the SLP had been twenty years before.

The position of this group, which was influenced by the increasing success of the British Labor party, was perhaps best stated in an editorial in *Justice* of July 16, 1920, welcoming the establishment of the National Farmer-Labor party in Chicago. It was true, the journal said, that the Farmer-Labor party was not a socialist organization and that it was composed of people with largely middle-class aspirations. But most of the planks it had adopted were similar to the immediate aims of the Socialist party, and it would be much more profitable for the socialists to agree on a common candidate in the 1920 presidential elections, rather than to persist in the "splendid isolation" which had characterized the party's position since America's entrance into World War I.[70]

This compromise position was as yet too advanced for many ILGWU members—as we have seen, they supported Debs in the election of that fall—but as time went on it came increasingly to be accepted, partly because Morris Hillquit (still the most respected socialist leader among the garmentworkers) pressed vigorously for it, and partly because the Socialist party continued in such obvious decline. The attitude of the union was also a matter of considerable interest to both the Farmer-Labor party and the Socialist party themselves, since to secure the endorsement of the ILGWU, despite its somewhat diminished membership, was still a glittering prize. Thus, William H. Feigenbaum, national publicity director of the Socialist party, wrote to *Justice* reproving the editor for his reference to the party's "isolation" and urging continued loyalty to the party cause, only to be up-braided in turn by Abraham Lefkowitz, a national official of the Farmer-Labor party, and also by its 1920 vice-presidential nominee, the veteran socialist Max S. Hayes. Radicals who opposed the Farmer-Labor party, the two men argued, "are attacking the most hopeful sign of political regenera-tion in America." "With the Socialist as a left-wing of the Farmer-Labor Party," they asserted, "it would be possible in 1924 or 1928, to do for America what the British Labor Party has done and is doing for England." [71]

In the event, the moderates won out in the ILGWU. The union adminis-tration welcomed the decision of the June 1921 convention of the Socialist party to seek the cooperation of other radical groups, calling it "a move in the direction of life and growth," and despite the misgivings of the more ardent socialists the union played a major role in the development of the Conference for Progressive Political Action—always, however, in the hope that a new radical political party would emerge. In July 1922 the So-cialist party and the Farmer-Labor party in New York united in a com-mon ticket for the state and local elections in the fall, with ILGWU Vice-Presi-dent Salvatore Ninfo among those nominated for office, and in December the ILGWU sent a high-level delegation to the CPPA convention held in Cleve-land, hoping to convert it to the idea of a third party then and there. A reso-lution to that effect was defeated by a vote of 64 to 52, once more bringing the doubts of loyal Socialist party members to the fore. To reassure such members, Secretary-Treasurer Baroff, who had headed the ILGWU delegation to the December 1922 conference, pointed out that the railroad brother-hoods and other unions which had opposed the resolution were more flexible and tolerant than they had been earlier and claimed that all the supporters of the Conference for Progressive Political Action would eventually come round to the third-party idea. In addition Morris Hillquit, who played a national role as liaison between the Socialist party and the CPPA, also attempted to reassure union members by suggesting that the Socialist party would take on a new lease of life by joining with the third-party activists in the movement. He wrote to an ILGWU member in New Hampshire:

> It is my hope and belief that it [the CPPA] will result in the formation of a labor party, at least in a rudimentary form. This does not mean that the So-cialist Party will cease to exist. On the contrary, I am of the opinion that with the beginning of a political labor movement . . . , the Socialist Party will have a more important function than ever in helping and guiding the new movement.[72]

For a time this hope continued to prevail, and when the CPPA conven-tion of July 1924 finally nominated Senator Robert La Follette and Sena-tor Burton K. Wheeler of Montana on an independent ticket, the ILGWU gave its enthusiastic support. The prospect of a major political figure such as La Follette lending his name to the independent political movement was an event of considerable significance, even if La Follette himself was far from being a socialist, and it seemed to many as though at last the search for a new, third party would be satisfied. William H. Johnston, of the International Association of Machinists, chairman of the CPPA, was given an ovation at the 1924 ILGWU convention, and much satisfaction was expressed that the Democrats chose the conservative John W. Davis instead of William McAdoo (who was more popular with labor) to ensure the largest possible vote for La Follette. Cloakmakers' committees were established to support Israel Feinberg in London's old district, running on a joint Labor-Socialist-Progressive ticket, as they were in other areas as well, and great hopes were placed on the fact that both the AFL and the Socialist party had joined in supporting the CPPA. One writer in *Justice* even suggested that a large vote for La Follette would in itself bring rejuvenation to the Socialist party because of the larger number of native-born workers who would be brought into contact with the party, if only indirectly, as a result of the campaign.[73]

It is difficult to assess what the exact consequences were for the ILGWU of the disappointing performance of the La Follette-Wheeler ticket in November 1924. The union had clearly been overoptimistic about the possible results of the campaign, and although it continued to express the hope that a new third party would result from the rump caucus of the CPPA which was held in February 1925—President Sigman and Secretary-Treasurer Baroff dispatched a telegram of support, although no delegate was sent—there was, inevitably, widespread disappointment. For some members of the union, the result simply confirmed their belief that the socialists should never have committed themselves to the venture, and they returned once more to the forlorn task of trying to rebuild the Socialist party. Others, on the extreme left, moved over into the Communist party.

For many, however, who had already been attracted by the popularity of the liberal Democratic governor of New York, Alfred E. Smith, there were signs for the first time of a definite drift toward the Democrats. After 1932 this drift turned into a stampede when President Roosevelt became a popular hero in the garment trades, as he did with workers in other low-income industries. The precise reasons for this change lie beyond the province of this book, although it should be noted that for a time many garment workers, along with President Dubinsky (who gave up his Socialist party card in 1936), managed, by supporting the American Labor party in New York, to combine independent political action at the local level with national support for the New Deal.[74]

Nevertheless, although by this time the Socialist party was very small, the radical spirit in the ILGWU lived on, as Norman Thomas testified in a letter which he sent to the ILGWU convention of December 1929. "May I tell you," he wrote, "how I look to you—all of you members—to take up again the pioneer work for the organization of the workers on the political field. We do not want a Socialist or labor party to run the unions" —a reference to the recently concluded struggle with the Communists. "But a political party, Socialist in principle and program, will be very weak without strong industrial organization of the workers. . . . Let us press on with courage." [75]

V

At the end of our period, in 1924, the ILGWU still had strong loyalty to the socialists, even if it appeared to have little means of expressing it. There were, of course, some signs of decline, indicated partly by a diminution in the number of votes received by socialist candidates in the garment-workers' districts, although because of the split with the Communists (who received many former socialist votes) this diminution is not a wholly reliable index. In 1922, for example, Meyer London was defeated for the last time in his bid for reelection to Congress, and after this date there were no further socialists elected to the New York State assembly.[76] More important was the increasing evidence of rapid upward mobility, especially in the second generation, among Jews who had formerly worked in the sweatshops.

Unlike the Italians (who became an increasingly important factor in the trade), the Jewish immigrant rarely instructed his children in the needle trades, urging educational advancement and the acquisition of property on them instead; and the contracting system enabled him to become self-employed in a manner not open to either the brewery workers or the shoemakers. "The desire to rise out of their class is very prevalent among the members of our craft," one observer wrote in 1915, "and they too often ignore their trade problems, believing, as many of them do, that very shortly they may have nothing to do with their present co-workers." At least one member of the ILGWU's General Executive Board resigned during our period to enter the trade as a manufacturer himself, and the small scale of operations in the garment shops reinforced the desire for independent employment by the close personal relations which it cultivated between employer and employee.[77]

Nevertheless, the persistence of socialist influences among the garment workers, despite the pressures and disillusionments brought about by World War I, the socialist-Communist split, and the failure of the CPPA, bears remarkable testimony to the strength of their radical traditions. It was also unique among the trade-unions examined in this book. What is to explain this remarkable tenacity? Fundamentally, it was the continuing and simultaneous strength of two separate factors which were noted at the beginning of this chapter, but were rarely found together in the same degree of intensity: both a strong ethnic or communal interest in socialist ideas, upheld by a dominant group of European immigrant socialists, and severe exploitation and low wages in the garmentworkers' trade. Usually only one of these sets of factors was present, or was dominant in the situation. In the Brewery Workers Union, for example, despite considerable initial exploitation of workers who lived in the breweries, the primary source of socialism was ethnic. In the BSWU, where the destruction of a traditional craft was an important cause, ethnic factors had very little role to play.

In the ILGWU, however, ethnic and industrial factors were of almost equal importance, and they both persisted far longer than they did elsewhere. The influx of Jewish radicals into the garment industry continued right up to 1914, and it was even resumed, in limited numbers, for a period after World War I. The influx of German socialists into the brewing industry, by contrast, diminished rapidly after the turn of the century, with consequences that have already been observed.

As to the internal conditions of the industry, although wages steadily increased and hours of work declined from the period of the Protocol of Peace onward, massive immigration ensured that only a small fraction of the first generation of workers in the industry were actually in a position to rise above the sweatshop; and because of the continuing influx of cheap, unskilled labor most of the basic problems of the industry—sweating, seasonal unemployment, and the contracting system—were not solved until the 1930's. This meant that for the average worker the industry remained depressed for a considerable period of time, providing a continuing incentive for radical social change. In addition, although the actual number of sweatshops in New York, where the ILGWU was strongest, did considerably decline, improvement was limited by the ability of the employer to move his factory elsewhere. In a mobile trade such as the garment industry, as one observer has put it, high standards can be maintained only by complete unionization or by effective national legislation or both. In the ladies' garment industry this did not occur until the period of the New Deal.[78]

Ideologically, the socialism of the ILGWU was characterized partly by an adherence to the tenets of Marxist doctrine, and partly by a traditional Jewish yearning for emancipation and for social justice. This was at once the main source of its strength and of its ultimate decline. For a people suddenly released from the oppression and hostility which they had traditionally found in eastern Europe, and yet confronted anew by discrimination and exploitation in the industry where they found themselves employed, it was not surprising that a significant number of Jews should have persisted in the socialist ideal of the cooperative commonwealth as a substitute for, or a complement to, the age-old yearning for a Promised Land. But it turned out that most characteristic practical manifestations of this ideal—workers' education, female suffrage, and widespread demands for better health and conditions—were found in the end to be consistent with the native American tradition of reform. As the ILGWU matured and became more successful in the economic field, the revolutionary purposes for which many of these programs were designed were abandoned, and social reform became a sufficient end in itself. For many Jewish socialists, in other words, neither Palestine nor the cooperative commonwealth, but America itself became an acceptable substitute for the Promised Land.

The economic successes of the ILGWU in raising standards, which date initially from the Protocol of Peace, point again to the underlying conflict between the collaborationist assumptions of collective bargaining and the revolutionary purposes of the socialists. Although a new—and in a sense more radical—leadership came to the fore under Benjamin Schlesinger in 1914, the policy of the new administration in preserving contractual relations with the manufacturers, even if not in the same form as the Protocol of Peace, gave the organization a new and powerful rationale for cooperation with the employers which became too valuable for it to discard. Although the cultural tradition of socialism among the garment workers was too deep for this to have any immediate effect, over the long run the material benefits which it brought played an important role in weakening the impetus for revolutionary change.

Nevertheless, the strength of the radical tradition in the Jewish labor movement was remarkable and greater than any to be encountered elsewhere. In the ILGWU, in particular, it outlasted by many years the disintegration of the socialist movement proper, and there can be little doubt that had the Socialist party not been so weak politically after World War I, or had a labor party emerged with any prospect of success, the ILGWU would have been one union which would have given it full support.

Notes

1. For general studies of the needleworkers' unions, and of the ILGWU in particular, see J. M. Budish and George Soule, *The New Unionism in the Clothing Industry* (New York, 1920); Joel Seidman, *The Needle Trades* (New

York, 1942); Louis Levine, *The Women's Garment Workers, A History of the International Ladies' Garment Workers' Union* (New York, 1924); and Benjamin Stolberg, *Tailor's Progress, The Story of a Famous Union and the Men Who Made It* (New York, 1944). For the role of the Jews, see William Leiserson, *History of the Jewish Labor Movement in New York City* (New York, 1908); Melech Epstein, *Jewish Labor in U.S.A.*, 2 vols. (New York, 1950–1953); and Aaron Antonovsky, *The Early Jewish Labor Movement in the United States* (New York, 1961). See also Moses Rischin, *The Promised City: New York's Jews, 1870–1914* (Cambridge, 1962); and Melvyn Dubofsky, "Organized Labor and the Immigrant in New York City, 1900–1918," *Labor History*, II (Spring, 1961), 182–201.

2. Seidman, *op. cit.*, 87; Epstein, *op. cit.*, I, 11–17, 305–306; Antonovsky, *op. cit.*, 18–50.

3. Melech Epstein, *Profiles of Eleven* (Detroit, 1965), 236–237; *Ladies' Garment Worker*, VI (October 1915), 19–22; VI (November 1915), 21–24.

4. Epstein, *Profiles of Eleven*, 51–109, 161–231. See also Morris Hillquit, *Loose Leaves from a Busy Life* (New York, 1934); and Harry Rogoff, *An East Side Epic, The Life and Work of Meyer London* (New York, 1930).

5. In the 1890's especially, a number of Jewish socialists in New York, particularly among the anarchists, attacked Judaism, as Marxists in general attacked Christianity, as a major obstacle in the path of converting the Jewish masses to socialism. This did not deter many American Jews from becoming socialists, as it did in the case of the Catholics, partly because Jewish religious bodies did not mount any consistent counterattack, and partly because socialist attacks on the Jewish religion were relatively short-lived. See Antonovsky, *op. cit.*, 246–271.

6. Stolberg, *op. cit.*, 51–53, 98–105, 117–123; *Ladies' Garment Worker*, I (December 1910), 1–2; V (July 1914), 2–3.

7. Stolberg, *op. cit.*, 4–5; Seidman, *op. cit.*, 55–56, 60–61; Jacob Riis, *How the Other Half Lives, Studies among the Tenements of New York* (New York, 1890), 123–124.

8. Seidman, *op. cit.*, 58–60; Stolberg, *op. cit.*, 10–12.

9. *The Men's Factory-Made Clothing Industry: Report on the Cost of Production of Men's Factory-Made Clothing in the United States* (Washington, 1916), 13–14, cited in Seidman, *op. cit.*, 56–57. *Report of the Factory Inspector of Illinois, 1894* (Springfield, 1894), 29, cited in Levine, *op. cit.*, 20.

10. Stolberg, *op. cit.*, 15–20.

11. *Proceedings, Second Convention of the International Ladies' Garment Workers' Union* (Philadelphia, 1901), 13; *Proceedings, Third Convention of the International Ladies' Garment Workers' Union* (New York, 1902), 18, 24, 28; *Proceedings, Fourth Convention of the International Ladies' Garment Workers' Union* (Cleveland, 1903), 32.

12. Seidman, *op. cit.*, 95–96.

13. *Ibid.*, 84; Levine, *op. cit.*, 42–43.

14. *Ladies' Garment Worker*, I (April 1910), 5; John Dyche to Gompers, January 11, 1906, January 16, 1908 (Gompers' Correspondence with Affiliates, AFL–CIO Collection).

15. Antonovsky, *op. cit.*, 219–245; Levine, *op. cit.*, 68–76, 84–91; Epstein, *Jewish Labor in U.S.A.*, I, 192–237.

16. Levine, *op. cit.*, 114–119; Antonovsky, *op. cit.*, 335; *Proceedings, Fourth Convention of the International Ladies' Garment Workers' Union* (Cleveland, 1903), 32.

17. Levine, *op. cit.*, 56, 87, 123, 434–436; *Ladies' Garment Worker*, I (December 1910), 5; A.F. of L. Organizer to Gompers, August 22, 1903, Hermann Grossman to Gompers, November 2, 1905, Dyche to Gompers, December 12, 1905 (Gompers' Correspondence with Affiliates, AFL–CIO Collection); Gompers to Dyche, January 6, 1906 (Gompers' Letterbooks, AFL–CIO Collection); Wilfrid Carsel, *A History of the Chicago Ladies' Garment Workers' Union* (Chicago, 1940), 43–44.

18. Levine, *op. cit.*, 124; Epstein, *Jewish Labor in U.S.A.*, I, 377–378; Paul F. Brissenden, *The IWW, A Study of American Syndicalism* (New York, 1957), 68.

19. Levine, *op. cit.*, 124–126, 142–143; Martin A. Cohen, "Jewish Immigrants and American Trade Unions" (M.A. Thesis, University of Chicago, 1941), 109–111.

20. Seidman, *op. cit.*, 98, 234–235; *Constitution*, International Ladies' Garment Workers' Union (1901), 8–9.

21. Stolberg, *op. cit.*, 51–53, 57–58; Levine, *op. cit.*, 120–121; *Ladies' Garment Worker*, I (December 1910), 1–2; Dyche to Gompers, January 16, 1908 (Gompers' Correspondence with Affiliates, AFL–CIO Collection). In 1926 Dyche wrote a semiautobiographical book attacking both the Communists and the socialists in the ILGWU. See John Dyche, *Bolshevism in American Labor Unions, A Plea for Constructive Unionism* (New York, 1926).

22. This, at ten cents per month, was one of the lowest in the AFL. But it must be remembered that the ladies' garment industry was, save for the cutters and other skilled groups, a low-wage industry at this time, so that the ILGWU's dues were likely to be lower than in many of the skilled craft unions in any event.

23. Seidman, *op. cit.*, 98; Levine, *op. cit.*, 121–122; *Proceedings, Sixth Annual Convention of the International Ladies' Garment Workers' Union* (New York 1905), 8–9, 11, 40–42; *Proceedings, Tenth Annual Convention of the International Ladies' Garment Workers' Union* (New York, 1910), 23–24.

24. *The Worker*, XVI (September 22, 1906), 1; New York *Call*, I (July 23, 1908), 1; Epstein, *Jewish Labor in U.S.A.*, I, 244–247; Levine, *op. cit.*, 143; Hillquit, *op. cit.*, 107–116; Charles L. Fox to Morris Hillquit, October 10, 1906 (Morris Hillquit Papers, Wisconsin State Historical Society). In the 1908 election the SLP put up a candidate against Hillquit, which may also have partly accounted for his losing the election. Ben Hanford, the Socialist party's vice-presidential candidate that year, strongly attacked DeLeon for allowing this to occur, going so far as to call him an "agent provocateur for the capitalist class." "With his miserable remnant of the once great party that he destroyed," he wrote to Hillquit just before the election, "he makes no effort towards Socialist propaganda or organization, but devotes his entire strength to defeat [*sic*] the election of Morris Hillquit to Congress." See Ben Hanford to Hillquit, October 15, October 26, 1908 (Morris Hillquit Papers, Wisconsin State Historical Society).

25. Levine, *op. cit.*, 144–195; Epstein, *Jewish Labor in U.S.A.*, I, 387–406.

26. See below, pp. 198–199.

27. This aid was not confined to New York. The socialists often raised money for garmentworkers' strikes elsewhere, as, for instance, in a major strike organized by the United Garment Workers in Chicago in the same year. See *International Socialist Review*, XI (January 1911), 385–394; "List of Socialist party contributors to union strike funds" (Socialist Party of America Collection, Duke University), labor file.

28. Levine, *op. cit.*, 155, 160–164, 192; Henry Cohen to editor of *Forward*, August 4, 1910, William Filene to Louis Brandeis, August 31, 1910 (Louis D. Brandeis Collection, University of Louisville).

29. Levine, *op. cit.*, 195, 205–206, 235.

30. *Ibid.*, 196–198, 237–241; Meyer London to Dr. Henry Moskowitz, January 26, 1911 (Louis D. Brandeis Collection, University of Louisville).

31. Seidman, *op. cit.*, 107; Levine, *op. cit.*, 249–250, 253–254, *passim*. Hourwich had been preceded for a brief period as chief clerk by Abraham Bisno, of Chicago, who had much the same temperament and outlook. See Joel Seidman (ed.), *Abraham Bisno, Union Pioneer; An Autobiographical Account of Bisno's Early Life and the Beginnings of Unionism in the Garment Industry* (Madison, 1967).

32. Julius H. Cohen to Louis Brandeis, January 26, 1911 (Louis D. Brandeis Collection, University of Louisville).

33. In order to suppress this criticism, as well as on grounds of economy, the Rosenberg administration sought to amalgamate all the publications of the union into a single journal under International control. This was opposed by rank-and-file elements on ethnic, free-speech, and local autonomy grounds, and it was not until 1919, with the publication of *Justice* as the sole official union journal, that amalgamation was finally achieved. See Levine, *op. cit.*, 258–259, 263, 265; *Ladies' Garment Worker*, VI (January 1915), 4–5; VI (June 1915), 26; VII (December 1916), 3–4; *Proceedings, Fourteenth Convention of the International Ladies' Garment Workers' Union* (Boston, 1918), 40, 210–216.

34. Hyman Berman, "Era of Protocol, A Chapter in the History of the International Ladies' Garment Workers' Union, 1910–1916" (Ph.D. Thesis, Columbia University, 1956), 2–3.

35. *Proceedings, Eleventh Convention of the International Ladies' Garment Workers' Union* (Toronto, 1912), 53–58, 85; *Proceedings, Twelfth Convention of the International Ladies' Garment Workers' Union* (Cleveland, 1914), 50, 65; "Report of debate between Morris Hillquit and William D. Haywood, January 11, 1912" (Morris Hillquit Collection, Tamiment Institute).

36. Levine, *op. cit.*, 250; *Ladies' Garment Worker*, II (May 1911), 5; III (September 1912), 1–2; V (January 1914), 8–15.

37. "Translation of article in the *New Post* June 20, 1913, by I. A. Hourwich." See also similar translations of articles and speeches by Hourwich on May 23, June 21, June 27, and October 4, 1913 (Louis D. Brandeis Collection, University of Louisville).

38. Levine, *op. cit.*, 265–272; *Proceedings, Twelfth Convention of the International Ladies' Garment Workers' Union* (Cleveland, 1914), 15–16, 36, 45–46, 58–60, 79–82, 175–176, 201–205.

39. Levine, *op. cit.*, 272–273; *Ladies' Garment Worker*, V (July 1914), 19–20; Dyche to Gompers, October 1, October 17, 1914 (Gompers' Correspondence with Affiliates, AFL–CIO Collection). It is worth noting that Gom-

pers himself implied strong support for Dyche and Rosenberg in their handling of the Hourwich affair. Never, Gompers said in a speech before the 1914 ILGWU convention, had he met "a set of men in authoritative position who have so thoroughly, unselfishly and intelligently safeguarded and protected the interests of the men and women [in the garment trade] as those you now have as officers of your organization." See *Proceedings, Twelfth Convention of the International Ladies' Garment Workers' Union* (Cleveland, 1914), 109.

40. Levine, *op. cit.*, 318; Seidman, *The Needle Trades*, 107.

41. Epstein, *Profiles of Eleven*, 238–239; Levine, *op. cit.*, 283–284; *Ladies' Garment Worker*, V (September 1914), 4–11; VI (January 1915), 1–6; VI (February 1915), 1–4; VI (May 1915), 1–4; *Proceedings, Thirteenth Convention of the International Ladies' Garment Workers' Union* (Philadelphia, 1916), 24–25, 51–52, 212–225.

42. Note, however, that it was alleged in some quarters that part of the AFL's motive in helping the ILGWU in this strike was its fear "that some more radical body will step in and organize the workers," presumably the IWW. See clipping from the New York *Sun*, May 17, 1916. See also clippings from New York *Call*, May 16, 1916, May 18, 1916, and the New York *Evening World*, July 13, 1916, and July 27, 1916 (Scrapbooks, ILGWU Headquarters).

43. Levine, *op. cit.*, 287–311, 318–319; *Ladies' Garment Worker*, VI (January 1915), 1–6.

44. Seidman, *The Needle Trades*, 100; Levine, *op. cit.*, 135–139. It is noteworthy that whereas the cutters in the shoe industry tended to become radical because of the undermining of their position through technological change, the cutters in the garment industry were less likely to become socialists for this reason, since at this time there was no satisfactory mechanical substitute for the hand-operated cutting knife, which required both skill and strength to operate.

45. Stolberg, *The Needle Trades*, 111; Seidman, *op. cit.*, 228; *Ladies' Garment Worker*, III (April 1912), 18; III (June 1912), 16–17; *Proceedings, Thirteenth Convention of the International Ladies' Garment Workers' Union* (Philadelphia, 1916), 154. Note also that Salvatore Ninfo, the leader of Local 48, had earlier been an IWW member and that Luigi Antonini, the leader of Local 89, later became a Communist for a time. See Stolberg, *op. cit.*, 111; Philip S. Foner, *History of the Labor Movement in the United States*, 4 vols. (New York, 1947–1965), IV, 551n.

46. Dyche indicated the strength of this antipathy toward the Democrats at an earlier date in a letter which he wrote to Gompers after the presidential election of 1908, when the AFL first gave signs of overt support for the Democratic party. Living as he did, Dyche said, "in the midst of quite a number of rabid socialists who were full of wrath against you and the A.F. of L. for supporting the Democratic Party, and prophesied the disruption of the A.F. of L. and the downfall of the President [that is, Gompers himself] for allieing [*sic*] the American Trade Union movement with 'Tammany Hall' as they expressed it, I had a hot time of it during the campaign." Dyche to Gompers, December 3, 1908 (Gompers' Correspondence with Affiliates, AFL–CIO Collection).

47. *Proceedings, Twelfth Convention of the International Ladies' Garment Workers' Union* (Cleveland, 1914), 22–23, 173–175.

48. In 1916, for example, the *Ladies' Garment Worker* asserted that the

1912 amendment gave "official sanction" to the earlier support which ILGWU members and locals had given to the Socialist party; and President Schlesinger even suggested that his administration had been elected in 1914 in part to give effect to this policy change. See *Constitution,* International Ladies' Garment Workers' Union (1913), 11–12; *Ladies' Garment Worker,* V (July 1914), 19–20; VII (November 1916), 8.

49. In 1910 London lost by 3,322 votes to 4,606 for the Democrat, Henry M. Goldfogle; and in 1912 by 3,646 votes to 4,592 for the same man. In 1916 he was reelected by 6,103 votes to 5,763, also over the Democrat. Hillquit lost the Twentieth Congressional District in 1916, by 4,129 votes to 4,542, to a Republican. See *The New York Red Book* (New York), 1912, p. 698; 1913, p. 672; 1915, p. 707; 1918, pp. 461–463. See also Rogoff, *op. cit.,* 48; Hillquit, *op. cit.,* 116–118; Epstein, *Profiles of Eleven,* 172–184; Epstein, *Jewish Labor in U.S.A.,* I, 357–360; *Ladies' Garment Worker,* VII (November 1916), 8; *Proceedings, Thirteenth Convention of the International Ladies' Garment Workers' Union* (Philadelphia, 1916), 271–274; M. Shamroth to Gompers, October 10, 1912; Gompers to M. Shamroth, October 25, 1912 (A.F. of L. Collection, Wisconsin State Historical Society).

50. *Ladies' Garment Worker,* III (January 1912), 14–15; V (June 1914), 11–12; VI (December 1915), 6–7; VII (November 1916), 8, 12; VII (December 1916), 7–8.

51. Levine, *op. cit.,* 115–117, 136–139, 272, 292; Stolberg, *op. cit.,* 93–94; Hillquit, *op. cit.,* 133–141. It is worth noting that although Gompers clearly favored the conservative leaders of the ILGWU wherever possible, as indicated by his evident support for the Rosenberg-Dyche administration in the Hourwich affair, and also by his close personal relationship with Dyche, his willingness to give the ILGWU help in its early strikes, and his endorsement of London in 1912 add somewhat of a corrective to the view that he was always and on every occasion antagonistic to socialist trade-unions.

52. Seidman, *The Needle Trades,* 150–151; *Ladies' Garment Worker,* I (December 1910), 3, 5; II (December 1911), 6–7; III (July 1912), 15–18; VI (November 1915), 3–4; VI (December 1915), 22–25; VII (January 1916), 6–7; VIII (December 1917), 7–8; *Proceedings, Twelfth Convention of the International Ladies' Garment Workers' Union* (Cleveland, 1914), 173–175; *Proceedings, Fourteenth Convention of the International Ladies' Garment Workers' Union* (Boston, 1918), 43–44, 200–201; *Proceedings, Sixteenth Convention of the International Ladies' Garment Workers' Union* (Cleveland, 1922), 90–92.

53. Moses Rischin, "The Jewish Labor Movement in America: A Social Interpretation," *Labor History,* IV (Fall, 1963), 235. For a further discussion of this aspect of Jewish socialism and its relation to Judaism in general, see Nathan Glazer, *American Judaism* (Chicago, 1957), especially 134–139.

54. *Proceedings, Thirteenth Convention of the International Ladies' Garment Workers' Union* (Philadelphia, 1916), 109–114, 129–131; *Proceedings, Fourteenth Convention of the International Ladies' Garment Workers' Union* (Boston, 1918), 99–101.

55. Seidman, *The Needle Trades,* 37–38, 227; *Proceedings, Eleventh Convention of the International Ladies' Garment Workers' Union* (Toronto, 1912), 91; *Proceedings, Thirteenth Convention of the International Ladies' Garment Workers' Union* (Philadelphia, 1916), 50; *Proceedings, Sixteenth Convention of*

the International Ladies' Garment Workers' Union (Cleveland, 1922), 106–108. It should be noted, however, that in its early attitude toward Asiatics, the ILGWU was considerably less liberal. Its 1902 convention adopted a resolution barring them from membership. This provision was soon repudiated, but it has been suggested that one reason why Hillquit lost in the Ninth Congressional District in 1908 was that he had proposed restricting the immigration of "backward races" at the Stuttgart congress of the Second (Socialist) International the previous year. See Seidman, *The Needle Trades*, 227; Epstein, *Profiles of Eleven*, 204–207.

56. *Ladies' Garment Worker*, II (February 1911), 3–4; VII (May 1916), 8–9; *Proceedings, Twelfth Convention of the International Ladies' Garment Workers' Union* (Cleveland, 1914), 34, 178, 184–185; *Proceedings, Fifteenth Convention of the International Ladies' Garment Workers' Union* (Chicago, 1920), 116–117.

57. Stolberg, *op. cit.*, 18–20; *Ladies' Garment Worker*, I (November 1910), 6; VI (November 1915), 8–9; VIII (July 1917), 13; VIII (November 1917), 10–11; VIII (December 1917), 8–9; IX (February 1918), 13; *Proceedings, Thirteenth Convention of the International Ladies' Garment Workers' Union* (Philadelphia, 1916), 86. For a further discussion of the role of women in the union, see Alice Henry, *Women and the Labor Movement* (New York, 1923), 65, 78–84; Edith Abbott, *Women in Industry, A Study in American Economic History* (New York, 1928), 215–245; Mabel Willett, *The Employment of Women in the Clothing Trade*, Columbia University Studies in History, Economics and Public Law, XVI, No. 1 (New York, 1902), 175–370.

58. Levine, *op. cit.*, 474–505; *Ladies' Garment Worker*, VI (January 1915), 4; VI (March 1915), 20; VII (January 1916), 18–19; VII (July 1916), 20–21; VII (November 1916), 5; VIII (October 1917), 10–11; *Proceedings, Twelfth Convention of the International Ladies' Garment Workers' Union* (Cleveland, 1914), 147–148; *Proceedings, Thirteenth Convention of the International Ladies' Garment Workers' Union* (Philadelphia, 1916), 18, 50–51, 197–198.

59. Seidman, *The Needle Trades*, 138–142; Levine, *op. cit.*, 327–338; *Ladies' Garment Worker*, VII (May 1916), 5–6; VIII (May 1917), 7–8; VIII (September 1917), 15.

60. *Ibid.*, VIII (September 1917), 15; VIII (November 1917), 12–14; *Proceedings, Fifteenth Convention of the International Ladies' Garment Workers' Union* (Chicago, 1920), 29, 107; *Proceedings, Sixteenth Convention of the International Ladies' Garment Workers' Union* (Cleveland, 1922), 101.

61. *The New York Red Book* (New York), 1919, p. 391; Hillquit, *op. cit.*, 180–210; Epstein, *Jewish Labor in U.S.A.*, II, 77–80; *Ladies' Garment Worker*, VIII (November 1917), 7–8; VIII (December 1917), 8–9; Hillquit to John P. Mitchel, October 10, 1917; Hillquit to Eugen Schoen, October 13, 1917; clipping from New York *World*, October 12, 1917 (Morris Hillquit Collection, Wisconsin State Historical Society).

62. Epstein, *Jewish Labor in U.S.A.*, II, 63–66; *Ladies' Garment Worker*, VIII (April 1917), 9–10; VIII (July 1917), 28–29; VIII (September 1917), 23–24; IX (February 1918), 31; *Proceedings, Fourteenth Convention of the International Ladies' Garment Workers' Union* (Boston, 1918), 42–43.

63. *Ibid.*, 38, 214–215.

64. *Justice* (New York), II (October 29, 1920), 4; *Proceedings, Fortieth An-*

nual Convention of the A.F. of L. (Montreal, 1920), 265–266; *Proceedings, Fifteenth Annual Convention of the International Ladies' Garment Workers' Union* (Chicago, 1920), 32–35, 66, 78, 105–106.

65. More extensive accounts of the conflict can be found in Carsel, *op. cit.*, 174–192; Jack Hardy, *The Clothing Workers, A Study of Conditions and Struggles in the Needle Trades* (New York, 1935), 38–54; and David M. Schneider, *The Workers' (Communist) Party and the American Trade Unions* (Baltimore, 1928), 87–104.

66. *Justice*, II (June 25, 1920), 4; *Proceedings, Seventeenth Convention of the International Ladies' Garment Workers' Union* (Boston, 1924), 29, 235–236. Rose Pesotta later became a vice-president of the ILGWU and an influential union leader, publishing her memoirs in 1944. See Rose Pesotta, *Bread upon the Water* (New York, 1944).

67. Seidman, *The Needle Trades*, 155–159; Levine, *op. cit.*, 352–356; *Proceedings, Sixteenth Convention of the International Ladies' Garment Workers' Union* (Cleveland, 1922), 50–54.

68. Levine, *op. cit.*, 356–359; Seidman, *The Needle Trades*, 159–169, 183–184; *Constitution*, International Ladies' Garment Workers' Union (New York, 1924), 37.

69. Levine, *op. cit.*, 342–352; *Ladies' Garment Worker*, IX (November 1918), 8–9; *Justice*, II (June 4, 1920), 2; II (June 11, 1920), 2; II (June 18, 1920), 2; II (June 25, 1920), 4; II (October 15, 1920), 1, 7; *Proceedings, Fifteenth Convention of the International Ladies' Garment Workers' Union* (Chicago, 1920), 2, 105.

70. *Justice*, II (July 16, 1920), 4; II (July 23, 1920), 4; II (November 12, 1920), 4; III (July 1, 1921), 4.

71. *Ibid.*, II (July 30, 1920), 6; II (August 6, 1920), 4; II (August 20, 1920), 3; II (August 27, 1920), 3; II (October 1, 1920), 3.

72. For this, see Morris Hillquit to Roland A. Gibson, February 20, 1924 (Morris Hillquit Papers, Wisconsin State Historical Society).

73. *Justice*, III (July 15, 1921), 4; IV (February 17, 1922), 7; IV (February 24, 1922), 1; IV (June 30, 1922), 3; IV (July 21, 1922), 2; IV (December 15, 1922), 1; V (December 29, 1922), 4, 8; VI (March 7, 1924), 4; VI (June 20, 1924), 3; VI (July 4, 1924), 1; VI (July 18, 1924), 5; VI (August 8, 1924), 1, 7; VI (September 19, 1924), 1; VI (October 31, 1924), 1; *Proceedings, Seventeenth Convention of the International Ladies' Garment Workers' Union* (Boston, 1924), 24.

74. For David Dubinsky's leadership of the ILGWU and his general contribution to the labor movement, see "David Dubinsky, the I.L.G.W.U., and the American Labor Movement," special supplement of *Labor History*, IX (Spring, 1968).

75. Stolberg, *op. cit.*, 192–193; *Justice*, VI (November 14, 1924), 7; VI (December 5, 1924), 6; VIII (February 20, 1925), 4; VIII (February 27, 1925), 1, 2; VIII (March 13, 1925), 4; *Proceedings, Twentieth Convention of the International Ladies' Garment Workers' Union* (Cleveland, 1929), 26–27.

76. Running on the Farmer-Labor as well as the Socialist party ticket, London lost heavily to the Democrat, Samuel Dickstein, by 5,900 votes to 11,027. See *The New York Red Book* (New York), 1923, p. 534. See also Epstein, *Jewish Labor in U.S.A.*, II, 84–85.

77. *Ladies' Garment Worker,* VI (February 1915), 16; VI (May 1915), 16–17. This increasing rate of mobility among Jews into business and the professions, which has frequently been commented on by scholars in various fields, was welcomed by antisocialists in the ILGWU such as Dyche as evidence that the socialism of the Jews was simply a surface phenomenon masking a more fundamental enthusiasm for the opportunities provided by American capitalism, and by socialists such as London with a mixture of admiration and regret. Nevertheless, it is noteworthy that many Jews retained their social idealism, if not their active support, for the Socialist party, for years after they had entered the ranks of the property-owning middle class. See *Ladies' Garment Worker,* II (May 1911), 5; *Proceedings, Fourteenth Convention of the International Ladies' Garment Workers' Union* (Boston, 1918), 288–292; Seidman, *The Needle Trades,* 83; Antonovsky, *op. cit.,* 336–345; Glazer, *op. cit.,* 80–83; Nathan Glazer and Daniel Moynihan, *Beyond the Melting Pot: The Negroes, Puerto Ricans, Jews, Italians, and Irish of New York City* (Cambridge, 1963), 143–159. For the impact of the small scale of manufacturing operations on labor relations in the industry, see Selig Perlman, "Jewish-American Unionism, Its Birth Pangs and Contribution to the General American Labor Movement," *Publication of the American Jewish Historical Society,* XLI (June 1952), 349–355.

78. Seidman, *The Needle Trades,* 68–69.

5

Populism, Socialism, and the International Association of Machinists

The trade-unions so far examined in this book differ from one another on sectional and ethnic, as well as on ideological and structural grounds. But each of them has so far been largely confined in its geographical area to the North and to the Midwest. This was not true of the International Association of Machinists, which was founded in Atlanta, Georgia, in 1888, and was the only important socialist union in the American labor movement to have originated in the South. Railroad machinists from small southern and western towns dominated the organization for some years, and it later spread north among machine shops producing machinery for industry under contract. As a result, it incorporated a variety of immigrants into its ranks. Fundamentally, however, it was native American in its composition and outlook, and such foreign influences as it had were British rather than continental in their nature. By 1901, with 57,000 members to its credit and headquarters in Chicago, the International Association of Machinists was one of the largest and most influential of the unions in the metal trades.[1]

The southern origins and native-born composition of the IAM made it ideologically less Marxist than the unions previously discussed, and more responsive to indigenous movements for reform. It was cautious, pragmatic, and moderate in its approach, and there were few impossibilists in its ranks. Although it had little specific connection with the People's party, its origins in the small-town railroad centers of the South and West gave a strong Populist orientation to its radicalism. For example, it shared the Populists' concern for economic and political democracy, as well as their antipathy toward the great corporations and the trusts. These influences persisted, in a changing form, right through the period of socialist administration in the union, which began in 1912. They also reappeared after World War I in the Conference for Progressive Political Action, in which the union played a prominent part.

In fact, the major importance of the International Association of Machinists lies in its contribution to the indigenous tradition of socialism in the American labor movement. It played a role in the indigenous wing of the movement comparable to that of the ILGWU in the immigrant wing. A review of socialist influence in the union gives conclusive proof that the appeal of socialism to the American workingman was not confined to the unskilled and the underprivileged or to unions dominated by Germans or Jews. It also had an important influence among the skilled craftsmen and the native-born Americans.

I

The International Association of Machinists was not a socialist union at first. In fact, in its early years it exhibited many of the characteristics typically associated with the conservative craft unionism of the AFL. The railroad machinists who established it were highly skilled engineers who worked in the roundhouses and repair shops of the railroads which were then spreading rapidly throughout the South and West. Most of them were native-born Americans, respectable artisans of English, Irish, or Scottish descent who had earlier been members of the Knights of Labor but who now, like other skilled workers, favored the establishment of an independent organization devoted solely to the preservation of their separate status and craft.[2] To this conservative background was added the exclusiveness of the South. Negroes were prevented from joining by the "white clause" in the Machinists' national constitution, and so were immigrants who were not yet American citizens.[3]

Thomas W. Talbot, the first grand master machinist, illustrates well the conservative origins of the IAM. Born on a South Carolina farm in 1845, he apprenticed himself to the North Carolina Railroad machine shops in 1865. Later, he opened his own machine shop in Sumter, South Carolina, and after this became active in the Knights of Labor. This experience led him to conclude that the machinists should have their own organization, and it was he who sent out the circular announcing the union's birth on September 10, 1888. The circular indicated that the purpose of the new organization was to resist wage cuts, establish union benefits, and fulfill the other traditional functions of a trade-union. But it also demonstrated the conservative and socially exclusive nature of the association. "Don't think for one moment," wrote Talbot in the circular, "that the writer is one of the so-called labor agitators, for I believe that the only right way of obtaining greater consideration is by persistently showing that we are more worthy men and better mechanics than formerly, thereby proving to our employers and the world at large that we are justly entitled to standing and distinction." [4]

Although he was a northerner, James O'Connell, who was grand master machinist from 1893 to 1912, continued to preserve the conservative traditions of the IAM. Born in Pennsylvania of Irish parents, and an active Catholic, he was a close associate of Gompers, and became third and then second vice-president of the AFL between 1895 and 1917. He was also a strong supporter of the National Civic Federation and president of the AFL Metal Trades Department. During his administration the membership of the union rose from about 8,000 in 1895 to 64,000 in 1911. [5]

In order to establish comprehensive and stable agreements with the employers, which was one of his major aims, O'Connell and his supporters sought to include in the union's membership not only the all-round machinists who could construct an entire piece of machinery from a blueprint, but also specialists who were skilled on only a few, or even one, of the machines traditionally associated with the machinists' craft. Thus, in 1897 the qualification for membership was expanded to include a variety of machine operators. This reform was similar to that which Gompers and Adolph Strasser had introduced earlier into the Cigarmakers International Union. [6] But, like them, O'Connell limited the Machinists' membership to skilled workers so far as he could. He had no wish to incorporate the unskilled into the union or to expand it into an industrial organization, as the socialists were later to urge. [7]

In other respects also O'Connell developed still further the IAM's commitment to "pure and simple" trade-unionism. He expanded the powers of the grand lodge—the national headquarters, which in 1895 were moved to Chicago, and later to Washington, D.C.—in order to secure control over the negotiation of local contracts, and he established strict rules concerning the authorization of strikes. He also raised the union's dues. [8] Politically, the machinists under O'Connell followed labor's traditional pattern of lobbying for legislation to protect the members' special interests, while at the same time avoiding overt entanglements with party politics. With its largely native American composition, the IAM endorsed legislative efforts to limit foreign immigration—a position which did not change even during its socialist period—and it sought apprentice laws and other concessions from the state legislatures. But political discussions were banned from local lodge meetings until 1899, and in a debate over politics which took place in the *Machinists' Monthly Journal* in 1893, most of the participants showed themselves favoring the nonpartisan tactics of the AFL. The editor, former Grand Master Machinist James Creamer, of Richmond, Virginia, expressed the official view when he stated that "the American workingman . . . should never tie himself to any political party, but should vote for the man and measure he represents, regardless of party connections." [9]

Paradoxically, the IAM first encountered socialist trade-unionism directly when it attempted to affiliate with the AFL. The AFL, true to its early idealism on the question of discriminating against Negroes, had refused to admit the IAM in 1890 because of the white clause in its national constitution. Instead, in 1891 it chartered the International Machinists Union, a small, separate organization of northern machinists which was established by a group of SLP members under the leadership of August Waldinger, of New York, and Thomas J. Morgan, of Chicago. By 1892 the International Machinists Union, which had less restrictive membership requirements than the IAM, fewer benefits, and an overtly Marxist Preamble to its constitution, had acquired over 2,000 members and twenty-three locals in New York, Philadelphia, and other northern cities.[10]

However, the International Association of Machinists was now moving into the North, and it grew much more rapidly than its rival. In fact, it absorbed several of the International Machinists Union's lodges in 1893 and 1894.[11] This put the AFL into an ambiguous position, for the jurisdiction of its own affiliate, in this case the socialist International Machinists Union, was being challenged by a union which it could not charter because of its discriminatory racial policy but which, in ordinary circumstances, it would certainly have preferred.[12] In the end, after considerable negotiation, the issue was settled by a compromise. In April 1895 Acting President James Duncan of the AFL (McBride was ill) agreed to withdraw official objections to issuing a charter to the IAM if the white clause was removed from its national constitution. This was done at the May 1895 IAM convention, but in order to pacify the southern lodges the white clause was incorporated into the secret rituals of the locals instead. Soon after this the IAM affiliated with the AFL, even though its locals continued to refuse admission to Negroes. This was the first important case in which the AFL chartered a national union whose locals followed a policy of open discrimination. At the December 1895 AFL convention the charter of the International Machinists Union was withdrawn, and its remaining locals either dissolved or joined the IAM.[13]

But although the Marxist and in some cases DeLeonite lodges which were now incorporated from the International Machinists Union exerted some influence in the IAM, it was not they who were primarily responsible for the development of radical sentiment in the trade. DeLeonite machinists were influential for a time in Cleveland, notably in Pearl Lodge No. 238, and in April 1896 there was a complaint from Hartford, Connecticut, that socialists had acted as scabs in a strike conducted by machinists there. But this simply helped to undermine the influence of the SLP in that town. Thomas J. Morgan, the influential Chicago machinist who had been prominent in the International Machinists Union, gave up the machinists' trade in 1893 to become a lawyer; [14] and the only real success of the SLP in the International Association of Machinists was in New York, where the union was for some years small and weak. Early in March 1896 the De-Leonites in Empire City Lodge No. 357, who were in a minority, obstructed the business of its meetings to such an extent that the majority of the members, who were not socialists, ceased to attend. The DeLeonites then succeeded in securing the passage of a resolution transferring Lodge No. 357 to the Socialist Trades and Labor Alliance. This was done despite the protests of the other members, and after an appeal to the General Executive Board, Lodge 357 was expelled from the international union for doing so. An attempt was made to do the same thing to a lodge in Brooklyn, which was composed of Swedish members, but this time the DeLeonites failed to win over the membership. [15]

Despite this, the rise of socialism among the machinists, as among the shoe workers, had much more to do with indigenous radical influences in the labor movement than it did with the Marxist socialism of the European immigrants. The southern founders of the union rejected the broad membership qualifications of the Knights of Labor. But they did not wholly divest themselves of the reformist social philosophy of the Knights. For some years the organization retained the secret ritual and fraternalistic nomenclature of the K of L, calling their officers grand master machinist and so on; and the early issues of the *Machinists' Monthly Journal* were imbued with a strong commitment to moral improvement, concern for local and state politics, and even some hope for the regeneration of society along cooperative lines. In addition, the IAM represented the revival of an earlier tradition of radicalism in the metal trades which went back before the Civil War and in many ways resembled that of the Knights of St. Crispin. The National Union of Machinists and Blacksmiths, founded in 1859, was largely set up to control the number of apprentices in the machinists' trade. But the union also provided the post-Civil War labor movement with some of its most famous theorists. Ira Steward, the great apostle of the eight-hour movement, was a machinist, and so was Terence V. Powderly. [16]

But the first indication that the machinists took an interest in politics which went beyond the nonpartisan position of the AFL came with the development of the People's party. Populism was a southern movement even more than a western and a midwestern one, and the Populists were influential in many of the small railroad towns in which the IAM at first had its greatest strength. It was also influential in such cities as Atlanta. For example, at its first anniversary meeting in May 1889, the Atlanta lodge heard Senator Hoke Smith of Georgia give a typically Populist address in which he asserted that the greater part of the wealth in the United States was in the hands of 10 per cent of the people. It is also likely that many southern-born machinists, with their concern at the rapid growth of European immigration, sympathized with the nativist aspects of Populism.

Although there is little direct evidence of involvement by machinists in the People's party as such, the union did send a delegate to the Populist convention which met in St. Louis in February 1892, and strong interest was expressed in the financial, antimonopoly, and democratic reforms proposed by the Populists at many levels in the organization. The editor of the union journal, for example, writing after the beginning of the severe depression in 1893, asserted that economic crises resulted from the control exerted by a few businessmen over the economy as a whole. Such crises would recur, he stated, "until the laws which allow the money sharks to control our finance are legislated out of existence." The popular election of officials and the initiative and referendum system of legislation gained wide acceptance in the organization in the 1890's, despite the opposition expressed by the O'Connell administration. The 1895 convention decreed that amendments to the national constitution should be made between conventions by means of the initiative and referendum, thereby increasing rank-and-file control. And at the 1897 convention, election of the union's delegates to the convention of the AFL was transferred from the convention to the referendum vote. Further Populistic reforms of this kind were undertaken in later years.[17]

But the most important link between the IAM and the Populists was their common hostility toward the railroad corporations. A majority of union members were railroad machinists until well after the turn of the century, and in March 1893 a correspondent to the union journal played on a familiar theme when he urged the IAM to endorse Populist demands for government ownership of the railroads. Otherwise the amalgamations which were continually taking place among the railroad companies would undermine the machinists' bargaining position and force them to work solely on the companies' terms. Political action, and that alone, the writer continued, could control the growing power of the railroads; and this must be taken by "the people," since the federal government was clearly in the hands of the "money power." These demands were evidently popular in the union as a whole, for at its convention in May 1893 the delegates adopted a resolution requesting government ownership of the railroads, as well as of the telegraph and telephone companies—another standard Populist demand.[18]

One year later, in the summer of 1894, the great Pullman strike took place, accelerating demands for the nationalization of the railroads and providing a spectacle of virtual class warfare which was not lost on the members of the IAM. The activities of the American Railway Union also raised the issue of industrial unionism in the organization for the first time. Coming at a time when many machinists were resentful of the AFL's refusal to give it a charter, the failure of the craft unions to give their support to the ARU crystallized the discontent in the union and impelled a growing number of machinists to go beyond their former Populist views and espouse the cause of socialism.

It will be recalled that the American Railway Union was established by Eugene Debs in June 1893 to enroll all the railroad workers into a single industry-wide organization and to give them more militant leadership than the conservative railroad brotherhoods had been willing to provide. In its first months the ARU spread rapidly along the midwestern and western lines, where the Machinists' own strength largely lay, and its early successes attracted considerable sympathy among the union membership, especially since they took place during the industrial depression when several of their own strikes had failed.

In addition, the ARU was, temporarily at least, much larger than the IAM, and it seemed to provide more immediate prospects of advance. Thus during the successful Great Northern strike which the ARU conducted early in 1894, quite a number of machinists not only joined the strike but also took out membership in the ARU. According to one report, railroad machinists on the Santa Fe system "from one end to the other embraced industrial unionism," while those on the Union Pacific were also strongly affected. One member of the General Executive Board, Peter J. Conlon, later suggested that the failure of the Pullman strike not only destroyed the ARU; it "very nearly wrecked the International Association of Machinists as well." "Whether it was the success of the strike or the belief that trades unions were a failure I cannot say," O'Connell later reported, speaking of the earlier Great Northern victory. "But some of our members in that system were inflicted to such an extent that they immediately began disorganizing our lodges." [19]

It is noteworthy that O'Connell was strongly opposed to the ARU, not only because of its challenge to the IAM's jurisdiction but also because of the industrial form of trade-unionism which it upheld. For many rank-and-file members of the IAM, however, the ARU appeared to offer a much more logical response to the giant railroad corporations than the separate craft unions in the industry, and when the Pullman strike began in May 1894 they gave it enthusiastic support. A number of the union's lodges were disbanded, and several thousand members joined the ARU. After the collapse of the strike the IAM soon made good its losses, but the tremendous spread of the strike, the widespread use of injunctions, and the prosecution and imprisonment of Debs all had a powerful impact on the union membership. Many members, especially in the West, saw in the episode evidence of the inadequacy and failure of the traditional weapons of craft unionism and the need for socialist political action and industrial unionism throughout the labor movement as a whole.

O'Connell's popularity suffered, in particular, and the most ardent supporters of the ARU in the IAM even charged him with having contributed to the failure of the strike. He denied the accusation, although he did admit that some members of the lodge in Richmond, Virginia, had acted as strike-breakers. The whole episode, in fact, only served to strengthen his adherence to the craft-union policies of the AFL. Time had shown the folly of sympathizing with the American Railway Union, he asserted at the IAM convention of 1895; and he claimed that the membership had come through with "a better understanding of the aims and objects of our organization than ever before." The claim was hardly justified, however. More apposite was the comment of a local lodge leader from Anaconda, Montana: "Brothers of the I.A. of M., it has been a recognized fact that labor organizations have steered clear of dabbling in politics, but I believe with E. V. Debs, that it is the only way now left open for us to get our just and equal rights." [20]

An even more important source of radicalism in the IAM was anxiety at the profound changes which were taking place in the machinists' craft. The main reason for establishing the organization, as we have seen, had been a desire to protect the position of the skilled worker in the trade. This was true to some extent of most of the craft unions which were being founded at this time. But in the IAM, as in the Boot and Shoe Workers Union, it took on particular urgency because of the technological advances which were rapidly undermining the status and the skill of the all-round machinist and reducing him from an independent artisan to little more than a factory hand. These changes were just as serious as those which occurred in the shoemaking trade, if not more so. But they began somewhat later, in the 1870's and 1880's rather than before and just after the Civil War, so that their effect on the labor force in the machine industry came somewhat later than it did in shoemaking. This may have been important in determining the period of socialist influence in the IAM.

Until about 1870 the machinist strongly resembled a carpenter who worked in metal instead of in wood.[21] He worked at a bench, usually in quite a small workshop, and used numerous small hand tools or lathes which required great skill to operate. The capital outlay involved in such an enterprise was not so great as to prevent individual journeymen from establishing a workshop of their own. But in the years which followed, the machinist's craft was revolutionized by the introduction of large and costly machinery driven by steam or electricity, most of it automatic, which was set up in large machine shops, very different from the workshops in which he had traditionally been employed.

This meant that the machinist, instead of being an independent craftsman who worked with his own hands and in his own time, became increasingly an operator of machine tools who worked in a factory. It also meant that self-employment was much more difficult to achieve, just as it was in the brewing and the shoemaking trades. By 1900 it was rarely possible to repeat the experience of Grand Master Machinist Talbot, who had owned his own machine shop in the early 1870's. The machinist still needed to learn how to use the machines he operated, some of which were highly sophisticated, but it was no longer necessary for him to become an all-round machinist who could construct a whole piece of machinery from a blueprint. Instead, he became a "specialist," a planer-hand or a slotting-machine hand who could do only part of the work and whose job consisted of little more than the manipulation of the levers on a machine.

These developments did not appear to have any very severe effects on wage levels, as they did in the shoe industry. In fact, wages continued to rise throughout the 1890's for both railroad and shop machinists, when the technological revolution was still in full swing.[22] Nevertheless, the psychological consequences of these changes, and their adverse effect on relations with employers in the industry, were severe. The machinist's craft had traditionally been so skilled and so well established, and his prestige with his fellow workmen and with his employer so much associated with it, that the threat posed by the introduction of machinery was regarded by many as little short of a disaster. In May 1898, for example, a correspondent in the union journal had this to say about the introduction of machinery into the trade: "The old feeling of mutual dependence between employers and men has disappeared under its blighting influences which have driven thousands of men into the streets of the cities and highways of the land as tramps and paupers without occupation for the present or hope or ambition for the future." The time had come, he said, for members of the union to face up to this problem if they hoped to live better than Chinese coolies.[23]

In addition, the widespread changes in the machinists' craft caused dislocation in the machine shops and brought temporary, and sometimes permanent, unemployment to thousands of skilled machinists. They also accorded well with the Marxist description of the development of industry under capitalism, and predictably the socialists in the union were quick to exploit them. One, writing in December 1898, said that technical changes had destroyed the independence of the machinist and rendered him a slave. "The division and sub-division of work done by both man and machine," he wrote, "eliminates the skilled machinist . . . and drives all skilled mechanics downwards to the level of all labor." The apprenticeship system, another wrote, was out of date, and the machinist's job would seem to be within the competence of any unskilled worker who chose to undertake it. The lesson was plain: the machinist could never hope to improve his condition so long as the machine, the great leveler, remained in private hands.[24]

For all these different reasons a number of skilled rank and file members of the International Association of Machinists became increasingly sympathetic toward socialism as the 1890's came to a close. So also, despite the continuing conservatism of O'Connell, did several of the union's officers. By 1898 the general secretary-treasurer, George Preston; the editor of the *Machinists' Monthly Journal,* Douglas Wilson; the union's general organizer, Stuart Reid; and the first vice-president, Peter J. Conlon, were all acknowledged socialists. Although the five-man General Executive Board usually supported O'Connell, at least in the early years of his administration, this meant that by the turn of the century most of the union's leading officials were socialists.

Characteristically, all these men were either British-born or native Americans, and they all upheld the moderate, gradualist form of socialism which had been developing among the rank and file in the previous decade. Although some had early sympathies with the SLP, they all preferred the evolutionary socialism of Debs and the Socialist party. Douglas Wilson, who edited the *Machinists' Monthly Journal* from 1895 until his death in 1915, perhaps exemplified best the type of socialist which the IAM produced. Scottish by birth, unlike many of the German or Jewish socialists in the labor movement he was not a socialist when he first arrived in this country. He began by apprenticing himself to a marine engineer in Charleston, South Carolina; and at first he upheld the somewhat exclusive moral and educational values which typified the southern founders of the union. Some of this remained with him as editor, with his advocacy of temperance and frequent reference to individual self-help. Then he ran, unsuccessfully, as a Populist for the Alabama legislature in 1894 and thereafter turned increasingly radical in his views. He also became a close personal friend of Debs. Wilson took a strong editorial interest in the growth of the British Labor party, as did many members of the IAM, and in the careers of its leading members—notably that of his fellow Scotsman James Keir Hardie—and he constantly urged the American labor movement to follow the English example. Also characteristically, however, he expressed little interest in ideological questions as such, contenting himself for the most part with urging his fellow workingmen to "vote for men from [their] own ranks." [25]

The general secretary-treasurer of the union between 1895 and 1917, George Preston, was an Englishman by birth, and unlike Wilson was a socialist before he came to America. In fact, he first became interested in labor politics in Nottingham, where he helped secure the nomination of John Burns (later a cabinet minister) as a socialist candidate for Parliament in 1885. Fundamentally, however, Preston, like Wilson, was a pragmatist. Thus he was critical of Gompers, and of his own union president, James O'Connell, for claiming that trade-unionism was the only answer to labor's problems. But he had little sympathy for the more revolutionary socialists. "To say that socialistic agitation and legislation affords the only measure of relief for our present ills," Preston wrote in 1897, "is just as inconsistent as to assert that trades unionism is all powerful to establish a regime of equality and justice." Stuart Reid, who resigned as general organizer in 1900 to become labor reporter for the Chicago *Daily News,* was another Scots-born moderate who deplored the division between socialists and trade-unionists in America, which, as he pointed out in May 1890, in Europe was being rapidly overcome.[26]

First Vice-President Peter A. Conlon also represented the socialism of the IAM in a characteristic form. Born in Brooklyn in 1869, Conlon moved to Sioux City, Iowa, early in his career and remained there for many years. Many of the reforms which Conlon first advocated, such as a national referendum on congressional legislation and municipal ownership of public utilities, were more Populist than socialist in content; and he began by supporting the Populists in Iowa, much as Douglas Wilson had supported Populism in the South. As late as October 1898 he wrote to an SLP member in Cleveland attacking the DeLeonites and urging Cleveland members to support the People's party. He wrote that the career of the SLP

> has been so blighted that us [*sic*] Western Socialists would have nothing to do with it, and look upon it as no more or less than a tail to the Tammany kite. . . . While you folks have been ranting about your significant Labor Party we have been silently coming together under the banner of the People's party. . . . I ask you to enquire into the platforms of [the] Kansas and South Dakota People's parties and [what] you will see there is nearly word for word the Socialist Labor Party platform, and this party is the dominant party of those states and the one that is now in power.[27]

Nevertheless, Conlon soon came to believe in some form of socialist party, if not the SLP, and with the collapse of Populism he turned, like so many machinists, toward the moderate reformism of Debs and the Social Democracy of America. He supported the colonization movement among socialists in the West and later became a strong and consistent member of the Socialist party itself.

It is important to notice that while Conlon was a socialist he was also a Catholic, as were quite a large number of machinists, both the northern Irish members and many of the native-born element. Douglas Wilson, as editor of the *Machinists' Monthly Journal,* was taken to task for expressing anticlerical views in 1894, and President O'Connell was a leading member of the Militia of Christ, the conservative and antisocialist Catholic work-ingmen's association. But Conlon's opinions indicate that the division be-tween socialists and antisocialists in the union was, as in the BSWU, not wholly a Catholic non-Catholic one. Interestingly, Conlon himself acknowledged that the Catholic faith precluded complete acceptance of the Marxist doctrine of class consciousness. But he espoused instead the idea of "social consciousness," which, he claimed, acknowledged the fatherhood of God while at the same time permitting a radical interpretation of the brotherhood of man.[28]

II

By the end of the 1890's, several of the leading officers of the IAM, to-gether with what appeared to be a significant proportion of the rank and file, demonstrated a growing sympathy with the moderate, reformist wing of what was soon to become the Socialist Party of America. They did so, moreover, despite the steady progress and growing strength of the Machin-ists as an economic organization. After the industrial depression, in the period between 1897 and 1899, 31 new lodges were organized, 125 exist-ing lodges increased the wages of their members by 10 per cent, and 39 se-cured a considerable increase in overtime pay. The IAM was now a truly national organization, with over 20,000 members distributed throughout the North and the Midwest as well as in the older areas of the South and West, and with lodges in most of the other states too.[29]

Up to this point little attempt had been made to commit the union to so-cialist policies as such. But at the eighth convention of the union, which was held at Buffalo, New York, in May 1899, proposals of a socialist na-ture were for the first time put forward and adopted. First, as a result of resolutions originating from the lodge at Sioux City, Iowa, of which P. J. Conlon was a member, a resolution was passed urging that government should again become "for the people and by the people, and not be used as a tool to further the ends of combination of capital for its own aggrandize-ment." This was little advance on the Populist sentiments which many machinists had earlier expressed, and its government "for the people and by the people," recalling Lincoln, had a particularly Populistic flavor. But the convention later went on to adopt a much more radical proposal which directly reflected the concern of the machinists at the undermining of their craft. "Whereas," the resolution ran, "the conditions under which we are at present laboring, are vitally different from those existing at the time we were first organized. And inasmuch as we are confronted by new problems which necessarily change our mode of action . . . Resolved that . . . [we] heartily approve and give . . . [our] support to that branch of political economy termed 'Public Ownership of Public Utility.' " O'Connell fought hard against the adoption of this motion. "I am a trade unionist all the way up, and all the way down, all through, and all around," he told the convention. "But I want to say that for our organization to deviate from our constitution and our platform, one iota along the political road, means . . . ripping up the back of our association." But he was overruled, and the convention adopted the resolution by a large majority.[30]

Although O'Connell was defeated on this issue and faced increasing criticism from various quarters because of his conservative policies, his administration still appeared to be in control of the union as a whole. As we have seen, the return of prosperity in 1898 brought renewed advances for the union, and in 1900, with the Murray Hill Agreement, O'Connell scored the greatest success of his career. Early in 1900 the IAM authorized strikes in Chicago, Cleveland, and Paterson, New Jersey, to secure the nine-hour day, the closed shop, and other reforms. This was a prosperous year, and the manufacturers, wishing to avoid a long and costly strike, agreed to negotiate with the union on a national basis. In March the strikes were called off, and O'Connell, Douglas Wilson, and other machinists' representatives met with delegates of the National Metal Trades Association at the Murray Hill Hotel in New York in May to draw up a national agreement for the industry at large. This included recognition of the union concessions on overtime and an agreement to introduce the nine-hour day throughout the industry after one year had elapsed.[31]

The Murray Hill Agreement was rightly regarded by O'Connell and most members of the IAM as a great advance. In the event, however, it proved to be a Pyrrhic victory. In May 1901, when the nine-hour day was due to be introduced, the union's officials found that the manufacturers intended to maintain the same hourly rates of pay, thus reducing the amount each machinist earned by 10 per cent. Remonstrance proving useless, the union, relying on a relatively well-filled treasury, ordered a general strike of machinists, and on May 20, 1901, over fifty thousand men came out. The manufacturers' association held that the IAM had violated that part of the agreement which provided that no strike should take place until all attempts at negotiation had failed. It declared war on the union, making the open shop its main objective. The employers organized a strikebreaking service and pooled their financial resources, and by midsummer the machinists realized that they were no match for the combined financial power of their adversaries. The union appealed, without success, to the good offices of the National Civic Federation, and in October 1901 O'Connell even wrote for help to President Theodore Roosevelt, also to no avail. The strike was lost, despite enormous financial expenditures on the part of the union, and with it went O'Connell's hopes of a permanent trade agreement in the industry.[32]

O'Connell's prestige suffered a further and even more severe setback as a result of the failure of the 1901 strike. His whole policy had been built on strict trade-union methods, cooperation with the AFL, and attempts to secure stable and lasting agreements with the employers; and now that the machinists had suffered a direct defeat in their own industry the radicals in the union challenged the traditional policies of the administration even more strongly than before. They did not propose withdrawing from the AFL, as extremists in a number of other unions had done. But when the implications of the 1901 defeat had sunk in, demands arose for increased political action, termination of the union's connections with the NCF— which had been unable to mediate the strike—and some concrete plan of industrial unionism to provide broader protection against the National Metal Trades Association than the individual metal unions had been able to provide. All of this took one step further the radicalism which had first appeared at the time of the Pullman strike.[33]

This new radical mood dominated the union convention held at Milwaukee in May 1903. First, the convention agreed, after considerable debate, to add to the Preamble of the national constitution a declaration that the IAM was "based upon the class struggle upon both economic and political lines, with a view to restore the common weal of our Governments to the people and using the natural resources, means of production and distribution for the benefit of all the people." It is noteworthy that although there were still Populist overtones here (in the reference to restoring the "common weal of our Governments to the people"), this resolution spoke explicitly for the first time of the "class struggle" and implicitly, also, of the need for collective ownership of the means of production. A resolution was next introduced which derived directly from the defeat of 1901. It asserted that the failure of the 1901 strike and the means which were used to combat it had demonstrated "that our interests as workers are separate from and opposed to the interest of the capitalistic class, both politically and industrially," and that "we must act unitedly with all the workers on the political field, as we have done on the industrial field." Even more important, it instructed the secretary-treasurer of the IAM to put to a referendum vote the question of whether or not the union should pledge its support to the Socialist party of America.[34]

This resolution was, in fact, defeated. But a further one, which instructed the secretary-treasurer to ascertain through a referendum vote whether the union membership favored industrial unionism, whether it favored the AFL's endorsing socialism, and whether it favored the reelection of Samuel Gompers as president of the AFL, was passed. The IAM's delegates to the 1903 AFL convention were to be bound by the result of the vote on these questions. They were duly submitted to a referendum vote. Although the membership refused (by 3,603 votes to 2,705) to oppose Gompers as a matter of policy, it did commit the union delegates (by 4,544 votes to 1,650) to voting in favor of industrial unionism and (by 4,403 votes to 1,963) to voting for the endorsement of socialism by the AFL. However, the union's delegates to the November 1903 AFL convention only partially obyed these instructions.[35]

After 1903 O'Connell and his supporters in the administration of the IAM were unable to reestablish their former authority, and they became increasingly isolated. This was partly because of the continuous and frequently bitter hostility of the employers in the National Metal Trades Association, which undermined still further O'Connell's moderate approach and his hope of establishing good relations in the industry. But it was also because the socialists were by now organized into a coherent and articulate group who were able to exploit their differences with O'Connell with considerable success, and who also took on many of the characteristics of an opposition party. Their main strength lay in the railroad roundhouses and small-town lodges of the South and West. But they had also now acquired considerable support among the big-city lodges of the North and East.[36]

The issue which commanded perhaps the most widespread interest in the union was that of industrial unionism. President O'Connell had modified his stand on this issue somewhat with the passage of time, and in 1903 helped to resuscitate an organization called the Metal Trades Federation, which in 1909 became the Metal Trades Department of the AFL. However, this organization, of which O'Connell became president, simply provided for cooperation between separate craft unions, not for industrial unionism as such. But it is also worth noting that the issue of industrial unionism was also a difficult one for IAM socialists to handle, on their side. Like the Brewery Workers Union, the Machinists organized workers from many different areas of industry,[37] and had either of the proposals which the socialists actually put forward—for an industrial union comprising all the railroad workers in the country, modeled on Debs's ARU, or for an industrial union consisting solely of metal-trades workers—in fact been carried through to its logical conclusion, the result would have been, not to expand the IAM's jurisdiction, but to divide its membership into two separate organizations. Not even the most ardent advocate of industrial unionism wanted that, and it was perhaps for this reason that the issue was not pressed so hard as might have been expected.

Nevertheless, after the defeat of the job machinists in the 1901 strike, some form of cooperation with the other metal workers' unions seemed particularly important, and at the September 1905 convention a number of socialist delegates proposed implementing "the principle of industrial unionism" by amalgamating all the metal-trades unions into a single organization. This was rejected by the O'Connell forces on the ground that it was impractical, and a milder resolution was adopted urging the president and the General Executive Board to negotiate with the other metal-trades unions on the subject of a common strike and lockout policy. Nothing came of this suggestion, however.[38]

Three months earlier, in June 1905, the IWW had been established, and it made various efforts to organize the machinists, as it had the other trades. In late 1905 and 1906 IWW organizers appeared at machinists' meetings in Chicago, Cincinnati, Buffalo, New York, and New York City, criticizing the IAM for its craft-union orientation and urging its members to join the IWW. But they had little success. Two union lodges joined the IWW in Schenectady, New York, one in Cleveland (where the DeLeonite ST & LA had been strong), and also three lodges from District 15 in New York City. As far as can be ascertained, however, none of these IWW lodges lasted more than two or three years. Predictably, the IAM leadership rejected the IWW categorically, both socialist and nonsocialist alike.[39]

Closely connected with the issue of industrial unionism was the question of membership qualifications and admissions policy. In 1897, as we saw earlier, the administration had broadened the membership qualification to include a variety of trained machine operators as well as the skilled, all-round machinists. But this was about as far as O'Connell wanted to go. He was willing to admit young apprentices to the union, but not unskilled handymen or helpers, even though they were grown men, a distinction which the socialists regarded as invidious. Thus in 1899 they succeeded in getting the membership qualification widened to include "every competent machinist who is actively engaged at the trade, or connected with it," a definition which admitted of pretty wide interpretation.[40]

However, the socialists found themselves in somewhat of a dilemma regarding this issue also. The decline in the position of the skilled machinist had been one of the major causes, if not the major cause, of the rise of socialism in the IAM; and despite their general policy of support for organizing the unskilled on humanitarian or ideological grounds, the socialists had to tread carefully where the interests of their own supporters in the union were concerned. Thus, at the 1901 convention there was a prolonged debate as to whether or not to leave out the word "competent" in the membership qualification (which would have broadened it still more), and a number of western delegates who were known to be socialists expressed doubts about the wisdom of doing so. The diluted admissions requirement was authorized, but a similar debate arose at the 1903 convention. A resolution to replace the word "machinist" by "person" was adopted by the small majority of 286 votes to 241, and again doubts were expressed by some socialist delegates. However, probably a majority of the socialists present voted in favor of the proposal, one of them pointing out the inconsistency of favoring the other 1903 socialist resolutions and then refusing "to sit in the lodge rooms on terms of equality with men lower than themselves." [41]

No such ambivalence affected the socialists' attitude toward political action. Now that the People's party had virtually disappeared, it was evident that many members of the IAM had transferred their allegiance to the rising Socialist party, despite the opposition of O'Connell and his supporters. Privately, O'Connell usually voted Democratic, as most of those in the union who were of Irish descent probably did also.[42] Publicly, however, O'Connell, together with Vice-Presidents Ames and Keppler and at least three members of the five-member General Executive Board, adhered firmly to their nonpartisan position and continued to oppose any attempt to commit the union to partisan politics. In his presidential report to the 1905 union convention, for example, O'Connell said, "We should see to it that our organization is not made the tail to anybody's kite." He was also a member of the Labor Representation Committee appointed by the AFL in 1906 to supervise its activities in the fall elections of that year.[43]

But in the early years of the AFL's political activism, when its pressure-group tactics seemed to be making little headway, O'Connell's political views were subjected to increasing criticism. In July 1908 Secretary Hourigan of District 15 in New York, now encompassing one of the largest groups of lodges in the union, protested at what he described as O'Connell's open attempt to commit labor's vote to the Democratic Presidential candidate, William Jennings Bryan. In May 1910 the IAM's business agent in Milwaukee, commending the victory of the socialists in the spring municipal elections there, attacked the AFL's nonpartisan policy and expressed the hope that socialist victories such as this would force the union to "take up the political fight . . . along close lines and quit flirting with the capitalist owned political parties as heretofore." There were numerous letters to the editor of the *Machinists' Monthly Journal* of a similar nature. And in August 1912 the editor himself, Douglas Wilson, openly scoffed at Gompers and the other AFL representatives for what he considered to be their fruitless journeys to the platform committees of both the Republican and Democratic conventions, despite the apparent success of their most recent visit. O'Connell was included, by implication, in these criticisms.[44]

Instead, at both the state and local levels, rank-and-file members of the IAM and local leaders, too, gave increasing evidence of support for the Socialist party. In November 1904 John Collins, of Chicago Unity Lodge 134, and J. E. Carney, of Pawtucket, Rhode Island, were nominated as socialist candidates for the governorship in their respective states. Two years later, in November 1906, Lodge 311 in Los Angeles voted unanimously to support the socialist ticket in the local elections, as it later did in 1911 when Job Harriman ran for mayor of the city. Also in 1906 Manhattan Lodge 402, of New York City, responded to Gompers' call for increased political activity by endorsing Charles Heyde, a member of Lodge 313 who was running for the state assembly on behalf of the socialists. And in the municipal elections of 1911, of the eighteen Socialist party members who were elected to run the city government in Schenectady, New York, no less than half were members of the IAM.[45]

Equally important were the political activities of the machinists in the Midwest. In 1910 Thomas Van Lear, the machinists' leader in Minneapolis, made the first of several attempts to win the mayoralty of that city for the socialists, with machinists providing "the backbone of the campaign." (He was to be successful in 1916.) And in Milwaukee machinists made a major contribution to the Socialist party's efforts. In November 1904 William J. Allridge, past president of Lodge 200, was elected to the Wisconsin state assembly on the socialist ticket. In May 1906 Max Grass, H. W. Grant, and Gustave Geerdts, of Lodge 66, were elected aldermen. And in the April 1910 municipal elections, at which Emil Seidel was elected mayor, four of the twenty-one successful socialist candidates elected to municipal office were members of the IAM.

It is not without significance that most of this political activity took place at the municipal level, where the moderate, reformist elements in American socialism enjoyed their greatest influence. Commenting on the 1910 victories in Milwaukee, Douglas Wilson, who had admired the municipal "gas and water" socialism which developed earlier in England, noted characteristically that

> although these men have been elected upon a strictly socialistic platform, nothing approaching a social revolution need be feared, neither will there be any free-love nonsense or the dividing up of property. Nothing but an ambitious desire to do the things that ought to be done in the proper administration of the cities' affairs with honesty and fairness towards all.[46]

By 1910 all these various developments—employer hostility, rising sentiment for industrial unionism, and the growth of strong socialist political sentiments—combined to make President O'Connell's position in the union increasingly difficult. In 1907 the National Metal Trades Association had begun using yellow-dog contracts to prevent the unionization of machine shops, and the railroads had an effective black-listing apparatus. The union's treasury was low, necessitating further increases in dues and highly unpopular special assessments: in 1909 an assessment of one day's pay for each of the following three years was voted, over considerable opposition. Union membership also remained static at about 50,000 members, another issue exploited by the socialists.[47]

More important was the decision, taken at the 1905 IAM convention, that all union officers, save for the assistant general-secretary, were to be elected by referendum vote, a development which O'Connell denounced as an example of "referendum madness." This change deprived him of the convention as a forum for justifying his policies. Even more significant, it exposed him for the first time to the judgment of the IAM rank and file. In the 1907 and 1909 elections he was reelected to the presidency, although by reduced margins. But in a hotly fought election two years later, in July 1911, in which allegations of cheating were made on both sides, he was defeated for reelection by the socialist William H. Johnston, of Providence, Rhode Island. The count was 15,300 votes to 13,321. No vote of thanks or gift was tendered to O'Connell, despite his long tenure of the presidency. He left office a bitter and disappointed man.[48]

III

William H. Johnston took office as president of the IAM in January 1912 and remained in the position until he resigned because of ill-health in 1926. His election was not, of course, simply and solely a victory for the socialists or for socialism. He and those who supported him for election campaigned on O'Connell's widespread unpopularity and on the administrative and trade-union problems which he had been unable to solve, as well as their own ideological differences with the philosophy of trade-unionism which O'Connell represented. Nor, although the 1912 victory did bring what had earlier been the opposition party to power in the union, were all those who formed the Johnston administration socialists. Several vice-presidents and members of the General Executive Board who had supported O'Connell in the previous administration remained in office; and at least one prominent socialist who had earlier helped to lead the socialist insurgency, General Secretary-Treasurer George Preston, opposed Johnston's election.[49] Nevertheless, his victory was hailed as a matter for congratulations by the Socialist party, which looked forward to continued and increasing support from the IAM.

Johnston himself came from the same sort of mold as the other British and native-born radicals in the union. Born in Nova Scotia in 1874, he was the son of a Scottish shipwright who had helped to build transatlantic tea clippers in the earlier part of the century. Johnston the younger was apprenticed to the Rhode Island Locomotive Works in Providence at the age of fourteen, then worked at various jobs both as a railroad and contract machinist before joining the union in 1895. Soon afterward he became president of Lodge 147, in Providence, and in 1905 was elected head of District 19, which included most of the lodges in New England. In 1909 he took on the even larger responsibility of running District 44, which comprised all the machinists in government employ, most of whom were on the east coast. In 1909 and 1910 he frequently urged marine and other government machinists to lobby for legislation to improve the federal eight-hour law. Even before this, however, there was evidence of more radical convictions. In 1907 he ran on the Socialist party ticket for governor of Rhode Island.[50]

In its early years the Johnston administration certainly gave promise of acting in a much more radical manner than the O'Connell administration which preceded it. In its relations with the AFL, for example, the IAM now became much more critical than it had been under O'Connell. This was partly because of a number of jurisdictional disputes with other unions—notably with the United Brotherhood of Carpenters and Joiners over the millwrights—which became quite serious during Johnston's period of office. And it was partly because of the continuing influence of O'Connell in the AFL, even though he was no longer president of the union. O'Connell remained head of the Metal Trades Department and second vice-president of the AFL until 1918, a fact which was strongly resented by the socialists in the IAM, who felt that Johnston should have been elected in his place. In 1912 the socialists at the AFL convention made a determined effort to have Johnston replace O'Connell as a member of the Executive Council, but to no avail.[51]

But the more hostile attitude toward the AFL was also due, predictably, to the fact that the leading members of the Johnston administration disagreed with the conservative ideological position of the AFL and sought to change it. At the AFL convention of 1915, for example, Thomas Van Lear, of Minneapolis (to be elected socialist mayor of that city the following year), introduced a resolution on behalf of the IAM delegation attacking the AFL's voluntarist attitude toward social legislation and urging it to secure the eight-hour day by political means rather than by relying on economic action alone. This resolution was defeated, although only by the narrow margin of 8,500 to 6,396 votes. But afterward Fred Hewitt, who had succeeded Douglas Wilson as editor of the *Machinists' Monthly Journal* earlier in the year, engaged in a verbal battle with Gompers over the whole issue of labor's political position.[52]

On matters of internal union policy, however, the Johnston administration turned out to be more moderate than might have been supposed. On the question of union finances, for example, in opposition Johnston had been critical of O'Connell's efforts to raise the union's dues—although not so critical as the impossibilists in some other radical trade-unions—arguing that it was more important to increase membership than to develop a large treasury. And in the election campaign of 1911 he had pledged himself against special assessments and higher per capita taxes. But when he became president he found the union's treasury empty; and within four months he was obliged to secure additional funds, first in the form of voluntary contributions, and then, when that proved insufficient, in the form of special assessments and higher dues.

Similarly, on the issue of union democracy and popular control, the socialists found that decentralization and local responsibility, which they had earlier supported, were impracticable in an organization operating in a competitive national market, as the IAM now did. In 1912 and 1914 the grand lodge increased its control over the financial affairs of local lodges. At the 1916 convention it was decided, on the initiative of the administration, to have regular quadrennial conventions instead of irregular ones called by referendum. The convention also agreed that officers should be elected for a four-year rather than a two-year term. And in 1920 the number of vice-presidents, who were largely under the president's control, was increased to ten.[53]

These issues had little dramatic appeal in the IAM, and they did not occupy the attention of more than a small proportion of the membership. Much more important was the attitude of the Johnston administration toward industrial unionism and political action, on both of which Johnston had publicly committed himself to a radical position before he was elected to office. First, as to industrial unionism. Despite the difficulties of securing industry-wide organization in either the railroads or the metal trades, the new administration was hailed as the champion of industrial unionism, and much was expected of it. At a conference of officers and business agents held in St. Louis in March 1914 it was authorized to approach the other unions in the Metal Trades Department of the AFL—which included the Boilermakers, Blacksmiths, Steam Fitters, Sheet Metal Workers, as well as several other unions—with a view to working out a plan for amalgamating them into a single industrial union.

This decision was later confirmed by referendum vote, and at the subsequent meeting of the Department in November 1914 the IAM's representatives put forward a resolution proposing consolidation of all the metal trades into a single organization. The resolution was defeated by a large majority, as was a similar proposal put forward by the IAM in 1915. In his public speeches and at conventions, Johnston maintained an officially favorable position toward amalgamation. But privately he acknowledged that since the other unions in the Metal Trades Department of the AFL were almost wholly opposed to the idea, genuine amalgamation of the metal unions was next to impossible. In a private circular sent to the other members of the General Executive Board in November 1915, Johnston pointed out that amalgamation was impracticable and would, moreover, "cause unlimited [jurisdictional] trouble." [54]

On the railroads it seemed at first as though greater progress could be made. In 1911, on the initiative of the socialists and against the advice of President O'Connell, joint committees of machinists, railway carmen, boilermakers, and other metal workers employed on the railroads (known as shop craft federations) had been established to coordinate the activities of their respective unions in negotiations with the railroad corporations. In 1912 the Federation of Federations was organized, providing for still further cooperation. None of this meant amalgamation, or industrial unionism in the sense of establishment of a single organization, and little attempt was made to secure the cooperation of the railroad brotherhoods, as, for example, the IWW was quick to point out.[55] Nevertheless, the Federation of Federations did represent somewhat of an advance.

Unfortunately, however, the IAM's relations with the Federation were strained by a prolonged strike involving the IAM and several other railroad shop craft unions, beginning in 1911, which took place on the Illinois Central and Harriman railroad lines. The Johnston administration at first enthusiastically supported the strike, and Johnston personally was eager to see it succeed in order to prove his commitment to industrial unionism.[56] But the payment of strike benefits proved costly, and since neither of the railroads ceased operating, it soon became clear that it was unlikely to be won. In December 1914 Johnston reported that the IAM's treasury was exhausted—it had paid out $700,000 in support of the strike—and that he was obliged to cease paying benefits. The machinists still participating in the strike voted to continue the stoppage, but in June 1915 the administration ended the union's official participation.[57]

An outcry immediately ensued, both among those who felt that Johnston had condemned members of the IAM unjustly to defeat, and also among those socialists who regarded the decision as an abandonment of the principle of industrial solidarity. Disquiet had already been expressed by the more radical element over Johnston's apparent unwillingness to press harder for amalgamation in the metal trades,[58] and his decision on the Harriman strike was strongly criticized, both inside the IAM and without. A circular was issued by a number of radical California lodges condemning Johnston and the General Executive Board as "traitors to the cause," and a resolution was adopted at the 1916 convention urging the administration to implement its 1911 promises on industrial unionism "if our Executive body are sincere in the wishes they at that time expressed." However, the strike was lost, and little further progress was made in cooperation with the railroad unions.[59]

Thus, on the issue of industrial unionism, as on those of union financing and popular control, the Johnston administration found itself obliged to behave in a much less radical manner than had originally been expected. To some extent this was due to circumstances beyond the union's control —continued employer hostility, for example, or the conservatism of many of the AFL unions with which it had to deal. And to some extent it reflected the inevitable compromises of any radical group when faced with the responsibility of power, unless it is determined upon revolution at all costs. Nevertheless, it also indicated the beginnings of a more general shift in the union's ideological position away from its earlier radicalism toward a more conservative union philosophy.

This is borne out when one examines the IAM's attitude toward politics in the years between 1912 and 1916. The socialists in the union had never distinguished as clearly as their more radical colleagues did between political action based on an exclusively workingmen's political party and effective lobbying for labor legislation within the existing political framework. Johnston himself, as we noted earlier, had run for the governorship of Rhode Island on the Socialist party ticket in 1907, while at the same time urging federally employed machinists to lobby in Congress for amendments to the eight-hour law. Nevertheless, in the campaign circulars before he was elected to office Johnston had openly condemned the "unholy alliance" which he claimed O'Connell had attempted to establish between the union and the Democratic party, and he urged the "heartiest cooperation between the trade unions and the working class political movement." As we have seen, before 1912 many local leaders and rank-and-file members had committed themselves openly to the Socialist party in New York, Wisconsin, California, and elsewhere, and now that the socialists were in control at the national level they expected it to support the party nationally also.

To some extent this did occur. No union convention was held in 1912, so the Socialist party could not be directly endorsed in the elections of that year. But the *Machinists' Monthly Journal* attacked both the Republican and the Democratic platforms for representing the "interests of special privilege"; and it indirectly urged union members to vote for Debs as well as local socialist candidates throughout the country. Numerous letters were received supporting this position, including one from the old southern bastion of the union, Atlanta, where the local business agent predicted "the largest socialist vote that has ever been cast in this part of the country."

Nor, evidently, was the IAM seduced to any great extent by Theodore Roosevelt's Progressive party, even though its moderate radicalism appeared likely to attract some of the urban, native-born members of the IAM. A Denver machinist named Evans was prevailed upon to run for the Colorado legislature on the Bull Moose ticket. But the union journal officially disapproved of Roosevelt, and a socialist leader in Chicago, H. J. Molley, urged members not to be "fooled" into voting for him. When the election was over, editor Douglas Wilson gave widespread publicity to the increased socialist vote and invited Debs to contribute a series of articles on socialism to the union paper.[60]

Despite all this, there was suspiciously little evidence of socialist activity by IAM members in the 1912 elections as such, and almost immediately after the Woodrow Wilson administration had taken office in 1913 there were signs that the attitude of the administration, at least, had begun to change. Numerous local union leaders, urged on by the Johnston administration, participated in the lobbying campaign conducted by the AFL on behalf of an anti-injunction law, and when the Clayton Act was finally passed and signed into law in 1914 *Journal* editor Douglas Wilson indicated clearly the dilemma into which many union members had been put by the reforming zeal of the Democratic administration. As a socialist, he maintained that labor's friends in Congress and in the Democratic administration could never be properly trusted and that the election of a large block of workingmen to political office was the only really effective way of securing labor legislation. It was extremely difficult, he argued, "to make the representatives of another class know what the working class really wants."

But as a pragmatist Wilson was forced to acknowledge that it was the lobbying pressures exerted by the AFL, the railroad brotherhoods, and the IAM itself which had been primarily responsible for securing the passage of the Clayton Act, and not the activities of the Socialist party. He pointed out that these two approaches were not necessarily mutually exclusive; but he also realized that once pressure-group tactics proved to be widely successful, it would be increasingly difficult to prevail upon trade-unionists to vote for the Socialist party.[61]

As time went on, it became increasingly clear that the machinists had benefited from the reforming legislation passed by the first Woodrow Wilson administration as much as, if not more than, any other labor organization. Besides the Clayton Act, which brought hopes of an end to the use of injunctions in railroad labor disputes (which had again been used in the Harriman strike of 1911–1915), the union derived especial benefit from the La Follette Seamen's Act, which improved conditions for marine engineers, the Locomotive Boiler Inspection Act, which promoted the safety of machinists working in railroad shops, and the addition of the Taverner amendment to a federal appropriation bill, prohibiting the use of time and motion studies in military and naval establishments. The latter was a direct result of lobbying on the part of the union. In addition, the union expressed gratitude to President Wilson and to Congress for promoting the eight-hour day on the railroads, which was incorporated into the Adamson Act of 1916.

As a result, when the 1916 elections came around the Johnston administration shifted perceptibly away from the radical position which it had adopted in 1912. There was little discussion of politics at the June 1916 convention, but in October the new editor of the union journal, Fred Hewitt, came near to endorsing Woodrow Wilson for reelection. He urged members to vote socialist where they thought it would be beneficial, but he added, in a highly significant editorial, that the Democrats had already implemented many of the Socialist party's most important immediate demands. "The time may come in this country when organized labor will have a party of its own," he concluded, "but until then labor will lend its sympathy to those in sympathy with its aims and objects." [62]

This change in emphasis on the part of the IAM leadership was paralleled by a comparable shift in the political outlook of part, at least, of the union's rank and file. It is not possible, of course, to ascertain with any degree of certainty just how union members voted. But there was a marked decline in the number of reports of machinists' participation in local Socialist party activities between 1913 and 1916, save to some extent in California and in Minneapolis, where Thomas Van Lear was elected socialist mayor in the latter year. Some socialist members objected to Hewitt's *Journal* editorial of October 1916—notably John M. Work, of Milwaukee, who argued that the Clayton Act was not due to labor's lobbying tactics, but to the fact that Congress was frightened by the prospect of a revolt among the working class. But the more conservative approach of the administration appeared to be greeted more with approbation than with dismay. In June 1916 a circular was dispatched throughout the membership from Lodge 211 of Chicago endorsing the administration's general political position, and although a second circular was sent criticizing its policies as insufficiently radical, the former received the majority of endorsements. J. J. Fox, of Oakland, California, went so far as to plead for a return to the "sound reasoning and successful methods employed by the worthy founder and pioneers of our organization." Those men, he said, had been imbued with a spirit "not of class hatred, but rather of determination to establish a more harmonious relationship between employer and employee." [63]

IV

Thus, already before World War I there were signs of a marked falling off in the radical zeal which had characterized the Johnston administration when it first came into office in 1912. Besides the reasons for this which have already been examined, the administration was impelled to further caution by its lack of adequate union funds and by a number of internal disputes which occurred at this time, notably over the recall from office by referendum vote of Secretary-Treasurer George Preston in 1916. Also in 1918 Peter J. Conlon, who with Preston had been one of the strongest early supporters of socialism in the union, was defeated in the union election. Johnston did not handle these internal disputes well. He made little attempt to conciliate the conservative elements which had opposed his initial election to the presidency, and he was now increasingly criticized by some of the more radical socialists on the left wing of the union also, who were disillusioned by his handling of the Harriman strike, by his change of tactics over union finances and popular government, and by his apparent inability to make progress on the question of industrial unionism. In fact, instead of broadening the base of his support in the union, Johnston had diminished it, and this was to be of crucial importance when the opposing faction increased its influence still further in the period following World War I.

However, the Johnston administration's difficulties were alleviated, temporarily at least, by the expansion which took place during the war. Both the prewar sale of arms to Great Britain and France, and American participation in the war itself, greatly expanded the number of machinists employed in the armaments industry and brought indirect benefits to machinists employed in other industries as well. In 1917 the eight-hour day was finally secured in a majority of shops and factories, the union was recognized by a large number of new employers, and membership rose by more than 25 per cent. Then 1918 saw even greater gains. In some cases wages rose by nearly 50 per cent, and total membership by the early part of 1919 was 331,449.[64]

Given the moderation and largely native-born composition of the IAM and its intimate involvement with the armaments industry, there was no question of its support for American involvement in the war itself. When the war broke out in Europe there were expressions of shocked surprise by a number of influential union figures, and the *Machinists' Monthly Journal* permitted a number of articles by Debs explaining the socialist position on the conflict. Two or three German lodges criticized America's predisposition in favor of the Allies, but ethnically speaking the Anglo-Saxon origins of many of the members carried far more weight. In April 1915 an English-born correspondent to the *Journal* defended Great Britain's war aims and took the Socialist party to task for opposing the war without distinguishing between the two sides. The 1916 union convention adopted a resolution upholding preparedness, and when America entered the war there was no doubt where the great majority of union members stood. President Johnston led a full IAM delegation to the AFL conference of March 1917 to pledge the union's support for the war, and later in the year the *Journal* gave full publicity to the patriotic declarations of the prowar American Alliance for Labor and Democracy, including, significantly enough, its denunciations of the antiwar stand of the Socialist party.[65]

Thus wartime prosperity, federal aid in securing union recognition, and a largely unquestioning loyalty to the American cause widened the gap between the IAM and the Socialist party, as it did in other trade-unions. In fact, the traditional zeal of the machinists for democracy, and their moralistic attitude toward political action generally, gave President Wilson's war aims a greater attraction to many members of the union than they had in unions with no particular radical tradition.

Even more important than this in affecting the machinists' political outlook was President Wilson's decision in December 1917 to take into public control all United States railroads, on which a considerable proportion of the union's membership was still employed. This not only gave the union an additional reason for gratitude toward the Democratic administration. It also implemented its most cherished political demand. Ever since the 1890's the IAM had advocated public ownership of the railroads, and this desire had, if anything, been increased by the failure of the Harriman strike and by the failure of the union's efforts to establish some form of large-scale industrial organization capable of combating the great economic power of the railroad corporations.

Earlier, while the hope of railroad nationalization remained largely academic, the union had maintained that the only way of gaining public control of the railroads was to elect enough trade-unionists and socialists to Congress to bring this about. In 1912, for example, it had supported Victor Berger's bill in Congress to nationalize railroads, telephones, and telegraph properties while at the same time asserting that the bill could never be passed until Congress "has a majority of workingmen in it." But now, even though federal control did not mean public ownership and was intended only for the duration of the war, the best way of maintaining it seemed clearly to be the exerting of political pressure on the Democratic administration and on favorably disposed congressmen of both political parties rather than using the union's political influence in support of third-party political action. "To our members employed on the railroads," a *Journal* editorial wrote in February 1918, "we say, 'Do your bit.' By doing so you will help win the war and also accomplish that which we advocate in our Platform, 'Public ownership of all public utilities.' " [66]

Thus, for the next two years the IAM devoted its main political efforts to securing the permanent, full-scale nationalization of the nation's railroads or, failing that, the maintenance of federal control. Significantly, however, it appeared to confine itself wholly to pressure-group tactics, and there is little evidence to suggest that it sought to make use of the Socialist party or of any other radical third party in its activities. In March 1918 the officers of the union, together with those of the railroad brotherhoods and two or three other unions, issued an appeal to the members of both parties in Congress not to fix a time limit for the return of the railroads to private control. In February 1919 a union delegation appeared before the Senate committee conducting hearings on the disposition of the railroads, and over a hundred lodges sent communications to their respective congressmen and senators opposing the end of public control. The union took a leading part—with the railroad brotherhoods and ten other unions—in drawing up the Plumb Plan for nationalizing the railroads, which was introduced into Congress in July 1919. And President Johnston and other officers of the union lobbied intensively in Washington for the passage of the bill.

Their efforts failed, however. In March 1920 the railroads were returned to private ownership under the Esch-Cummins Act, and the period of federal control was brought to an end. Politically speaking, this put the IAM in a quandary. Johnston and his supporters were determined to do all they could to restore the railroads to public control, but neither support for the Democratic administration—to which the union had in effect been openly committed throughout the war—nor the lobbying tactics which it had employed in 1918 and 1919 had brought the success which it wanted.

For a time it seemed as though the union would confine itself to the AFL's political methods in order to get the Esch-Cummins Law reversed. In June 1920 the IAM's delegation to the AFL convention was influential in securing the passage of a resolution favoring government ownership of the railroads (the first time the AFL had agreed to this). And in the fall elections of that year Johnston cooperated with the other railroad unions in establishing a campaign committee which gave its full support to the "reward your friends, punish your enemies" policy followed by the National Non-Partisan Committee of the AFL. But when President Harding and an overwhelmingly antilabor Congress were elected, Lawrence Todd, leader of the influential District 15 of New York, declared that the AFL's tactics had elected "the most reactionary set of men who have sought election or appointment in this republic since Grant's day." And President Johnston himself, reacting angrily to the election results, called upon the representatives of organized labor to hold a conference to establish a national labor party to fight the congressional elections of 1922.[67]

There were other, more familiar, causes of the IAM's resurgent radicalism. The sudden termination of war orders threw a considerable number of union members out of work, exacerbating the effects of the immediate postwar depression, and the employers revived their open-shop campaign of prewar years, pressing hard for company unionism and the American Plan. In addition, although the IAM had no sympathy for the extreme left and later on became strongly anti-Communist, the progressive elements in the union were shocked by the excesses of the 1919 Red Scare and showed considerable sympathy for the aims and purposes of the Russian Revolution. The September 1920 union convention authorized President Johnston and the attorney of the union, Frank L. Mulholland, to visit Soviet Russia in order to seek out contracts for the export of machinery, despite an official American embargo on trade. Although they were unable to secure entrance to Russia itself, Johnston and Mulholland did visit Europe, and in a report on their trip they expressed "great sympathy for Russia and her people in this period of struggle for something better than the absolute despotism of the Tsarist regime." [68]

There was also continued resentment at the position of the IAM in the AFL. Although it was now one of the largest unions in the AFL, the union still had no direct representative on the Executive Council, and its position became even more isolated when O'Connell's term as second vice-president ended in 1918. With O'Connell's departure there were high hopes that Johnston would replace him on the Executive Council. However, at the June 1920 convention of the AFL Johnston was defeated for seventh vice-president by the narrow margin of 19,929 to 18,125 votes, and the September convention of the IAM was so incensed at this defeat that it adopted a resolution favoring the referendum election of all AFL officers. The 1921 AFL convention rejected this proposal, and the union's delegation cast its entire vote against Gompers and in favor of John L. Lewis.[69]

Predictably, also, the IAM took a strong interest in the amalgamation movement which developed among industrial unionists in the AFL after World War I. As we have seen, the Johnston administration had been unable to make much progress on this issue in the prewar period. After the war, however, it took up the issue once more. At the June 1921 convention of the Metal Trades Department of the AFL the machinists' delegation again introduced a resolution favoring the closer affiliation or outright amalgamation of the metal-trades organizations. The resolution was defeated, and the editor of the *Machinists' Monthly Journal* took strong exception to allegations made by other delegations that the IAM secretly favored the IWW and the advocates of One Big Union. In fact, this was a long way from the truth. In 1919 in Philadelphia, and in 1920 in Detroit, Johnston successfully brought charges of dual unionism against these factions, and at two separate conferences of officers, organizers, and business agents held in Kansas and in Washington, D.C., in December 1920, a campaign was agreed upon to eliminate IWW elements from the union.[70]

It seemed, therefore, as though the IAM would be in a better position than almost any other labor organization to take the initiative in the movement for a postwar political labor party. It had a strong radical tradition which had been enhanced, if anything, by its disillusionment with the major parties after the end of World War I, and its desire for the nationalization of the railroads gave it a strong independent motive for political involvement. Moreover, its traditional moderation meant that it was not divided, as the ILGWU had been, by doubts over whether to continue supporting the Socialist party alone, while its strategic position in the labor movement—with one foot in the independent railroad unions and the other in the radical and dissatisfied wing of the AFL—made it acceptable to a wide variety of opinion.[71]

There were certainly signs, in the immediate postwar period, that the union might play this role. Although no official delegation was sent from the IAM, more than thirty lodges from all over the country sent representatives to the National Labor party convention which met in Chicago in November 1919. A similar number, led by Thomas Van Lear, of Minneapolis, attended the July 1920 convention of the National Farmer-Labor party. Numerous local lodges passed resolutions in favor of a labor party in 1921 and 1922; Lodge 78 of Cleveland, Ohio, for example, asserting in December 1921 that the establishment of a broadly based national labor party was the only effective way of opposing the businessmen and reactionaries who had taken over in the 1920 elections.[72]

Equally important was the fact that President Johnston himself at first appeared to favor the establishment of an independent political party. Although he did not act immediately on the suggestion which he himself made after the elections of 1920, in 1921 he worked hard to broaden the political activities of both the railroad unions and the AFL,[73] and he was head of the committee of railroad organizations which issued the call for the first conference of the Conference for Progressive Political Action which met in Chicago on February 21–22, 1922. At that conference he also was elected chairman of the Committee of Fifteen, which subsequently directed the efforts of the CPPA, and its main office was established in the union's headquarters in Washington, D.C. The important point, however, was that although this first convention of the CPPA disavowed the establishment of a third party and committed itself instead to campaigning on behalf of liberal candidates in both major parties, Johnston himself, in an April 1922 circular to the union membership which he attached to his report on the CPPA founding convention, expressed the hope that the movement could "ultimately result in the creation of a new party, . . . in the workers marshalling their forces on the political field of action under a common banner for the purpose of electing their own representatives to our legislative bodies." [74]

In the event, however, the advocates of third-party action in the IAM were to be disappointed. This was primarily because it soon became apparent that the return of the railroads to public control, which was the major reason why the union had become involved in the CPPA, was more likely to be achieved by securing the political support of congressmen from both major parties who had voted against the Esch-Cummins Act of 1920 than it was by attempting to turn the CPPA into a new political party. In addition, the railroad brotherhoods, which were influential in the CPPA and were the major allies of the IAM in seeking public control over the railroads, were conservative in their general outlook and had no interest in the establishment of a permanent labor party. Finally, the IAM itself, although one of the largest unions to support the CPPA, was well aware that it needed other allies besides the railroad unions in its campaign for railroad nationalization and feared to alienate other trade-unions by pressing too hard on the third-party issue.

Thus, in the congressional elections of November 1922, despite what Johnston had said in the previous April, the IAM went no further than to distribute to its lodges a detailed list of CPPA-endorsed candidates for election, pointing out especially the voting record of each congressman on the Esch-Cummins Act. The results of this election appeared to confirm the effectiveness of the nonpartisan approach. According to an estimate by *Labor,* the official organ of the railroad organizations, 21 senators friendly to the repeal of the Esch-Cummins Act were elected in the 1922 elections and 169 members of the House. Thus, at the crucial second national convention of the CPPA, held on December 11–12, 1922, the IAM delegation voted against the resolution to launch a third political party, on the ground that this would "destroy its effectiveness" in Congress, lessen its influence among liberal voters generally, and create serious dissension in the CPPA itself. After the conference was over, Andrew T. McNamara, of Pittsburgh, an influential local Machinists' leader, wrote: "Although I advocate a Labor party and had hoped such a party would emanate from the convention of the conference, I have to admit that the non-partisan plan does bring results." [75]

Whatever continuing support there was for third-party action in the IAM received an additional setback from the further decline, and then the virtual collapse, of the Johnston administration's electoral support throughout the union as a whole. As we have seen, the prosperity of World War I and the growth of union membership had temporarily concealed the administration's internal difficulties. But with the postwar depression and the return of employer hostility they had again come increasingly to the fore. In January 1922 the union lost a bitter two-year-long strike against the American Can Company, for which the Johnston administration was widely blamed. Partly as a result of this, Johnston's own majority in the June 1922 union elections fell by a substantial amount—the General Executive Board becoming anti-Johnston by a bare majority—and the left-wing critics of the administration, including the small Communist element in the union, voted against him.[76]

Johnston's personal position was still further undermined by the disastrous defeat of the nationwide railroad shop craft-union strike (not unlike the prewar Harriman strike, but on a much larger scale), which lasted from July 1922 to 1924 and in which the machinists were extensively involved. During this strike Attorney-General Daugherty secured a sweeping injunction against the strikers, and Johnston, realizing that he could not possibly win, negotiated a separate agreement with the Baltimore and Ohio Railroad, known as the B&O Shop Plan. For this he was sharply criticized in a manner which recalled the attack on O'Connell after the failure of the 1901 strike, and in the June 1924 elections his administration came near to total defeat. J. F. Anderson, Johnston's opponent for the presidency, attacked the administration on a wide variety of issues, pointing to the precipitous decline in membership which had taken place since the war— from 288,857 in 1921 to 111,677 in 1924—and criticizing by implication Johnston's extensive activity on behalf of the CPPA. "Men devoting too much time to . . . extraneous activities," he said—including in his remarks the recent acquisition of a cooperative machine shop and part ownership in a savings bank, in both of which the administration took part— "lose the common touch." The Communists again voted against Johnston,[77] and although he won by the narrow margin of 18,021 votes to 17,076, there were widespread charges of fraud. J. F. Anderson, in a pamphlet entitled *The Story of the Big Steal,* alleged that Johnston and his supporters had rigged the election; and although Johnston remained in office, the acrimony which the conflict engendered destroyed much of his remaining influence in the union, among friend and foe alike.[78]

In view of these circumstances, it was not surprising that neither Johnston nor his remaining supporters on the General Executive Board (including Peter J. Conlon, who had been reelected first vice-president in 1921 and who headed the CPPA organization in Virginia) felt willing to commit the IAM to any renewed campaign for independent political activity. In 1924 there appears to have been a falling off, also, in rank-and-file support for the CPPA. Whereas in 1922 and 1923 union members, with help from the administration, had given over $2,000 to the CPPA, an appeal issued by Johnston for financial contributions to the organization's funds early in 1924 yielded only the insignificant sum of $193. Interestingly enough, this money came largely from the smaller lodges in the Midwest, and also in the South, where radicalism in the IAM had first developed.

In the early part of 1924 President Johnston maintained to the full his own activities on behalf of the CPPA. But when he came to deliver his chairman's keynote speech at the July 4 nominating convention of the organization, even though it was only nominating Robert M. La Follette and Burton K. Wheeler on a separate presidential ticket, he came down firmly against transforming the CPPA into a new political party. At the second national convention of the CPPA (which had defeated the third-party resolution by 64 votes to 52), he said, there had been numerous advocates of third-party action. But "time and results have proved the wisdom of . . . [that] decision." "There is no obstacle to prevent our supporting independent candidates for President and Vice President," he went on, "while we are engaged in reelecting our Progressive friends to Congress, regardless of the party ticket upon which they may appear. They may be Democrats, Republicans, Socialists or Farm-Laborites. We do not care." In effect, the only difference between this statement and that of any AFL statement on political action was the willingness to endorse socialists for office.

Privately, or semiprivately, at the subsequent IAM convention in September 1924, Johnston acknowledged that there might still be a case for a labor party on the British model at some future date in the United States. But he asserted that the CPPA had, by its nonpartisan methods, already "accomplished more . . . than all of the third parties combined," and he insisted that the organization stick to its established tactics through the elections of 1924. Various voices were raised against the policy from some of the old socialist lodges in the union—from St. Paul, Chicago, and Los Angeles, and even from Johnston's old local in Providence, Rhode Island. Despite this, however, support for the CPPA's general nonpartisan strategy in the campaign was endorsed by a simple voice vote.[79]

It is difficult to assess fully the impact of the defeat of the La Follette candidacy on the IAM in November 1924, just as it was in the case of the ILGWU. In December the *Machinists' Monthly Journal* expressed strong disappointment at the failure of the Progressive ticket to do better and mentioned vague hopes that the CPPA might be kept going, although it did not propose that it be transformed into a new political party. But there was remarkably little reaction from the membership as a whole. The political mood of the labor movement, and of the country at large, had by now changed so much that the idea of independent political action, and even of returning the railroads to public control, seemed hopelessly utopian. Johnston personally—and in some ways paradoxically, in view of his earlier statements—kept alive the hope of a third political party, and he attended the February 1925 rump convention of the CPPA as an advocate of the idea. Later he was for a short time president of the tiny Progressive party which was established there. But by this time he was virtually isolated in the IAM hierarchy, and the General Executive Board specifically enjoined him from representing the union as such, a decision which was reflected in his speeches at the 1925 meetings. In his main address to the convention, for example, he said: "As president of one of the labor unions, and as one who believes in a new alignment, I could not speak for my organization as such." [80]

The end came for the Johnston administration, and with it the period of radical or socialist control in the IAM, somewhat fortuitously. In September 1925 Johnston suffered a stroke, and in May 1926 he resigned the presidency. Even had he not done so, however, his defeat or removal was almost certainly a matter of time. The General Executive Board appointed Arthur O. Wharton to fill out Johnston's unexpired term, and in 1927 he was elected president without opposition. Wharton was President of the AFL Railroad Department and a moderate conservative in the mold of J. F. Anderson and, before him, James O'Connell. "If we are wise," he wrote in his introductory circular to the membership in July 1926, "we will be less visionary and more practical by concentrating our efforts in the direction of securing immediate and material benefits." We should insist, he went on, appealing to the older and more conservative craft-oriented members, "that the members of our Association shall perform the work of our craft, whether it be in the manufacture, erection, installation or maintenance thereof." He concluded his circular with these words: "To reduce strikes to a minimum, to establish cooperative relations with every employer who is willing to recognize our Association and establish mutually satisfactory contractual relations." Conservative policies on these lines were to dominate the IAM for the next ten years. [81]

V

Socialist influence in the International Association of Machinists developed out of what appeared at first to be a most unlikely context: the socially conservative and industrially backward South. Thus it was not dependent on the presence of an unassimilated generation of European radicals, as in the case of the Brewery Workers Union, or to a considerable extent in the case of the ILGWU. Immigrants from Great Britain and Ireland helped found the union, and English influence persisted in the organization for some time, manifested in admiration for the British Labor party. But there were signs of prejudice against more recent immigrant groups—as well, of course, as against Negroes—and it is unlikely that foreign influence determined the machinists' radicalism to more than a very limited extent. Instead, this grew essentially out of the conditions and consequences of American industrialization.

Of these consequences the most important was the steady erosion of the machinist's traditional skill, undermining the independence and the status of the artisan and reducing him, within the space of a generation, to little better than a factory hand. After 1890 few machinists could establish themselves in a machine shop of their own, as Thomas W. Talbot had done in the 1860's.[82] This technological revolution was similar to that which took place in other industries. As in the case of the shoe industry, however, its consequences for the machinists were especially severe. It also occurred somewhat later and lasted somewhat longer than in other industries, which may well have had an effect in prolonging the period of radical discontent among the machinists until World War I and beyond.

Moreover, whereas in the shoe industry the technological revolution was exploited in our period primarily by the extremist DeLeonites of the SLP, in the IAM it generated a variety of radical movements: Populism, industrial unionism, and moderate reformist socialism, in part because of the union's ethnic and geographical characteristics, and in part because of its dissatisfaction with the craft-oriented policies of the other trade-unions in the railroad and the metal-trades industries. Paradoxically, the IAM later found itself in political alliance with the conservative railroad brotherhoods, in order to secure public control over the railroads. The limited objectives of these unions, and the generally conservative attitude toward politics and toward the industrial unionism of most of the other unions with which the machinists had to deal, were important reasons for the frustration and ultimate failure of its radical policies.

In some ways, however, the third-party orientation of the IAM proved remarkably durable, stimulated as it was by demands for nationalization of the railroads and by the resurgent radicalism of the labor movement after World War I. Interestingly, the war experience as such appeared to have very little influence on the machinists' radicalism, which was at its most characteristic in the postwar movement for a labor party—a movement which was ideologically more suited to the moderate, reformist traditions of the machinists than it was to more revolutionary organizations such as the ILGWU. Yet the wartime assertion of public control over the railroads by the Democratic administration, and the subsequent decision of the Conference for Progressive Political Action to press for its political objectives primarily by nonpartisan means, put the IAM into a dilemma which was not essentially different from that of the Brewery Workers Union when faced by the prospect of Prohibition. Ideologically, probably a majority of the IAM members still favored some form of third-party political action after World War I. Pragmatically, however, when the only available radical coalition of any size, the CPPA, sought to return the railroads to public control by nonpartisan means, it seemed more realistic for the union to exert political pressure in the existing two-party system than to devote its limited resources in an attempt to reestablish a viable third party. As one influential union official put it in April 1920: "If we are to obtain beneficial legislation we must play the game with the old two parties, using one against the other." [83]

There were other, earlier, causes of the decline of socialism in the IAM. The reforms enacted by the first Woodrow Wilson administration between 1913 and 1916 undoubtedly undermined the union's predisposition in favor of the Socialist party. In fact, the IAM provides the best evidence of this phenomenon of all the unions examined in this book. Moderate reform socialists of the type which led the organization were never very far away from the radical wing of the Democratic party, and although there were some reservations expressed in 1912 about Woodrow Wilson's overly intellectual background, the achievements of the first Democratic administration probably did more than anything else to erode political support for the socialists.

Another cause of decline was the difficulties and disappointments associated with the performance of the Johnston administration. The socialists never succeeded in securing complete control of the IAM as they did in the case of the ILGWU, and Johnston's change of position on dues policy, on centralization, and on other issues disillusioned the extreme left in the union while at the same time reinforcing the conservative elements who eventually returned to power. Many of these problems—the inability to make progress on the question of amalgamation, for example—were not of Johnston's own making, and to some extent they simply represented coming to terms with reality. But they also reflected genuine changes in the administration's ideological position, as well as pointing to the difficulty of attempting radical action in a labor movement dominated by the conservative AFL.

The question of broadening the union membership, axiomatic in socialist doctrine, also raised problems for the socialists in the IAM, as it did elsewhere. It was clear, as O'Connell recognized, that inroads on the machinists' craft made it necessary for bargaining purposes to incorporate some of the machine operatives in the industry—more of them, in practice, than O'Connell was willing to accept. The socialists pressed hard for still further expansion of the membership when in opposition, but since their electoral support in the union came from precisely those skilled machinists whose skill had been undermined, they found it necessary to softpedal this demand when they secured power. Thus the egalitarian assumptions of socialist theory conflicted with their major base of political support in the union, a dilemma which was later exploited by conservatives such as J. F. Anderson and Arthur O. Wharton, Johnston's successor as president.

Closely connected with the issue of expanding the union membership was the question of the ethnic and religious affiliation of the machinists. The limited evidence available here supports the view, with certain important exceptions, that the division between socialists and nonsocialists in the organization was to some extent a division between the southern and midwestern native-born or assimilated radicals and the largely northern, Irish, and Catholic conservatives: a conclusion which certainly challenges the assumption that most of the socialist influence in the American labor movement came from unassimilated European radicals. Yet the evidence must be read with care. Although socialism in the union originated primarily among the Anglo-Saxon machinists in the South and West, an analysis of the lodges who voted for Johnston in 1911 indicates that quite a lot of his support came also from the larger, big-city lodges of the North and East. And it would be unwise to attribute the decline of the Johnston administration simply to an increase in Catholic, Irish sentiment: in 1919, of 1,299 lodge secretaries in the union, more than half still had Anglo-Saxon names.[84] It seems more likely that the more assimilated, or second-generation, Irish in the union, of whom there were quite a number in the early days in the South, as well as elsewhere, reacted to industrialization in a manner which did not necessarily preclude support for socialism, any more than it did in the BSWU. The response of the Anglo-Saxon element, on the other hand, was probably not dictated to any great extent by religious or ethnic affiliations.

At all events, socialist and third-party sentiments displayed considerable strength in the IAM, as they did in the ILGWU, although of a more moderate kind. Had a labor party emerged in America after World War I with any permanent prospect of success, the machinists, like the garment workers, would in all probability have given it their support.

Notes

1. Mark Perlman, *The Machinists: A New Study in American Trade Unionism* (Cambridge, 1961), 3, 33. For other general studies of the International Association of Machinists, see Mark Perlman, *Democracy in the International Association of Machinists* (New York, 1962); *Half a Century with the International Association of Machinists* (Washington: The Union, 1938); and Harold M. Groves, "The Machinist in Industry: A Study of the History and Economics of His Craft" (Ph.D. thesis, University of Wisconsin, 1927). Also useful are J. O. Fagan, *Labor and the Railroads* (Boston, 1909); and Terence V. Powderly, *The Path I Trod* (New York, 1940), for the period before the union was established.

2. In May 1889 the International Association of Machinists had thirty-three lodges, and their secretaries all had English, Irish, or Scottish names save one, who was German. It is worth noting, in particular, that the English played an important role in the machinists' trade. In 1861 the Amalgamated Society of Engineers, one of the oldest of the English craft unions, established branches for its members in the United States, and by 1890, according to one account, nearly one-tenth of all machinists in America were British immigrants. The Amalgamated Society of Engineers was a leading advocate of high benefits and dues, which may have helped to determine the conservatism of the IAM in its early years. Its American branches, numbering about 2,000, merged with the IAM in 1920. See Perlman, *The Machinists*, 3–5; *Proceedings, First Convention of the International Association of Machinists* (Atlanta, 1889), 5; Rowland T. Berthoff, *British Immigrants in Industrial America, 1790–1950* (New York, 1953), 73–74, 89–90, 100; Clifton K. Yearley, *Britons in American Labor: A History of the Influence of the United Kingdom Immigrants in American Labor, 1820–1914* (Baltimore, 1957), 56–57 ff.

3. *Constitution,* International Association of Machinists (1889), 5.

4. *Circular,* International Association of Machinists, September 10, 1888, cited in Perlman, *The Machinists,* 5.

5. Perlman, *The Machinists,* 9–10, 15–17, 33; American Federation of Labor, *American Federation of Labor: History, Encyclopedia and Reference Book* (Washington, 1919), 428–429; Philip Taft, *The A.F. of L. in the Time of Gompers* (New York, 1957), 218–219; Marguerite Green, *The National Civic Federation and the American Labor Movement, 1900–1925* (Washington, 1956), 169n; Samuel Gompers, *Seventy Years of Life and Labor,* 2 vols. (New York, 1925), II, 336–337; *Proceedings, Twelfth Convention of the International Association of Machinists* (St. Louis, 1907), 79–80.

6. For this, see "Gompers and Business Unionism, 1873–90," *Business History Review,* XXVII (September 1954), 249–271; H. M. Gitelman, "Adolph

Strasser and the Origins of Business Unionism," *Labor History*, VI (Winter, 1965), 71–83.

7. Perlman, *The Machinists*, 22–23, 34; Perlman, *Democracy in the International Association of Machinists*, 13–14.

8. *Ibid.*, 14–15; Perlman, *The Machinists*, 152, 158; *Constitution*, International Association of Machinists (1907), 13, 28.

9. *Monthly Journal of the International Association of Machinists*, IV (August 1892), 193; V (October 1893), 376–378; *Constitution*, International Association of Machinists (1899), 34.

10. Perlman, *The Machinists*, 7, 16–17; Taft, *op. cit.*, 308–309; Philip S. Foner, *History of the Labor Movement in the United States*, 4 vols. (New York, 1947–1965), II, 195; Sterling D. Spero and Abram L. Harris, *The Black Worker: The Negro and the Labor Movement* (New York, 1931), 88; American Federation of Labor, *A.F. of L. Year Book* (New York, 1892), 1; *Constitution*, International Machinists' Union (1891), 5–6, 19–20; "Declaration Relative to Political Action adopted by first Annual Convention of the International Machinists' Union in Philadelphia, June 1892" (Thomas J. Morgan Collection, University of Illinois Historical Survey). In several of these accounts the International Association of Machinists is referred to as the National Association of Machinists. It was called this from 1889 to 1891, when it changed its name. The union is called the International Association of Machinists throughout this chapter in order to avoid confusion.

11. Just why this occurred is not altogether clear, especially since the IAM was still largely southern at this time. It may have been the result of a deliberate policy on the part of the IAM, which had been sending organizers into Pennsylvania, New Jersey, and elsewhere in order to forestall the growth of its rival. Or it may have been that since most machinists were native-born Americans or of Anglo-Saxon background, the nonsocialist members of the International Machinists Union found the higher standards, superior benefits, and greater respectability of the International Association of Machinists more congenial than the alien and largely German International Machinists Union. See Perlman, *The Machinists*, 7.

12. Although the AFL had been largely responsible for establishing the International Machinists Union in 1891 and was prepared to defend its jurisdiction up to a point, there is considerable evidence to suggest that it preferred the IAM and that it did not deal fairly with the International Machinists Union. Thomas J. Morgan made just this allegation at the 1893 convention of the AFL. His views may well have been biased since he was a leader of the organization concerned. But there is further evidence also. In May 1895, after the IAM had removed the "white clause" from its national constitution, negotiations were instituted between the two unions for a merger—negotiations in which the International Association of Machinists demanded acceptance by the International Machinists Union of all the remaining provisions in its national constitution including, significantly, its higher qualifications for membership. These terms were unacceptable to the International Machinists Union, but the AFL nevertheless proceeded to charter the IAM irrespective of the fact that the International Machinists Union was already an affiliate and that its policy was to charter only one union in any given trade. Moreover, at the December 1895 AFL convention, O'Connell sponsored the passage of a resolution declaring that no

trade should have dual representation in the AFL, as a result of which the charter of the International Machinists Union was withdrawn. The negotiations for merging the two unions were never, in fact, completed, as stated in the accounts given by Foner and by Spero and Harris. The locals of the International Machinists Union either joined the larger union one by one or lost their separate identity. See Foner, *op. cit.*, II, 348; Spero and Harris, *op. cit.*, 88; *Monthly Journal of the International Association of Machinists*, V (January 1894), 525–527; VII (July 1895), 236; VII (January 1896), 528; John McBride to T. J. Morgan, May 16, 1895 (Letterbooks of Samuel Gompers, AFL-CIO Collection).

13. Perlman *The Machinists*, 17; Taft, *op. cit.*, 309–310; Foner, *op. cit.*, II, 348; Spero and Harris, *op. cit.*, 88.

14. Morgan did not develop any contacts with the national leadership of the International Association of Machinists, and in the next decade (he died in 1912) he wrote only one article in the union's monthly journal. See Yearley, *op. cit.*, 107–123; *Machinists' Monthly Journal*, XXI (January 1909), 117–119; "Autobiographical Notes of Thomas J. Morgan" (Thomas J. Morgan Collection, University of Illinois Historical Survey).

15. *Monthly Journal of the International Association of Machinists*, VIII (April 1896), 125–126; X (December 1898), 719–720; *Proceedings, Seventh Convention of the International Association of Machinists* (Chicago, 1897), 220.

16. Perlman, *The Machinists*, 3; John R. Commons et al., *History of Labor in the United States*, 4 vols. (New York, 1926–1935), II, 6, 56–58, 111–112; *Monthly Journal of the International Association of Machinists*, IV (July 1892), 131–132; IV (September 1892), 221–222; V (September 1893), 301–302.

17. Perlman, *The Machinists*, 8, 36; Foner, *op. cit.*, II, 301; *Constitution, International Association of Machinists* (1897), 9; *Monthly Journal of the International Association of Machinists*, V (September 1893), 330–331.

18. *Ibid.*, V (March 1893), 53–54; *Proceedings, Fifth Convention of the International Association of Machinists* (Indianapolis, 1893), 56.

19. Almont Lindsay, *The Pullman Strike: The Story of a Unique Experiment and of a Great Labor Upheaval* (Chicago, 1942), 107–113; Foner, *op. cit.*, II, 247–278; *Monthly Journal of the International Association of Machinists*, V (November 1893), 428; XXXIV (July 1922), 235; *Proceedings, Sixth Convention of the International Association of Machinists* (Cincinnati, 1895), 6. See also Ray Ginger, *The Bending Cross: A Biography of Eugene Victor Debs* (New Brunswick, 1949), 93–183; Norman Pollack, *The Populist Response to Industrial America, Midwestern Populist Thought* (Cambridge, 1962), 52–57; and Donald L. McMurry, "Federation of the Railroad Brotherhoods, 1889–1894," *Industrial and Labor Relations Review*, VII (October 1953), 73–92.

20. Perlman, *The Machinists*, 17–18; *Monthly Journal of the International Association of Machinists*, VI (November 1894), 423–427; *Proceedings, Sixth Convention of the International Association of Machinists* (Cincinnati, 1895), 2–6.

21. For this account of changes in the machinists' craft, see William H. Buckler, "The Minimum Wage in the Machinists' Union," in Jacob H. Hollander and George E. Barnett (eds.), *Studies in American Trade Unionism* (New York, 1912), 114–116, 136. See also Groves, *op. cit.*, 75–85.

22. For this, see *Nineteenth Annual Report of the Commissioner of Labor* (Washington, 1905), 64, 86.

23. *Monthly Journal of the International Association of Machinists*, X (May 1898), 278. Fifteen years earlier, in 1883, John Morrison, a New York machinist, had described the effects of mechanization to a Senate committee as follows: "The trade has been subdivided and these subdivisions have again been subdivided, so that a man never learns the machinist's trade now. Ten years ago he learned, not the whole of the trade, but a fair portion of it. Also there is more machinery used in the business, which again makes machinery. In the case of making the sewing machine, for example, you find that the trade is so subdivided that a man is not considered a machinist at all. . . . In that way machinery is produced a great deal cheaper than it used to be formerly, and in fact, through this system of work, 100 men were able to do now what it took 300 or 400 men to do fifteen years ago." *Report of the Committee of the Senate upon Relations between Labor and Capital* (Washington, 1885) I, 755.

24. *Monthly Journal of the International Association of Machinists*, VII (April 1896), 90–91; X (December 1898), 711–724. Morrison's testimony before the Senate committee also gave evidence of this decline in status. "When I first went to learn the trade a machinist considered himself more than the average working man. He liked to be called a mechanic. Today he recognizes the fact that he is simply a laborer the same as the others. Ten years ago even he considered himself . . . a mechanic, and he felt he belonged to the middle class; but today he recognizes the fact that he is simply the same as any other ordinary laborer, no more and no less." *Report of the Committee of the Senate,* I, 756.

25. *Monthly Journal of the International Association of Machinists,* VI (September 1894), 315; VII (July 1895), 232–237; X (July 1898), 385–386; XIII (April 1901), 231; XVI (January 1904), 9; XVI (February 1904), 2; XVIII (September 1906), 785; XX (September 1908), 772–773; XXVII (June 1915), 486, 490–491, 496; XVII (July 1915), 637; *Proceedings, Seventh Convention of the International Association of Machinists* (Kansas City, 1897), 225.

26. Perlman, *The Machinists,* 187; *Monthly Journal of the International Association of Machinists,* VIII (May 1896), 146–148, 157–159; IX (April 1897), 96–97; XV (May 1903), 402–403. See also Berthoff, *op. cit.,* 90.

27. *Monthly Journal of the International Association of Machinists,* VIII (September 1896), 360–362; IX (March 1897), 61–62; IX (August 1897), 366–369; X (April 1898), 225; X (July 1898), 417; X (October 1898), 594–595; XI (March 1899), 148; XV (May 1903), 402–408.

28. Marc Karson, *American Labor Unions and Politics, 1900–1918* (Carbondale, 1958), 244, 247, 252–253; *Monthly Journal of the International Association of Machinists,* VI (March 1894), 70–72; VI (April 1894), 111; VI (May 1894), 143–145.

29. Perlman, *The Machinists,* 206; *Machinists' Monthly Journal,* XVI (January 1904), 71–85; *Proceedings, Eighth Convention of the International Association of Machinists* (Buffalo, 1899), 329, 331.

30. *Ibid.,* 350–351, 362, 398.

31. Perlman, *The Machinists,* 25–27; *Proceedings, Eighth Convention of the International Association of Machinists* (Buffalo, 1899), 409–409; *Proceed-*

ings, *Tenth Convention of the International Association of Machinists* (Milwaukee, 1903), 642.

32. Perlman, *The Machinists*, 27. Notice that the socialists attempted to improve their position among the machinists still further as a result of the strike. In May 1901 James F. Carey and Martha Avery, of the Massachusetts Social Democratic party, addressed a mass meeting of two thousand machinists in Hartford, Connecticut. See *The Worker*, XI (May 26, 1901), 1.

33. Perlman, *The Machinists*, 27–28. For a discussion of the IAM's relations with the National Civic Federation, see Green, *op. cit.*, 20–24, 466 ff.

34. *Proceedings, Tenth Convention of the International Association of Machinists* (Milwaukee, 1903), 522.

35. *Ibid.*, 50, 637; *The Worker*, XIII (June 7, 1903), 4; *International Socialist Review*, IV (January 1904), 435–436; *Proceedings, Twenty-third Annual Convention of the A.F. of L.* (Boston, 1903), 198–199.

36. Perlman, *The Machinists*, 28–32. For an extremely interesting discussion of the concept of the two-party system in the trade-unions, see Seymour M. Lipset *et al.*, *Union Democracy: The Internal Politics of the International Typographical Union* (Glencoe, 1956).

37. Notice, however, that the machinists, although employed by different kinds of firms, were all engaged in the same kind of task. The Brewery Workers Union organized workers of wholly different skills who were employed in the same firm.

38. Perlman, *The Machinists*, 32, 37; *Proceedings, Eleventh Convention of the International Association of Machinists* (Boston, 1905), 67.

39. *The Worker*, XV (June 24, 1905), 2; *Machinists' Monthly Journal*, XVII (December 1905), 1123, 1125–1126, 1129; XVIII (January 1906), 45–46; 51–52; XVIII (March 1906), 244; XVIII (June 1906), 534–535, 541; XVIII (November 1906), 984–985; XVIII (December 1906), 1180–1111; XIX (January 1907), 85–98; *Proceedings, Thirteenth Convention of the International Association of Machinists* (December 1909), 1044–1079.

40. Perlman, *The Machinists*, 34; *Constitution*, International Association of Machinists (1899), 3.

41. *Proceedings, Ninth Convention of the International Association of Machinists* (Toronto, 1901), 565–567; *Proceedings, Tenth Convention of the International Association of Machinists* (Milwaukee, 1903), 586–591.

42. In 1896 O'Connell endorsed the Democratic-Populist candidate, William Jennings Bryan, and indirect evidence indicates that he remained a Democrat later on, rather than moving to the left to support Debs and the Socialist party, as many of the radical ex-Populists among the machinists did. See Foner, *op. cit.*, II, 336; *Machinists' Monthly Journal*, XVIII (November 1906), 1021–1023; XXIV (November 1912), 9081–9082.

43. Karson, *op. cit.*; 45; *Machinists' Monthly Journal*, XVII (April 1905), 41–42; XVIII (June 1906), 511–512; *Proceedings, Eleventh Convention of the International Association of Machinists* (Boston, 1905), 913.

44. *The Call*, I (July 17, 1908), 1; *Machinists' Monthly Journal*, XXI (July 1909), 600–601; XXII (May 1910), 456–457; XXIV (August 1912), 675–678.

45. In Rhode Island, Carney received a minimal vote for the governorship, securing only 743 votes to 32,965 for the Democrat and 33,821 for the victorious Republican. In Illinois, John Collins received 59,602 votes for the gover-

norship, as against 334,880 for the Democrat and 634,029 for the victorious Republican. See *Rhode Island Manual, 1912* (Providence, 1912), 121; *Illinois Blue Book, 1919–1920* (Springfield, 1919), 596–597. See also *The Worker*, XVI (September 1906), 1, 6; *The Call*, V (September 12, 1912), 5; *Machinists' Monthly Journal*, XVI (October 1904), 923; XVI (November 1904), 1005; XVIII (November 1906), 923; XXIV (January 1912), 48, 53.

46. Running on the socialist ticket for mayor of Minneapolis in 1916, Van Lear won by 87,926 votes to 73,241 for his Republican opponent. *Legislative Manual of the State of Minnesota* (Minneapolis, 1917), 591. See also *Machinists' Monthly Journal*, XVI (November 1904), 1005; XVIII (June 1906), 536; XVIII (July 1906), 651; XXII (May 1910), 406–408, 456–457.

47. Perlman, *The Machinists*, 30–35; *Proceedings, Fourteenth Convention of the International Association of Machinists* (Davenport, 1911), 84–85.

48. Perlman, *The Machinists*, 33, 36–37; *Machinists' Monthly Journal*, XIX (September 1907), 903; XXI (September 1909), 913; XXIII (August 1911), 797–798; XXIII (September 1911), 901–903; XXIII (October 1911), 985–987, 1017; *Proceedings, Eleventh Convention of the International Association of Machinists* (Boston, 1905), 923–924, 1017–1018; *Proceedings, Twelfth Convention of the International Association of Machinists* (St. Louis, 1907), 968.

49. Preston disapproved of the way in which Johnston's supporters issued campaign circulars on behalf of their candidates. He may, however, have had ambitions for the presidency himself. See *Machinists' Monthly Journal*, XXIII (September 1911), 902–903.

50. Perlman, *The Machinists*, 39; *Machinists' Monthly Journal*, XIX (October 1907), 1003; XXI (November 1909), 1092; XXII (February 1910), 155; XXIV (January 1912), 59–60.

51. Not in 1916, as Mark Perlman states. See Perlman, *The Machinists*, 44–46; *Machinists' Monthly Journal*, XXIV (June 1912), 546; XXIV (September 1912), 851; XXV (January 1913), 36; XXVI (September 1914), 903; XXVII (January 1915), 82–83; *Proceedings, Thirty-second Annual Convention of the A.F. of L.* (Rochester, 1912), 374–376. At the November 1912 AFL convention the IAM delegation also voted against Gompers and for the socialist Max Hayes in the contest for AFL president. Four years later Frank Duffy, secretary of the United Brotherhood of Carpenters and Joiners, sent Gompers the copy of a letter from Johnston to an unidentified member of the IAM complaining about the degree of support which O'Connell had received from fellow Catholic delegates in his reelection to the third vice-presidency. "When you consider that they," Johnston wrote, referring to the delegates who had voted for O'Connell, "were assisted by two Catholic priests who were busily engaged for more than a week lining up the votes for O'Connell, we done [*sic*] exceedingly well and the progressives all feel encouraged and feel confident that by the time the next [that is, the 1913] convention rolls around our numbers will be increased in sufficient numbers to enable us to break into the Council and probably defeat Gompers." Frank Duffy added a postscript of his own to Johnston's letter asking Gompers "what had us Catholics [*sic*] ought to do when we are tricked like this, he [Johnston] has a machine and it is knifing the Catholics for re-election. Watch and see." Gompers subsequently wrote to Johnston sending him a copy of this letter and demanding an explanation. It is not known whether he received any reply. See Frank Duffy to Gompers, Feb-

ruary 4, 1916; Gompers to William Johnston, April 4, 1916 (Gompers' Correspondence with Affiliates, AFL-CIO Collection).

52. *Machinists' Monthly Journal,* XXVIII (February 1916), 116–119; XXVIII (April 1916), 339–343; XXVIII (May 1916), 530–535; *Proceedings, Thirty-fifth Annual Convention of the A.F. of L.* (San Francisco, 1915), 484–504; *American Federationist,* XXII (May 1916) 316–318.

53. Perlman, *The Machinists,* 50–51, 68; *Machinists' Monthly Journal,* XXIII (August 1911), 797–798; *Proceedings, Fourteenth Convention of the International Association of Machinists* (Davenport, 1911), 84–95; *Proceedings, Fifteenth Convention of the International Association of Machinists* (Baltimore, 1916), 851–852, 931–933.

54. *Machinists' Monthly Journal,* XXIII (August 1911), 797–798; XXVI (April 1914), 375–376; XXVI (June 1914), 544–546; XXVI (September 1914), 903; XXVI (November 1914), 1035–1038; XXVII (January 1915), 46; XXVII (March 1915), 252–253; XXVIII (January 1916), 21; XXXI (July 1919), 625–626; unprinted circular to General Executive Board, November 19, 1915, cited by Perlman, *The Machinists,* 45.

55. *Solidarity,* VI (September 2, 1925), 1.

56. In February 1912 Congressman Victor Berger, in the hope of securing some relief for the strikers, proposed that a congressional investigating committee be established to enquire into the strike. The suggestion was not carried out. See National Executive Committee Correspondence, Socialist Party of America (Socialist Party of America Collection, Duke University).

57. Perlman, *The Machinists,* 40–42.

58. For example, an article appeared in the *International Socialist Review* in March 1913 asking, "What excuse have the machinists for remaining a craft organization?" See *International Socialist Review,* XIII (March 1913), 669.

59. *Machinists' Monthly Journal,* XXVII (March 1915), 253; XXVII (April 1915), 355–356; XXVII (July 1915), 648–650; XXVII (November 1915), 1022–1025; *Proceedings, Fifteenth Convention of the International Association of Machinists* (Baltimore, 1916), 40, 83.

60. *Machinists' Monthly Journal,* XXII (August 1910), 744–745; XXIII (August 1911), 797–798; XXIV (August 1912), 675–678, 736; XXIV (September 1912), 831; XXIV (October 1912), 925–927, 942, 944, 950; XXIV (December 1912), 1092–1093; XXV (March 1913), 283; XXVI (February 1914), 129–131; XXVII (May 1915), 399–400.

61. *Ibid.,* XXV (November 1913), 1203–1205; XXVI (November 1914), 943–946; XXVII (April 1915), 296–300.

62. *Ibid.,* XXVII (April 1915), 296–300; XXVIII (August 1916), 811–812; XXVIII (September 1916), 880–882, 887–888; XXVIII (October 1916), 1026–1029; XXVIII (December 1916), 1215–1217.

63. *Ibid.,* XXV (April 1913), 382–383; XXVII (October 1915), 878–880; XXVIII (June 1916), 541–542; XXVIII (July 1916), 643–644; XXVIII (September 1916), 881–883; XVIII (December 1916), 1181, 1197.

64. Perlman, *The Machinists,* 46–54; *Machinists' Monthly Journal,* XXX (January 1918), 80–81; XXXI (June 1919), 507.

65. *Ibid.,* XXVI (September 1914), 843–844; XXVI (December 1914), 1131–1134; XXVII (February 1915), 103–104; XXVII (April 1915), 308–309; XXVIII (January 1916), 6–7; XXIX (March 1917), 355–357, 365–366; XXIX

(October 1917), 805–808; XXIX (December 1917), 1044–1045; XXX (April 1918), 344; *Proceedings, Fifteenth Convention of the International Association of Machinists* (Baltimore, 1916), 40, 89–90.

66. *Machinists' Monthly Journal,* XXIV (March 1912), 193–196; XXIV (November 1912), 1054; XXVI (August 1914), 739–742; XXVII (February 1915), 103; XXIX (March 1917), 254; XXX (February 1918), 129, 160–161; XXXVI (October 1924), 10.

67. *Ibid.,* XXX (March 1918), 270–271, 296; XXX (September 1918), 822; XXXI (February 1919), 133, 154; XXXI (March 1919), 210–219; XXXI (April 1919), 335; XXXII (July 1920), 662–664; XXXII (October 1920), 910; XXXII (December 1920), 1085–1086; *Proceedings, Fortieth Annual Convention of the American Federation of Labor* (Montreal, 1920), 283, 399–406, 407–420.

68. Perlman, *The Machinists,* 56–57; *Machinists' Monthly Journal,* XXXI (February 1919), 133; XXXII (July 1920), 667; XXXII (December 1920), 1139–1140; XXXIII (June 1921), 505–506; XXXIII (September 1921), 739–743; XXXIII (October 1921), 834–839; *Proceedings, Sixteenth Convention of the International Association of Machinists* (Rochester, 1920), 271–275, 319–326, 577.

69. *Machinists' Monthly Journal,* XXXII (August 1920), 720–722, 741; XXXIII (August 1921), 682–683; XXXIII (September 1921), 748; XXXIV (September 1922), 621–626; *Proceedings, Sixteenth Convention of the International Association of Machinists* (Rochester, 1920), 194–200; *Proceedings, Fortieth Annual Convention of the A.F. of L.* (Montreal, 1920), 448–449; *Proceedings, Forty-first Annual Convention of the A.F. of L.* (Denver, 1921), 455–456.

70. Perlman, *The Machinists,* 64; *Machinists' Monthly Journal,* XXVII (June 1915), 546–547; XXVII (September 1915), 832; XXX (May 1918), 457; XXXIII (January 1921), 41–43; XXXIII (July 1921), 602–603; *Proceedings, Sixteenth Convention of the International Association of Machinists* (Rochester, 1920), 129–140, 224–226; *Proceedings, Thirteenth Annual Convention of the Metal Trades Department of the A.F. of L.* (Denver, 1921), 67–70.

71. Vic Gautier, a socialist who had been elected to the General Executive Board, put this well in a letter which he wrote in December 1921 urging the Johnston administration to press for the establishment of an American Labor party on the British model. Both of the major political parties were now "controlled by the enemies of labor," he wrote, and Communists could be dismissed "as hopeless theorists." But the National Farmer-Labor party, the Farmers Non-Partisan League, the Committee of Forty-Eight, and the remnants of the prewar Socialist party, together with the organized labor movement, could be welded together into a strong national party if the appropriate action were taken. It should have been the duty of the AFL to do this, he went on. "Unfortunately, there is no hope from that quarter—the leaders of the A.F. of L. are opposed to political action . . . except through the old parties. The one organization in [a] position to render this service is our own I.A. of M. We have the confidence of the progressives and radicals alike, both in and out of the labor movement." See *Machinists' Monthly Journal,* XXXIII (December 1921), 996–999.

72. *Machinists' Monthly Journal,* XXXII (August 1920), 754–755; XXXIII

(March 1921), 197–198; XXXIII (April 1921), 293–295; XXXIII (December 1921), 996–999; *Proceedings, First National Convention of the Labor Party of the United States* (Chicago, 1919), 126–131.

73. This was not an easy task, since the railroad brotherhoods were not affiliated with the AFL at this time, and the latter was sensitive about any legislative action which might seem to encroach on its own political preserve. In February 1921 Johnston presided over a meeting of the railroad organizations to which the AFL was not at first invited, much to Gompers' annoyance. On April 12 another meeting was held, at which the railroad organizations indicated reservations about cooperating with the AFL. And at a third meeting at which the People's Legislative Service was established (held in Senator Robert La Follette's office), the AFL once more expressed reservations. This time Johnston became angry, asserting that "all the wisdom of the labor movement is not in the Executive Council of the A.F. of L., and if the A.F. of L. is not represented as such, a great many of the nationals and internationals will be represented." Nevertheless, he clearly did his best to bring the AFL and the other labor elements together. He was also active in the People's Reconstruction League, the All-American Cooperative Commission, and other Farmer-Labor groups, as well as being on the Executive Committee of the National Farmer-Labor party. See *Machinists' Monthly Journal,* XXXIII (March 1921), 197–198; XXXIII (April 1921), 293–295; Taft, *op. cit.,* 466–467, 480–481; J. G. Brown to J. H. Walker, September 7, 1921 (John H. Walker Papers, University of Illinois Historical Survey).

74. Kenneth C. MacKay, *The Progressive Movement of 1924* (New York, 1947), 60–65; Nathan Fine, *Labor and Farmer Parties in the United States, 1828–1928* (New York, 1961), 398–402; *Machinists' Monthly Journal,* XXXIV (April 1922), 269–273.

75. *Machinists' Monthly Journal,* XXXIV (September 1922), 618–619; XXXIV (November 1922), 709–718, 751; XXXIV (December 1922), 796, 798, 807–809; XXXV (January 1923), 53; XXXV (May 1923), 255–256; XXXV (August 1923), 400–401; XXXV (November 1923), 542.

76. In February 1923 Gompers drew Johnston's attention to the fact, which the union had already ascertained for itself, that the Communists in the union had been specifically instructed to vote for William R. Hudson against Johnston in the June 1922 union elections. Hudson received 9,241 votes to Johnston's 13,829. See Gompers to W. H. Johnston, February 21, 1923 (Gompers' Correspondence with Affiliates, AFL-CIO Collection). For further information on the role of the Communists in the IAM, see Perlman, *The Machinists,* 64–65; David M. Schneider, *The Workers' (Communist) Party and the American Trade Unions* (Baltimore, 1928), 8–25; *Machinists' Monthly Journal,* XXXVI (August 1924), 339–342; *Proceedings, Sixteenth Convention of the International Association of Machinists* (Rochester, 1920), 129–140.

77. In the 1924 union elections the Trade Union Educational League issued a circular on behalf of the International Committee for Amalgamation in the Metal Trades Industry, a Communist-controlled organization, urging all "militants" to support the Anderson slate of candidates. "We consider that the defeat of Johnston at this time," the circular said, "in view of the coupling of his name with the class collaboration schemes like the B. & O. plan, would be a sign of a revival of the fighting spirit of the union and a repudiation of the cor-

rupt and treacherous Johnston administration. It would be a real achievement that would have a far-reaching effect in the labor movement." Note also that the Johnston administration further antagonized the Communists by issuing an anti-Communist circular at the height of the campaign. See Schneider, *op. cit.,* 10–25; Perlman, *The Machinists,* 70; Circular of the Trade Union Educational League (Gompers' Correspondence with Affiliates, AFL-CIO Collection).

78. It is interesting to note that in the 1924 union elections the issue of Catholicism versus socialism again came to the fore. The antiadministration candidates, who were on the whole conservative, were called Catholics, and the pro-Johnston candidates Masons. The Masons were, as Mark Perlman points out, largely old Populist-Socialists, railroad machinists and southerners, while the Catholics were for the most part the big-city members employed in job shops and erection work. However, it should be pointed out that the Mason-Catholic differentiation was not wholly a socialist-nonsocialist one. J. F. Anderson, the *de facto* leader of the Catholic party, was a Mormon, while, as we have noted, P. J. Conlon, one of the few remaining supporters of Johnston's radicalism, was a Catholic. See Perlman, *The Machinists,* 57–60, 68–70; *Machinists' Monthly Journal,* XXXIII (November 1921), 919–920; XXXIV (August 1922), 555–557; XXXIV (October 1922), 688–691; XXXIV (November 1922), 753; XXXVI (May 1924), 212–213; XXXVI (October 1924), 450–454.

79. MacKay, *op. cit.,* 75–76, 118–120, 134–135, 146–149, 188; *Machinists' Monthly Journal,* XXXVI (February 1924), 77–78; XXXV (August 1924), 339–343, 382–383; *Proceedings, Seventh Convention of the International Association of Machinists* (Detroit, 1924), 15–19; *The Facts: La Follette-Wheeler Campaign Text-Book* (Chicago La Follette-Wheeler Campaign Headquarters, 1924), 4.

80. *Machinists' Monthly Journal,* XXXVI (December 1924), 594–599; XXXVII (February 1925), 87; XXXVII (April 1925), 240; *Report of the Proceedings of the National Progressive Convention* (Chicago, 1925), 3, cited in MacKay, *op. cit.,* 230–231, 233, 236, 238.

81. Perlman, *The Machinists,* 71–77; *Machinists' Monthly Journal,* XXXVIII (July 1926), 324–325.

82. Testimony before an 1883 Senate committee confirmed this. John Anderson, a New York machinist whose opinions were cited earlier, gave evidence as follows: "I understand that at this present day you could not start in the machinist's business to compete successfully with any of those large firms with a capital of less than $20,000 or $30,000. That is my own judgment. There have been cases known where men started ten or fifteen years ago on what they had earned themselves. One of these firms is Floyd & Sons, on Twentieth Street. That man started out of his own earnings, he saved enough to start a pretty fair-sized shop, and he is occupying it today; but since that time it appears the larger ones are squeezing out the smaller, and forcing more of them into the ranks of labor, thus causing more competition among the workers."

83. In this letter the same official made an illuminating comment on the collapse of the Socialist party. "The Socialists," he said, "have claimed for years to be the party of the workers . . . yet the workers will not or have not joined hands with them, which leads me to think the worker is not a party man, or to

put it another way, the worker can be counted on as being a non-partisan voter." See *Machinists' Monthly Journal,* XXXII (April 1920), 339–342.

84. *Ibid.,* XXIII (October 1911), 1025–1032; XXXI (May 1919), 464–479. This, of course, gives only a rough idea of the ethnic composition of the union, since apart from the difficulty of associating names to ethnic background it reflects only the local leadership, not the rank and file. But since the German, the Scandinavian, and to some extent the Irish lodges in the union were differentiated ethnically, it is of some significance.

6

Socialism, Industrial Unionism, and the United Mine Workers of America

With the United Mine Workers of America, founded in 1890 in Columbus, Ohio, we enter a world which was in many ways quite different from that of the skilled, urban, largely eastern labor movement which we have considered in the earlier chapters of this book. The UMWA was much larger than any of our other unions. By 1905 it had more than 300,000 members, most of them semiskilled or unskilled pick-and-shovel workers employed at the coal face. It also included engineers, laborers, machinists, coal hoisters, pumpmen, and more than forty other classified occupations "in and around" the coal mines of over twenty states.

This not only made the United Mine Workers by far the largest union in the AFL. It also made it much the most important organization in the labor movement to embrace the principles of industrial unionism. In addition, the autonomous character and isolated location of many of the coal fields —stretching from West Virginia and the southern Appalachians to the flatter districts of Indiana and southern Illinois, and on again to the mountains of Colorado—brought to its radicalism elements which were quite different from those of the unions which we examined above.[1]

The socialists were never able to capture the national administration of the UMWA. The only national officer who was an active member of the Socialist party was Frank Hayes, who was elected international vice-president in 1910, and president between 1917 and 1920. But they did succeed in developing considerable influence in several of the district unions, most notably in Illinois, which was numerically the largest and most powerful state-wide organization in the union. Although its character varied somewhat from area to area, the influence of the socialists grew essentially out of a strong and militant sense of misuse and oppression, which derived in turn from a long tradition of bitter and often violent conflicts with the coal operators. This tradition was not syndicalist, save in a few western areas such as Colorado District 15. But it was volatile, tough, and highly individualistic, while at the same time putting a high premium on industry-wide cooperation and working-class solidarity.

Ethnically, the United Mine Workers was dominated in this early period by immigrants from Great Britain, despite a large influx of Slavs and Italians into the Pennsylvania anthracite fields and elsewhere after 1880. The relative isolation of the coal fields also brought it into even closer contact with rural populism than in the case of the International Association of Machinists. Ideologically, therefore, the major radical influences in the union were non-Marxist, reformist, and evolutionary in character, despite the presence of a number of militant direct-action advocates on the extreme left. This was manifested in strong enthusiasm for a broadly based labor party after the English model. Although formal socialist influences had declined in the union by 1917, demands for a national labor party, and for such collectivist measures as nationalization of the coal mines, re-emerged strongly after World War I. The United Mine Workers played relatively little role in the Conference for Progressive Political Action. But its radical traditions persisted, albeit in a somewhat different form, as its prominent role in the CIO later showed.

I

The growth of socialist influence in the United Mine Workers of America can be traced to a variety of different causes. In the first place, there was a tradition of political activism among the membership going back beyond the time when the union was first established. Of the eleven principal planks laid down in the United Mine Workers constitution of 1890, more than half involved demands for legislation: to provide adequate safety laws, to prevent the employment of Pinkerton detectives and armed guards during strikes, and to secure the enactment of legislation for the grading and weighing of coal.[2] This was reinforced by the political background and experience of many of the English, Welsh, and Scottish miners who first built up the organization. Quite a number of the early leaders of unionism in the industry had been Chartists—participants in that great social and political movement in Great Britain which in the 1830's and 1840's had attempted to secure political representation for the English working class. When Chartism failed in 1848, like the more radical revolutionary movements on the European continent, a number of ex-Chartist miners from Great Britain emigrated to the United States. For example, Thomas Lloyd, a Welshman, and Daniel Weaver, who founded the American Miners Association in 1861, were both ex-Chartists. John Hinchcliffe, a Yorkshire-born miners' leader active in Illinois in the 1870's, had also been affected by Chartism. So had a considerable number of coal miners in other states.[3]

For those immigrants from Great Britain who were too young to remember the Chartists, there was the tradition of political independence which had been established by the British coal miners themselves. This was begun in 1874 when Thomas Burt, from a mining district in Northumberland, and Alexander MacDonald, the great Scottish miners' leader, were elected to the House of Commons.[4] Thereafter the English miners were rarely without a representative in Parliament, and by 1905 they had fourteen M.P.'s of their own in the House of Commons. In keeping with this tradition, the American miners' unions were among the few trade organizations in this country to permit their members to run for political office while retaining official positions in the union. By 1900 a considerable number of them had already served in their state legislatures. Among them were John Hinchcliffe and William Scaife, of Illinois (where the tradition of political activism was strongest), and Robert Watchorn, in Pennsylvania. There was also John McBride, in Ohio, who was elected to two terms as a Democrat to the Ohio state legislature before he became president of the UMWA in 1892.

Another socialist idea which the British miners brought over with them was cooperatively owned provision stores, which were established to avoid dependence on the company store. Such ventures were relatively common among the miners in England and Scotland, and they were introduced here with considerable success. In 1874 John Siney, the earliest important leader of the coal miners, also proposed the establishment of producers' cooperatives by suggesting the purchase of a cooperatively owned mine in Tennessee. But nothing came of this idea.[5]

Not all the early British immigrants in the coal mines were political radicals. John B. Rae, the first president of the UMWA, and William B. Wilson, later international secretary-treasurer, were opposed to political action outside of the traditional party framework. Others, who may have been radicals in the Old World, found it inappropriate to behave like socialists in the New. In August 1895, for example, the *United Mine Workers' Journal* reproved James Keir Hardie, the Scots-born socialist then touring America (who was also originally a miner), for advocating the "red flag" in a New York speech. This was acceptable in England or Scotland, the editor said, but was foreign "to the life and ideas of the New World." Also, in the early period quite a few of the ex-British miners, by virtue of their previous experience, rose relatively rapidly in the mining industry to become foremen, superintendents, and mine inspectors, probably depriving the rank and file of some of its potentially more radical leaders. Nevertheless, the tradition of political activism which the English-speaking miners brought to the country had a considerable effect in determining the political outlook of American miners. It helped to create a strong interest in politics as a means of solving labor's problems. And especially after the turn of the century, it also led to frequent pleas that the American miners follow the example of their English brothers by helping to establish an independent labor political party.[6]

A second cause of radical discontent was the special hazards of the miners' task. Before adequate safety legislation was adopted, which in most states was not until well after 1900, mining was among the most perilous of industrial occupations. Besides the natural dangers of working underground, such as cave-ins, seepage of gas, the threat of falling coal, and lung disease from the inhalation of coal dust, mine disasters were frequent and death and injury commonplace. Even after the turn of the century more than ten thousand miners a year continued to be killed or injured as a result of mine accidents. This figure was higher than in any western European country, and it was needlessly inflated by indifference on the part of many operators and by lax enforcement of the law. For example, in the great Monongahela River disaster in Fairmont, West Virginia, which took place in 1907, as many as four hundred coal miners were killed by a single explosion of gas. It had been left to the miners themselves to discover the presence of gas, and after the accident union officials in West Virginia complained angrily about the carelessness of the state inspector of mines. When disasters occurred, wives and children hastened to the pitheads to wait for their husbands and fathers to be brought out of the mines—some dead, some burned beyond recognition, and others maimed for life. Coal miners could rarely purchase life insurance to secure their families against the loss of the breadwinner, and union death benefits in the early days were either nonexistent or pitifully small.[7]

In the third place, the geographical isolation of many of the mining camps and the great political and economic power of the coal operators put the miners at the mercy of their employers in a manner virtually unparalleled elsewhere. In remote areas of the Alleghenies, for example, where several of the largest anthracite and bituminous fields were located, the coal miner depended on the coal company for virtually all the necessities of life. His house belonged to the coal company. He bought his tools, powder, food, and clothing at the company store. Powder was notoriously expensive, and prices in general ranged from 10 per cent to 40 per cent higher than in outside stores. If the miner's wife were sick, she went to the company doctor. When his sons needed employment, they took jobs alongside of him in the company's mines. State law notwithstanding, the miner was often paid in "scrip," which was not negotiable at ordinary stores. Sometimes he was cheated even out of part of this when the cars carrying the coal he had mined passed through the breaker screens and removed good coal, as well as dust and shale, reducing still further the amount of money he was entitled to receive.

In good times wages for English-speaking miners were quite high, ranging from \$1.25 to \$2.00 a day. But the coal industry was subject to seasonal changes in demand, and when demand was low the miner would work only three or four days a week, or even go without work altogether. Moreover, coal mining, like the shoe industry and the garment trades, experienced a period of acute instability and competition in the period which followed the Civil War. As new coal fields were opened up—in Kentucky, Tennessee, and Alabama in the South, Missouri and Kansas in the Midwest, and Colorado and Washington in the West—a national instead of a series of local markets emerged, bringing competitive conditions which were for a time little short of chaotic. Operators would drop their prices in order to remain competitive, frequently following this by a cut in wages also. During the major periods of depression in the industry, in the 1870's and 1890's, a further general lowering of wages occurred. As a result, average daily wages in the coal industry fell from \$1.65 in 1872 to \$1.10 in 1879. There was a brief recovery during the prosperous years of the mid-1880's, but by the depression of 1893 they had fallen back to \$1.15, a figure which was not exceeded with any consistency until after 1903.[8] In this period many of the smaller companies went out of business, accounting for much periodic unemployment. At this time, also, the railroads acquired extensive holdings in the coal lands. This presented the miners with an even more formidable adversary to confront, and one which, because of absentee ownership, it was even more difficult for them to control.[9]

In addition, there were the severe problems which the miners experienced in establishing a viable, national trade-union. After the demise of the American Miners Association in 1873, numerous district organizations appeared, sometimes overlapping into several states and coal fields. Their separate existence contributed to a tradition of conflict over district versus central autonomy which the socialists, as in other unions, were later to exploit. But for almost thirty years after 1861, when the first efforts at union organization had begun, the miners were unable to maintain a viable national union for long. When they did attempt to organize, the miners were discharged, black-listed, or evicted from their houses by company guards or Pinkerton detectives. If they struck, strikebreakers would be brought in, frequently Negroes from the southern coal fields. Or they would be served with an injunction and threatened with a riot bill from friends and agents of the coal companies in county courtrooms, sheriffs' offices, or state legislatures. John Siney made the first attempt at a national miners' organization, called the Miners National Association, in 1873. But it disappeared in the depression of the mid-1870's. Siney was widely admired during the brief period when the Miners National Association was successful. But he was quickly repudiated when he urged caution and restraint in the 1870's depression, establishing another important precedent for rank-and-file discontent which the socialists were to exploit later on.[10]

The task of organizing the miners was rendered even more difficult by the influx of Slavs into the anthracite regions of eastern Pennsylvania and elsewhere. In 1878 these immigrants—Bohemians, Slovaks, Croatians, Serbians, and Lithuanians from the Austro-Hungarian empire, together with some Poles and Italians—formed less than 2 per cent of the foreign-born mining population. By 1900 they constituted over 46 per cent. Ex-peasants ignorant both of the English language and of industrial conditions, the Slavs were more easily manipulated by the coal operators than the English-speaking miners and more willing to work for lower wages also. This threatened still further the earnings of the English-speaking miners and caused widespread resentment.[11]

The English-speaking miners did not exclude the Slavs from their unions, because of the danger of their being used against them during strikes. For the same reason they also accepted Negroes, who in the 1890's constituted a higher proportion of the national membership—possibly as high as 15 per cent—than they did in most other trade-unions. Indeed, the career of Richard L. Davis, a Negro miners' leader from Ohio who was elected to the National Executive Board in 1896 and 1897, suggests that the UMWA took a more sympathetic attitude toward the Negro than did almost any other labor organization in this period, although there is little evidence to suggest that this was a cause particularly espoused by the union's radicals.[12] Nevertheless, in the 1880's and 1890's competition from Slavs and other recent immigrants caused a large number of English-speaking miners to leave the anthracite fields, seeking jobs in the bituminous fields farther west. So it was no coincidence that Illinois, to which many of these miners moved, became a major center of socialism in the trade.

Finally, there came the great depression of 1893–1896, which affected coal mining more severely than almost any other industry. With a market glutted with coal even before the depression began, hundreds of mines were closed, and so many miners were thrown out of work that the governors of several midwestern states had to issue public appeals for aid. In a desperate attempt to avert further wage cuts, the 1894 UMWA convention ordered a general strike of miners, to begin on April 21. With only 13,000 paid-up members and $2,600 in the national treasury, over a hundred thousand miners came out and stayed on strike for a period of eight weeks. "The miners are on strike because they must," DeLeon's *The People* declared. "Their condition was unbearable." And he went on to cite, as an example, the near-starvation conditions in which a family of miners was living in Ohio.[13]

The 1894 strike was an almost total failure. Wage reductions were temporarily checked in some of the coal fields. But President McBride was forced to abandon his hope of a nationwide conference with the operators, and the UMWA emerged from the conflict almost totally destroyed. With barely 8,000 members, the union was too poor to defray the expenses of International Executive Board meetings, and within months the downward trend in wages was resumed. "Hardly a letter or a bit of mining news [comes] from any part of the country," wrote the editor of the *United Mine Workers' Journal* in December 1894, "which does not contain news of hunger, cold and rags." Some of the miners went to the cities in search of work; others joined "General" Jacob S. Coxey's march on Washington. But most stayed near the mines, scraping food together from the vegetable patches behind the company shacks. In most of the coal districts the UMWA had lost virtually all its influence, and hundreds of local strikes broke out, despite warnings from the national officials that they were bound to fail. "We would strike [for] three, four, or six months," recalled one Ohio miner years later, "go back to work when starved to it; work until we had a barrel of flour and a side of bacon ahead, and then we would give them another tussle." Another miner, this time from Kansas, remembered these years as the most disastrous period of his life. "Out of work more than half the time; ill paid and disheartened while working; insecure at all times, not knowing whether we would strike or be forced to strike; no certainty of a home anywhere"—this was an experience he never wished to repeat.[14]

In 1897 a second national strike took place, ending this time in something like success. In July nearly 150,000 miners laid down their picks, in what President Ratchford described as "nothing less than the spontaneous uprising of an enslaved society." At a meeting held in Pittsburgh on September 3 an average advance in wages of about 21 per cent was agreed upon, with the understanding that the joint interstate agreement should also be resumed. At a further conference, held in Chicago in January 1898, representatives from both sides agreed upon a locally adjusted mining scale which covered the entire central competitive field of Ohio, Illinois, Indiana, and western Pennsylvania. The eight-hour day was accepted, as well as the checkoff system of paying union dues, under which the operators deducted the fee automatically whenever wages were paid. In addition, a system of arbitration was established for negotiating disputes. With some local variations, this joint interstate agreement has provided the basis for negotiations in the industry ever since.[15]

II

With this background, the surprising thing was not that radical sentiments should have developed among the coal miners, but that these sentiments were not more widespread than they were. Politically, the national leadership of the UMWA had begun by warning against the "misunderstanding and very often disruption" which could result from mixing partisan politics with union affairs. "It seems to us," the *United Mine Workers' Journal* stated editorially in May 1893, "that the interests of the mining craft will be best conserved by electing miners to office regardless of party or political affiliations. Miners—not politicians—are best qualified to represent miners on the floor of our Legislative halls, no matter what party or faction they represent." This was not quite the orthodox AFL approach. The emphasis on electing miners themselves to office, instead of "politicians," showed a concern for bringing workingmen directly into politics, which was considerably more radical than the general position of the AFL, in addition to its Populist overtones. But with its indifference to third-party political action, the statement appeared to bring cold comfort to advocates of a more radical course.[16]

Despite this, the socialists had by this time made some progress at the grass-roots level, although, as in the case of other unions, their progress was impeded by the hostile tactics of the Socialist Labor party. In his report to the Socialist Trades and Labor Alliance convention of 1897, Ernest Boehm claimed that several ST&LA groups had been established among the miners in Pennsylvania. But available information confirms the existence of only one, organized at Buena Vista in the Pittsburgh District 5 by Thomas Hickey, who was later to become active as a socialist in the Boot and Shoe Workers Union. The Buena Vista local followed the usual pattern of the ST&LA by refusing to conform to District 5's agreement with the operators, and by opposing the union's official policies on every possible occasion.

Dual unionism, therefore, was one reason for the failure of the SLP. Another was the fact that the SLP was primarily an eastern, urban party, with neither the money nor the organization to conduct extensive organizing in the coal fields. Also, the United Mine Workers was dominated just as much as the IAM had been by British or native-born workers who had little sympathy with the continental Marxism of the SLP. In addition, the Socialist Laborites went out of their way to denounce not only the United Mine Workers' leadership but also the gullibility of the rank and file. The *Arm and Hammer,* for example, a labor monthly issued by the party in Missouri, denounced the national officers of the union thus: "[as] blackhearted, corrupt and ignorant a set of crooks as ever sold out for gold and silver since the days that Judas sold Christ." And *The People,* while commiserating with the miners in the depression, blamed a large part of their ills on the fact that they had been "deluded by the fakirs at their head." [17]

Nevertheless, interest in radical politics was manifested in other ways. During the 1890's depression correspondents to the *United Mine Workers' Journal* from Ohio, Kansas, West Virginia, and Illinois urged "direct political action" against the operators, electoral alliances with "advanced elements and socialists," and even wholesale nationalization of the mines. And in November 1893 an English correspondent, commenting on the recent formation of the Independent Labor party in Great Britain, pointed to the lack of "genuine labor representatives" in the various state legislatures and urged the American miners to follow the "independent course" of their English friends. Widespread enthusiasm developed for Thomas J. Morgan's 1894 Political Program, especially for Plank Nine, which called for government control of the railroads, telegraphs, and mines. Despite some misgivings about Plank Ten (requiring collective ownership of all the means of production and distribution), the April 1894 convention of the UMWA adopted the Program *in toto.*[18]

But the People's party was the first radical third-party movement to capture the attention of the coal miners on any scale. In fact, for a brief period it appeared as though the UMWA would give the Populists even more overt support than the International Association of Machinists had done. This was not surprising. The rapid centralization of ownership in the coal mining industry, and the widespread influence of the coal operators in the courts, the administrative offices, and the legislative halls, provided a classic example of the fusion of political and economic power which the national People's party sought to redress. Coal miners were also in more frequent contact with farmers than the urban workers were, by virtue of the rural location of many of the mines. Quite a number of miners supplemented their reduced income in the summer by working in the fields, a process which was reversed in the winter when some of the farmers worked in the coal mines. In fact, in the depression years so many miners went to work on the farms that the 1894 national convention of the UMWA found it necessary to pass a "corn huskers" resolution, reminding the absentee members to keep up with their union dues.[19]

The first overt sign of Populist sentiment among the miners came when a number of them joined in antirailroad demonstrations in 1892. This was followed, after the financial panic of 1893, by a variety of typically Populist fulminations in the *United Mine Workers' Journal* against Wall Street, the trusts, and the "money power." In Kansas members of District 14 persuaded the Populists to add weekly wage payments and a mine screen law to their state platform in 1892: concessions which they had been unable to secure from the Democrats or the Republicans. And in West Virginia the People's party included government ownership of the mines in their state platform, thereby winning considerable union support. But it was in Illinois, where a Labor-Populist-Socialist [20] alliance was temporarily established, that the miners played their most active role. The condition of the southern Illinois miners, after many had been discharged or black-listed in the great strike of April 1894, was particularly deplorable—so bad, in fact, that W. J. Guyman, secretary-treasurer of District 12, predicted in all seriousness in January 1895 that unless conditions improved, a revolutionary outburst might occur. Guyman himself was an active Populist, and President J. A. Crawford of District 12, departing from his earlier practice of lobbying the major parties, attended a Labor-Populist-Socialist convention in July 1894 to plan concerted action. Later, he was nominated for Congress on the Populist ticket in Springfield. Several other miners also ran for the Illinois state legislature on behalf of the Labor-Populist alliance. [21]

For a time it seemed as if the international officers of the UMWA might also come out openly in support of the People's party. In August 1894 International President McBride broke publicly with the Democrats and declared for Populism. McBride, together with International Executive Board member John Fahy and an Ohio official, John Kane, summoned a conference of trade-unionists in Columbus to plan joint political action with the Populists, somewhat like the Illinois Labor-Populist alliance. When it met, on August 15–16, the convention endorsed the Omaha Populist platform, with the addition of several other labor planks, including Plank Ten of the Morgan Program; and it ended with an agreement to run a joint Labor-Populist ticket in the state elections of Ohio in November 1894.

In the event, however, this political alliance did not develop very far. The depression made it difficult to raise money for campaigning, and in Ohio the total vote cast for the Populists in the 1894 election was under 5 per cent. In Illinois the percentage was somewhat better, but the labor coalition still failed to elect any of its candidates to office. The Populist vote increased in a number of the southern Illinois mining counties, but the popularity of the liberal Democratic governor, John Peter Altgeld, kept it down elsewhere. [22]

The Populist episode provides the first concrete evidence of the central problem which third-party voting was to pose for the coal miners throughout the entire period under review: namely, the danger of alienating support in the Democratic and Republican parties by transferring their allegiance elsewhere. The concentration of the mining population in certain specific areas gave union officials an important means of exerting influence in either, or even both, of the two major parties, should they choose to do so. It was an influence, moreover, which had already been used effectively on behalf of safety or other mining legislation in several states. As a result, coal miners in general had little incentive to make any permanent or extensive commitment to a third political party, unless both of the major parties became extremely unresponsive, or unless the miners' discontents became so great as to disaffect them from the two-party system as a whole.

Thus, in Kansas, where the Populist administration which the miners had helped to elect in 1892 failed to enact weekly wage payments or a mine screen law, many influential union members lost their enthusiasm for the party and urged a return to their former political loyalties. In Indiana a similar development occurred. In January 1896 Dan O'Leary, a member of the District 11 executive board, reported that the Populist party in Indiana had been a disappointment, because it had given very little attention to interests of ordinary workingmen. The only real way for the miners to advance politically, he contended, was to secure the nomination of an "honest miner" to the ticket of whichever of the two major parties was in power. It was in vain for W. J. Guyman to retort (with some exaggeration) that the miners had followed this practice in Illinois with little effect for more than twenty years. O'Leary pointed to the considerable amount of legislation which the Indiana miners had secured by this bipartisan method —screen laws, laws providing for mine inspectors, for checkweighmen, and for a variety of safety regulations—and he expressed his conviction that the miners had enough votes in the mining counties of eastern Indiana to continue this policy with success.[23]

However, implementation of mining legislation alone was not enough to fulfill the aspirations of the more active radicals in the UMWA, and once the Populist-Democratic fusion had taken place in 1896 interest in the activities of the socialists began to return. The UMWA, as an industrial union, had expressed strong sympathy for the American Railway Union in 1893 and 1894. This was especially true in Illinois, where turmoil over the Pullman strike had played an important part in forming the Labor-Populist alliance of 1894. The *United Mine Workers' Journal* expressed a strong interest in Debs' transition from Populism to socialism, and his declaration for socialism in the *Railway Times* of January 1, 1897, aroused so much interest that the editor felt obliged to reproduce it in full. A considerable amount of attention was also paid to the plans of the Social Democracy of America to establish a cooperative colony in the west, if only because it offered the miners some hope, however illusory, of relief from unemployment.[24]

Then came the great coal strike of July 1897, in which Debs also played an important role. The crucial field proved to be West Virginia, where numerous miners continued production, threatening the success of the strike as a whole. At the request of President Ratchford, Debs left a speaking tour in the Midwest to spend about a month visiting the strike areas of West Virginia, where he proved to be by far the most popular speaker. On July 26 an injunction was issued against him, as well as against Grand Master James R. Sovereign of the Knights of Labor and President Ratchford, for their activities in the strike. All three men ignored the injunction and continued with their work. But it was Debs who received the most publicity and applause, recalling the furore which had been raised by the Pullman injunction of 1894. He attended a rally organized by the miners in St. Louis on August 30 to protest the injunction and served as chairman of a further meeting on September 27, at which a resolution was adopted urging "unification of all labor and reform forces along national political lines." During the strike Debs also secured financial contributions for the strikers from Social Democracy of America branches in various parts of the country.

The leaders of the UMWA were grateful to Debs for his help in the 1897 strike, and his popularity among the membership generally increased a thousandfold. "No name is more revered," the union journal reported in August 1898, "nor no [*sic*] voice accorded a more respectful, attentive hearing than that . . . [of] Mr. Debs." Miners' locals in Illinois, Indiana, and Ohio invited him to speak at their meetings, and the evidence suggests that he complied with the requests more frequently than he did with those of other labor organizations. In 1900, the first year that Debs ran for the United States Presidency, the *United Mine Workers' Journal* commented that "his personality will draw many votes for the party that it could not possibly obtain otherwise." And in January 1902 the national secretary of the Socialist party, Leon Greenbaum, sent a telegram to the annual convention of the union urging it to declare for socialism. Nothing came of this proposal, however.[25]

The socialists were also able to exploit the frequent criticisms which were leveled by rank-and-file elements in the union against the terms of the joint interstate agreement which was renegotiated by the national officials of the UMWA in the spring of each year. Strikes were forbidden during the period of the agreement, necessitating a degree of self-discipline which the miners, like the garment workers under the Protocol, were reluctant to exert. In addition, negotiation of the agreement was an extremely complex matter, involving a wide variety of conditions and terrain; and coal miners sometimes had to accept a lower wage in one district in order to ensure the competitive equality of another. Also, the miners' frequent conflicts with the operators, and the severe poverty which had visited many of them over the previous decade, made them extremely sensitive toward concessions made during negotiations, as well as toward any suspicion of excessive collaboration with "the other side."

This cautious and suspicious attitude on the part of the miners toward their own leaders was already apparent in the 1870's with the treatment of Siney; and it reappeared during the 1894 strike, when there were widespread criticisms of McBride. But it was in 1902 that it was first exploited in any major way by the socialists, as a result of the great anthracite strike which took place in that year. This began on May 12, 1902, when the operators refused to meet with the miners to agree on a new wage scale. More than a hundred thousand anthracite miners in eastern Pennsylvania —virtually the entire labor force in that section of the industry—came out. Violence spread, the militia were summoned, and tension rose as the shortage of hard coal became acute. As one socialist newspaper in New York put it, this was a situation to "make socialists," and the Socialist party exploited it to the full. The Pennsylvania state committee of the party sent out organizers to distribute literature and help organize the strikers. National Secretary Leon Greenbaum issued an appeal to all party members for funds to help in the strike, which realized over $9,000. And in the November elections J. W. Slayton, the socialist gubernatorial candidate, got four times the vote Debs had received in Pennsylvania in the presidential election of 1900. Several new Socialist party locals were organized in the anthracite area as a result.

The most important development, however, occurred after President John Mitchell had persuaded the miners to go back to work pending the award of an arbitration commission appointed by President Theodore Roosevelt. On March 18, 1903, the commission awarded a 10 per cent wage increase, a reduction in hours, and permission to use checkweighmen, as well as denouncing the use of sheriffs' deputies by the coal and railroad corporations. Some of the miners were satisfied with these results. Mitchell had consulted with President Roosevelt and the leading coal operators at the White House during the strike, and this resulted in a great increase in his prestige. But there was also widespread disappointment that the settlement had not secured a larger wage increase. *The Worker,* a prominent socialist paper, belabored Mitchell for putting the settlement into the hands of a tribunal. The socialist John Spargo, who had worked in the strike, criticized Mitchell for his "friendship with T.R." And Debs, referring to Mitchell's failure to call a general strike of all the miners in support of the anthracite workers, bluntly called the settlement a "farce." [26]

Similar conflicts followed the annual review of the interstate agreement with the operators in the central competitive field and in other areas where comprehensive agreements had now been established. For example, the joint interstate conference for the central competitive field held in February 1903 secured an increase of 10 per cent in mining rates over the previous year, and many miners hoped for a comparable increase in 1904. However, by this time a major strike was under way in Colorado, a downward trend was evident in business, and the operators, instead of agreeing to an increase, demanded a reduction of 15 per cent. At first, Mitchell and the other leaders of the union stood firm against the proposed reduction. But after further negotiation they recommended that the membership accept a compromise reduction of 5½ per cent. A referendum vote adopted the proposal by 102,000 votes to 68,000, but criticism from many quarters followed. Illinois, which by now had by far the largest district membership, voted solidly against the reduction. Max Hayes, well known as a socialist leader at AFL conventions, urged the miners to repudiate the agreement by voting for the Socialist party in the fall elections of 1904—the only party, he asserted, which had declared that "the miners shall have . . . a 'fair share' of the wealthy [*sic*] they produce, not a reduction of 5½ per cent." And Debs, whose ties to the coal miners continued to remain strong, delivered a tirade against President John Mitchell in the Milwaukee *Social Democrat Herald*. "You not only yielded everything you had originally demanded, but you agreed to a reduction," Debs said. "Not only this, but you did all in your official power to enforce [it]." "Verily," he wrote to his young coal miner friend Adolph Germer, of Mount Olive, Illinois, "these are days for miners to think and see for themselves. The ballot-box is the only place where they can vanquish the operators and come into their own." [27]

It was no coincidence that Debs should have written to Adolph Germer on this point, for it was in Illinois that the center of socialist influence in the UMWA had now crystallized. Until 1900 the socialists had no clear geographical basis of support in the union, and such radical criticism as had been made of the organization's policies had come largely from outside. But by 1903 Illinois District 12—which contained about 80,000 members, or more than a quarter of total union membership—had come largely under the control of the socialists, who made it the basis for their operations throughout the United Mine Workers as a whole.

There were a number of reasons why the coal fields of Illinois, in the southwestern part of the state, became the center of radicalism in the UMWA. For one thing, as already noted, they absorbed a considerable number of the English-speaking miners who had been driven westward by the depression and had suffered from the incursion of cheap Slav and Italian labor into an industry which they had formerly controlled. For another, despite the collapse of the Labor-Populist-Socialist alliance in 1894, the earlier tradition of radicalism in the state had been exploited by the socialists in a uniquely successful way. This was partly because of the extensive use of socialist speakers and campaign literature—much of it from the Debs Standard Publishing Company in Terre Haute, across the state line in Indiana—and partly because of the proximity of the Socialist party's national headquarters in Chicago. But it was also due to the efforts of a new generation of young socialists in the Illinois Miners Union who were to control most of the leading offices in District 12 for more than fifteen years.

The oldest of these men was John H. Walker, of Braceville, born in Scotland in 1872 and president of District 12 between 1906 and 1913. He was also president of the influential Illinois State Federation of Labor from 1915 until the end of our period and beyond. Walker was a convinced socialist and an active member of the Socialist party. But he was also a moderate, and he did not allow his radicalism to interfere with a close personal friendship with John Mitchell. Another Scots-born moderate was Duncan McDonald, secretary-treasurer of the district between 1910 and 1917. Frank Hayes, the redheaded and popular young trade-union leader who became international vice-president in 1910, and then president of the United Mine Workers as a whole between 1917 and 1920, was also for many years a member of the Socialist party in Illinois, although less active in it than some of his colleagues. Hayes was a native-born American, having been born in Iowa in 1879. He was, moreover, a Catholic. But the most influential as well as the most radical figure in Illinois was Adolph Germer himself, who first joined the Socialist party in 1900 and became its national secretary between 1916 and 1919. Germer was born in Germany in 1881, came to the United States in 1888, and began work in the mines at Staunton, Illinois, at the age of ten. In 1907 he was elected vice-president, and then secretary-treasurer, of the Belleville subdistrict, which contained about 20,000 of the 80,000 United Mine Workers' members in Illinois. Although Germer was German-born, it should be noted that he had come to the country far too young for his socialism to have been determined simply by a previous commitment to German Social Democracy.[28]

These Illinois socialists were not wholly in control of District 12. A number of the other officers of the district were nonsocialists, including the influential International Executive Board member from Illinois, Frank Farrington. Nor did they constitute, by any means, the only center of opposition to the policies of the Mitchell administration. Nevertheless, the Illinois socialists were responsible for most of the radical initiatives which were made in the United Mine Workers up to World War I. Their first interest was in establishing an alliance with the militant metal miners' movement of Colorado and the Far West, which had now become of considerable importance.

III

Since its inception the UMWA had been by far the most powerful advocate of industrial unionism in the AFL. The geographical location of the industry, and the great preponderance of pick-and-shovel workers in it, made it impractical to maintain a wide variety of craft-union locals for the minority of skilled craftsmen who worked in the separate coal fields. And in the complex negotiating procedures of the interstate joint agreements, it was essential for the bargaining position of the union to have as much control as possible over the different types of workers who were employed. However, in their approach to the question of industrial unionism the coal miners had hitherto been influenced more by pragmatic considerations regarding their own jurisdiction than by questions of working-class solidarity as such. In 1899 and 1900, for example, the Brotherhood of Blacksmiths demanded a right to organize in the mining communities, and jurisdictional disputes also occurred with the Engineers, the Machinists, the Hoisting Engineers, and other unions. It was in response to these conflicts that the January 1901 convention of the union adopted a resolution asserting its right "to organize into the United Mine Workers of America all engineers, firemen, blacksmiths, carpenters and others who may now be members of other trade organizations." And it was largely in response to them that the AFL Scranton Declaration of December 1901 was passed. The two main arguments heard in favor of it in the UMWA were that by controlling the craft workers' ability to strike, the miners' own agreements with the operators would be preserved; and, along the same line of reasoning, that when others struck, the miners themselves were less likely to be thrown out of work. Neither argument was particularly radical in its tone.[29]

For this reason there had for some years been disappointment among the socialists in the UMWA at the union's evident unwillingness to press for industrial unionism in the AFL in more militant and ideological terms, and a corresponding enthusiasm for the rise of the Western Federation of Miners, which had been founded in 1893. Although much smaller than the UMWA—its membership never rose much above 30,000—the WFM was at this time an openly revolutionary organization with an aggressive and militant leadership, and to many socialists in the AFL it was the archetype of an aggressive, revolutionary, industrial trade-union. From the beginning, therefore, the idea of cooperating with the WFM, and even of uniting with it in the cause of industrial unionism and of revolutionary socialism generally, had been a matter of considerable interest to the radicals in the UMWA. It was to become of crucial importance when the WFM became the major force behind the founding of the Industrial Workers of the World in 1905.

Official relations between the Western Federation of Miners and the United Mine Workers of America remained relatively cordial throughout the 1890's, despite the somewhat acrimonious withdrawal of the WFM from the AFL in 1897. In 1899 President John Mitchell even recommended "consolidation" of the UMWA with the WFM as a means of facilitating the transfer of miners from one organization to the other. But after the Western Federation of Miners had helped organize the radical Western Labor Union in 1898 and begun openly to challenge the AFL, the official position of the UMWA leadership rapidly changed. Rank-and-file UMWA members in the West, who had no particular affection for the AFL, but felt strong sympathy for the metal miners in their repeated struggles with the employers, continued to give them financial and moral support. But the United Mine Workers' administration first became cautious, and then openly hostile, as the American Labor Union (formed out of the Western Labor Union in 1902) began to attack Mitchell, together with Gompers and the other leaders of the AFL, as "fakirs" who wined and dined with the operators while the miners "starved." But this did not deter the Illinois socialists from keeping in close touch with the WFM. Adolph Germer corresponded frequently with John M. O'Neill, editor of the WFM official journal, *Miners' Magazine,* and with Clarence Smith, secretary-treasurer of the American Labor Union. He solicited subscriptions to both the *Miners' Magazine* and the *American Labor Union Journal* throughout the coal fields of southern Illinois, in order to "extend the influence of a really aggressive labor organization." [30]

Then came a major coal and metal miners' strike in Colorado in 1903, involving members of both the United Mine Workers and the WFM, which served at once to draw the radical members of both organizations closer together, while at the same time antagonizing still further their respective leaders. In August 1903 President Charles Moyer of the WFM addressed a District 15 convention of the coal miners in Colorado urging them to strike, both on their own account and in order to relieve the pressure on the WFM, which had for some time been conducting a bitterly fought contest of its own. The Indianapolis headquarters of the UMWA reluctantly agreed. But soon after the strike had begun it advised the coal miners in the northern part of the state to make a separate settlement, since the operators offered them substantial gains. In November 1903 this was done—by secret ballot of the miners themselves, it should be added—leaving the more numerous strikers in the southern part of the state to continue the struggle alone. To

the socialists, including Mother Jones, the colorful radical figure now working in Colorado on behalf of the United Mine Workers, and to other members
of both unions, this seemed like an act of betrayal. It was made all the
worse by the fact that President Mitchell was absent in Europe at the time,
thus depriving the strikers of his experience and prestige.

After a prolonged struggle, accompanied by evictions, forced marches
over the mountains, and wholesale arrests, the strike in southern Colorado
was lost. This brought a bitter attack on Mitchell from a variety of
sources, including the influential socialist paper *Appeal to Reason,* as well
as from the more radical delegates at the January 1905 United Mine
Workers Convention. Delegate Robert Randall, a member of the Socialist
party who had also been active on behalf of the WFM, declared that had
the northern miners stayed out

> it would have meant victory for both the coal and the metalliferous miners
> of the West. . . . The day the northern miners returned to work, the dis-
> couraged southern miners were defeated, and the strike was lost. The Denver
> Citizen's Alliance, the Victor Fuel Company, and the Colorado Fuel and
> Iron Company, with the able assistance of John Mitchell, won a victory over
> the miners of the West that has forced them into a state of abject peonage
> and closed upon them the door of hope for years to come.

This speech gave a tremendous boost to the prestige and influence of the
socialists throughout the United Mine Workers as a whole, even though
Mitchell's conduct was defended by Secretary-Treasurer W. B. Wilson, by
Vice-President Tom Lewis, and by various other members of the UMW
International Executive Board.[31]

The chief importance of these developments, however, was in the effect
which they had on the coal miners' attitude toward the IWW, which was established, largely through the efforts of the WFM, in June 1905. Predictably, despite its own form of industrial unionism, the UMWA administration
would have nothing to do with the new organization and denounced it in
much the same terms as the other trade-unions of the AFL had used. In the
early part of the year, when preparations for the IWW were being made,
the editor of the *United Mine Workers' Journal* dismissed the idea of industrial federation as "impossible," since it meant "abolishing all existing
trade unions." And when the IWW had actually been established the antagonism became even more intense. In 1905 and the early part of 1906,
Debs, DeLeon, and President Charles Moyer of the WFM all made
speeches criticizing the UMWA on behalf of the IWW. All three were denounced by the *Journal* as "defamatory rascals and self-seekers." [32]

The crucial area for the United Mine Workers' response to the IWW,
however, was Illinois. No Illinois miners were present at the preliminary

planning conference for the IWW which met on January 2, 1905. But two locals from other states—from Red Lodge, Montana, and Pittsburgh, Kansas—joined the organization at its founding convention in Chicago in June. More important was the fact that the February 1905 convention of District 12 appointed a committee of observers to attend the meeting. Precisely who constituted this committee, and what its recommendations were, are not known. But Adolph Germer was certainly a member of it, and Gompers was sufficiently concerned about its possible influence that on May 13, 1905, he wrote to W. D. Ryan, secretary-treasurer of the Illinois district, urging him to try to persuade its members not to attend. The IWW was already claiming that the "Illinois miners are with the movement," Gompers wrote, and if the Illinois committee attended the June convention "still greater capital will be made of it, to the detriment of not only your State organization and the interests of the miners, but also the entire labor movement, and the interests of the working people of the country." Ryan, however, responded that since the delegates were going simply "to listen and learn, and report their opinion of the meeting," he did not see that there could be any harm.[33]

In the event, the high hopes placed by the IWW on the affiliation of the Illinois miners failed to materialize. In 1906 and 1907 twenty-four locals of the IWW were organized in the coal fields, encompassing about 2,000 men—a very small number compared to the more than 300,000 miners who were now in United Mine Workers as a whole. Fourteen of them were in Illinois, three in Texas, two in Kansas, four in Pennsylvania, and only one in Colorado—a remarkably low figure for the latter state, in view of the weakness of the United Mine Workers there and the resentment which had developed against the UMWA leadership as a result of the loss of the 1903 strike. At the second IWW convention, in June 1906, Secretary-Treasurer William E. Trautmann reported that IWW organizers had "come into contact with . . . thousands of coal miners in Illinois, Ohio, Pennsylvania" who were, he said, prepared to join a "true revolutionary industrial union" if given the chance. But the only coal miners' delegate actually present was John M. Francis, of Du Quoin, Illinois, and even he represented his local unofficially and against the wishes of its officers. At the 1907 convention there were no coal miners' delegates at all. One new United Mine Workers local had joined the IWW in the intervening year. But the official optimism expressed by Trautmann, who claimed that "at least one-third of the locals in the State of Illinois" might soon join the organization, was wholly unjustified. As far as can be ascertained, only three new coal miners' locals were established by the IWW in the next four years.[34]

One of the reasons for this lack of success was clearly doubt and disapproval at the virulent attacks made by the IWW on the UMWA and the AFL generally, which was felt even in Illinois. Germer, McDonald, and Frank Hayes were themselves critical of the conservative policies of the United Mine Workers' administration. But by the end of 1906 it had become clear to them that the IWW was losing more friends than it gained by its indiscriminately hostile approach. There were also the IWW's inadequate financial resources and its inability to mount a sustained organizing drive. Despite what Trautmann had said at the 1906 IWW convention, Francis reported that the Illinois miners had felt neglected by the organization, even though some of them had been predisposed in favor of it after the Chicago convention of June 1905. More important than this, however, were the commitments which the coal miners customarily made under the contracts with the operators, which in the case of the Illinois miners ran until June 1908. At this time the IWW repudiated the whole concept of time contracts, but the Illinois miners had by now learned enough of the value of agreements to be unwilling to repudiate them without the guarantee of some better method of advance.[35] The checkoff system, under which the operators deducted the union dues from the miners' wages, also tended to tie coal miners to the United Mine Workers rather than to any other union.

By early 1907 it had become clear that not only the conservative Illinois leaders, such as W. D. Ryan and Frank Farrington, but also the socialists had lost patience with the IWW. By this time the WFM, with which the Illinois socialists were still in close touch, was also having strong doubts about its association with the IWW—although it did not finally break with it until July 1908—and at a convention of District 12 of the UMWA, held in Springfield in February 1907 (and attended by James O'Neill of the WFM), a decision was formally taken to campaign against the IWW throughout southern Illinois. A rival meeting held by Trautmann and other IWW representatives on February 24 was of no avail, and at least one coal miners' local, at Blue Mound, Illinois, was broken up and the members run out of town because of their IWW associations. The national officers of the IWW roundly condemned the Illinois miners for this decision. At the September 1907 convention of the organization Trautmann described Walker, McDonald, and Germer as "brain[less] and spineless tools of the capitalist class." But this, predictably, simply served to harden their opposition. Although a few IWW locals lingered on among the miners, President John Mitchell was right when he reported to the January 1908 UMWA convention that the organization had failed to "pervert the minds of the mine workers." [36]

Despite their hostility toward the IWW, the socialists in the UMWA continued to press for third-party political action. In Illinois itself Germer ran for state office on the Socialist party ticket in 1904, and he did his best to help

Debs' presidential efforts in that year by attempting to secure a list of all UMWA locals for Debs' use during the campaign. Charles P. Gildea, of Pennsylvania, sought to develop Socialist party sentiment in the anthracite districts. And at the national level there were signs for the first time of an interest in a labor party on the British model. The *United Mine Workers' Journal* had always contained a great deal of English news, due to the British background of so many of the coal miners, and after the great Liberal victory at the end of 1905, when fifty-one labor M.P.'s were elected to the House of Commons, the Northumberland correspondent of the *Journal* strenuously urged the American miners to follow the English example. "This election has special interest to organized labor in the United States," he wrote in February 1906, "which has not one Congressman where it could elect sixty, not a Senator where it could have sixteen, and in the legislatures of the various states it has three or four scattered here and there." [37]

This comparison was all the more apt since the American miners were now suffering, like the machinists, from an abuse which had done much to drive the English workers into politics: namely, the excessive use of labor injunctions by the courts.[38] In 1907 President John Mitchell was named as one of the defendants in the Buck's Stove and Range Case, and at the national union convention shortly afterward D. B. Robb, of District 6, Ohio, introduced a resolution asserting that the "absolute power" of judges in labor disputes was "a menace to the independence of . . . the wage-workers" and urging the United Mine Workers to "encourage, in spirit and in fact, the promotion of a national labor party."

In support of this motion Robb argued that "in Great Britain the miners, machinists, boiler-makers and workers of every other description in mine, mill and shop have closed up the ranks and are working together. All I ask is that we do that in America and save us from having less all the time." Several of the Illinois delegates spoke in favor of the resolution, including John H. Walker. But a majority of speakers in the debate were opposed. Typical were the arguments of International Secretary-Treasurer W. B. Wilson, who said that it was better for the miners to continue their traditional policy of electing their own members to office on one of the major party tickets, "forcing the man who is on the outside to take a stand in our favor. Then we can use them to force concessions." Wilson also argued that conditions in England—and in Germany—were quite different from those in America, which was less industrialized and in which the larger number of farmers, who were "not as far advanced in economic freedom of thought as the wage workers," made political unity of the workers impossible.

Interestingly enough, Adolph Germer also objected to the idea of a labor party, although on very different grounds. There already was a labor party in America, he argued, namely, the Socialist party, which was committed to fighting the class struggle on behalf of the entire working class. He added that the evil of injunctions, although serious, was insufficient to serve as the sole basis for political action. "The abuses of which we complain," he said, "spring from the capitalist class, and as long as this class struggle exists, . . . you can organize as many labor parties as your mind is able to invent, and so long as you fail to strike at the vital issue, so long will your independent labor party be of very little value." In expressing these opinions Germer reflected clearly the official policy of the Socialist party at this time, which feared that a broadly based labor party would be insufficiently radical in its program.[39]

The convention debate over a labor party proved to be largely academic, however, for the proposal was heartily defeated. In March 1906 the UMWA welcomed the AFL's Bill of Grievances, especially the plank on injunctions; and in the November 1906 elections it pursued its traditional policy of attempting to secure the nomination of its own members on the ticket of one of the two major parties and of supporting other favorably disposed candidates where this was impossible. In fact, 1906 was one of the union's most active political years. More than thirty miners ran for political office in Pennsylvania, West Virginia, Illinois, Kansas, Oklahoma, and Ohio. John Nugent, president of District 17, was elected to the West Virginia state legislature. Peter Hanraty was elected to the constitutional convention in Oklahoma, and there were numerous other successes elsewhere. The most important of them was in Pennsylvania, where International Secretary-Treasurer W. B. Wilson, following his own advice at the union convention, was elected to Congress as a Democrat in the Fifteenth Congressional District, thereby marking the start of an important political career. T. D. Nicolls, president of District 1 in the anthracite region, was also elected as a Democratic congressman, although only for a single term. Nevertheless, this gave the UMWA two out of the three trade-union congressmen elected in the AFL's first really active political year. Five coal miners, all of them Democrats, were also added to the union's representation in the Pennsylvania legislature.[40]

President John Mitchell campaigned actively on behalf of the UMWA candidates in the 1906 elections. His reputation had become nationwide as a result of the anthracite settlement and of the sudden growth which had taken place in the size of the union at the turn of the century. Indeed, he had been mentioned as a possible candidate for governor of Illinois as early as 1902.

Mitchell turned down this offer, as he did all subsequent political offers; and in October 1907, seriously ill and affected by heavy bouts of drinking, he announced his resignation from the presidency of the United Mine

Workers as of the following March. In the 1908 union elections he was succeeded by Vice-President Tom L. Lewis, of Ohio. In all likelihood this would have been the end of Mitchell's official connection with the miners had he not, while still remaining a member of the union, accepted a full-time post as chairman of the Trade Agreements Department of the National Civic Federation at a salary of $8,000 a year. At the same time a boom developed to draft him as Vice-Presidential candidate on the Democratic ticket, to run with William Jennings Bryan.[41] The result was perhaps the most important public clash between the socialists and their opponents in the history of their relations throughout the labor movement at large.

Mitchell had from the first been one of the most enthusiastic supporters of the National Civic Federation, having been a member of its national committee since 1900 and having used its services extensively during the anthracite strike of 1902. The socialists had earlier criticized Mitchell for his NCF connections, and now that he had become an officer of the organization they attacked him remorselessly, charging him with "wining and dining" with employers, selling out the interests of the miners to the operators, and becoming the "little tin god of the capitalist class." The situation was exacerbated by the fact that the NCF itself was now becoming increasingly conservative and antisocialist, a development which was to characterize its later years. A list of all the United Mine Workers' locals also got into the hands of the Democratic National Committee—probably through the AFL—and the Democrats sent out literature to large numbers of the miners' locals. This caused Mitchell "severe embarrassment" and forced him to explain publicly in the *United Mine Workers' Journal* that the posters were sent out without his knowledge or consent.[42]

It thus became easy for the socialists in the UMWA to suggest to the rank and file that Mitchell was "playing politics" with the union and even that he had "gone over" to the employers. President Tom L. Lewis was also on bad terms with Mitchell and was evidently jealous of the fact that Mitchell remained second vice-president of the AFL, reproducing to some extent the situation in the International Association of Machinists after the defeat of O'Connell in 1912. Thus at the January 1911 convention of the union Lewis gave administration support to a series of resolutions, sponsored by the socialists, declaring that "all United Mine Workers who are connected with the Civic Federation sever their connection with that body" and that all union members were prohibited, "under penalty of expulsion, from affiliating with or rendering aid, financial or otherwise, to the aforesaid Civic Federation." [43]

This motion would have had less importance had it not been for Mitchell's widespread reputation throughout the country and had it not been clearly directed against him personally, as much as against the NCF as such. The situation was made all the more dramatic because Mitchell was at that time defending himself against a Supreme Court indictment in the Buck's Stove and Range case and was unable to attend the 1911 convention to defend himself. In the debate a number of the more extreme radicals in the union attacked Mitchell openly, arguing that men like him were "nothing more nor less than sheep in wolves' clothing," who associated with great capitalists like Judge Gary of the United States Steel Corporation, where men were "murdered day by day and others are kept in abject slavery."

But some of the Illinois leaders, aware of Mitchell's strong following and unwilling to oppose him openly when he was under indictment along with other leaders of the AFL, were more cautious in their approach. This was not true of Germer, who openly denounced him, recalling the defeat of the 1903 strike in Colorado and asking angrily of those who pointed to the Supreme Court indictment, "What have these men from whom we expect favors in the Civic Federation done for the men in the Colorado jail?" But Duncan McDonald expressed concern that Mitchell was not present to defend his connection with the NCF; and Walker was instrumental in moderating the tone of the original resolutions. In the end a constitutional amendment was adopted by 1,213 votes to 967, which had the same effect. But it avoided use of the word "expulsion" and simply stated that any union member who was also a member of the National Civic Federation was to forfeit his membership in the UMWA.[44]

Mitchell now had to choose between resigning from the union and leaving his job with the NCF. Mitchell himself tended to favor the former course of action. But Gompers, in a private letter, urged him to leave the Civic Federation and to fight for his own good name in the United Mine Workers. If he left the union, Gompers argued, Mitchell would have no platform from which to fight back against the socialists, and he would, moreover, play into the hands of those who alleged that he was "in league with the NCF." In February 1911 Mitchell decided to leave the Civic Federation. Immediately afterward, in a letter to Mitchell that this time was highly publicized, Gompers described the action taken by the UMWA convention as unjust to the Civic Federation, unjust to the labor movement, and unjust to Mitchell himself. Any feeling which had been created against the NCF, he claimed, was the fault of "partisan Socialists," who "mask behind a pretended interest in and friendship for labor."[45]

There were numerous socialists who felt that the successful attack on Mitchell was their greatest success in the UMWA up to that time. This was questionable, however. The humiliation of Mitchell had only succeeded because President Tom Lewis and other elements in the union had given it support, and it was not followed by the election of a national socialist administration, such as occurred in the IAM after the defeat of James O'Connell. Comments on the "egregious blunder" of the union came from as far away as Canada, and Gompers was probably to a great extent successful—although no doubt unjust—when he sought to blame Mitchell's defeat on the socialists alone. Protests were received from a variety of UMWA locals throughout the country, and a resolution condemning the action was even brought before the February 1911 convention of Illinois District 12. It was adopted by a large majority, despite the fact that this was the socialists' stronghold. Germer sought to belittle the matter, asserting that none of the locals in his Belleville subdistrict had supported the resolution, and that Frank Farrington had deliberately misrepresented the socialists' stand. On balance, however, the whole affair probably did more harm than good to the socialist cause.[46]

Nevertheless, in other ways the socialists appeared for a time to maintain, if not actively to expand, their area of influence in the UMWA. In the union elections of 1910 the socialist Frank Hayes had been elected international vice-president, a post which he retained until 1917 before succeeding to the presidency for a brief term. Hayes was not an assertive nor a particularly successful union officer, and by 1915 he had lost much of his former radical zeal. But he was openly identified as a socialist when he ran for office, and it was considerable testimony to the socialists' strength that he managed to get elected at all.[47] In addition, once the Western Federation of Miners had withdrawn from the IWW, friendly relations were resumed between the two miners' unions, and the idea was revived of uniting them into one. In 1910 the United Mine Workers gave strong support to the WFM's application for AFL membership, and there was even a suggestion that the coal miners might disaffiliate from the AFL if the metal miners were not given a charter covering as broad a jurisdiction as their own. After prolonged and somewhat delicate negotiations the WFM entered the AFL in May 1911. A Mining Department was established along the lines of the other trade departments in the AFL.

There is no doubt that part of the purpose behind this maneuver was to force the AFL into taking a more radical stand on the issue of industrial unionism; and the United Mine Workers' leadership, both in its support for the WFM and in its more general arguments in favor of industrial organization, now took a more militant position than it had over the Scranton Declaration of 1901. At the January 1912 convention of the union a resolution was proposed that the UMWA withdraw from the AFL and help establish a genuine "industrial organization of labor" which would have as its object "the emancipation of the wage workers from the yoke of industrial slavery." The proposal was voted down and replaced by a more moderate resolution urging the coal miners' delegates to work for the idea of "organization by industry" in the AFL. Nevertheless, the more radical proposal received a surprising amount of support. At the same convention a resolution favoring "government ownership of all industries" slipped past the Committee on Resolutions almost without notice, to be adopted by a voice vote. Even more significant, the Preamble to the constitution was amended, endorsing the miners' right to the "full social value of their product," again without any major dissent.[48]

The problem with proposals for unification with the Western Federation of Miners, however, was that the United Mine Workers was now very much the larger and more successful of the two organizations, so that if a merger was to take place the coal miners would have had to take responsibility for the organizing difficulties and frequent conflicts with the western mining operators with which the WFM was faced. In October 1914 committees from both unions met in Butte, Montana, to consider unification. But it was found that the accession of the Western Federation to the coal miners' union, with only 17,000 members out of a potential labor force of 200,000, would have placed an excessive burden on the organizing resources of the United Mine Workers. In addition, it was pointed out that "the product of the metal miner [in] nowise enters into competition with that of the coal miner; in fact, his relationship to coal mining is not so near nor so important in terms of industrial strife, as is that of men employed in the transportation industry." Thus, negotiations for consolidation of the two unions were abandoned. Although relations between them remained quite close, a renewed plea from Debs for the secession of both organizations from the AFL, and the establishment of a new, revolutionary trade-union federation, went unheeded by both sides.[49]

Debs' call for the secession of the UMWA from the AFL probably alienated the coal miners' leadership from him still more, and it reflected an aberrant preoccupation with dual unionism on his part which continued to do the socialist cause considerable harm. Nevertheless Debs and the socialists generally had been able to recoup some of their former popularity with the miners by the help which they gave in the year-long West Virginia coal strike, which began in April 1912. West Virginia still remained largely unorganized, threatening the stability of the agreements made in the Central Competitive Field. After an extremely bitter struggle, conducted much of the time under martial law—in which machine guns were used against a miners' tent colony in Holy Grove, and numerous deaths resulted from clashes with the Baldwin-Felts mine guards—a compromise agreement was negotiated which included the nine-hour day, recognition of the union, and the right to trade in noncompany stores. The National Executive Committee of the Socialist party sent a memorandum to President Wilson demanding an investigation into mining conditions in the state (the Senate did, in fact, conduct an inquiry), and it appointed Debs, Victor Berger, and Adolph Germer to carry out an investigation of its own. In May 1913 the socialist committee toured the strike areas, drawing attention to the strong-arm tactics of the operators and the appalling conditions in the mines. They were also able to secure the release from jail of a number of strike agitators, including John Brown, the socialist organizer for West Virginia, and the eighty-year-old Mother Jones.[50]

Another area in which the socialists made progress was in helping to establish cooperative retail supply stores in the mining camps, as a means both of avoiding the extortionate prices of the company stores and of lessening the miners' dependence on them during strikes. In 1909 an Iowa local suggested that the international union invest some of its considerable funds in purchasing mining land and mining equipment and go into cooperative coal production as well. This was rejected, probably because of the risks and the high costs involved; but by 1916 there was quite a network of retail cooperative stores in Illinois, Ohio, Pennsylvania, and other states. In Illinois there were over thirty of them, operating mainly in the mining camps where the socialists were strong. A primitive cooperative medical plan was also established, involving five doctors and a makeshift hospital at West Frankfurt, Illinois. This was especially valuable because of the frequency of accidents and the need for objective evidence concerning insurance claims which the company doctors were often unwilling to supply. In 1919 Duncan McDonald was made secretary of the socialist-controlled Central States Cooperative Society, and John H. Walker was a member of the Executive Board.[51]

But despite these continuing evidences of radicalism and dissent, there were by 1916 unmistakable signs that the position of the socialists in the UMWA was in decline. One measure of this was the familiar shift in political interest from the bipartisanship of earlier years to virtually open endorsement of President Wilson's Democratic administration. In 1912, union members had as usual run for various political offices on both of the major party tickets. But there was also prolonged and serious discussion of a resolution to endorse the Socialist party at the UMWA convention of that year, and a number of coal miners ran for local offices on the party's ticket. Although the resolution endorsing the party failed by 515 votes to 155, it generated widespread interest and support. In addition, the *United Mine Workers' Journal* reproduced the entire Socialist party platform—a privilege it did not extend to the other parties—and in a preelection editorial drew a comparison between the increasing success of the Labor party in England and the absence of any comparable body in America. "Let us emulate our brothers on the other side," the editorial ran. "Let us send men to the Congress of the United States who can really represent us. Men from our own ranks. Men with our own point of view."

In the 1916 elections, by contrast, as far as can be ascertained no member of the union ran for state or national office on the socialist ticket, and while keeping its options open on the local level, the enthusiasm which the national administration had displayed in 1912 for independent political action was now directed largely at reelecting Woodrow Wilson. For the benefit of the membership the union journal spelled out the list of labor measures passed by the Democratic administration—the Clayton Act, the Anti-Child Labor Act, the La Follette Seamen's Act, and the Adamson Eight Hour Law for the railroads—and it reproduced the AFL's circulars indirectly urging labor to vote Democratic. "The workers should see to it," the *United Mine Workers' Journal* added, "that the friends of these progressive and humane laws should be placed in a position to administer them." After the election was over it expressed open pleasure at President Wilson's victory over Republican Charles Evans Hughes, despite the fact that at the local level several members of the union had run for office on the ticket of the Republican party.

It is probable that much of this change, as in other unions, was due to satisfaction with the record of the Democratic administration, especially with the passage of the Clayton Act, which seemed to promise even more to the United Mine Workers than it did to the International Association of Machinists. But a special factor was the appointment of ex-International Secretary-Treasurer W. B. Wilson as the first Secretary of Labor. Wilson had been defeated for reelection to Congress in 1912 by a narrow margin. But during his congressional term he had taken a prominent part in securing the adoption of legislation establishing the Federal Bureau of Mines (for research into the safety and health of workers underground), as well as working on early drafts of other important measures such as the Clayton Act, the Seamen's bill, and the Anti-Child Labor Act. These legislative successes had already brought convincing evidence of the value to the miners of working through the existing party system. But Wilson's appointment as Secretary of Labor gave them even stronger reasons for gratitude to the Democratic party.[52]

Economic recovery also sharply undercut the popularity of the socialists. Average daily wages throughout the coal industry rose from $1.80 in 1904 to over $2.00 in 1915. Because of inflation, they were to rise still further during the period of World War I. The membership of the UMWA also continued to increase, until by 1917 the union was in a strong position in virtually all the major coal fields. All of this lessened the bitterness and friction which had marked industrial relations in the coal industry before the turn of the century and for the first time gave the miners confidence in the future of their organization. In addition, widespread recognition of the union under the interstate agreements, and annual meetings with the operators to agree on a mining scale, gave the miners' leaders a new sense of participation, as well as of responsibility. The interstate agreement was negotiated on the basis of "current business ideas, competitive equality and upon well recognized principles of justice," the *United Mine Workers' Journal* had written in November 1898. Future negotiations with the employers were largely determined by this approach. As in many other unions, union recognition and economic success satisfied many of the aspirations of the leadership, even if they did not do so wholly for the rank and file.[53]

The position of the socialists was also undermined by the increasingly overt attacks which were made on them by the UMWA administration, at both the national and the district levels. This was particularly noticeable during the administration of President John P. White, which lasted from 1911 to 1917. As early as November 1911 there were allegations that President White had sought, unsuccessfully, to prevent the reelection of Duncan McDonald as secretary-treasurer of District 12 by sending International Executive Board member Frank Farrington and several international organizers back to Illinois to help campaign against him. Three years later, in 1914, a much more serious storm blew up over an attempt to frame Adolph Germer with evidence of treacherous conduct in his activities as international organizer during the Colorado coal strike of 1913–1914. On September 18, 1914, a mysterious circular was issued from Walsenburg, Colorado, asserting that Germer had consorted with prostitutes, given strikers' guns to the militia, and in other ways betrayed the miners' cause. Germer immediately denied the allegations, and a committee of officers from District 12 which visited Colorado found that several of those allegedly responsible for the circular had no knowledge of the document. The important point, however, was that it came out on the eve of another District 12 election, in which Germer was running against Farrington for the International Executive Board. Farrington was reelected, and Germer demanded another investigation, this time by international officials, who eventually cleared his name. But by this time quite a lot of damage had been done to his reputation, and Germer, together with other socialists (including both Eugene and Theodore Debs), became convinced that the Walsenburg circular was part of a general attempt by the administration to malign him and other socialists in the UMWA.[54]

Finally, there were increasing defections and divisions among the socialists themselves. International Vice-President Frank Hayes left the Socialist party sometime before 1915, because he was threatened with censure for having endorsed two nonsocialist candidates for the office of sheriff in a

Colorado coal town. Two years later John H. Walker left the party under not dissimilar circumstances. For some time Walker's political activities as president of the Illinois State Federation of Labor (which followed the regular "reward your friends, punish your enemies" electoral policy of the AFL) had put a strain on his relations with the local socialists; and in the November 1916 elections Walker caused quite a stir by endorsing simultaneously the reelection of President Wilson and the Republican candidate for governor of Illinois, Dunne. Soon afterward he was charged with disloyalty by his local Socialist party branch, in Danville, Illinois. Walker defended himself by saying that a majority of the membership of the State Federation of Labor, 25 per cent of whom were socialists, had favored the endorsements and that he had felt bound to support them. Despite this, he was expelled from the Socialist party.[55]

These strains and tensions among the socialists in the UMWA were increased after America's entry into World War I. As with the International Association of Machinists, there was no question of the United Mine Workers' support for American participation. In fact, the development of its attitude closely paralleled that of the IAM, and it ended up by being perhaps even more chauvinistic. In 1916 the coal miners expressed strong distaste for the war as a solely European conflict, both out of traditional American hostility toward militarism, and also because of a fear that the expansion of the military for wartime purposes would be used against labor at home. Once war came, however, the UMWA rallied immediately to the national cause. As many as 53,812 union members served in the armed forces (an average of sixteen men to each union local), and the union administration, ironically now headed by the former socialist President Frank Hayes, gave strong support to the antisocialist American Alliance for Labor and Democracy.[56]

Adolph Germer, who had now become national secretary of the Socialist party, was the only one of the former group of Illinois socialists to support the party's St. Louis antiwar declaration of April 1917. Early in 1918 he was prosecuted, along with other leading socialists, for allegedly obstructing the draft and enlistment laws. Even before this, however, he was publicly denounced by both Hayes and Walker as pro-German and a traitor to the American cause. An exchange of letters between the three men at the end of 1917 illustrated dramatically the destructive impact which the superpatriotic mood of the country now had on the already weakened state of relations between the Socialist party and the labor movement as a whole.

In response to the criticisms which had been made of him by Walker and Hayes, Germer protested that he opposed Prussian militarism as strongly as anyone and that he hoped, like many socialists, for a revolution in Germany which would create a more just and democratic society there, as well as in the United States. Nevertheless, Walker treated him almost as if he were an outcast, even though he had known him well for nearly twenty years. "I want you and your like," he wrote to Germer on October 29, "who want to [make] . . . the German Kaiser the Emperor of the World, and put everybody under the heels of his military, to know that there isn't anything I can think of or do, that I won't do, to prevent you and your kind from accomplishing your purpose." Similarly, President Hayes indignantly rejected Germer's reproaches at his strong support for the war, writing him on February 22, 1918:

> I suppose if you occupied this position, knowing that every act of yours reflected itself into the lives of two million people, you would follow the tactics of the I.W.W., and forever destroy the influence of our organization in the industrial and political life of America. . . . We have secured some very substantial benefits for our people during the past year, but, of course, . . . these have been entirely overlooked by you and your pro-German supporters.[57]

IV

The disintegration of the Illinois alliance of socialists between 1916 and 1918 marked virtually the end of organized socialist influence in the United Mine Workers of America. But it did not bring an end to radicalism or to third-party sentiments as such. As in the IAM, there was a strong, if temporary, revival of radical tendencies among the coal miners after World War I. This development was largely the work of a new set of radical leaders, most of whom were not, and never had been, members of the Socialist party. Only John H. Walker and Duncan McDonald remained influential of the older group. Although most of the issues involved were similar, it was also a broader and more heterogeneous movement than the prewar socialist one, and it involved Pennsylvania, Kansas, and other states, equally with Illinois. Nevertheless, for a time the postwar movement evoked as strong an upsurge of radical sentiments as any which had preceded it, and it coincided also with the emergence of the dynamic but ambiguous figure of John L. Lewis.

In one sense, John L. Lewis was himself the figurehead of a new challenge to the conservative leadership of the AFL. As already noted, Lewis ran against Gompers for the AFL leadership in 1921. He also continued to champion the more traditional forms of industrial unionism. But he ran roughshod over any sign of opposition in the UMWA, and in his leadership of the organization he exemplified the modern brand of tough, pragmatic, business unionism more completely than any of his predecessors had done. Politically, Lewis was at this time a conservative Republican; it was not until the 1930's that he became for a brief period a political radical.[58]

As in other unions, one of the causes of the postwar radical revival in the United Mine Workers was disillusionment and indignation at the profiteering, unemployment, and rising prices which had accompanied the ending of the European war. Although the union maintained a postwar membership of over 400,000, making it still by far the largest organization in the AFL, wartime demands had overstimulated coal production to such an extent that in 1919 the mines were producing 60 per cent in excess of peacetime needs. As soon as the demand for coal abroad diminished, a large number of miners were laid off or employed only irregularly.

Equally important was the miners' acute dissatisfaction with the wartime accord drawn up with the United States Fuel Administration, known as the Washington Agreement. This had brought initial wage increases, as well as other advantages. But it had also involved a no-strike clause and was to run for the entire period of the war, provided that this did not continue for longer than two years after April 1, 1918. By this time the bituminous miners had received no wage increases for three years, despite the soaring cost of living, and when the Armistice came, in November 1918, they immediately demanded a major increase, assuming the Washington Agreement to be at an end. The federal government, however, insisted that the agreement was still binding because the state of war with Germany was not officially terminated, and it refused to concede any of the union's demands. An outcry among the miners immediately arose. Numerous unauthorized strikes broke out, and at the September 1919 UMWA convention resolutions were adopted demanding the "nationalization and democratic control of the mines" and, what was more important, the establishment of a national labor party.

The nationalization resolution was adopted unanimously, as were others pledging the cooperation of the United Mine Workers with the railroad workers to secure government ownership of the railroads under the Plumb Plan. So also was the labor-party resolution, which represented the culmination of a prolonged campaign by the radicals in the union, who now had few militant Socialist party members to oppose them. It described the lobbying tactics of the AFL as "a miserable failure"—a major *volte-face* for a union which had always encouraged the AFL's involvement in politics —and it instructed the officers of the union and the International Executive Board to call a conference of representatives of various trade-unions, the AFL, the Nonpartisan League, the farmers' organizations, and state federations of labor "for the purpose of taking action on the question of organizing and launching a national Labor Party." Such a party, the resolution concluded, "could wield a tremendous power and assure the enactment of legislation for the nationalization of coal and other basic industries in the interests of the workers." The UMWA was by far the largest and most important trade-union in 1919 to give its official blessing to the labor-party idea.[59]

The new radical movement was also given powerful impetus by the insurgency which took place in both Illinois District 12 and Kansas District 14 against the policies of the national administration. This began in Illinois on July 4, 1919, when the operators enforced a penalty clause in their agreement against miners who had joined a five-day strike for the release of Tom Mooney, the labor organizer who had been convicted after a Preparedness Day parade in San Francisco in 1916 and whose case became symbolic for all postwar radicals. Then, in August, the officers of District 12 refused rank-and-file demands for a convention to consider negotiations for a new central competitive scale. A widespread unauthorized strike took place, with Belleville, Germer's old district, the center of the revolt, and on August 20 an insurgent district convention was held, with two hundred delegates from 141 locals. Farrington and President Lewis cooperated in suppressing the revolt, and twenty-four Illinois locals were expelled, after two days of acrid debate at the September 1919 national UMWA convention. In Kansas, the rebellion arose over Lewis' failure to support Alexander Howatt and the bulk of the membership of District 14 against a reactionary Industrial Court Law passed by Governor Henry J. Allen in order to suppress illegal strikes and other labor activities. Howatt and four other District 14 officers were convicted and sent to jail for refusing to terminate an unauthorized strike. But Lewis and the International Executive Board, instead of supporting them, upheld the operators' contention that the miners had violated their contract. Howatt was suspended by the administration, eighty-one locals loyal to him lost their charters, and a new group of officers was installed in District 14.[60]

These developments made a popular hero of Alexander Howatt, and they brought a greater show of hostility toward President John L. Lewis than against any United Mine Workers' president since Mitchell. Rank-and-file resentment was compounded still further by Lewis' refusal to continue a nationwide coal strike which had begun on November 1, 1919. On November 8, the United States District Court in Indiana declared the strike illegal because of the Washington Agreement; and on November 10, Lewis, having previously taken a bold stand, called off the contest with the statement that "I will not fight my government, the greatest government on earth." The *United Mine Workers' Journal* protested strongly, although it accepted the need to obey the injunction. John H. Walker told the aged Mother Jones that Lewis' "surrendering and bowing in abject submission, allowing the men to be driven back into the mines like cattle, without a fight at all, . . . makes the decent Mine Workers, who understand what it means, blush with shame." And John Brophy, president of District 2 in Pennsylvania, who was to emerge as probably the most influential of the postwar radicals, declared that he was "disgusted by the cheap hypocrisy of the talk about patriotism and law and order." He immediately set about popularizing a new *Miners' Program,* based on mine nationalization, workers' education, and demands for the thirty-hour week. In the union elections which took place in the fall of 1920 the old radical element which had supported Walker in 1916 and 1918 transferred its support to Robert Harlin of Washington District 10, running against Lewis for the presidency, and to Alexander Howatt for international vice-president. Lewis won, but there were widespread charges of fraud.[61]

There were also extensive indications of support for the labor-party movement at the local level. More than fifty miners' delegates from Illinois, Indiana, Ohio, Pennsylvania, and Kansas attended the National Labor party convention which met in Chicago on November 22, 1919—more even than from the IAM—and John H. Walker became vice-chairman of the party organization. William Mitch, president of District 11, took a prominent part in the labor-party movement in Indiana, as did Robert Harlin in the state of Washington. In Pennsylvania, Brophy was now pressing hard for mine nationalization, and Altoona, a mining town in Blair County, elected its mayor and several other officers on a labor-party ticket in the fall elections of 1919.

The year 1920 seemed to be equally encouraging. In Illinois, Walker became national chairman of the National Farmer-Labor party and ran for governor of the state in November on that party's ticket, despite the presence of an opposing Socialist party candidate. Robert Harlin and Alexander Howatt both attended the July 1920 convention of the National Farmer-Labor party; and Frank Farrington sent Walker a $100 personal contribution to his campaign expenses, even though he had been an implacable enemy of the socialists before the war. During the year strong support also developed for old-age pension legislation, a federal inheritance tax, and compulsory health insurance. And in April 1921 Alexander Howatt, at Walker's request, sent round an appeal for funds to District 14 on behalf of the National Farmer-Labor party, asserting that there was "no class of workmen in America today, who realize the necessity of the workers uniting at the ballot-box, more than the miners of Kansas, as there is no other state in the nation where they have an industrial court law, such as they have in Kansas at this time." [62]

It seemed, therefore, as though the frustrated postwar efforts for industrial progress were now to be translated into political action, and that the UMWA might give stronger support to the third-party element in the Conference for Progressive Political Action than either the IAM or the

ILGWU had done. But this did not prove to be the case. Violent strikes continued to mark the union's efforts in West Virginia and in many other coal fields, and 1922 saw more coal miners out on strike than in any previous year. It also saw the terrible massacre of June 1922, in Herrin, Illinois, in which nineteen strikebreakers and two union members were killed. Equally bitter strife continued to characterize the union's internal life, which was to culminate in John Brophy's challenge to Lewis for the presidency in 1926 and the ultimate establishment of the Progressive Miners of America as a separate organization in Illinois, Kansas, and elsewhere.[63] But the UMWA as such took very little interest in the CPPA. International Secretary-Treasurer William Green attended the first conference of the organization in February 1922, and the miners were unofficially represented by one delegate at the second meeting, in December of that year. Rank-and-file members also contributed $3,000 to the CPPA's funds. This was a larger total than the sum collected by the IAM in that same year. But in view of the much larger size of the United Mine Workers of America, it was in relative terms a much smaller sum of money.[64]

One reason for this relative lack of interest was disappointment at the failure of the initial postwar labor-party movements to do better than they did. In Illinois, there had been an unfavorable reaction in the state legislature as soon as the National Labor party had appeared. Thus at their June 1921 convention the Illinois branch of the party decided not to put up candidates in areas where such action would simply ensure the election of men favored by the coal operators or the Chicago packing-house interests, and Walker busied himself cultivating a close relationship with the Republican governor, Len Small. In Kansas, Howatt's enthusiasm for the Farmer-Labor party had also by this time largely disappeared. In July 1921 Howatt decided to attempt organizing both the farmers and the miners in Kansas into the Republican party, in order to try to elect an administration which would repeal the Industrial Court Law. Instead of discouraging him, Walker told Howatt that he and J. G. Brown, national secretary of the National Farmer-Labor party, had "come to the conclusion that we must work on a practical basis, if we are to get anywhere"; and that as far as he was concerned Howatt was at liberty to use such strength as the party had in Kansas "in whatever way will be most helpful in the practical situations that we are dealing with at the time." [65]

Another problem was President John L. Lewis' indifference, and then his increasing opposition, to third-party politics and to the whole program of mine nationalization and social legislation which had been proposed by the radicals. As already indicated Lewis was at this time a conservative in matters of social policy, as well as being a registered Republican—he endorsed Coolidge in 1924—and it is ironic that the man who was to become the outstanding leader of radical trade-unionism in the 1930's should at this time have opposed the progressives in the UMWA. Lewis had acquiesced in the passage of the nationalization proposal at the 1919 convention; and he remained, in theory, favorably disposed toward it through 1921, evidently in an attempt to secure the full support of the miners' delegation in his contest with Gompers at the AFL convention of that year.[66] But he did nothing to forward the proposal and later sabotaged it altogether by publicly testifying before the House Committee on Labor that "government ownership is an impossibility under present circumstances." He also hampered the work of the union's Nationalization Research Committee, which was headed by John Brophy of District 2, by refusing to permit publicity for the proposal in the *United Mine Workers' Journal* and by effectively preventing it from continuing its work.[67]

Lewis' actions in regard to the labor-party proposal were very much the same. At the 1919 convention he had acquiesced in the passage of the labor-party resolution directing the union to call a conference to establish such a party. But in the convention debate over the proposal, he ruled, as chairman of the session, that adoption of the resolution would simply serve as "a declaration of principles" and that it would not interfere with the provision in the UMWA constitution specifying that the organization would not transgress the freedom of individual union members to vote as they pleased. After this Lewis, and the International Executive Board along with him, simply ignored the labor-party resolution, despite its specific instructions; and although at the September 1921 convention another motion was passed reaffirming the proposal, it was so hedged around with reservations as to make practical implementation impossible.[68]

Lewis kept up the pressure on the radicals in other ways, too. In April 1920, for example, he successfully prevented John H. Walker from running as a candidate in the union elections for delegate to the AFL, on the ground that Walker held a salaried position as president of the Illinois State Federation of Labor. Since other union members had been elected delegates in previous years while holding a salaried position (such as W. B. Wilson when he was a member of Congress), this was a transparent attempt to deny Walker an opportunity to run in the election. Similarly, in the fall of 1920 Lewis sought to prevent Robert Harlin of District 10 from running against him in the elections for international president, alleging that Harlin had only worked for three years in the mines, whereas the UMWA constitution specified that any candidate for union office must have worked as a miner for five. When Harlin produced evidence that he had worked in the mines for sixteen years Lewis backed down, but not before numerous locals had passed resolutions of censure against him "for again, as . . . in the past, attempting to misconstrue the plain provisions of our International Constitution." Even earlier than this, when Lewis was vice-president of the organization, he had unsuccessfully tried to pressure John Brophy into opposing the reelection of the prominent socialist James Maurer as president of the Pennsylvania State Federation of Labor.[69]

A third difficulty was the issue of Communism, which divided the radicals in the union and was also used by President John L. Lewis as a weapon against them. There were not a large number of actual Communists in the UMWA. A mixture of Communist and old IWW members succeeded in bringing over District 18, in western Canada, to the One Big Union movement in the summer of 1919. And a similar development occurred in 1923 in Nova Scotia, when District 26 went so far as to apply for membership in the Third (Communist) International of Trade Unions. Lewis dealt with both episodes as he did with Alexander Howatt in Kansas, by suspending the officers of the districts and installing district executive boards favorable to the international administration.[70] The important point, however, was that very little effort was made, as, for example, it was in the ILGWU, to distinguish between Communists, socialists, and other kinds of radicals; and Lewis was not above denouncing his opponents as "bolsheviks" or "reds," even when there was very little evidence as to what their actual opinions were. He had used his patriotic Americanism in defending the sudden termination of the 1919 national strike; and it was particularly unfortunate for advocates of third-party action that the National Farmer-Labor party, which had initially appeared so attractive, should have been captured by the Communists at its convention in July 1923.[71]

Equally important was the impact of this anti-Communist propaganda on the fortunes of the Progressive International Committee of Miners, which was established at a conference held in Pittsburgh in February 1923 in order to bring about reforms in the internal policies of the UMWA. There were certainly Communists present in this organization, and in the end they were probably able to secure control. William Z. Foster was active in the founding of the committee, and Tom Myerscough, a self-confessed member of the Communist party, was secretary. It was ostensibly because of Communist influence that Lewis declared the committee a dual organization and expelled its leading members. But the initial purpose of the Progressive International Committee was to unite the various radical and reforming elements in the union behind a moderate program of reform, and its program—mine nationalization, election of international organizers, reinstatement of Howatt and his followers, and reform of the union's electoral system so as to prevent the stealing of elections—was one which in earlier years any moderate socialist could reasonably have been expected to support.

Yet neither Brophy nor Walker would join the Progressive Committee because of its Communist associations, and Howatt himself was the only one of the leading postwar radicals to do so. In a revealing letter to his friend John Steele, of Pittsburgh, Walker indicated the damage which had been done by the intrusion of the Communist issue into the movement for moderate reform. The influence of the Communist party in the Progressive International Committee was "leaving matters in very bad shape," he wrote. "If he [Howatt] flirts around with the I.W.W.'s, or has anything to do with the worker's party, or a dual union, no man who knows anything about the labor movement will support him." His words were borne out by the subsequent January 1924 United Mine Workers' convention, when the case for Howatt's reinstatement—now described by the editor of the union journal as "Alexandervitch Howatt"—was rejected virtually out of hand. So also were nearly all the resolutions put forward by the radicals, even though most of them were quite moderate in their tone.[72]

All of this goes far to explain the failure of the postwar labor-party movement in the United Mine Workers of America and of the campaign for nationalizing the mines. But it does not quite account for the union's indifference to the Conference for Progressive Political Action. The CPPA was not Communist-influenced, and its tactic of exerting pressure on the old party candidates, coupled with support for the La Follette-Wheeler presidential ticket, would seem to have been highly attractive to the miners as a whole. One explanation for the union's relative indifference, aside from President Lewis' personal support for Coolidge, lies in the miners' traditional fear of alienating their friends in each of the two major parties, if they were to identify themselves openly with an independent political cause.

Another factor was the well-publicized attempt of ex-Secretary of Labor W. B. Wilson, who still had considerable prestige among the miners, to dissuade Gompers and the AFL Executive Council from endorsing La Follette and Wheeler and to support the Democratic candidate, John W. Davis, instead. Detailed evidence of the miners' behavior in the November 1924 elections is scarce. Brophy attempted to stir up interest in the CPPA in Pennsylvania, and a miners' committee for La Follette was established briefly in Illinois. But the more general attitude of the coal miners may be seen from a resolution adopted at the twenty-ninth convention of the union, a few months before the election took place:

As a labor organization we are organized to increase the wages, lower the hours of labor, and generally improve the economic conditions of the workers in the coal industry. Having these principles in view, we would consider it unwise at this particular time to attempt to directly affiliate our economic organization with any political organization of this country.[73]

V

Because of the UMWA's large size, it was more important for the social-ists to secure control of the United Mine Workers of America than any of the other trade-unions in the AFL, if they were to have a real chance of making the American labor movement socialist. But they were unable to do so. The only union district in which they enjoyed real power was Dis-trict 12, in Illinois. Elsewhere, their influence was local and sporadic. Nev-ertheless, political radicalism and enthusiasm for a broadly based third party of labor, especially in the period just after World War I, clearly had a considerable effect.

This radicalism did not derive from the socialism of continental Europe, any more than it did in the case of the Boot and Shoe Workers Union or the IAM. English influences were powerful among the coal miners—more so than elsewhere—and there are a number of interesting parallels to be drawn between the position of the miners in Great Britain and in Amer-ica, particularly in their relationship to the idea of a labor party. But it must not be assumed that the United Mine Workers were influenced by their English origins toward such a party more than to a very limited ex-tent. It was not, after all, until 1919, when most of the leaders of the union were native-born Americans, that the UMWA seriously considered helping to establish a third political party. Moreover, the strength of radi-calism in the postwar period emphasizes, as in the case of the IAM, the danger of assuming that the experience of World War I itself necessarily brought an end to radical tendencies in the labor movement during this pe-riod. Since the radicals in the UMWA were very largely the Anglo-Saxon el-ement, not the Italians, Slavs, or other eastern Europeans who by now constituted more than half of the mining labor force, it also shows the dan-ger of assuming that most of the militants in the labor movement were for-eign-born.

Radical discontent among the miners did not derive, either, from loss of skill, as it did in several other unions. Machine mining was widely intro-duced during the period under review, and it did cause some displacement and temporary unemployment. But it appears unlikely that many coal miners had previously been self-employed, and the impact of mechanization as such was nothing like so severe as it was in the metal and shoemaking crafts. Instead, the sources of radicalism are to be found in company control, ill-treatment by the operators, and the frequent hostility of the courts, the state militia, and other agents of the state. In addition, severe competitive condi-tions in the years before 1900, and static or temporarily declining wage levels, were also of considerable importance. The relative loss of earning power and of status which this occasioned among the English-speaking miners in relation to the Italians and Slavs, may have had a crucial effect.

Once these problems had been overcome, at least partially, the appeal of socialism, although not necessarily of a more broadly based form of radicalism, began to lose its effect. In the absence of an established ideological tradition, such as existed in the ILGWU, relative economic security and a recognition of the legitimacy of the union's aspirations rapidly undermined any desire for revolutionary change, at least at the top. Radical influences persisted longer at the lower levels of the union and were never actually lost. After a brief resurgency following World War I, however, these also declined, for a variety of reasons, among them the strong opposition of John L. Lewis and the fear of Communism, the consequences of which are clearer in this chapter than anywhere else.

But the most important reason for the failure of third-party politics in the United Mine Workers was its fear, expressed on innumerable occasions, of destroying its influence in the two major parties. Because of the geographical character of the industry the UMWA had considerable influence in both of the two old parties, particularly at the local level, and its discontents were never great enough to warrant risking that influence. To some extent, this was similar to the experience of other unions in the AFL also. But because of its exceptionally strong traditions of political activism, the United Mine Workers gives us an insight into that experience which was not to be reproduced in most other unions until the 1930's and beyond.

Notes

1. There are numerous general studies of trade-unionism in the coal-mining industry, but no satisfactory one-volume history. Among the most important works are: David J. McDonald and Edward A. Lynch, *Coal and Unionism: A History of the American Coal Miners' Unions* (Indianapolis, 1939); McAlister Coleman, *Men and Coal* (New York, 1943); Frank J. Warne, *The Coal-Mine Workers: A Study in Labor Organization* (New York, 1905); Andrew Roy, *A History of the Coal Miners of the United States: From the Development of the Mines to the Close of the Anthracite Strike of 1902* (Columbus, 1907); Chris Evans, *A History of the United Mine Workers of America, 1860–1900*, 2 vols. (Indianapolis, 1900); William A. McConagha, "History and Progress of the United Mine Workers of America" (Ph.D. Thesis, University of Illinois, 1925).

2. *Constitution*, United Mine Workers of America (1890), 1–2.

3. As late as 1898 the *United Mine Workers' Journal* reproduced the Chartist platform, together with an article on Ernest Jones, a prominent Chartist

leader, for the edification of the membership. See Roy, *op. cit.*, 125–145; Clifton K. Yearley, *Britons in American Labor: A History of the Influence of the United Kingdom Immigrants in American Labor, 1820–1914* (Baltimore, 1957), 124–126; *United Mine Workers' Journal*, VII (January 20, 1898), 5.

4. In 1867 and 1869 Alexander MacDonald visited a number of mining communities in America, greeting fellow Scotsmen and exhorting the American miners to organize. See Yearley, *op. cit.*, 126–129.

5. Yearley, *op. cit.*, 134–135; McConagha, *op. cit.*, 41; Roy, *op. cit.*, 260–261, 272–273; G. D. H. Cole and R. Postgate, *The Common People, 1746–1946* (London, 1946), 398, 459; *Proceedings, Second Annual Convention of the United Mine Workers of America* (Indianapolis, 1892), 5; *Denver Times*, December 19, 1894 (clipping in Thomas J. Morgan Collection, Illinois Historical Survey); R. MacIntosh to John H. Walker, April 25, 1916 (John H. Walker Papers, University of Illinois Historical Survey).

6. McDonald and Lynch, *op. cit.*, 29; Edward A. Wieck, *The American Miners Association: A Record of the Origin of Coal Miners' Unions in the United States* (New York, 1940), 77; *United Mine Workers' Journal*, V (August 29, 1895), 4.

7. Roy, *op. cit.*, 81–85, 186–214, 267–272, 281–289, 370–379, 427–440; John Brophy, *A Miner's Life* (Madison, 1964), 38–46; *United Mine Workers' Journal*, XVIII (December 12, 1907), 1; XXII (January 11, 1912), 4.

8. For these figures on wages, see *Nineteenth Annual Report of the U.S. Commissioner of Labor* (Washington, 1904), 242–243.

9. McConagha, *op. cit.*, 37, 43, 50–51; William Green, *Labor and Democracy* (Princeton, 1939), 5–9; *Autobiography of Mother Jones* (Chicago, 1925), 63–70, 89–93, 149–171, 232–235; Elsie Glück, *John Mitchell, Miner: Labor's Bargain with the Gilded Age* (New York, 1929), 3–18.

10. McConagha, *op. cit.*, 40–48; Warne, *op. cit.*, 18–194; Coleman, *op. cit.*, 41–44. For the use of Negro strikebreakers in the early period, see Herbert Gutman, "Reconstruction in Ohio: Negroes in the Hocking Valley Coal Mines in 1873 and 1874," *Labor History*, III (Fall, 1962), 246–264. For the use of Pinkerton detectives, see Morris Friedman, *The Pinkerton Labor Spy* (New York, 1907). This refers primarily to the activities of the Pinkertons against the Western Federation of Miners, but similar tactics were used against the coal miners.

11. Evans, *op. cit.*, II, 257; Frank J. Warne, *The Slav Invasion and the Mine Workers, a Study in Immigration* (Philadelphia, 1904), 65–83, 88–90. For a more extensive study of the impact of the Slav immigration, see Peter Roberts, *Anthracite Coal Communities: A Study of the Demography, the Social, Educational and Moral Life of the Anthracite Regions* (New York, 1904).

12. For this, see Herbert Gutman, "The Negro and the United Mine Workers of America, The Career and Letters of Richard L. Davis and Something of Their Meaning: 1890–1900," in Julius Jacobson (ed.), *The Negro and the American Labor Movement* (New York, 1968), 49–127.

13. *The People*, IV (June 10, 1894), 1.

14. McConagha, *op. cit.*, 66–70; Warne, *The Coal-Mine Workers*, 212–216; Evans, *op. cit.*, II, 350–357; *United Mine Workers' Journal*, IV (April 26, 1894), 1; IV (May 10, 1894), 1–2; IV (June 28, 1894), 1, 5; IV (July 19, 1894), 1; XXIII (November 14, 1912), 4.

15. Roy, *op. cit.*, 323–350; Warne, *The Coal-Mine Workers,* 219–221; John R. Commons *et al., History of Labor in the United States,* 4 vols. (New York, 1926–1935), IV, 25–30; *United Mine Workers' Journal,* VII (August 12, 1897), 2, 4–5.

16. *Ibid.*, III (May 4, 1893), 8.

17. *Ibid.*, IX (October 6, 1898), 1; IX (October 20, 1898), 8; IX (October 27, 1898), 2–3, 8; IX (November 10, 1898), 1; *The People,* VII (August 1, 1897), 1) *Arm and Hammer* pamphlet, July 1899 (Daniel DeLeon Collection, Wisconsin State Historical Society).

18. *United Mine Workers' Journal,* III (April 13, 1893), 2; III (June 29, 1893), 1; III (August 18, 1893), 4; III (October 12, 1893), 4; III (November 2, 1893), 4; IV (April 19, 1894), 2; IV (May 10, 1894), 1, 5; IV (August 2, 1894), 1; IV (October 18, 1894), 4. In the official call which President McBride sent out for the April 1894 convention of the United Mine Workers, he erroneously stated that the December 1893 convention of the AFL had already endorsed Morgan's Political Program, when in fact it had simply referred it to affiliated unions for their consideration. Gompers wrote to McBride notifying him of this error, no doubt in the hope of reducing the probability that the union as a whole would endorse the Program. Even though the union convention did adopt the Program, however, not all its delegates voted in favor of it at the AFL convention of December 1894, causing considerable criticism at the next UMW convention, held in February 1895. See *United Mine Workers' Journal,* IV (February 21, 1895), 5; *Proceedings, Fourteenth Annual Convention of the A.F. of L.* (Denver, 1894), 36–40; Gompers to McBride, March 26, 1894 (Letterbooks of Samuel Gompers, AFL-CIO Collection).

19. Relations between farmers and coal miners were not always good, however. Miners' leaders sometimes had to warn their members against treating the farmer as "a jay or a rube with goat whiskers and one suspender," and there was resentment against the farmers who competed for winter jobs in the mines. Politically, however, there was much in this period on which they could combine. See Coleman, *op. cit.*, 56; *United Mine Workers' Journal,* XVI (June 15, 1905), 4; *Proceedings, Seventeenth Annual Convention of the United Mine Workers of America* (Indianapolis, 1906), 123.

20. The small group of SLP members in the United Mine Workers opposed the miners' interest in Populism, just as they did in other unions. In January 1894, O'Neill McDarragh, of District 6 in Ohio, attacked the Populists as a middle-class party which was concerned only with superficial reforms, and in July he was backed up by DeLeon, writing in *The People.* "A political party that stands upon and pledges its loyalty to the Omaha platform," he wrote of the Kansas Populists, "is a party hostile to the working class." DeLeonite hostility toward Populism may have been another reason for the miners' relative indifference to the SLP. See *The People,* IV (July 1, 1894), 1; *United Mine Workers' Journal,* III (January 1894), 5; IV (November 8, 1894), 4.

21. *United Mine Workers' Journal,* III (June 8, 1893), 1; III (March 22, 1894), 5; IV (April 19, 1894), 2, 4; IV (August 2, 1894), 1; IV (October 25, 1894), 5; IV (November 15, 1894), 5; IV (January 17, 1895), 1; Chester M. Destler, *American Radicalism, 1865–1901: Essays and Documents* (New London, 1946), 166–171, 175, 179, 207.

22. *Ibid.*, 207–208; McDonald and Lynch, *op. cit.*, 39–40; John D. Hicks,

The Populist Revolt: A History of the Farmers' Alliance and the People's Party (Lincoln, 1961), 337; *United Mine Workers' Journal,* IV (April 19, 1894), 2; IV (August 9, 1894), 4–5; IV (August 16, 1894), 5; IV (August 23, 1894), 4; VI (April 16, 1896), 1, 8.

23. *The People,* IV (July 1, 1894), 1; *United Mine Workers' Journal,* V (January 30, 1896), 5; V (February 6, 1896), 5; V (February 13, 1896), 5.

24. Destler, *op. cit.,* 179–180; *United Mine Workers' Journal,* V (December 26, 1895), 1; VI (January 23, 1896), 4; VII (January 30, 1897), 1.

25. Commons *et al., op. cit.,* IV, 20–24; *United Mine Workers' Journal,* VII (July 15, 1897), 4; VII (August 26, 1897), 1–5; VII (September 2, 1897), 1; VII (October 26, 1897), 4; IX (August 4, 1898), 4; IX (August 12, 1898), 4; IX (April 6, 1899), 1; X (March 15, 1900), 4; *Proceedings, Thirteenth Annual Convention of the United Mine Workers of America* (Indianapolis, 1902), 129; Ray Ginger, *The Bending Cross: A Biography of Eugene Victor Debs* (New Brunswick, 1949), 196–197.

26. Commons *et al., op. cit.* IV, 40–47; Glück, *op. cit.,* 102–156; Warne, *The Slav Invasion,* 106–108; *The Worker,* XII (May 18, 1902), 1; XII (May 25, 1902), 1; XII (June 1, 1902), 1; XII (October 26, 1902), 1; *United Mine Workers' Journal,* XIII (August 14, 1902), 3; Ira Kipnis, *The American Socialist Movement, 1897–1912* (New York, 1952), 139–141; *International Socialist Review,* III (July 1902), 79–85; III (April 1903), 618–620.

27. Glück, *op. cit.,* 157–170; *The Worker,* XIII (February 7, 1904), 2; XIV (September 18, 1904), 1; *International Socialist Review,* IV (April 1904), 657; Eugene Debs, "Reply to John Mitchell" (Pamphlet in Wisconsin State Historical Society); Debs to Germer, March 4, 1904 (Adolph Germer Collection, Wisconsin State Historical Society).

28. Glück, *op. cit.,* 85; Biographical notes on John H. Walker (John H. Walker Papers, University of Illinois Historical Survey); Biographical notes on Adolph Germer (Adolph Germer Collection, Wisconsin State Historical Society); Theodore Debs to Germer, May 11, May 27, June 25, 1904, March 7, 1905 (Eugene Debs Collection, Tamiment Institute); Philip S. Foner, *History of the Labor Movement in the United States,* 4 vols. (New York, 1947–1965), IV, 116n.

29. *United Mine Workers' Journal,* XI (November 22, 1900), 4; XI (December 20, 1900), 1; XI (January 17, 1901), 4; *Proceedings, Twelfth Annual Convention of the United Mine Workers of America* (Indianapolis, 1901), 62–63; Philip Taft, *The A.F. of L. in the Time of Gompers* (New York, 1957), 194–198.

30. John O'Neill to Germer, June 19, 1903, August 18, 1905; Clarence Smith to Germer, July 24, August 18, 1903, January 6, 1904 (Adolph Germer Collection, Wisconsin State Historical Society); *Proceedings, Seventeenth Annual Convention of the United Mine Workers of America* (Indianapolis, 1906), 159–160.

31. Glück, *op. cit.,* 167–178; *Autobiography of Mother Jones,* 94–113; *United Mine Workers' Journal,* XV (January 26, 1905), 4; XVI (May 25, 1905), 2. Note, however, that a resolution to expel Randall from the convention was put forward by John H. Walker, of Illinois. This was in part to offset criticisms of the Socialist party, which had been made by several speakers in the debate. But it was also a sign of Walker's personal friendship for Mitchell,

which later drew strong criticism from Germer and other socialists. See *Proceedings, Sixteenth Annual Convention of the United Mine Workers of America* (Indianapolis, 1905), 175–232.

32. *United Mine Workers' Journal*, XVI (May 25, 1905), 2; XVI (June 8, 1905), 4; XVI (August 13, 1905), 4; XVI (September 21, 1905), 4; XVI (March 1, 1906), 4; XVI (March 22, 1906), 1.

33. Gompers to W. D. Ryan, May 13, 1905; Ryan to Gompers, May 15, 1905 (Gompers' Correspondence with Affiliates, AFL-CIO Collection); *Proceedings, First Convention of the Industrial Workers of the World* (Chicago, 1905), 83–90; Paul F. Brissenden, *The IWW, A Study of American Syndicalism* (New York, 1957), 115n; *United Mine Workers' Journal*, XVIII (December 12, 1907), 1. At the January 1906 convention of the UMWA, Acting Secretary-Treasurer James Kirwan of the Western Federation of Miners reported that the Illinois district had taken a referendum vote on the question of affiliating with the IWW, presumably in the latter part of 1905. I have been unable to discover any other evidence as to whether this actually occurred. See *Proceedings, Seventeenth Annual Convention of the United Mine Workers of America* (Indianapolis, 1906), 5.

34. *Proceedings, Second Convention of the Industrial Workers of the World* (Chicago, 1906), 50–51, 323–327; *Industrial Union Bulletin*, I (September 21, 1907), 5; *United Mine Workers' Journal*, XVIII (January 25, 1908), 1; XX (January 27, 1910), 1; XXIII (November 28, 1912), 1.

35. In his account Brissenden suggests that the mine workers' locals at Barrow, Muddy Valley, and Elkville in Illinois "reported themselves at the second convention as desirous of admission" to the IWW, but unable to join because of the union contract. This is somewhat of an exaggeration. No representatives of these locals attended the convention, and John M. Francis, who reported on the situation in Illinois, simply stated that he had visited these locals and secured the signatures of a number of rank-and-file members who would have liked to join the IWW. In general, Brissenden overrates the influence of the IWW in the UMWA. See Brissenden, *op. cit.*, 115; *Proceedings, Second Convention of the Industrial Workers of the World* (Chicago, 1906), 323.

36. Brissenden, *op. cit.*, 115; Glück, *op. cit.*, 211; James Kirwan to Germer, August 18, August 27, 1906, January 16, January 21, January 25, January 29, February 4, February 15, March 11, 1907 (Adolph Germer Collection, Wisconsin State Historical Society); *Industrial Union Bulletin*, I (September 21, 1907), 5.

37. Debs to Germer, July 25, July 30, August 1, 1904 (Adolph Germer Collection, Wisconsin State Historical Society); *United Mine Workers' Journal*, X (August 17, 1899), 2; XII (October 31, 1901), 4; XVI (February 1, 1906), 4; XVII (October 4, 1906), 1.

38. The Taff Vale case of 1900, in which an English union was successfully sued for damages incurred as the result of a strike, helped to consolidate trade-union support for the Labor Representation Committee, which eventually became the Labor party. See Henry Pelling, *The Origins of the Labour Party, 1880–1900* (London, 1954), 225–228.

39. *United Mine Workers' Journal*, XIV (March 17, 1904), 4; *Proceedings, Twentieth Annual Convention of the United Mine Workers of America* (Indianapolis, 1909), 405–417.

40. The 1906 electoral alliance with the Democratic party in the mining counties of Pennsylvania appeared to be a classic example of the Democrats exploiting their traditional appeal for working-class, and especially immigrant, votes, to their electoral advantage. Although both major parties openly competed for the support of the Slavs by purchasing their citizenship papers and by paying with liquor and cash for votes at election time, the Democratic machine was evidently the more successful. See *United Mine Workers' Journal,* XVII (October 25, 1906), 2; XVII (November 8, 1906), 1; Warne, *The Slav Invasion,* 106–108; Roberts, *op. cit.,* 316–342; Roger W. Babson, *W. B. Wilson and the Department of Labor* (New York, 1919), 122–125.

41. In addition, the Illinois State Federation of Labor again tried to draft Mitchell as a Democratic candidate for governor of Illinois; and he was also mentioned for the U.S. Senate. In July 1908 G. H. Hendren, of the Indiana State Democratic Committee, asked Gompers whether Mitchell could appear in the Indiana coal fields on behalf of the Democrats, in order to counteract the rumor that he was supporting the Republicans because of his earlier associations with President Theodore Roosevelt. Gompers passed the request on to Mitchell, adding that "a few addresses by you in this campaign will have a tremendous influence." And Grant Hamilton, the AFL's general organizer in Chicago, asserted on October 3 that "if there are any doubts regarding Mr. Bryan's election, they would be dispelled should you [Mitchell] decide to take a prominent part in the fight against his opponent." See Mitchell to Alfred Broad, November 26, 1902; S. J. Young to Mitchell, March 9, 1908; Mitchell to James Dunlavey, October 6, 1908 (John Mitchell Papers, Catholic University of America); G. H. Hendren to Gompers, July 28, 1908; Gompers to Mitchell, July 31, 1908 (Letterbooks of Samuel Gompers, AFL-CIO Collection); Grant Hamilton to Gompers, October 3, 1908 (Gompers' Correspondence with Affiliates, AFL-CIO Collection); Alvah E. Staley, "History of the Illinois State Federation of Labor" (Ph.D. Thesis, University of Chicago, 1928), 336; Marguerite Green, *The National Civic Federation and the American Labor Movement, 1900–1925* (Washington, 1956), 146–150.

42. In a letter to Frank Morrison, secretary of the AFL, Mitchell enquired as to whether Morrison had released the list of locals, adding that the miners "resent what they charge as an attempt on my part to dictate . . . for whom they shall vote" and that the incident had got him "into about as much trouble as I have had in my life." See Mitchell to Grant Hamilton, October 12, 1908; Hamilton to Mitchell, October 17, 1908; Mitchell to F. Morrison, October 20, 1908 (Gompers' Correspondence with Affiliates, AFL-CIO Collection).

43. Glück, *op. cit.,* 228–233; M. Green, *op. cit.,* 8–20, 43–54, 151–153.

44. *Proceedings, Twenty-Second Annual Convention of the United Mine Workers of America* (Columbus, 1911), 519–575 ff.

45. M. Green, *op. cit.,* 156–158; Mitchell to Gompers, February 2, 1911; Gompers to Mitchell, February 16, 1911 (Gompers' Correspondence with Affiliates, AFL-CIO Collection).

46. M. Green, *op. cit.,* 163, 168; Germer to Thomas Kennedy, March 15, 1911 (Adolph Germer Collection, Wisconsin State Historical Society).

47. Hayes' difficulties were increased by the highhanded behavior of President Tom Lewis, who informed him soon after he was elected that the office of in-

ternational vice-president was no longer to be maintained at national headquarters and that his function as head of organization work was to be abolished. As a result, the socialists in the union turned against Lewis and in 1911 ran John H. Walker for the presidency of the UMWA, the first of many occasions on which Walker was to run. See Glück, *op. cit.,* 231; M. Green, *op. cit.,* 151; Frank Hayes to Germer, October 30, 1912, January 25, February 25, 1918; Germer to Hayes, February 22, 1918 (Adolph Germer Collection, Wisconsin State Historical Society); *Proceedings, Nineteenth Annual Convention of the United Mine Workers of America* (Indianapolis, 1912), 281–283.

48. *Proceedings, Twenty-second Annual Convention of the United Mine Workers of America* (Indianapolis, 1912), 191, 194–213, 258–271, 432–434; Vernon H. Jensen, *Heritage of Conflict, Labor Relations in the Nonferrous Metals Industry up to 1930* (Ithaca, 1950), 238–243.

49. *Ibid.,* 370–371; Nathan Fine, *Labor and Farmer Parties in the United States, 1828–1928* (New York, 1961), 290. For a further discussion of relations between the UMWA and WFM, see below, pp. 260–262, 269–272.

50. The socialists ran a strong ticket in the November 1912 West Virginia elections, in the hope of capitalizing on the intense bitterness engendered by the strike, as they had in the Pennsylvania anthracite districts in 1902. This did not yield any great results, as the West Virginia miners were mostly Democratic. However, the Socialist party committee's endorsement of the compromise settlement raised quite a furore in the party, because it was negotiated with Governor Hatfield, who had been critical of some of the union's tactics, and it was opposed by the more radical socialists in the state. Debs dismissed these critics as "IWW calamityites," indicating that on this occasion he dissociated himself from the left wing of the party. See Ginger, *op. cit.,* 258, 320–321; Commons *et al., op. cit.,* IV, 329–335; *Autobiography of Mother Jones,* 148–171; *International Socialist Review,* XIII (October 1912), 295–303; XIII (November 1912), 391–393; XIII (January 1913), 541–543; XIII (April 1913), 729–735; XIII (June 1913), 895; XIV (July 1913, 12–24; Germer to Robert Hunter, December 23, 1912 (Adolph Germer Collection, Wisconsin State Historical Society); Debs to Germer, May 13, May 14, June 1, June 2, June 4, June 19, July 11, 1913 (Debs Collection, Tamiment Institute); Mother Jones to Terence V. Powderly, May 1, 1913 (Mary Harris Jones Papers, Catholic University of America).

51. *United Mine Workers' Journal,* (January 7, 1904), 4; XIV (January 21, 1904), 4; *Proceedings, Twentieth Annual Convention of the United Mine Workers of America* (Indianapolis, 1909), 417; *Proceedings, Twenty-fifth Convention and Second Biennial Convention of the United Mine Workers of America* (Indianapolis, 1916), 596–615; "Minutes of meeting of Board of Directors of the Central States Cooperative Society, January 26, 1919" (John H. Walker Papers, University of Illinois Historical Survey).

52. Babson, *op. cit.,* 127–129, 134–146; W. Green, *op. cit.,* 26–27; *United Mine Workers' Journal,* XXII (January 4, 1912), 8; XXIII (May 23, 1912), 7; XXIII (June 13, 1912), 1; XXIII (June 27, 1912), 1; XXIII (July 25, 1912), 4; XXIII (September 19, 1912), 1; XXIII (October 24, 1912), 4; XXIII (March 6, 1913), 4; XXVII (October 26, 1916), 11; XXVII (November 2, 1916), 4; XXVII (November 16, 1916), 4; *Proceedings, Twenty-first Annual Convention of the United Mine Workers of America* (Indianapolis, 1910), 524–529; *Pro-*

ceedings, Twenty-third Annual Convention of the United Mine Workers of America (Indianapolis, 1912), 215–238, 244–246.

53. *United Mine Workers' Journal,* IX (November 3, 1898), 4; XXIII (June 2, 1913), 4; XXVII (October 11, 1916), 2–3; XXVII (October 17, 1917), 1; *Thirty-third Annual Report of the U.S. Commissioner of Labor* (Washington, 1918), 218–220.

54. On February 12, 1916, for example, Eugene Debs wrote to the editor of the *Argus-Star,* published in Charleston, West Virginia, saying that he had given up hope that the United Mine Workers would ever become a genuinely radical trade-union. In 1914, Debs recalled, he had given "the U.M.W. credit for coming nearest [to] being a real industrial union and revolutionary in spirit" and had advised it to leave the AFL in order to lead the way toward a new "industrial organization." But now the most reactionary elements in the organization had come to the fore. "They have succeeded in checking the revolutionary tendency and making the union quite respectable, safe and sane, pure and simple, and in all regards satisfactory to the operators." Newspaper clipping (Mary Harris Jones Papers, Catholic University of America). See also John P. White to Germer, November 8, 1911; Germer to Elvis Williams, January 14, 1915; Germer to Edgar Wallace, January 20, 1915; Theodore Debs to Germer, April 26, June 14, 1915; Officer Commanding Militia at Walsenburg, Colorado, to Sheriff of Huerfano County, December 4, 1913; "Report of Secretary-Treasurer McDonald and District Member Franckney to Officers and Members of District 12, December 2, 1914" (Adolph Germer Collection, Wisconsin State Historical Society); *Proceedings, Twenty-fifth Consecutive and Second Biennial Convention of the United Mine Workers of America* (Indianapolis, 1916), 228–318.

55. Frank Hayes to Germer, February 2, 1918; Germer to Hayes, February 25, 1918 (Adolph Germer Collection, Wisconsin Historical Society); Harriet Reed to John Walker, July 12, 1915; Luke Grant to Walker, September 23, 1916; William Mitch to Walker, November 2, 1916; Fred Weidenburner to Walker, November 6, 1916; Walker to Fred Weidenburner, November 8, 1916; Walker to Germer, November 14, 1917; Walker to John P. White, November 17, 1916 (John H. Walker Papers, University of Illinois Historical Survey).

56. Coleman, *op. cit.,* 89–90; Commons *et al., op. cit.,* IV, 469; *United Mine Workers' Journal,* XXVI (January 16, 1916), 1; XXVII (April 12, 1917), 4; XXVIII (July 19, 1917), 4; XXVIII (October 25, 1917), 4; XXVIII (November 29, 1917), 5; XXVIII (March 28, 1918), 4; *Proceedings, Twenty-fifth Consecutive and Second Biennial Convention of the United Mine Workers of America* (Cleveland, 1919), 101–102, 124–128.

57. Germer to Walker, October 23, November 2, 1917, January 3, 1918; Walker to Germer, October 29, 1917 (John H. Walker Papers, University of Illinois Historical Survey); Germer to Hayes, January 25, February 25, 1918; Hayes to Germer, February 22, March 4, 1918 (Adolph Germer Collection, Wisconsin State Historical Society).

58. Charles A. Madison, *American Labor Leaders: Personalities and Forces in the Labor Movement* (New York, 1950), 174–177. For full-length biographies of John L. Lewis, see Saul Alinsky, *John L. Lewis, An Unauthorized Biography* (New York, 1949); Cecil Carnes, *John L. Lewis, Leader of Labor* (New York, 1936). For radical critiques of Lewis and his leadership of the

UMWA, see Anna Rochester, *Labor and Coal* (New York, 1931); and Eric Hass, *John L. Lewis Exposed* (New York, 1938).

59. Madison, *op. cit.*, 176; Commons *et al.*, *op. cit.*, IV, 470–471; *Proceedings, Twenty-seventh Consecutive and Fourth Biennial Convention of the United Mine Workers of America* (Cleveland, 1919), 392–397, 631–632, 841–849, 854–859, 867–870.

60. Commons *et al.*, *op. cit.*, IV, 470–476; Sylvia Kopald, *Rebellion in Labor Unions* (New York, 1924), 50–123. See also H. W. Perrigo, "Factional Strife in District No. 12, United Mine Workers of America, 1919–1933" (Ph.D. Thesis, University of Wisconsin, 1933); and Edward D. Wickersham, "Opposition to the International Officers of the United Mine Workers of America" (Ph.D. Thesis, Cornell University, 1951).

61. Commons *et al.*, *op. cit.*, IV, 471–472, 476; Alinsky, *op. cit.*, 30–34; Taft, *op. cit.*, 406–411; Brophy, *op cit.*, 138–143, 154–156; *United Mine Workers' Journal*, XXX (November 15, 1919), 2–3; Walker to Mother Jones, March 16, 1920; Robert Harlin to Walker, July 6, 1920; Walker to Harlin, July 13, 1920; Walker to Howatt, January 12, 1921; Walker to Farrington, January 15, 1921 (John H. Walker Papers, University of Illinois Historical Survey).

62. *United Mine Workers' Journal*, XXXI (August 1, 1920), 9; Staley, *op. cit.*, 521–528; Harry B. Sell, "The A.F. of L. and the Labor Party Movement of 1918–1920" (M.A. Thesis, University of Chicago, 1922), 81–94; *Proceedings, First Convention of the Labor Party of the United States* (Chicago, 1919), 126–131; Walker to Mother Jones, March 16, 1920; William Mitch to Walker, July 6, 1920; Harlin to Walker, July 6, July 21, 1920; Walker to Howatt, July 10, 1920; Farrington to Walker, September 16, 1920; "Circular of Alexander Howatt to District 14, April 21, 1921" (John H. Walker Papers, University of Illinois Historical Survey).

63. For a detailed study of this organization, see Dallas M. Young, "A History of the Progressive Miners of America, 1932–1940" (Ph.D. Thesis, University of Illinois, 1940).

64. Commons *et al.*, *op. cit.*, IV, 479–488; Brophy, *op. cit.*, 200–218; *United Mine Workers' Journal*, XXXIV (March 18, 1923), 4; XXXV (November 15, 1924), 7; Kenneth C. MacKay, *The Progressive Movement of 1924* (New York, 1947), 69, 76; James Weinstein, *The Decline of Socialism in America, 1912–1925* (New York, 1967), 276.

65. Fine, *op. cit.*, 390–391, 394–395; Staley, *op cit.*, 531–533; Walker to Farrington, September 16, 1920; Walker to Howatt, July 13, 1921; Walker to Governor Len Small, July 21, August 21, 1921 (John H. Walker Papers, University of Illinois Historical Survey).

66. Lewis did not succeed in this. At the June 1921 AFL convention three of the eight United Mine Workers' delegates, Alexander Howatt, Frank Farrington, and Robert Harlin, voted against Lewis and for Gompers, thereby increasing Lewis' antagonism toward the radicals. See *Proceedings, Forty-first Annual Convention of the A.F. of L.* (Denver, 1921), 455–456; John L. Lewis to Brophy, June 27, 1921 (John Brophy Papers, Catholic University of America).

67. Brophy, *op. cit.*, 157–175; Brophy to Ellis Searles, April 11, April 22, 1921; Searles to Brophy, April 13, 1921 (John Brophy Papers, Catholic University of America).

68. *Proceedings, Twenty-seventh Consecutive and Fourth Biennial Convention of the United Mine Workers of America* (Cleveland, 1919), 870; *Proceedings, Twenty-eighth Consecutive and Fifth Biennial Convention of the United Mine Workers of America* (Indianapolis, 1921), 1137.

69. Brophy, *op. cit.*, 132–133; John L. Lewis to Walker, April 5, April 12, 1920; Walker to Lewis, April 9, 1920; Lewis to Robert Harlin, September 18, 1920; Harlin to Lewis, September 23, 1920; Officers of Local 4069 U.M.W. of A., Zeigler, Illinois, to Lewis, October 11, 1920 (John H. Walker Papers, University of Illinois Historical Survey).

70. For this and further information about Communist influence in the United Mine Workers, see David M. Schneider, *The Workers' (Communist) Party and the American Trade Unions* (Baltimore, 1928), 38–59.

71. Alinsky, *op. cit.*, 34–35, 49–50; Fine, *op. cit.*, 429–431; *United Mine Workers' Journal*, XXXV (January 15, 1924), 8–9; XXXV (February 15, 1924), 5. President John Brophy of District 2 attended this convention and joined with John Fitzpatrick and other moderates in a vain attempt to prevent the Communist takeover. Brophy retained his interest in forming a labor party for some time after this, but felt that little could be done in the UMWA since Lewis would "brand all those opposing him as communists." "I believe," he added, "that until they [the Communists] . . . have run their course in the American labor movement they will do what the conservatives in the trade union movement would be unable to do, that is, prevent progress by those who, like myself, are trying to follow a middle course." See Brophy to Arthur Gleason, July 12, 1923 (John Brophy Papers, Catholic University of America).

72. Schneider, *op. cit.*, 45–48, 50–52; Brophy, *op. cit.*, 205; *Proceedings, Twenty-ninth Consecutive and Sixth Biennial Convention of the United Mine Workers of America* (Indianapolis, 1924), 20–23, 252–253, 268–277, 379–380, 383–384, 411–503, 547–552, 845–851; *United Mine Workers' Journal*, XXXV (August 1, 1924), 6; Walker to John Steele, June 14, 1923 (John H. Walker Papers, University of Illinois Historical Survey).

73. Taft, *op. cit.*, 484–485; *Illinois Miner*, IV (July 12, 1924), 1; IV (August 16, 1924), 1; IV (August 23, 1924), 1–2; IV (September 13, 1924), 1; *Proceedings, Twenty-ninth Consecutive and Sixth Biennial Convention of the United Mine Workers of America* (Indianapolis, 1924), 199–209.

7

Syndicalist Socialism and the
Western Federation of Miners

The revolutionary socialism of the Western Federation of Miners,[1] which was founded in Butte, Montana, in 1893, was in some ways a more radical manifestation of tendencies which were apparent in several districts of the UMWA. Company pressures, radical Populism, and a strong commitment to the principles of industrial solidarity all helped to bring about the development of socialist beliefs. The isolated and autonomous character of the mining camps, which was even more evident in the Rocky Mountain states than it was in the coal lands farther east, permitted open and direct confrontations between labor and capital during strikes. Given the more primitive conditions of western society, it also made possible an even more overt alliance between the mine operators and the courts, the militia, and the other agents of the civil state. In addition, there was a greater willingness to resort to violence in settling labor disputes, which stemmed in part from the relatively recent experiences of the frontier.

Nevertheless, there were important differences between the two organizations. Whereas the United Mine Workers was willing to cooperate with the operators in bringing some measure of stability to the coal industry after the conclusion of the interstate agreement in 1898, the Western Federation of Miners at first rejected the use of trade agreements and made little effort to discipline its men. Instead, it gave its temporary support to the IWW and conducted a series of violent conflicts with the operators which were even more bitter and more continuous than they were in the coal industry, while at the same time being considerably less successful. As a result, unlike the United Mine Workers the WFM was unable to organize more than a small proportion of the total labor force in the industry. At its peak, in the early 1900's, it enrolled only about 30,000 members, out of a total of over 200,000 workers in the metal mines. Impossibilist doctrines concerning the "failure" of conventional trade-unionism therefore played an important role in its philosophy. But whereas in other unions, notably in the Boot and Shoe Workers Union, impossibilism was exploited by the DeLeonites, in the conditions of the western mining camps it took the form of an unsophisticated type of syndicalism.

The intensely revolutionary period of the WFM's history did not last very long. It broke with the IWW in 1907, returned to the AFL in 1911, and in other ways assumed a more conservative position in the years before World War I. Nevertheless, it still faced strong employer opposition, and this, coupled with the attacks on it of IWW members and other extreme radicals both inside the union and without, combined to reduce it to a shadow of its earlier self. By 1924 it had only a few thousand members. In consequence, it played very little part in the revival of radicalism after World War I or in the Conference for Progressive Political Action. For a period in the early years of the century, however, it presented a more revolutionary spectacle than any of the other unions considered in this book.

I

Like several other trade-unions which later became socialist, the Western Federation of Miners was not particularly radical at first. Few details exist concerning the convention of forty delegates from Colorado, Montana, Idaho, and South Dakota who met in Butte in May 1893 to establish the organization. But there is little to suggest that any of them were socialists before the union was founded. Ethnically, they reflected the composition of the metal mining industry as a whole. Some of the metal miners were Irish immigrants, Canadians, or ex-tin miners from Cornwall, in southwestern England. There were also a few Germans and Scandinavians among them, and a number of oriental workers were employed. But the great majority of them were native-born Americans. Census figures indicate that virtually every metal mining center in Colorado, Idaho, and Montana had a native-born majority at this time. An unusually large number of the immigrants in the industry were also naturalized citizens.[2] There was no evidence of European socialist influences among them, or of a previous tradition of political independence, such as characterized the English immigrants in the UMWA.[3]

Nor, despite a bitter strike which had been fought between the operators and the metal miners in the Coeur d'Alene district of Idaho in 1892, did the first convention of the WFM advocate any revolutionary aims. The Coeur d'Alene strike betrayed all the elements which were shortly to characterize labor relations throughout the industry at large. It followed a lockout over wage reductions, which the employers' Miners Protective Association claimed were necessitated by exorbitant railroad freight rates. Despite this a heated conflict had taken place in the narrow canyons and mountainous areas of the Coeur d'Alene, near the Idaho-Washington border. Imported strikebreakers were held off at gunpoint, company property was dynamited, and pitched battles, with several dead, were fought between miners and company guards. When this failed to bring order, court injunctions were issued, federal troops were called in, and several hundred miners were imprisoned in hastily erected bull pens. Among the prisoners was Edward Boyce, who was shortly to become president of the Western Federation of Miners. In fact, according to one account it was in the Coeur d'Alene bull pen that the plans for the union were laid.[4]

In spite of this, the Preamble to the constitution adopted by the 1893 convention modestly announced that the union would seek safety legislation, "an earning fully compatible with the dangers of employment," and payment of the miners in lawful money instead of scrip. Protests were entered against company stores, convict labor, Pinkerton detectives, and other abuses against which the coal miners had also complained. But the general tenor of the document was protective and conservative, rather than revolutionary. On relations with the employers, for example, the Preamble proposed "to use all honorable means to maintain friendly relations . . . and endeavor by arbitration and conciliation, or other pacific means, to settle any difficulties which may arise between us, and thus strive to make contention and strikes unnecessary." [5]

If the WFM was not overtly radical in its initial declarations, however, a number of circumstances soon conspired to make it so. One of these was a strong commitment to the principles of industrial solidarity, induced in part by the familiar influence of the Knights of Labor. Although there were few actual K of L assemblies reported among the western metal miners, the absence of any significant AFL influence in the Rocky Mountain states at this time made the impact of those that did exist all the greater. Moreover, while in the East the K of L was in decline, in the West the industrial depression appeared to give it a temporary new lease on life. In January 1894, for example, Montana labor papers reported that the Knights of Labor were advancing in that state more rapidly than they had for years.

In Idaho, former Grand Master Workman James R. Sovereign became editor and publisher of the Wallace *Tribune,* which was also the Coeur d'Alene miners' union official publication. And as late as 1902 a WFM member from Slocan, British Columbia, claimed in the *Miners' Magazine* that "there are thousands of old-line K. of L.'s in the W.F. of M." [6]

Thus it appeared natural that the relatively few craft workers in the isolated mining camps and towns, most of whom pursued occupations which were in some way dependent on the mines, should belong to the same union as the metal miners themselves. At its first convention the WFM authorized the organization of "all persons working in and around the mines, mills and smelters." But from the first it interpreted its jurisdictional responsibilities more broadly than the United Mine Workers had done. The May 1894 convention invited M. J. Elliott, of the American Railway Union, to address it "on the necessity of federation." [7] In 1897 President Boyce advised the miners to "open our portals to every workingman, whether engineer, blacksmith, smelterman, or millman." And three years later Boyce broadened the union's scope still further. "We will at all times and under all conditions espouse the cause of the producing masses, regardless of religion, nationality or race," he declared in the first published issue of the *Miners' Magazine.*[8]

It was broad declarations such as these which were later to bring jurisdictional conflicts with the AFL, besides indicating that the industrial unionism of the WFM was based not simply on expediency, as it was largely in the case of the UMWA, but also on an ideological commitment to the proletarian solidarity of the working class.

Equally familiar was the influence of the Populists, which took on a special significance in the contest of the Rocky Mountain states. Unlike other areas of the nation, where Populism was primarily a movement of agrarian protest, the People's party in Colorado, Montana, and Idaho received overt support from many elements of the working class. The metal miners, especially, had strong reasons for giving the Populists their support. Many of them were employed by large-scale mining corporations owned by absentee capitalists in the East: a fact which encouraged the growth of anti-eastern sentiments among the miners which were later turned against the Washington-based AFL. In addition, the big railroad corporations exerted at least as much influence over the location and operation of the metal mines as they did in coal, as the dispute over freight rates in the 1892 Coeur d'Alene contest had shown; and the 1893 WFM convention committed the union to supporting government ownership of the railroads, just as the UMWA had done. It approved the Populists' support for measures to secure the eight-hour day, which was to be one of the union's own most persistent legislative demands. And it enthusiastically endorsed the principles of the initiative and referendum, which accorded particularly well with the grass-roots character of western democracy.[9]

As a result, between 1892 and 1896 mining districts in various parts of the Mountain West elected miners' candidates to office on labor or Populist tickets to an even greater extent than the coal miners in the UMWA had done. In Butte, where metal miners dominated the local labor movement, the local Trades and Labor Assembly urged all lower-class groups to unite behind the Populists. In Anaconda, another WFM stronghold in Montana, the *Populist Courier* was edited by a member of the union. At Coeur d'Alene, Edward Boyce was elected briefly to the state legislature on the Populist ticket. And the union as a whole gave enthusiastic support to the prolabor Colorado Populist Governor Davis Waite, who was elected to office in November 1892. Miners' votes undoubtedly helped to account for the large Populist tally registered in Idaho, Nevada, and Colorado in that year, and also to a lesser extent in 1894.

Western miners' support for Populism was also enhanced by the issue of free silver. A considerable proportion of the WFM membership mined silver for a livelihood, and they naturally supported the political struggle to resume the coinage of silver at a ratio of 16 to 1 in gold. Throughout the 1880's the price of silver had been falling, and by the onset of the 1893 panic it was worth only sixty-two cents an ounce, far less than it had been only a few years before. The May 1893 convention of the union grumbled at the "untold loss, misery, and crime" which had resulted from the earlier demonetization of silver, and the effects of the depression in the industry were aggravated by the repeal of the Sherman Silver Purchase Act in August of that year. The 1895 WFM convention gave its "undivided support to the party [Populist] advocating the principles contained in the Omaha platform"; and in the presidential election of 1896 virtually all the mining counties in Colorado, Idaho, and Montana went for Bryan.[10]

But Populist and industrial-union sentiments were not in themselves enough to turn the WFM into a class-conscious, revolutionary organization, any more than they were in other socialist trade-unions. In the mid-1890's many western mine owners and businessmen as well as miners gave their support to the People's party—a fact which tended to obscure class differences instead of accentuating them—and in several of the mountain states both the old parties endorsed free silver also. More significant than Populism itself was the collapse of the People's party after fusion with the Democrats in 1896, which appeared to leave many miners angry and frustrated, or so President Boyce indicated when he denounced "the silver barons of the west" in a speech to the May 1897 union convention. The silver operators of both the major parties, he declared, "are as bitter enemies of organized labor as the gold bug Shylock in his gilded den on Wall Street." [11]

The implication of this was that the metal miners should turn to a more radical party to do for them what Populism had been unable to do.

Equally important in developing revolutionary tendencies among the western miners was the social and economic character of the metal mining industry and the nature of the mining labor force. Wage levels were usually higher in metal mining than in coal, owing to the generally higher cost of labor in the West. They ranged from $2.00 a day to $3.50 or even more in certain mines, and although wage reductions were often the cause of strikes, the general level of wages was quite high and destitution was rarely a serious problem. Nor did the great depression of the mid-1890's appear to have such serious consequences for metal miners as it did for coal miners, despite periodic pockets of unemployment.

In other respects, however, virtually all the factors which had created disaffection among the coal miners were present to a still greater degree. Safety legislation was even more necessary in the metal mines than it was in coal, owing to the more primitive conditions of the western mining settlements and the reckless speed with which the ore was extracted in the hope of acquiring sudden wealth. But in practice there was even less safety legislation than there was in the coal mines; and it was also less well enforced. By 1900 a safety law had been passed in Colorado, but it was regarded as "entirely inadequate" because of the insufficient number of mine inspectors. "In practice," said one witness before the U.S. Industrial Commission in 1899, "no mine is inspected except when a man has been killed." In Utah there was no law for the inspection of metal mines, and in Idaho it was described as a "perfunctory affair." In addition, the health of miners and smeltermen was undermined by the fumes of arsenic, sulphur, and lead. To the other hazards of mining noted in coal, there must be added the climatic rigors of working underground in intense heat, while the surrounding temperature, in the high mountain camps, was extremely cold. Ascending to the surface brought nausea and dizziness, as well as the danger of pneumonia. "To describe in detail the manifold ways in which men have lost their lives in these mines," wrote one observer in 1883, "would be a needless catalogue of horrors." [12]

The operators' influence over the lives of the metal miners was also very extensive. Company stores were less prevalent than in the coal mining states. But the renting of company-owned tenements and boardinghouses —often no more than shacks—at prices considerably above those in surrounding towns was standard practice in most mining camps. So was the use of company doctors and hospitals. If the operators wished to get rid of a man, they had only to refuse to rent him a house. In case of strikes, those living in company houses and trading at company stores could be forced back to work, or compelled to leave the community, by the threatened withdrawal of housing or of credit. Employment was unstable for other reasons, too. The industry was characterized by sudden, spasmodic fluctuations in production and in employment, as new mines were discovered and old ones played out, as well as by changes in the nature of the market, as in coal. In the early period, especially, the life cycle of a mining town—from wilderness to boom, and then to the status of a ghost town—could be as short as a dozen years. Improved technology made assessment of the potential life of a mine more predictable. But frequent job changes, sudden periods of unemployment, and insecurity of work characterized metal mining to an even greater extent than they did coal.

The corollary of these developments were similar difficulties in establishing a viable and successful trade-union. Competition from oriental immigrants helped to undermine the solidarity of WFM strikes, although this type of labor was much less numerous than were Slavs and Italians in the coal mines. The WFM was relatively successful at first. By the turn of the century it had nearly 30,000 members and quite strong organizations in the major mining communities of Montana, Idaho, Nevada, Colorado, and Utah. But this was a relatively small number compared to the total labor force in the industry. Moreover, it represented the peak of the WFM's membership, comparing very unfavorably with the much larger numbers which the UMWA was able to organize once its initial 1898 break-through had been made.[13]

Technological and other industrial developments also had greater importance in metal mining than they did in coal. In the coal industry self-employment was virtually impossible after 1885, save for the highly talented or the highly fortunate who rose up through the company hierarchy. By contrast, in the metal mines at this time there were a large number of ex-artisans, speculators, or prospectors who had earlier come out west in the hope of finding gold.[14] This was usually found in its relatively pure state, in stream beds or as a free ore in separate veins, and it could be mined with fairly simple tools by one or two prospectors, operating an individually owned grubstake. Silver could also sometimes be handled in this way. But more usually silver was found mixed with lead, zinc, or copper, requiring advanced technology, considerable capital, and large milling and smelting facilities to mine. Within a remarkably short space of time individual grubstakes had to be abandoned, to be replaced by relatively large-scale industrial communities, complete with smelting factories, milling plants, and extensive underground mines.

The result, in the 1880's and 1890's, was the rapid growth of an at least partially previously self-employed mining labor force which was dependent on large-scale mining corporations for a livelihood. Companies such as the Amalgamated Copper Company and Phelps-Dodge dominated the copper industry. Other large corporations exploited lead and silver, and the American Smelting and Refining Company and the United States Reduction and Refining Company largely monopolized the refining and smelting of ores. In 1901 President Boyce of the WFM complained bitterly against these trusts, which had, he said, in the eight years of the union's history transformed the industry so much that now "less than a dozen men control the metalliferous product of the United States and Canada, and dictate to owner and workmen alike the value of their property and the schedule of wages paid workmen for their labor."

How many members of the WFM were actually former prospectors who had become mine employees is difficult to assess, since workingmen in the West generally were highly mobile, and quite a large number of union members were professional miners who had previously been employed in coal. But a desire to recover self-employment, and an awareness of its loss, certainly seemed present in the minds of those members who in 1894 protested a proposed new federal assessment on miners' claims; in numerous plans, never realized, for the union itself to employ prospectors to examine mining claims; and in the rhetoric of union officers, who frequently urged the "reassertion of control" by the miners over "the wealth [which] they produce." [15]

Last, there were the extremely repressive tactics of both the mining operators and the governmental authorities in the Rocky Mountain states themselves. These tactics were also used, of course, in coal mining and in other industries, but in metal mining they led to an unparalleled series of violent conflicts between the mine owners and their employees which had many of the characteristics of class war. The miners were able to absorb the first defeat at Coeur d'Alene in 1892 without abandoning their commitment to traditional trade-union principles. But a similar and even more violent conflict occurred in the same area in 1899, when the ore concentrator at Wardner was dynamited, to be followed almost immediately by the summoning of federal troops, the arrest and confinement of union members in bull pens without warrants, and a declaration from the representative of Idaho Governor Steunenberg that only miners with permits from the state authorities could be employed in the mines. The first of the celebrated conflicts at Cripple Creek in Colorado, in 1894, was also accompanied by bombings, extensive use of court injunctions, and another open battle between deputies and miners, conducted with an almost military sense of tactics for control over the mines. [16]

Each of these disputes was characterized by a resort to violence extremely early in the conflict, and over grievances—such as wage reductions, eight-hour shifts, or the employment of nonunion men—which in most eastern cities would almost certainly have been settled either by direct negotiation or by some other form of compromise. But in the western mining communities, located in mountainous areas which were still relatively sparsely settled, and isolated even more than the coal camps were from the moderating influences of large-scale urban life, both sides tended to resort readily to violence as a means of resolving their differences.[17]

This tendency was enhanced by the absence of any large, relatively neutral business or professional class to mediate disputes in the mining towns. There were, of course, middle-class elements present in Butte, Anaconda, and other large mining centers. But since they were nearly always dependent on the mines in one way or another for their livelihood, in a clash these groups tended to align themselves with either the miners or the owners, whichever appeared to be the stronger. They could not afford to support the losing side. And since the WFM proved itself, over the long run, to be the weaker of the two groups, the business and economic community tended to ally with the operators, sometimes even despite their predispositions. This development did not take place all at once, of course. Before the development of large-scale mining corporations, the metal miners retained a considerable number of allies among local merchants, professional men, and farmers. Even so radical a commentator as Bill Haywood, for example, acknowledged that before the major strike of 1903–1904 in the Cripple Creek district, miners and businessmen associated with each other in a number of different ways.[18] But once important economic cleavages had developed between the miners and the operators, the middle-class elements frequently found themselves forced to choose sides.

The absence of any large, uncommitted reservoir of public opinion to enforce moderation in industrial disputes—such as was present, for example, in New York to help foster the Protocol of Peace in the garment industry in 1910—meant that it was left to the state, to a greater extent than it was elsewhere, to keep the peace between the two sides. It is in this fact that we find the major explanation for the frequent interference of state authorities in labor disputes in the metal mines. Western traditions of law enforcement helped determine their role, as did frequent propaganda accusations by the operators that the miners were anarchists who needed to be restrained by military force. But the important point, as in coal mining, was that the political and economic influence of the mining operators over the state governments was such that the state authorities, while claiming to dispense justice fairly, in practice nearly always backed the operators when a disagreement arose. The Populist governor of Colorado in the mid-1890's, Davis H. Waite, was one of the few prominent public officials who sought to prevent the state authorities from automatically supporting the operators during strikes, and he was hailed as a hero by the miners as a result. In general, however, the handling of labor disputes was notorious for the suspension of habeas corpus, the incarceration of miners in bull pens without proper charges being brought, deportations to other states, and the outright imposition of military rule.

President Boyce reflected on these developments in his report to the WFM convention of May 1901. Corporate interests, he said, had waged a campaign of repression in the mining industry through the agency of the courts, the press, the state legislatures, and the state militia which was "fast robbing the laborer . . . of all the rights he is by nature's law entitled to enjoy. The industrial warfare of today," he went on, "has reached such an acute stage that neutrality is no longer possible, and he who assumes such a position should be regarded as an enemy of labor." The WFM was better off in 1901 than it had ever been before, both financially and in terms of numbers. But compared to the tremendous power now wielded by the capitalists in the industry, the miners "have made no progress whatever." What was needed, Boyce concluded, was for the miners to recognize that it was the industrial system itself which was responsible for these ills. "Change from the old policy of [pure and] simple trade unionism," Boyce urged the convention. Adopt instead a new, revolutionary policy that would rally the miners in the industry, and convince them to "march bravely on until they reach the final goal where the men and women who labor shall possess every dollar of the wealth they produce with their own hands." [19]

II

A final element in alienating the WFM from the typically conservative pattern of American trade-union development was disillusionment with the AFL. We have already noticed the suspicious attitude toward the eastern labor movement which had been created among the western miners by geographical and temperamental differences, and by their preference for industrial methods of organization. They disapproved, also, of the AFL's failure to give its support to the Populists in the early 1890's and of its negative attitude toward the Knights of Labor. Nevertheless, at its May 1896 convention the WFM decided to apply for an AFL charter on the ground that the "only true" way of accomplishing labor's aims was "the federation of all organizations under one head working for the same cause and voting as one man." [20] It was shortly to find, however, that the AFL's idea of federation was very different from its own.

At the same time as the WFM joined the AFL in 1896, a bitter strike broke out at Leadville, Colorado, over a wage reduction, and the WFM decided to test the value of its new affiliation by appealing to the AFL for financial aid. No action was taken by the AFL until its December 1896 convention six months later, by which time the strike was virtually lost—although Debs, it should be noted, had responded promptly to a request to speak on the strikers' behalf. The 1896 AFL convention did ultimately pass a resolution urging all its affiliates to "extend to them [the Leadville strikers] our moral and financial support." But so little money was gathered by this appeal that it scarcely covered the costs of canvassing, and when Boyce again wrote to Gompers requesting assistance in February 1897, his letter was apparently mislaid.[21]

Already rumors were circulating that the WFM intended to withdraw from the AFL and establish a separate, western labor federation. In March 1897 President Gompers earnestly sought to dissuade the union from this course, pointing out that the AFL had no defense fund of its own and could not in any event have helped the Leadville strikers any more than it had, and indicating also the serious consequences that could flow from a division between the eastern and western wings of the labor movement. "As to the fact of attempting to divide the workers on sectional lines," he wrote to President Boyce on March 9, "it seems to me, if the thought should be harbored by anyone, a gross misconception of our duties to ourselves and our fellow-workers." And he went on to apply the same logic to sectional division that he did to dual unionism within the AFL itself: "We all maintain that it is morally wrong for a worker engaged at his trade or calling to remain outside of the union of his trade. It follows that it is . . . equally wrong for any national union of a trade to remain outside of the great family of trade unions of the country." [22] Boyce was unimpressed. He had been greatly disillusioned by what he regarded as the ineffective and ultraconservative character of the AFL as he had seen it in operation at the December 1896 Federation convention—the first time he had been East in fifteen years—by the apparent lack of rank-and-file influence in the organization, and by the "low intellectual plane of its deliberations." "Do not think me egotistical," he replied to Gompers on March 16, 1897, "when I say that I think the laboring men of the West are one hundred years ahead of their brothers in the East. . . . You know I am not a trades unionist; I am fully convinced that their day of usefulness is past."

President Boyce's March 16 letter also gave the first evidence of the syndicalist direction in which the WFM was now moving:

There is an easier way of winning the battles of labor, much easier than sitting down in idleness until the capitalists starve us to death in idleness and hunger. . . . I never was so much surprised in my life as I was at that convention, when I sat and listened to the delegates from the East talking about conservative action when 4,000,000 idle men and women are tramps upon the highway, made so by a vicious system of government that will continue to grind them further into the dust unless they have the manhood to get out and fight with the sword or use the ballot with intelligence.

Gompers was shocked by these assertions. "It grieves me . . . ," he replied on March 26, "to learn that you believe that there is an 'easier' way of winning the battles of labor than as you describe them 'sitting down in idleness until capitalists starve us to death in idleness and hunger.' This is not the language of the man I imagined as the hero of the Leadville strike," he said, adding that if the AFL had faults, it was the duty of all workingmen to improve it. "As for your suggestion that the resort must be to the sword, I prefer not to discuss [it]."

But by this time Boyce had become adamant. He wrote to Gompers on April 7, 1897:

> The trades union movement has been in operation in our country for a number of years, and through all these years the laboring masses are becoming more dependent. In view of these conditions, do you not think it is time to do something different than to meet in annual convention and fool away time in adopting resolutions endorsing labels and boycotts? . . . I can assure you that, no matter what action the western miners take with reference to the American Federation of Labor, it will not be hasty, nor calculated to injure the labor movement; but now, as ever, I am strongly in favor of a Western organization.

At its May 1897 convention, the WFM decided to withdraw its affiliation from the AFL.[23]

Despite the assertion that it would not act hastily in the matter of a separate western labor federation, the pressure of events caused the WFM to act more quickly than seemed likely at first. In November 1897 the State and Labor Council of Montana, a non-AFL organization which included the powerful Butte Miners Union and several Knights of Labor assemblies, complained at the "incapacity of labor of the East to aid us" and adopted resolutions urging an alternative western federation of labor. Other western groups quickly followed suit. So, in order not to lose the initiative, at its December 28 meeting the General Executive Board of the WFM decided to send round circulars to its locals asking the question: "Do you favor extending an invitation to various labor organizations of the West to meet with us for a two or three day discussion for the purpose of bringing all labor organizations in the West into closer touch?" The majority of locals replying in the affirmative, a conference of representatives of western labor was called at Salt Lake City for May 10, 1898. It was at this conference that the Western Labor Union was born.[24]

Although there had been other groups which supported the establishment of a separate western labor federation, the Western Labor Union was to a great degree an extension of the WFM. Of the 119 delegates who attended the Salt Lake City convention, for example, 77 were metal miners of various kinds. Daniel McDonald, leader of the Butte Molders Union and vice-president of the Montana State Trades and Labor Council, was elected president of the new organization, and it set out to organize a wide variety of trades. According to one estimate, in October 1899 the Western Labor Union had sixty-five affiliates in Montana, Colorado, and Idaho—as well as one in Rossland, British Columbia—which included cooks, waiters, butchers, clerks, musicians, lumbermen, bricklayers, and stonemasons. But the WFM was by far the largest and strongest of these organizations, and throughout the Western Labor Union's history it continued to play the dominant role.

In the Western Labor Union's general philosophy and outlook, therefore, a great deal of the WFM's own emerging brand of radicalism may be seen. The aim of the WLU was to organize "unattached bodies of workmen," especially the unskilled, "irrespective of occupation, nationality, creed or color, [who] are determined that no corporation, trust, syndicate, or injunction shall longer deprive them of their inherent rights." This was a reflection of the principle of industrial solidarity which the metal miners had realized to be essential if they were to be successful in their frequent clashes with the employers. Structurally, the Western Labor Union was to be modeled on the federal system of the United States government—with each state organization to be responsible for the workers in their respective states—together with "a selection of representatives from each state to guard and protect the general welfare." The announced plan was "an exact duplicate of our governmental plan of representation," save that the national convention would not have as much power as Congress. Instead, the "initiative and referendum and imperative mandate" were to be used in running the union. Although each worker was to be a member of the common organization, the principle of separate trade organization was recognized.

Ideologically, the emphasis on democracy in the Western Labor Union and the references to "inherent rights" and the "trusts" indicated an extreme, almost revolutionary form of Populism rather than a commitment to socialism as such. There were references at the founding convention to the changes which had taken place in methods of production in the mining industry. But the convention oratory was thoroughly American in its allusions and spoke of the western workers' plight in terms of disappointed hope rather than of inevitable decline. This was evident, for example, in the speech of John O'Neill, later to be editor of the *Miners' Magazine:*

In the dawn of the twentieth century we hear no longer the whip of the master, instead we hear the exultant shout of the millionaire over the poverty of the people. The government of the people, by the people, and for the people has been supplanted by government by injunction, which annuls the Declaration of Independence. Socialism has written a declaration of independence which will gather together the scattered shreds of liberty. Lincolns would spring upon its defense.[25]

Despite the declared intention to concentrate on organizing only "unattached bodies of workmen," the ambiguity of the Western Labor Union's policy, which allowed workers to remain within the AFL while at the same time organizing them for itself, soon brought the two organizations into conflict. At the December 1898 AFL convention, for example, Gompers indicated his concern at the division in the labor movement which the establishment of the WLU had created and expressed the hope that it could soon be brought to an end. But the temperamental and ideological differences between the two branches of the movement, coupled with the strong antipathy which many western workers felt for the AFL, made conflict between them almost inevitable. "We must try to teach our benighted brothers in the 'jungles of New York' and [in] the East what we have learned here in the Progressive, enterprising West," wrote a Gilman, Colorado, miner to the *Miners' Magazine* in December 1901. The westerners were also irritated by the sudden interest which the AFL now displayed in organizing in the Rocky Mountain area, having paid little or no attention to it before. In Denver AFL organizers tried actively to destroy WLU locals, and elsewhere sought to bring Western Labor Union members back into the AFL camp.[26]

In spite of these increasing tensions with the AFL, the leaders of the WFM continued to give their full support to the Western Labor Union, with the clear intention of creating a revolutionary western labor organization which would ultimately force the American labor movement as a whole into more radical and militant paths. The WFM agreed to exchange membership cards with the WLU, an arrangement which occasionally caused difficulty when metal miners and other mine workers who would normally have been organized into the WFM were enrolled into the WLU. The conventions of the two organizations were held simultaneously, with joint sessions on labor tactics and matters of general policy, and in 1902 a proposal was narrowly rejected which would have established a joint journal between the two bodies.[27]

In all these ways the WFM indicated that it was moving toward a much more radical position than it had adopted when it was first founded in 1893. Politically, the *Miners' Magazine* indicated plainly that with the collapse of Populism after 1896 it had moved sharply toward the left. As the election of 1900 approached, for example, the journal roundly censured President McKinley for his imperialist foreign policy, for having authorized the sending of federal troops to the Coeur d'Alene strike in 1899, and for his general support of the "moneyed people." But it also criticized the Democratic national convention for having ignored "the Populists and the silver Republicans." Instead, it urged the metal miners to vote for the Debs-Harriman socialist ticket: for Debs, because of his support for the miners in the 1896 Leadville strike, and for Harriman because he had written the only "true history" of the 1899 Coeur d'Alene strike in a pamphlet called *Class War in Idaho*. This leftward movement was also indicated by the passage of a resolution at the May 1901 WFM convention asserting that the "capitalist class" was in complete control of the Populist party, as well as of the Democrats and the Republicans. The resolution urged the miners to "take such steps politically as to completely separate them as a political body from all parties controlled by the capitalist class." [28]

This was not yet a declaration for socialism, and the metal miners indicated that at the local level, at least, they were not ready to give their full support to the Socialist party. In 1900, for example, the Colorado Supreme Court declared unconstitutional a state eight-hour law, for which the miners had contended for years, and Colorado members were urged to vote against the judge who handed down the decision "irrespective of political party." A similar recommendation was made to vote against Governor Steunenberg of Idaho. It was also evident, whatever disapproval the national leadership of the WFM may have felt for the fusion of the Populists with the Democrats in 1896, that many miners had earlier voted Democratic and would continue to do so. Colorado, for example, where a considerable proportion of the union membership lived, went Democratic after Governor Waite lost in 1896, and in 1900 the *Miners' Magazine* found that its efforts to persuade for the Debs-Harriman ticket were largely made in vain. It argued strongly that although Bryan and Stevenson (the Democratic vice-presidential candidate) were good men in themselves, the political bosses who had controlled the party under Grover Cleveland were still influential, "and not one of them has any sympathy with labor." Nevertheless, in the November 1900 election, the mining counties of Colorado, Montana, and Idaho all went overwhelmingly for Bryan.[29]

However, in June 1902, President Boyce reported to the tenth convention of the WFM, meeting in Denver, in an even more perturbed state of mind than he had the previous year. Although there had again been a slight rise in the over-all membership, the general position of the metal miners had continued to decline. The main object of the union when it was established in 1893, Boyce recalled, had been to secure higher wages and a shorter work day. But the union's campaign to introduce the eight-hour day had largely failed, and although wages had risen somewhat after the depression, it had almost always proved impossible to prevent reductions when the operators demanded them. In the nine years of its existence the union had had to conduct over fifty strikes protesting wage reductions and other deprivations, and in almost "all instances the forces of government have been used against us." There were now more unemployed men in the industry than there had been in 1893, Boyce claimed, due largely to the speculative activities of absentee mine owners in the East who manipulated the industry in total disregard of the welfare of those who worked in it.

The main reason for all these troubles, Boyce continued, was that the WFM had for years been pursuing the wrong policy. It could never succeed so long as it concentrated on wages and hours alone and ignored what was coming to be more and more obviously the root of the evil, the capitalist system itself:

> Trades unions have had a fair trial, and it has been clearly demonstrated that as presently conceived they are unable to protect their members. They . . . surrender their most sacred rights to boards of arbitration composed of men who have in the past proved to be labor's bitterest enemies. There are only two classes of people in this world: one is composed of men and women who produce all; the other composed of men and women who produce nothing. Realizing this to be a fact the time has arrived when this organization should array itself upon the side of the producers and advise its members to take political action and work for the adoption of those principles that are destined to free the people from the grasp of the privileged classes. . . . The most important action which you can take at this convention is to advise the members of your organization to adopt the principles of socialism without equivocation.[30]

The Socialist party encouraged the miners to act on Boyce's plea. National Secretary Leon Greenbaum sent a telegram to the WFM convention declaring solidarity with the miners, and Eugene Debs spoke to a mass meeting of the delegates in the Denver Coliseum Hall in terms which were very similar to Boyce's own. "You have tried the strike and the boycott," Debs declared, "and have been defeated; your organizations have been wrecked by your masters." It was now the duty of the miners "to combine in the political field, where you are invulnerable." To the socialists' great pleasure, the convention took their advice. After considerable debate, a resolution was adopted asserting, "We, the tenth annual convention of the Western Federation of Miners do declare for a policy of independent political action, and do advise the adoption of the platform of the Socialist Party of America by the locals of the Federation." It was adopted by a vote of 129 to 70.[31]

At the same time that the WFM convention was held, the delegates of the Western Labor Union were also meeting to consider the future of that organization. Secretary Morrison and Vice-President Thomas Kidd of the AFL, continuing Gompers' policy of attempting to reconcile the two wings of the labor movement, were sent by the Executive Council of the AFL to discuss proposals for unity between the AFL and the WLU. The emissaries of the AFL were well received until Debs, in a defiant speech, urged the WLU to retaliate against the attacks of the AFL on its jurisdiction by endorsing the principles of socialism, by declaring the Western Labor Union a national organization, and by changing its name to the American Labor Union so as to broaden its base of operations. All of this was done, despite the fact that the threat of dual unionism against the AFL caused widespread misgiving in the center and right wings of the Socialist party.[32]

The important point for our purposes, however, was that the WFM gave its full support to these moves. The *Miners' Magazine* declared scornfully:

> The western workingmen are not yet prepared to follow Mr. Gompers into Mark Hanna's wigwam [the NCF] to be scalped with the knife of capitalistic arbitration. . . . The Western Federation of Miners and the Western Labor Union are ready to join forces with any labor organization that offers a remedy, but they don't propose to be led like sheep into a slaughter pen to await the butcher's knife without a struggle.[33]

Thus by 1902 the WFM had repudiated conservative, craft unionism in all its forms and had embarked on an overt revolutionary policy, in open defiance of the AFL. Yet the precise nature of this policy, looked at in the spectrum of socialist ideology, remained unclear. In his 1902 speech, as just quoted above, President Boyce went beyond radical Populism to embrace a Marxist analysis of society, comprised of two conflicting classes, one "composed of men and women who produce all; the other composed of men and women who produce nothing." Equally clearly, the WFM had by this time become disillusioned with the conventional methods of trade-unionism and had adopted a revolutionary view of the purpose of trade-union tactics, much as the Boot and Shoe Workers Union had done several years before. The WFM continued to use the traditional weapons of trade-unions. Indeed, it conducted more strikes than most. But in this period they were not undertaken as part of a bargaining process with the employers, in order to secure negotiating concessions. Instead, either they were defensive, used as a means of resisting wage cuts or other depredations, or else they were a form of direct action, employed as a means of promoting open confrontations with the employers.

In fact, it was in its use of the strike weapon that the WFM came nearest to endorsing the syndicalist philosophy. But the form which this direct action took bore little resemblance to the classical syndicalism of France or the European continent, which repudiated politics in favor of economic tactics such as sabotage and local and general strikes undertaken as a deliberate means of provoking revolution by bringing the economy to a standstill. Violence and the destruction of property continued to character-ize the miners' disputes with the operators, and their leaders occasionally condoned the use of violence as deliberate policy, as in Boyce's letter to Gompers of March 16, 1897, or, on a more famous occasion, when he urged union members to carry rifles at the WFM convention of that same year. "Every union should have a rifle club," he said, in a much-quoted speech. "I strongly advise you to provide every member with the latest im-proved rifle, which can be obtained from the factory at a nominal price. I entreat you to take action on this important question, so that in two years we can hear the inspiring music of the martial tread of 25,000 armed men in the ranks of labor." But the reason for this kind of appeal was usually given as self-defense, or the need for the citizen to uphold his traditional liberties (sometimes coupled with an appeal to the principles of 1776), not any rationally conceived plan to use violence as a means of securing power in the state.[34]

Overt syndicalist characteristics were also evident to some extent in the refusal of the WFM to enter into direct negotiations for contracts with the employers. It did this because it believed that contracts tied the hands of labor organizations and corrupted their leaders; that each part of the labor movement should be free to go to the assistance of any other part at any time; and that economic concessions should be forced from employers by means of a direct confrontation, not by means of negotiations. Some form of revolutionary purpose which went beyond the usual functions of a labor organization was also suggested by proposals for a training scheme on "how to deal with the employers"—implying a kind of military training, the exact nature of which was never specified. In addition, there were suggestions that the various schemes of the union to purchase mining land, none of which ever came to fruition, were partly intended to provide an al-ternative means of sustenance in case of a revolutionary conflict with the employers.[35]

But in its wholehearted commitment to socialist political action, not as a supplement to economic action, but indeed sometimes as a substitute for it, the revolutionary policy which Boyce outlined to the 1902 convention de-parted wholly from syndicalist theory. Again and again President Boyce, and Charles Moyer who succeeded him in the union presidency in 1903, pointed out what they considered to be the increasing economic degrada-tion of the metal miners and of the American workers in general, asserting that little or nothing could be done for them by trade-union methods and that the only hope lay in political activity on behalf of the Socialist Party of America. The mere acquisition of union members, Moyer said at the WFM convention of 1903, recalling what John F. Tobin had said to the Boot and Shoe Workers convention in 1896, has brought us no nearer to the solution of the industrial problem than we were at the beginning. The American Labor Union and the Western Federation of Miners in declaring for independent political action [in 1902] have done more to advance the members of your organization, and the laboring people in general, than have the combined promises and useless resolutions of organized labor since the inception of the trade union movement.[36]

III

The new revolutionary policy which the Western Federation of Miners adopted in 1902 was not accepted wholeheartedly by all the union's members. The seventy delegates who had voted against the resolution endorsing the Socialist party at the union convention represented a powerful body of opinion which was skeptical of President Boyce's repudiation of traditional trade-union methods and reluctant to commit itself entirely to a policy of party political action. Some felt that politics were irrelevant to the union's purposes; others that the main emphasis should be on organizing; still others that there was "too much division along political lines in our ranks" to tolerate support for a single political party. Vice-President Mills, of Nelson, British Columbia, even went so far as to say that too few miners understood the principles of socialism to carry out the new policy intelligently. "There must be a great deal of education before we are ready for a great change," he said, "and I believe it would be a mistake to ally ourselves with the Socialist Party at this time." In addition, there was considerable resentment against the union administration for insisting, at the end of the 1902 convention, that a motion be adopted pledging each delegate individually to carry out the terms of the socialist resolution, especially since it was accompanied by covert suggestions that those who had voted against it "were working in the interest of [the] corporations." [37]

Those who worked in the better-organized centers, such as Butte, also objected to the union's official opposition to making contracts with the employers, while the more skilled elements in the union, such as the hoisting engineers, were reluctant to allow themselves to be organized in mixed locals together with the unskilled and semiskilled men. In fact, in 1902 the hoisting engineers in Local 83 threatened to leave the WFM altogether if they were not granted a separate charter, on the ground that their demands for higher wages had consistently been voted down by the majority of semiskilled (and less well paid) pick-and-shovel men in their local. In their plea to the national administration the engineers acknowledged that all members of the WFM were "in a certain sense, in the same class and on the same plane." But they insisted that the administration recognize the difference between unskilled and skilled workers and acknowledge that "skilled labor is entitled to greater remuneration than unskilled." The General Executive Board attempted to find a compromise on this issue, agreeing that some wage differential should be permitted. But it refused to grant the hoisting engineers a separate local, as a result of which they left the union and joined the appropriate craft organization of the AFL. It is significant, also, that these same hoisting engineers who insisted on a wage differential had also been among those who opposed the resolution endorsing the Socialist party at the union convention of 1902.[38]

Despite these signs of opposition, the WFM leadership continued to give its support to the Socialist party and to the American Labor Union, and if anything its militancy increased, rather than diminished, in the period between 1902 and 1905. Two factors, in particular, helped to sustain its revolutionary zeal. One was the savage industrial conflict which resulted in the defeat of the Cripple Creek strike of 1903–1904, in which the employers set out to destroy the WFM in Colorado, one of the states in which it was most firmly entrenched. Starting out from a relatively minor protest over the discharging of union members at Colorado City, the conflict grew into a bloody and protracted struggle between union members, on the one hand, and mine guards, imported strikebreakers, and members of the state militia, on the other. In addition, the militia was ordered out relatively early in the dispute by the strongly antilabor Republican governor of Colorado, James H. Peabody.

Every device was used by the operators against the strikers in this contest. Union halls were raided, safes broken into, and records taken; strikebreakers were armed and incited to violence. Cooperative stores established by the union were entered by mobs without hindrance from the authorities, and their entire contents destroyed. The homes of union men were sacked. More than 175 union members, including President Charles Moyer and Secretary-Treasurer Haywood, were imprisoned in local bull pens; and more than 400 union miners were forcibly deported from the state. The *Miners' Magazine* called the conflict "the most lawless and brutal that was ever carried on against any labor organization in the history of this country"; and President Moyer, writing from prison, said that the defeat of the strike was the clearest possible evidence of the correctness of the 1902 declaration in favor of the Socialist party. "Can Peabody be defeated unless labor goes into politics?" he asked. The response was no; independent political action along socialist lines was the only answer to the problems confronting the WFM.[39]

The other factor was deteriorating relations, not only with the AFL but also with the United Mine Workers of America, which, as we saw in the previous chapter, had maintained cordial relations with the Western Federation of Miners until the end of the 1890's and had tried to keep the lines of communication open between the western miners and the labor movement as a whole.[40] But with the establishment of the Western Labor Union in 1898, and the subsequent founding of the American Labor Union in 1902, official relations between the two organizations, as we have seen, rapidly began to cool. John O'Neill, the fiery editor of the *Miners' Magazine,* included President John Mitchell along with Gompers in his attacks on the AFL, and there was widespread bitterness and resentment at the UMWA's abandonment of the 1903 Colorado coal strike, which many metal miners felt contributed to their own disastrous defeat in the Cripple Creek section nearby.[41]

Relations between the two unions were also damaged by allegations that WFM members had acted as scabs in the Colorado coal strike and that the union intended deliberately to invade the UMWA's jurisdiction by adding a coal miner to its General Executive Board. The first allegation—that metal miners had scabbed on the coal miners—brought indignant protests from the officers of the Western Federation, who claimed that they had used their own money on behalf of the coal miners' strike and had treated it almost as if it were their own. The General Executive Board of the WFM issued circulars denying the accusation, and Secretary-Treasurer Bill Haywood sent a number of them to Adolph Germer, urging him to distribute them on behalf of the WFM's friends in District 12, Illinois. "We cannot permit such a statement coming from Mitchell to go unrefuted," Haywood wrote to Germer. "He knew when he made the statement it was a falsehood and a base calumny. No member of the Western Federation of Miners ever took the place of a striking coal miner in Colorado. . . . In nearly all of the printed matter that we published the coal miners' strike received the same prominence as our own troubles in Cripple Creek and Telluride." [42]

As to the second allegation, the WFM had, in fact, included a number of coal miners in its membership ever since it was founded in 1893, although in the early years it was not clear how far these joined as a result of a deliberate organizing policy, and how far they were simply coal miners working temporarily in the metal mines. But in 1904 Secretary-Treasurer Haywood reported that twenty-one coal miners' locals had been chartered in places as far apart as Michigan, Missouri, Alabama, and Illinois. The June 1904 WFM convention also adopted a proposal to include a coal miner on its Executive—a decision which was later reversed by referendum vote of the membership as a whole. But to many rank-and-file miners, the question of whether they were members of one union or the other had little significance, especially under the conditions of a serious and widespread strike. For many WFM members, also, the controversy brought home once again the folly of separate, trade-oriented labor unions.[43]

In fact, the main effect of both the Cripple Creek strike and the dispute with the UMWA was to isolate the WFM still further from the general labor movement, while at the same time demonstrating even more clearly its need for friends and allies. The American Labor Union had been of little use in helping the WFM in its labor struggles. By the end of 1904 it had lost its momentum, as well as many of its members, and it had clearly failed to establish itself as a viable alternative to the AFL. And so, even before the smoke of the bitter Colorado conflicts had cleared away, the twelfth annual convention of the WFM, held at Denver in June 1904, authorized the General Executive Board of the union to take "such action as might be necessary" to bring the representatives of organized labor together to outline plans "for the amalgamation of the working class into one general organization." In the fall, WFM officials conferred with William E. Trautmann, editor of the *Brauer-Zeitung,* George Estes, president of the United Brotherhood of Railway Employees, and various other leaders of dissident trade-unions; and President Charles Moyer, Secretary-Treasurer Haywood, and editor John O'Neill represented the union at the January 2, 1905, Chicago conference which was called as a preliminary to establishing the IWW.[44]

Even at this late date there were skeptics among the metal miners who doubted the value of forming yet another separate trade-union federation and feared the consequences of a further acrimonious conflict with the AFL. In June 1904, in another attempt to heal the breach with the western labor movement, a special delegation from the AFL Executive Committee met with WFM officers to discuss the possibility of reaffiliation. The AFL promised not to interfere with the WFM's industry-wide jurisdiction, and terms for reentry to the federation were seriously canvassed. But the ideological gap between the two organizations was too wide to be easily bridged, and the proposal was rejected by the WFM because, among other reasons, the AFL did not submit its decisions to a referendum vote of its entire membership. The WFM leadership was also convinced that with less than 30,000 members of its own it would have been unable to exert any great influence over the conventions of the AFL.

In addition, WFM leaders were outraged by an AFL executive circular of March 21, 1905, recommending that AFL affiliates cease making donations to striking metal miners, on the ground that the union's attendance at the January 2 Chicago conference had been detrimental to the interests of the labor movement as a whole. "That representatives of organized labor should recommend that the wives and little ones of the persecuted miners of Colorado should be deserted," President Moyer commented, "while their husbands and fathers, blacklisted by the corporations, were tramping the highways and seeking employment, is almost beyond belief." In any event, Moyer added, the AFL had done precious little for the metal miners, even though they on their part had always responded generously to financial appeals for other workingmen. The June 1905 convention of the union endorsed the proposed new industrial federation by a vote of almost four to one; and it selected five delegates to the June 27 IWW founding convention, with the deliberate plan of writing the two bodies into one. "It is plain and evident that the champions of trade and craft autonomy are becoming uneasy," wrote O'Neill enthusiastically to Adolph Germer on June 19, 1905. "The fact that the Executive Board of the A.F. of L. are sending out their ablest rostrum speakers [as observers] is convincing proof that Gomperism is trembling for its perpetuation." [45]

The WFM's major purpose in helping to establish the IWW, aside from its general aspirations for the labor movement as a whole, was its hope that the IWW would finally succeed in creating a coalition of powerful and likeminded labor organizations in the West which could provide it with allies in its frequent and debilitating struggles with the employers. Of the organizations which actually joined the IWW, the Western Federation of Miners was by far the largest, with 27,000 of the approximately 50,000 members which the IWW had at the end of 1905. President Moyer became an Executive Board member, and John Riordan, also of the WFM, served as assistant secretary-treasurer. Bill Haywood, the fiery and influential secretary of the WFM, held no official position in the IWW at this time, although he was later to play an extremely important role. The WFM transformed itself into the Mining Department of the new organization—enabling it to organize coal miners as well as workers in the metal mines—and it provided the IWW with most of its initial financial support.

But the high hopes with which the WFM entered upon its new affiliation were soon to be severely dashed. In February 1906 President Moyer, Secretary Haywood, and George Pettibone were arrested on charges of complicity in the murder of former Governor Frank Steunenberg of Idaho, leading to one of the most famous trials in the history of American labor.[46] This was not only a severe setback for the IWW. It also deprived the metal miners of experienced leadership at a time when they could ill afford to lose it, besides preoccupying them with the problems of maintaining their own organization at a time when they had intended to devote their energies to furthering the Wobbly (IWW) cause. Then came the disastrous second IWW convention of September 1906, which split the organization into two warring factions and led to serious divisions in the ranks of the WFM itself. Three of the five metal miners' delegates to the convention, Acting President Charles Mahoney, John McMullen, and Dan McDonald, supported Charles O. Sherman and the IWW administration which had been elected in 1905. But Albert Ryan and Vincent St. John, the other two delegates, gave their support to the group of convention dissidents headed by Daniel DeLeon and William E. Trautmann.[47]

The 1906 IWW convention also took several other steps of which the metal miners in general disapproved. It decided that all matters passed upon by the convention should be submitted to an initial referendum vote of the membership and then be allowed to stand as part of the general laws of the organization until the membership disapproved. This appeared to limit, even if only in a small way, the democratic methods of operation which were regarded as extremely important by the miners and had been one of their main reasons for refusing to rejoin the AFL in 1904. And the WFM was disconcerted also by the passage of a resolution opposing endorsement of any political party, which ran counter to Moyer's repeated assertions of support for the Socialist party. The convention even went so far as to instruct the Denver IWW local to withdraw its support for Bill Haywood, who, although in prison awaiting trial, was running for governor of Colorado on the Socialist party ticket in that year. This move, in fact, indicated the growing dominance of the more overtly syndicalist faction in the organization, which culminated in the repudiation of political action altogether at the IWW convention of 1908.[48]

The WFM was even more dismayed by the sharp disputes and personal antagonisms which characterized the internal operations of the IWW, especially at a time when it was desperately in need of strong and reliable support of its own. "I am bitterly opposed to the 'DeLeon' factional methods and tactics as one can possibly be," wrote Haywood to James Kirwan on October 10, 1906. "The acrimony and ill feeling engendered will take a long time to dispel." A week earlier President Moyer had written to Kirwan in much the same indignant vein:

> By the gods, I have suffered too much, worked too hard to ever tamely submit to the Western Federation of Miners being turned over to Daniel De-Leon, to take the place of his defunct trades and labor alliance. . . . I desire you to say to Vincent St. John and Albert Ryan that if they lent themselves to DeLeon, Veal, Trautmann and Riordan . . . they were not only acting without authority, but without any semblance of fairness, and that such [a] policy will never receive the support of myself, neither do I believe the rank and file of the Western Federation of Miners will ever sanction such damnable work.[49]

In consequence of this, the WFM ceased paying dues to the IWW, and the July 1907 union convention, although it adopted a new and much more radical Preamble than the earlier one of 1893, decided not to recognize either the Trautmann-DeLeon or the Sherman faction, but to try to refashion the IWW on a more solid base of organized trade-union support. A call was issued to all labor bodies interested in industrial unionism, including the Brewery Workers Union, the United Mine Workers, and both factions of the IWW, to meet in convention with the WFM in Chicago on October 1,

1907, "for the purpose of re-establishing and strengthening the Industrial Workers of the World." Because of doubts expressed by several groups who might have attended, the proposed convention was delayed until April 6, 1908, when a new invitation was sent out. But only one group, the Sherman faction of the IWW, accepted the invitation. The Trautmann faction sent an insulting reply. As a result, at its next convention, held in Denver in July 1908, the WFM gave up the idea of a new federation and decided on an absolute divorce from the IWW and all its works.[50]

Not unnaturally, the IWW resented the abrupt withdrawal of WFM support. The *Industrial Union Bulletin* condemned the 1907 peace proposal as "reactionary" and urged WFM locals sympathetic to the IWW to continue their loyalty to the Wobbly cause. On October 8, 1907, the Tonopah, Nevada, WFM local adopted a resolution urging the WFM Executive to pay its dues to "the stronger faction of that organization [the IWW], and by so doing assist in promoting the only true unionism of the working class." On October 22 a similar resolution was passed unanimously by Local 220 of Goldfield, also in Nevada. This latter development was particularly ominous as soon afterward a major strike was lost in Goldfield partly as a result of the rift between the WFM and the IWW—an occurrence which was to become increasingly frequent in later years. At the July 1908 WFM convention a resolution was also debated from IWW supporters in Butte and various other centers criticizing the administration's handling of the divisions in the IWW and accusing the administration of "throttling" the IWW when they "should be the first to recognize [its] . . . potency." [51]

Reviewing the whole IWW episode at the 1908 convention, it became clear that disappointment at the failure of dissatisfied AFL unions to join it was the main ingredient in the WFM's withdrawal of support. In particular, exaggerated faith was placed in the belief that the Brewery Workers Union and District 12 of the United Mine Workers would immediately join the industrial federation and start a general exodus of socialist trade-unions from the AFL. The failure of these organizations to join the IWW meant, as President Charles Moyer put it, that the WFM had been obliged to "again stand the brunt of the battle in the attempt to plant the seed of industrial unionism." "After a careful study," Moyer went on later, "it occurs to me . . . that industrial unionism is by no means popular, and I feel safe in saying that it is not wanted by the working class in America." Every effort which had been made by the union to found a militant, revolutionary organization—the Western Labor Union in 1898, the American Labor Union in 1902, and the IWW in 1905—had been rejected by "an overwhelming majority." The WFM "was not called upon to continue doing that which, for the time being, has proved impossible," he declared. Though continuing to conduct a campaign of education in favor of political action to end the capitalist system, the union should turn its chief attention to "the primary object of our organization, which is to better the condition of those employed in the mining industry, under the present system." [52]

These declarations of President Moyer, which were endorsed by the 1908 convention, did not mean that the WFM had become an ultraconservative trade-union overnight. Other evidence suggests that the unpopularity of industrial unionism, to which Moyer pointed, referred only to dual organizations of the IWW type, not to the idea of industrial unionism as a whole. Indeed, the delegates later went on to "reaffirm our allegiance to the principles of industrial unionism, and hereby pledge ourselves to work together for the solidarity of the working class." [53] Nevertheless, Moyer's views constituted the first overt sign of increased moderation on the part of the union and of a retreat from the reckless militancy of earlier years. One factor in this tendency was a belief on the part of many WFM members that the arrest of Moyer, Haywood, and Pettibone in 1906 was largely due to their connection with a revolutionary body such as the IWW. Widespread publicity attended the trial, and President Theodore Roosevelt went out of his way to condemn the defendants as "men who have done as much to discredit the labor movement as the worst speculative financiers and most unscrupulous employers . . . have done to discredit honest capitalists and fair-dealing businessmen." [54]

There was also a growing belief that the WFM's association with revolutionary socialism was one of the factors in increasing the mining operators' hostility toward it. The operators frequently published indictments of the miners' behavior during strikes, using them as a means of securing public support for their own activities. They took care to contrast the lawlessness and violence which accompanied these conflicts with the peaceful negotiations which terminated most other industrial disputes. Perhaps the most famous of these indictments was a pamphlet entitled *The Criminal Record of the Western Federation of Miners,* compiled in 1904 by the Colorado Mine Operators Association, which quoted Edward Boyce's 1897 speech urging the miners to buy rifles and recounted the acts of violence allegedly committed by union members from 1894 through 1904. Politicians also exploited the radical connections of the WFM to their advantage. Running for reelection in the fall of 1904, for example, Governor James H. Peabody of Colorado declared: "I sincerely believe that organized labor has no more dangerous enemy than the Western Federation of Miners, which is seeking, under the cloak of organized labor, to protect itself . . . in the promulgation of its dishonest socialist theories, which recognize no right to private property, and from the result of its anarchistic tenets and tendencies." The union also suffered from adverse publicity resulting from frequent state or federal investigations into its activities.[55] These condemnations would have mattered less had the WFM by this time secured official recognition by the mining companies as a bona fide labor organization, as other socialist unions like the ILGWU did. But the WFM still officially refused to negotiate contracts with the employers, even though it had been seriously weakened in the Cripple Creek conflict of 1903–1904.

Another source of disappointment to the metal miners' leadership was the failure of rank-and-file members to carry out with any great enthusiasm the request to vote socialist which had been made on numerous occasions since 1902. In the spring of 1903 the Socialist party made quite a flourish in the Rocky Mountain area by running candidates for municipal office in Butte, Anaconda, and Billings, Montana; in Spokane, Washington; in Wallace, Idaho; and in Telluride, Silverton, and Cripple Creek, Colorado. Several councilmen and other municipal officials were elected on this and subsequent occasions, culminating in the election of a socialist mayor in Butte in 1911. David C. Coates, a member of the International Typographical Union who had been elected lieutenant-governor of Colorado as a Populist in 1900, also received considerable publicity when he declared himself a socialist in the summer of 1902. When the large-scale and persistent character of the industrial conflicts in the mining industry is borne in mind, however, the actual size of the Socialist party vote in the early years of the century was small. In 1900 the socialist vote for governor of Colorado, where the party was strongest, was 684, compared to 142,321 for the successful Republican candidate. It jumped to 7,431 in November 1902, five months after the initial WFM declaration for socialism had been made, only to fall back to just over 2,000 in 1903. The successful Republican ticket in the state elections of that year received more than 153,000 votes.[56]

But the greatest disappointment came in the fall elections of 1904, only a few months after the end of the brutal and repressive Cripple Creek labor war. The Socialist party put up a strong candidate for governor of Colorado, A. H. Floaten, a Telluride storekeeper who had been run out of town for selling goods to union members during the strike. The socialist press gave widespread publicity to the election, denouncing "Peabodyism" as a "czaristic dictatorship." The Socialist party National Executive issued a statement attacking Republican Governor Peabody and his supporters as the "real anarchists" in the dispute. And Ben Hanford, the party's 1904 vice-presidential candidate, wrote a pamphlet entitled *The Labor War in Colorado,* which received considerable attention.

However, concern was expressed early in the campaign that the miners, instead of voting socialist, would vote Democratic as a means of unseating the Republican Peabody. On May 21, for example, the Milwaukee *Social Democratic Herald* reported that the leaders of the WFM were fearful that the great mass of the miners would "stupidly resent Peabodyism by . . . electing the Democrats in the coming state elections, instead of putting class-conscious Socialists at the head of the State administration, as they would doubtless be able to do by massing their own and their sympathizers' vote." This, according to the election results, is largely what happened. Alva Adams, the Democratic candidate for governor, beat Peabody by 97,420 votes to 86,543. A. H. Floaten, the socialist candidate, received only 2,498, a third of the socialist vote in 1902.[57]

But the most important evidence of increasing moderation on the part of the Western Federation of Miners was its decision, taken in the spring of 1910, to apply for readmission to the AFL. Tactically, this move was not wholly unexpected, in view of the break with the IWW, renewed contacts which had been made with the AFL in 1907, and the failure of the whole series of separate labor federations—going right back to the Western Labor Union in 1898—to provide the WFM with the necessary degree of labor-union support. "The Western Federation of Miners," wrote editor O'Neill in the *Miners' Magazine* of February 24, 1910, "standing alone and apart from the labor movement of the country, cannot hope to win a victory from the combinations that are backed by the armed power of the state and nation." Every major conflict which the union had undertaken with the operators on its own initiative, O'Neill continued, had been lost. In addition, the AFL was now much stronger in the Rocky Mountain area than it had been in the 1890's, and it was potentially in a much better position, therefore, to provide the support which the WFM so desperately needed. Also, its conservative trade-union policies were less likely to prove offensive to the operators, and to public opinion generally, than the aggressive militancy of the IWW.

Nevertheless, ideologically speaking, in view of the strong antipathy with which the WFM had earlier regarded the American Federation of Labor, there can be no doubt that the decision represented a distinct move to the right. Whereas the WFM, not unlike the administration of the Boot and Shoe Workers Union in the 1890's, had responded to its early defeats on the economic field by increased militancy and by emphasizing the importance of political action, it now realized that attempts to change existing economic relationships in the industry by revolutionary means were beyond its strength. The union "should, at all times, assume a position of absolute fairness towards the employers," President Moyer told the WFM convention of 1910. "While firm in our claims, we should be ever ready to listen to the other side and exert every effort to prevent a conflict." This was heresy according to the canons of syndicalist ideology, but in view of the tremendous opposition which the WFM's earlier policies had stirred up, it seemed to Moyer the only course which it was now possible to take. The

Miners' Magazine tried hard to convince itself that the AFL was more radical in 1910 than it had been in the 1890's, pointing to the establishment of trade departments in 1907–1908 and the greater flexibility over political action since the elections of 1906. "If militant, industrial unionism is logical," ran a journal editorial, "then it seems that it will be an easy matter for the advocates of industrial unionism to crystallize a sentiment on the floor of an A.F. of L. convention, that will ultimately relegate the present policy of the American Federation of Labor to the scrapheap." But this, as other socialist trade-unions had found, was easier said than done.[58]

The actual process of affiliating the WFM to the AFL took place with the help of the UMWA not because it approved of the radical ideological position of the metal miners' union, but because the affiliation raised important jurisdictional issues of concern to both organizations. A joint conference was held between representatives of the two unions in January 1910, at which it was agreed that the WFM should apply for reaffiliation provided that the jurisdiction of both the UMWA and the WFM remained unchanged and that a Mining Department, similar to those for the Building Trades and for the Metal Trades, should be established in the AFL. This agreement was put to a referendum vote of the WFM membership and approved by a margin of more than seven to one, with only 5 out of 265 local unions showing a majority against. The WFM therefore made formal application for a charter from the AFL in May of 1910. Considerable jurisdictional wrangling ensued between the Western Federation, the International Association of Machinists, and other AFL unions which had members working in the metal mining camps. Finally, under pressure from the UMWA, a compromise was reached, and the metal miners reentered the AFL on May 11, 1911, with its jurisdiction largely intact. But despite the hopes of the WFM, there is no evidence to suggest that the new Mining Department which was established as a result of these negotiations was any more radical than the other industrial departments of the AFL.[59]

Although reaffiliation with the AFL had been supported by a large majority of the WFM membership, the response of those who disapproved was predictably intense. *Solidarity,* the IWW paper, dismissed the move as a "reactionary step." The "once militant" Western Federation of Miners, it went on, was "drifting backwards" by "trying to suck its way into the A.F. of L." The Butte Mill and Smelterman's Local 74, at its February 9, 1911, meeting, entered a protest against what it called "the proposed retrograding affiliation," urging other locals to reject what it considered a violation of the principles of industrial organization. And ex-Secretary-Treasurer William D. Haywood, writing in the increasingly IWW-oriented *International Socialist Review,* declared that when the WFM rejoined the AFL it had become "poisoned and polluted with the virus of the pure and simple trade union that has representatives on the Civic Federation proclaiming the identity of interests of capital and labor." [60]

IV

The United Mine Workers' support for the WFM's entry into the AFL indicated that relations between the two miners' organizations had now much improved. This was partly because of John Mitchell's departure from the presidency of the UMWA, and partly because of continuing underlying sympathies between the rank and file of the two trade-unions. But it was also because the WFM's increasing moderation rendered it more acceptable to the United Mine Workers' official leadership than it had been before. In a message of greeting to the August 1911 convention of the WFM, for example, President Tom Lewis welcomed the fact that the WFM now took a "more pragmatic view" of labor developments than it had before. [61]

The WFM had refrained from enrolling UMWA members into its organization as early as 1906, in order not to offend the coal miners' union, and after it had officially broken with the IWW the practice of exchanging transfer cards between members, which had been temporarily broken off by the United Mine Workers, was resumed on both sides. The metal miners also swallowed their former objections to the conservative character of the UMWA leadership and gave their full encouragement to negotiations for unity between the two organizations. Bill Haywood—who was later to be expelled from the WFM because of his encouragement of the IWW element —was permitted to address the January 1908 United Mine Workers' convention on the subject of closer relations between the two miners' unions; and the UMWA responded by appointing a committee to explore the possibilities of unity between the two organizations at the WFM convention of July 1908. [62]

These developments were greeted with great enthusiasm by socialists generally who saw in them the hope of a major strengthening of the forces of radicalism throughout the entire labor movement. The New York *Call* commended the speeches made by the United Mine Workers' delegates to the 1908 WFM convention as "thoroughly progressive"; and the further discussions which were held between the two unions demonstrated, according to the *International Socialist Review*, that the "coal miners, like their brothers in the metalliferous mines, are becoming thoroughly class-conscious, politically and industrially. Socialist speakers who had traveled about in the mining regions," that journal continued with exaggerated optimism, "declare, almost without exception, that the miners will lead the vanguard of the American working class."

Nevertheless, as we saw in the previous chapter, the substantive negotiations which were held in October 1914 to amalgamate the two organizations ended in failure, despite the enthusiastic support which was given to them by Debs and other socialists. Calling upon both unions to unite and pull out of the "Civic-American Federation of Labor," and urging at the same time a reunification between the Socialist party and the SLP, Debs expressed the hope that a new industrial-union federation could be established which would draw to itself "all the trade unions with industrial tendencies" and that the "reactionary federation of craft unions [could] be transformed within and without into a revolutionary organization."

However, the WFM, whose basic purpose in pressing for unity was to try to secure much-needed support in its attempts to organize the metal miners, needed the amalgamation far more than the United Mine Workers did. It was even willing to sacrifice its sovereignty and independence by becoming a district organization of the UMWA. But, as previously indicated, the small size of the WFM in relation to the industry's labor force—about 17,000 members out of some 200,000 eligible for membership—and the sacrifices which the United Mine Workers would have had to make in order to bring the WFM up to its own level meant that the negotiations for unity ended in failure. "To amalgamate the two organizations under present conditions," the negotiating committee declared, "could not strengthen the organized metal miner without weakening the organized coal miner." [63] In any event, the WFM had already been so debilitated by its numerous conflicts with the employers that it is unlikely that the amalgamation, even if it had been secured, would have altered significantly the balance of radical forces in the AFL.

The failure to secure amalgamation with the United Mine Workers did not mean that the WFM turned away angrily to some other form of federation, as it had done in 1897 after its initial experience with the AFL, or again in 1905. The union was now tied firmly to the general labor movement, and it was in any event too feeble to launch out into further experiments of its own. Although some progress had been made in organizing since the break with the IWW, the WFM was in no position to undertake any major new campaign. Only a small fraction of the eligible metal workers in the country at large had joined the union, and the WFM did not have the organizers to cover the whole of the Rocky Mountain territory, still less to answer calls for assistance in the East. Despite this, efforts to organize copper and other metal miners in Missouri, Michigan, and Minnesota were made, most of which ended in failure.

President Moyer insisted that the reaffiliation with the AFL had not affected the basically socialist (although no longer perhaps revolutionary) purposes of the WFM. "I want to again, regardless of our affiliation with the American Federation of Labor," he said in July 1911, "reaffirm my position . . . that the Western Federation of Miners will continue . . . to advocate the industrial idea of organization on the economic field and united political action on the political field." [64] Nevertheless, at its convention in 1912 the union took a step which in many respects destroyed its unique position in the American labor movement: it decided to give up its opposition to time contracts and to follow the example of the United Mine Workers and of other AFL unions, whose progress was felt to be due largely to their joint agreements with the employers. The convention also empowered the president to appoint an auditor to audit the books and accounts of local unions and, with the consent of the Executive Board, to revoke the charters of any local for violation of the unions' constitution or bylaws. In some cases the checkoff system of the coal miners was also adopted, in spite of a feeling among many members that this system gave employers too great a hold on the union. After 1912, in places where the union was recognized, such as Butte, Telluride, Salt Lake City, and Denver, numerous contracts with the employees were drawn up.

These decisions were violently opposed by a minority of the WFM membership, even though they were subsequently approved by referendum vote. The proposal for the appointment of auditors and for the expulsion of dissident locals were not in themselves controversial, save for the group of IWW supporters, against whom the expulsion powers were largely directed. But for some members they represented a "tendency to centralize the powers of the organization," which was thought to be reactionary and a departure "from the democratic control of the organization."

It was against the decision to adopt contracts, however, that the critics directed their sharpest barbs. During the time period covered by a contract, they argued, the cost of living often rose, so that a wage scale negotiated at one point in time was usually inadequate when the contract expired. Contracts afforded the workers no real protection, since the employers would break them if they failed to accord with their interests. Moreover, they prevented one group of workers from going to the assistance of another when the need arose. But the basic objection to contracts, a member from Butte Local No. 1 declared, was that they involved a recognition that there were some common interests between the operators and the miners. "The very essence of industrial unionism is the recognition of the common interest of all the workers, while the very antithesis of this is the recognition of an identity of interest between employer and employee." This opinion was echoed on behalf of the IWW by Bill Haywood, who went out of his way to chastise the organization for signing a contract with the Anaconda Copper Company, where large numbers of WFM members were employed.[65]

Despite this, the decision to establish contracts was adopted, and in several places it was followed up by negotiated agreements with the operators, although the district-wide type of agreement of the UMWA was not used. But save in a few mining areas, the tradition of hostility was now embedded so deeply that the operators were suspicious of entering into contracts with the union. In addition, the WFM was by now so small and weak that many of the operators refused to recognize the organization, and they continued to import nonunion men during strikes. Thus, violence and mistrust continued to mark relations in the industry, despite the renewed efforts of the union to present itself as moderate and responsible. In 1913, for example, the leadership entered with reluctance into a major strike in the Michigan copper range. This time the AFL gave considerable help—as also did the Socialist party—issuing two appeals for financial aid from all its affiliates and sending ex-UMWA President John Mitchell and AFL Treasurer John Lennon into the Calumet district on the strikers' behalf. It also put pressure on the Department of Labor to secure an investigation into the conditions of the copper mines. Despite this, the usual tactics were employed by the other side. The governor of Michigan summoned the national guard, citizens' alliances were formed, and armed strikebreakers were brought in, resulting in several gun battles. President Moyer was deported from the state, and the strike ended in failure.[66]

In July 1916, President Moyer once more analyzed the weaknesses of the WFM and counseled a further step toward moderation. The lack of progress in the WFM, he told the union convention of that year, was attributable to the refusal to adopt trade agreements and the checkoff system earlier, so that the mine owners might recognize the union as a responsible institution; to the mistake of not remaining affiliated with the AFL in the first place; and to the public commitment to socialist political principles which were not held by a majority of workers in the industry. Because of the union's political stand, not only had employers refused to recognize it but many rank-and-file workers had kept away from it also. "Instead of devoting a greater part of its time and energy as it has in the past in attempting to teach our fellow trades unionists the only correct form of economic and political organization," Moyer said, "[the union] must become a business institution, directing its efforts to the objects for which it was organized, namely to unite the various persons working in the mines—into a central body, to increase their wages and improve their conditions of employment." In response to Moyer's suggestions, the 1916 convention removed the radical Preamble from the union's constitution, replacing it with a much more conventional one listing the aims of the union as "increasing wages, shortening hours, and improving working conditions." [67]

Two years earlier a similar analysis had been made of the condition of the union by Guy E. Miller, a member of the General Executive Board.

Tracing the history of the union from its earliest years, he blamed President Boyce for "indignantly spurning" the AFL when it had failed to help in the Leadville strike of 1896, even though he was aware that it had few financial resources of its own, and for helping to launch the Western Labor Union as "a dual movement separate and apart from the American Federation of Labor." The purpose of the Western Labor Union, Miller said, and of the American Labor Union and the IWW after it, had been "laudable, but the method has been proven to have been extremely faulty." The trouble, Miller went on, was that once the WFM had been committed to one or other of these organizations, its whole policy was shaped by whether its actions would advance the revolutionary ideology of the federation to which it was attached, instead of the interests of the metal miners themselves. Their conventions had been filled with socialist rhetoric, instead of with realistic, practical consideration of the actual conditions in the industry. "In my judgment," Miller said, "one of the supreme mistakes that have been made by the Western Federation of Miners for many years, was their failure, when they came into convention, to take up the issues before them, and to consider calmly whether a wise business policy had been followed or not." Part of this error had been that "our position in regard to the opposition to the contract system was not well founded, although it took about eight years for that idea to sink into the minds of the membership."

Miller also confirmed the degree to which both the mining companies and the state authorities had been antagonized by the WFM's commitment to socialism and had used it as an excuse to make further attacks on the union. The declaration of the 1902 convention, he said, had not succeeded in converting all the union's members to socialism. He added:

> But I want to tell you that it was sufficient to arouse and inflame the minds of the mine owners. It is my opinion that the historic conflict of 1903 and 1904 was largely brought about, was largely caused, by the bitter opposition of the mining companies of this state, and the antagonism of the state officials was increased many, many fold because of that declaration of our membership. Resolutions do not educate men in the principles of political economy and unionism; they were not organized to withstand the terrific onslaught that was made upon them.[68]

The reversion of the WFM toward a more conservative form of trade-unionism was not made without opposition. Ever since the WFM had withdrawn from the IWW, attempts had been made by a small group of IWW loyalists and other extreme radicals to disrupt the organization, or else to capture it from within. In addition, numerous efforts were made to unseat President Moyer, as the leader of the more conservative wing. The left wing circulated personal attacks against him and other officials, charging them with responsibility for the failure of the union to grow and with other offences. An accusation was even made that Moyer had stolen $14,000 from the union treasury. The 1912 convention exonerated him and expelled a number of members who had made the accusation. But the attacks went on.

In 1914 Butte Miners No. 1, the strongest local in the wfm, became the focus of this unrest. Butte had traditionally been the major center of unionism in the industry, with more than 5,000 organized members divided between conservatives, radicals, and iww sympathizers. It had also been one of the centers of opposition to the changing policies of the wfm.[69] In the June 1914 union elections the so-called "progressives" in the union— including Wobblies and their sympathizers, as well as union members —ran a separate ticket against the proadministration local officers, accusing them of being company-supported. When the local refused to sanction the use of voting machines in the election, the insurgents, angered also by recent union assessments, invaded Miners No. 1 hall, destroyed most of the files and records, and threatened to bolt the organization altogether. The *Montana Socialist,* attempting to summarize the dispute, said that the local administration had succumbed to corporation espionage, discrimination against miners who opposed local officers, and political interference by agents of the Amalgamated Copper Company. The insurgents, for their part, were characterized by the "disruptive tendencies of a militant, anarchistic minority seeking destruction of any form of American Federation of Labor unionism." [70]

President Moyer sought to calm the situation by holding an investigation and authorizing new elections, but the problem was rendered immensely more complicated by the dynamiting of Butte Miners No. 1 hall on June 23, 1914, which attracted widespread publicity and attention. Just who was responsible for this was never properly ascertained. Some believed it to be company agitators; others, dissatisfied union insurgents. But the predominant opinion was that the iww had a major hand in the work. President Moyer and the wfm administration quarreled with Mayor Duncan and the socialist administration of Butte over the matter, accusing them of condoning the violence by failing to keep law and order and in general of siding with the iww and the insurgents. Eugene Debs, on the other hand, supported the wfm in the dispute, writing in the *Miners' Magazine* that "there is not a man in the labor movement who has gone through more that is calculated to try men's souls and break their hearts than has Charles Moyer during the last ten years." [71]

Whatever the exact truth about the Butte bombing, the result was disastrous for the union as a whole. In July 1914 the Butte Miners Union was formed as a dual organization to Butte Miners No. 1, the operators repudiated their contract with the WFM, and a bitter fight developed between the two rival unions, which virtually destroyed organized trade-unionism in Butte. Taking courage from this, the IWW conducted a ceaseless campaign against the WFM in Arizona, Salt Lake City, and various other centers, weakening the union still further. By 1917 the membership as a whole was under 15,000, the national administration had lost control over many of the remaining locals, and in most areas the mining companies were as antagonistic toward the union as ever.

The effect of these developments on the former radicalism of the WFM could not have been more marked. President Moyer appealed to Gompers for help in the Butte affair, asking him to send either William Green or John L. Lewis out to Butte in order to counteract the efforts of the IWW. Gompers regretted that he could not send either of these men, but assured Moyer that the Executive Council of the AFL would do "everything in its power to be helpful in the effort to bring the miners of Butte back to a realization of their duty to themselves and their fellow-workers." [72] But despite the failure to provide immediate help in the Butte affair, assimilation to AFL policies and values on the part of the WFM went on unchecked. When the Democrats were elected in 1912, the WFM, despite continuing socialist rhetoric, in practice followed the path of other previously radical trade-unions. The *Miners' Magazine* greeted the prospect of Woodrow Wilson's election with the opinion that he was a "professional aristocrat" who, despite all his "pretended sympathy for the masses of the people," would in fact "make no assault on the murderous system of exploitation, which puts the few in palaces and the multitude in hovels." And it affected distaste for the reformism of the Democratic administration for a number of months after the election of 1912.

But President Moyer reflected more accurately the actual behavior of the union when he welcomed the establishment of the Department of Labor in 1913 (noting that W. B. Wilson, of "our sister organization," the United Mine Workers of America, was its first secretary) and described in detail the successful lobbying efforts which union officials had made on behalf of mine ventilation, antiblacklist legislation, and other reforms in Arizona, Montana, Idaho, and elsewhere. He also urged union members to write to their United States congressmen and senators on behalf of federal legislation which would penalize corporations engaging in interstate commerce if they required surrender of union membership as a condition of employment. "All political parties," Moyer told the July 1914 WFM convention, "are invariably seeking the support of labor, and in particular of the organized workers, and should be told in no uncertain way that these demands shall be inserted in their party platform." [73]

The most interesting development in the case of the Western Federation of Miners, however, was that for a union which had earlier committed itself to socialism with such devotion, there should be so little sign of radical political activity in the later years of our period. This was partly because the iww became the official champion of the dissidents in the union. The iww had had bad official relations with the Socialist party ever since the recall of Bill Haywood—who was no longer connected with the WFM —in 1913; and many of the syndicalist iww members were opposed to political action. It was partly because the earlier declarations in favor of the Socialist party had been regarded as coercive by many members of the rank and file, whose support was now essential if the union were to hold together. But it was mainly because the WFM was now so weakened [74] and divided by internal disputes that it could no longer afford to run the risks of further internal disruption by following political policies which were not acceptable to the union membership as a whole. As James Kirwan, an influential WFM leader and one-time acting president, put it in 1915: "Too much time has been spent on resolutions and debates over so-called theoretical questions, with the loss of many members. The miners are through with 'resolutions.' We must keep on a narrower track." [75]

At all events, none of our other radical trade-unions, with the possible exception of the Boot and Shoe Workers Union, appeared to pass more completely over to AFL orthodoxy than the WFM. The union failed to send a delegate to the March 1917 AFL conference pledging labor's support to World War I, but it did so because it could not afford to send a delegate, rather than because it opposed the purpose of the meeting. In May 1917 the *Miners' Magazine* was critical of conscription, but by November it had openly endorsed America's war effort; and in 1918 the union administration vociferously protested its loyalty to the American cause in order to dissociate itself from the antiwar stand of the iww.[76] After the war there was little sign of a return to radicalism, despite the continuing hostility of the employers. "Our organization has passed through an experience with partisan politics that, while educational, proved unwise," President Charles Moyer told the August 1920 convention, urging the union to support the Non-Partisan Campaign Committee of the AFL.

> This Committee proclaims that organized labor owes allegiance to no political party. . . . Whenever candidates for re-election have been friendly to labor's interests they should be loyally supported; whenever candidates are hostile or indifferent to labor's interests they should be defeated. I therefore recommend that this convention give its unqualified endorsement to the declaration and political plans of the American Federation of Labor, and when the delegates return to their homes that they urge their constituents to apply every legitimate means and all the power at their command to accomplish the defeat of labor's enemies who aspire for public office.

The recommendation was adopted unanimously, without any debate or overt sign of dissent. After 1920 the union made numerous attempts to achieve a recovery, notably in Michigan and in other states where the copper industry had grown rapidly as a result of the war. But decline had now gone so far that any immediate improvement, given the reactionary character of the postwar years, was impossible to achieve. The twenty or so remaining locals in the WFM lacked money, adequate leadership, or an effective organization, and both Communists and One Big Union members as well as the IWW, such as it now was, continued in their unremitting hostility, further weakening the union's ability to act. It was not until the 1930's that the International Union of Mine, Mill, and Smelter Workers, as it then came to be called, was able to recover something of its former strength.[77]

V

As already indicated at the beginning of this chapter, the sources of radicalism in the Western Federation of Miners were in some respects quite similar to those in the UMWA. There were important differences, of course. There were no English radical influences present, nor any particular tradition of independent political action on the part of the metal miners themselves. But mining hazards, company control, and the antagonism of the state authorities were obviously marked.

But the metal miners' response to these conditions was much more intense than it was in coal. This was partly because these pressures were even more powerful than they were in the coal industry. In the isolated and relatively primitive conditions of a semifrontier society, both the operators and the state authorities were able to take greater liberties with dissidents than they could in the Midwest and the East, and the tradition of independence and violent action associated with the frontier made the metal miners even quicker to respond with direct action of their own. Thus a deep legacy of antagonism was established which neither side was willing to overcome. In addition, whereas in coal mining the period of small-scale operation was over, for the most part, by the Civil War or just after, the intense hostility of the metal mining operators coincided also with the loss of self-employment in the western mines—a matter of great symbolic importance—as well as with a period of rapid technological change.

Two other factors were important. One was the collapse of western Populism, which in the western mountain states had much more of a revolutionary flavor than it did elsewhere and to which the metal miners had committed themselves much more overtly than in coal. The other, related factor, was an antieastern psychology, deriving in part from the Populist experience, which took the form of an intense antipathy for the Washington-based AFL.

Thus the WFM cut itself off from all the elements of traditional trade-unionism and from 1902 up until a period ending shortly after 1912 resorted to a form of revolutionary activity which, although it had a number of syndicalist characteristics, in fact largely resembled the DeLeonite impossibilism of the Boot and Shoe Workers Union in the 1890's. Like Tobin, Edward Boyce and Charles Moyer attempted to dismiss conventional trade-unionism as irrelevant and ineffective. Like Tobin, they tried to substitute political for economic action. And like Tobin, also, they found that this approach, taken by itself, would not work. Not only was it unacceptable to a substantial portion of the union's rank and file. It was also in practice largely a matter of rhetoric, and it did not conform to the actual practice of the union to more than a limited extent.

In the end, the WFM was forced to recognize reality and to accept the need for a more practical, as well as for a more conservative, form of trade-unionism. Thus it broke with the IWW and rejoined the AFL. In the interests of better labor relations it went further and by adopting contracts with the employers mitigated its radicalism still more. But whereas in the shoe industry and elsewhere this permitted the growth of a strong and viable trade-union, in the case of the WFM this did not occur. The indiscipline of the miners, the antagonism of the operators, and the legacy of animosity in the industry were too strong. Thus the WFM, which in the early part of the century had provided the main basis of support for the IWW, ended our period in dislocation and defeat, in part because of the hostility of the IWW itself. It is not too much to say that with the reentry of the Western Federation of Miners into the AFL, and with its failure to generate a new form of trade-union federation, went the last hope of a radical alternative in American trade-unionism until the rise of the CIO.

Notes

1. The only full-length treatment of the history of the Western Federation of Miners is Vernon H. Jensen, *Heritage of Conflict, Labor Relations in the Nonferrous Metals Industry up to 1930* (Ithaca, 1950). For the development of radicalism in the industry and its relation to the IWW, see William D. Haywood, *Bill Haywood's Book* (New York, 1929); Paul F. Brissenden, *The IWW, A Study of American Syndicalism* (New York, 1957); John G. Brooks, *American Syndicalism* (New York, 1913); Philip S. Foner, *History of the Labor Movement in the United States,* 4 vols. (New York, 1947–1965), Volume IV.

Two useful articles are: Louis Levine, "The Development of Syndicalism in America," *Political Science Quarterly,* XXVIII (September 1913), 451–479; Melvyn Dubofsky, "The Origins of Western Working Class Radicalism, 1890–1905," *Labor History,* VII (Spring, 1966), 131–154.

2. In order to rebut charges that all "dissatisfied" workers were foreigners, *The People* in June 1894 produced figures to show that more than 80 per cent of the Miners Union of Cripple Creek, Colorado, were American citizens. *The People,* IV (June 3, 1894), 2.

3. *Proceedings, First Annual Convention of the Western Federation of Miners* (Butte, 1893), 1–2; *Compendium of the Eleventh Census: 1890* (Part I, Population) (Washington, D.C., 1892), 472, 483, 490, 551–553; *Twelfth Census of the United States Taken in the Year 1900* (Part I, Population) (Washington, 1901), 490–491, 501, 739–741, 1155–1160. See also *Report of the Industrial Commission on the Relations and Conditions of Capital and Labor Employed in the Mining Industry* (Washington, 1901), 313, 377, 485, 572, 588, 595, hereafter cited as *Capital and Labor Employed in the Mining Industry.*

4. See Robert W. Smith, *The Coeur d'Alene Mining War of 1892, A Case Study of an Industrial Dispute* (Corvallis, 1960), 31–114.

5. *Constitution and By-Laws,* Western Federation of Miners (1893), 1–2.

6. Butte *Bystander,* January 20, 1894; Montana *Silverite,* April 20, 1894, cited in Dubofsky, *op. cit.,* 140. See also *Capital and Labor Employed in the Mining Industry,* 389; *Miners' Magazine,* III (April 1902), 3–31.

7. The convention also exaggeratedly commended the recent ARU victory in the Great Northern strike (conducted, it was noted, "under the able leadership of the Hon. E. V. Debs") as the "greatest victory gained by labor in the last quarter of a century." *Proceedings, Second Annual Convention of the Western Federation of Miners* (Salt Lake City, 1894), 3.

8. *Constitution and By-Laws,* Western Federation of Miners (1893), 2; *Miners' Magazine,* I (January 1900), 16–18.

9. *Proceedings, First Annual Convention of the Western Federation of Miners* (Butte, 1893), 19.

10. *Ibid.;* Dubofsky, *op. cit.,* 140–141; Percy F. Fritz, *Colorado, the Centennial State* (New York, 1941), 352–360; John D. Hicks, *The Populist Revolt: A History of the Farmers' Alliance and the People's Party* (Lincoln, 1965), 263, 337; Edgar E. Robinson, *The Presidential Vote, 1896–1932* (Stanford, 1934), 150–155, 174–177, 256–261.

11. Hicks, *op. cit.,* 264–267; Butte *Bystander,* V (May 15, 1897), 1.

12. *Capital and Labor Employed in the Mining Industry,* LXI–LXIV, LXXVII–LXXX; Edward Lord, *Comstock Mining and the Mines* (Washington, 1883), 319, 397–399, 403.

13. *Miners' Magazine,* I (September 1900), 18–19; III (November 1902), 11–12; VII (April 1906), 8; *Capital and Labor Employed in the Mining Industry,* LXVIII–LXXII; *Proceedings, Ninth Annual Convention of the Western Federation of Miners* (Denver, 1901), 74–75; *Proceedings, Eleventh Annual Convention of the Western Federation of Miners* (Denver, 1903), 123; Rodman W. Paul, *Mining Frontiers of the Far West, 1848–1880* (New York, 1963), 143–144.

14. "The Western mines," wrote one observer in 1906, "are full of long-limbed, frank-eyed men who have adventured . . . far and wide upon the face

of the earth. There are Eastern miners who were blacklisted after leading un-successful strikes. There are cowboys tired of the trail. There are farmers who preferred prospecting to plowing. There are city men who burst the bars of their cages to breathe the open air of the West. These adventurous characters, going out into a new country and plunging into the virgin, everlasting hills, where it would seem that at last all men would stand on the same footing, have suddenly discovered that amid these primitive surroundings the modern in-dustrial system is not only found, but found at its worst." See William Hard in *Outlook*, LXXXIII (May 19, 1906), 126–127.

15. Paul, *op. cit.*, 136–138, 195–196; Jensen, *op. cit.*, 4–9; *Capital and Labor Employed in the Mining Industry*, 191–618, *passim;* Dubofsky, *op. cit.*, 133–134; *Proceedings, Second Annual Convention of the Western Federation of Miners* (Salt Lake City, 1894), 7; *Proceedings, Ninth Annual Convention of the Western Federation of Miners* (Denver, 1901), 8–9; *Proceedings, Tenth Annual Convention of the Western Federation of Miners* (Denver, 1902), 103–105.

16. There are numerous accounts of these and other disputes. See, for exam-ple, Benjamin M. Rastall, *The Labor History of the Cripple Creek District, A Study in Industrial Evolution* (Madison, 1908), 15–58; *Report on Labor Dis-turbances in the State of Colorado from 1880 to 1904* (Washington, 1905), 68–111; Clifton H. Johnson, "The Western Federation of Miners, 1892–1906, A Study in Frontier Activism" (M.A. Thesis, University of Chicago, 1949), 26–61. The summary above is taken from Jensen, *op. cit.*, 20–53, 72–87.

17. Dubofsky argues that these conflicts were the product of rapid indus-trialization and urbanization, similar to that which took place in the East, and were not in any sense a response to geographical isolation or to the previously pioneer character of the western mining frontier. It is true that by 1890 many of the mountain mining settlements had developed beyond the frontier stage and that such cities as Cripple Creek, Colorado, and Butte, Montana, had ac-quired some, at least, of the characteristics of an urbanized society. Further, it is true, of course, that there were major industrial conflicts in more settled east-ern urban centers, such as at Homestead in 1892, Pullman in 1894, and Law-rence, Massachusetts, in 1912, even though these centers were in no sense influ-enced by the frontier. But these were relatively isolated episodes in their respective industries. Although there were comparably rapid technological and economic changes in the machinists' trade, or in shoemaking, for example, they did not result in the extreme violence which characterized virtually all the con-flicts, both major and minor, which took place in the metal mines from the 1880's right through to the 1920's and beyond. While the dislocations brought about by rapid economic change undoubtedly had some effect on this phenom-enon, its persistent and repetitive character must be seen also in the context of a society which was still influenced to some extent by the independent and sometimes lawless spirit of the frontier. See Dubofsky, *op. cit.*, 129–139, espe-cially n. 23. For other views and interpretations of these developments, see Foster R. Dulles, *Labor in America* (New York, 1949), 209; Lewis Lorwin, *The American Federation of Labor, History, Politics, and Prospects* (Washing-ton, 1933), 84–85; Selig Perlman, *A History of Trade Unionism in the United States* (New York, 1922), 213; John R. Commons *et al.*, *History of Labor in the United States*, 4 vols. (New York, 1926–1935), IV, 169–189.

18. Haywood, *op. cit.*, 117–128.

19. *Proceedings of the Ninth Annual Convention of the Western Federation of Miners* (June 1901), 8–11.

20. Foner, *op. cit.*, III, 408.

21. Jensen, *op. cit.*, 57–60; *Miners' Magazine*, I (September 1900), 5–6.

22. This correspondence between Boyce and Gompers is taken from "A statement of the Executive Council, American Federation of Labor, May 1, 1897," addressed to the WFM in convention at Salt Lake City. Reproduced in *Labor Troubles in Idaho*, 56th Congress, 1st Session, Senate Document 42 (Washington, December 14, 1899).

23. According to Foner, the WFM did not return its charter to the AFL at this time, but simply ceased paying dues, since it was described in March 1898 as a member of the AFL which was not in good standing. It must have returned its charter at some time subsequent to this, however, for when it reaffiliated with the AFL in May 1911, it was issued a new charter. See Foner, *op. cit.*, IV, 490n; Jensen, *op. cit.*, 238–243; *Miners' Magazine*, X (May 1911), 5.

24. Jensen, *op. cit.*, 63.

25. Foner, *op. cit.*, IV, 414–415; Jensen, *op. cit.*, 64–66; Philip Taft, *The A.F. of L. in the Time of Gompers* (New York, 1957), 153.

26. Foner, *op. cit.*, IV, 414; *Proceedings, Eighteenth Annual Convention of the A.F. of L.* (Kansas City, 1898), 17; *Miners' Magazine*, III (February 1902), 42–43.

27. *Miners' Magazine*, I (November 1901), 14; *Proceedings of the Tenth Annual Convention of the Western Federation of Miners* (June 1902), 59, 132.

28. *Miners' Magazine*, I (June 1900), 3–5; I (July 1900), 2–3; I (September 1900), 5–6; *Proceedings of the Ninth Annual Convention of the Western Federation of Miners* (June 1901), 89.

29. *Miners' Magazine*, I (May 1900), 14–18; I (September 1900), 5–6; I (October 1900), 5–6; Robinson, *op. cit.*, 73–74; 78–79; 98–99.

30. *Proceedings of the Tenth Annual Convention of the Western Federation of Miners* (June 1902), 8–14.

31. *Ibid.*, 93–96; *Chicago Socialist*, IV (May 31, 1902), 1; *The Worker*, XII (June 8, 1902), 1.

32. In September 1902 the Local Quorum of the party in St. Louis, which had power to make policy statements between meetings of the National Executive Committee, issued a statement criticizing Debs and other party members who had supported the American Labor Union for "misrepresenting the attitude of our party and compromising it in their attempts to build up a rival organization to the American Federation of Labor." At the next meeting of the NEC, held in January 1903, a statement was issued reaffirming the friendly attitude of the Socialist party toward the AFL. Nevertheless, the left succeeded in getting Leon Greenbaum, who had criticized Debs for his support of the ALU, replaced as national secretary. See *International Socialist Review*, III (November 1902), 257–265; III (January 1903), 410–411; Ira Kipnis, *The American Socialist Movement, 1897–1912* (New York, 1952), 144–145; Ray Ginger, *The Bending Cross: A Biography of Eugene Victor Debs* (New Brunswick, 1949), 218–221.

33. Foner, *op. cit.*, III, 416–422; *Miners' Magazine*, III (June 1902), 4, 14–16; III (December 1902), 33–42.

34. *Criminal Record of the Western Federation of Miners, From Cripple Creek to Coeur d'Alene, 1894–1904* (Colorado Springs, 1904), 7.

35. Jensen, *op. cit.,* 67; *Miners' Magazine,* III (November 1902), 18; V (October 1904), 8–9; V (November 1904), 11; VII (March 1906), 8–9.

36. *Proceedings of the Tenth Annual Convention of the Western Federation of Miners* (Denver, 1902), 95–96; *Proceedings of the Eleventh Annual Convention of the Western Federation of Miners* (Denver, 1903), 10–22.

37. *Proceedings of the Tenth Annual Convention of the Western Federation of Miners* (Denver, 1902), 65–69, 87–89, 104, 177–178.

38. *Ibid.,* 67, 156–160; *Proceedings of the Eleventh Annual Convention of the Western Federation of Miners* (Denver, 1903), 206–207.

39. Jensen, *op. cit.,* 118–159; Emma F. Langdon, *The Cripple Creek Strike* (Victor, 1904), 44–248; *Miners' Magazine,* V (June 1904), 5; VI (May 1905), 18–19; *Proceedings of the Twelfth Annual Convention of the Western Federation of Miners* (Denver, 1904), 199–203. Moyer may have been aided in this judgment by the support which socialists gave to the miners in the Cripple Creek strike. State secretaries of the Socialist party called public meetings to protest the treatment of the strikers, and several thousand dollars were raised on their behalf (Socialist Party of America Collection, Duke University), State of Colorado file.

40. See above, pp. 207–208.

41. *Miners' Magazine,* IV (February 1903), 34; VI (January 1905), 6.

42. William D. Haywood to Adolph Germer, July 18, September 4, 1904 (Adolph Germer Collection, Wisconsin State Historical Society).

43. *Miners' Magazine,* VI (January 1905), 6; *Proceedings, Seventeenth Annual Convention of the United Mine Workers of America* (Indianapolis, 1906), 160–161; *Proceedings of the Twelfth Annual Convention of the Western Federation of Miners* (Denver, 1904), 28, 168.

44. Jensen, *op. cit.,* 161–162.

45. *Proceedings of the Twelfth Annual Convention of the Western Federation of Miners* (Denver, 1904), 248–250, 254; *Proceedings of the Thirteenth Annual Convention of the Western Federation of Miners* (Salt Lake City, 1905), 17–22; John M. O'Neill to Germer, June 19, 1905 (Eugene Debs Collection, Tamiment Institute).

46. The trial of Moyer, Haywood, and Pettibone, in which they were finally acquitted, evoked widespread sympathy throughout the labor movement, especially in the UMWA. Debs wrote and spoke out widely on behalf of the defendants, mass meetings were held to protest their forced removal from Colorado to Idaho, and the Socialist party raised several thousands of dollars for their defense. The NEC of the party received support from twenty national unions in its request for a special convention of the AFL to consider the trial, but this was refused by a majority of the Executive Council even though President John Mitchell, of the UMWA, favored it. See *The Worker,* XVI (January 19, 1907), 1; XVI (February 2, 1907), 2; XVI (March 23, 1907), 1; XVII (June 8, 1907), 1, 6; XVII (August 3, 1907), 1; Subscription list to Moyer-Haywood-Pettibone Defense Fund (Socialist Party of America Collection, Duke University), Labor file; John O'Neill to Germer, April 6, 1906 (Eugene Debs Collection, Tamiment Institute); Ginger, *op. cit.,* 244–256; Taft, *op. cit.,* 157–158; *United Mine Workers' Journal,* XVI (March 22, 1906), 1; XVII

(January 24, 1907), 1–2; David H. Grover, *Debaters and Dynamiters, The Story of the Haywood Trial* (Corvallis, 1964), 77–82.

47. The differences between the two factions were partly personal and partly ideological, but they arose initially over the attempt of DeLeon and the remnants of the ST & LA to secure control of the IWW. In 1908 the DeLeonites were expelled from the IWW, to found a separate organization in Detroit. The Chicago IWW and the Detroit IWW continued separately until 1914, when the latter changed its name to Workers International Industrial Union before expiring completely in 1925. See Jensen, *op. cit.,* 160–196; Brissenden, *op. cit.,* 71–104. For other studies of the IWW, see Foner, *op. cit.,* IV, *Industrial Workers of the World, 1905–1917;* Brooks, *op. cit.;* John S. Gambs, *The Decline of the IWW* (New York, 1932); and Patrick Renshaw, *The Wobblies, The Story of Syndicalism in the United States* (New York, 1967).

48. Renshaw, *op. cit.,* 102; *Proceedings, Second Convention of the Industrial Workers of the World* (Chicago, 1906), 190–121, 243–244.

49. *Proceedings of the Fifteenth Annual Convention of the Western Federation of Miners* (Denver, 1907), 579–580, 582–585.

50. *Ibid.,* 788; Jensen, *op. cit.,* 189–193.

51. Jensen, *op. cit.,* 219–235; *Industrial Union Bulletin,* I (July 13, 1907), 1; I (July 28, 1907), 1; I (August 24, 1907), 1; I (October 26, 1907), 1; I (November 9, 1907), 2. *Proceedings of the Sixteenth Annual Convention of the Western Federation of Miners* (Denver, 1908), 332–336.

52. *Ibid.,* 16–19; *Miners' Magazine,* X (July 1908), 4–8.

53. *Proceedings of the Sixteenth Annual Convention of the Western Federation of Miners* (Denver, 1908), 339–341.

54. Quoted in *Outlook,* LXXXIV (May 4, 1907), 1–2; Roosevelt also attacked Debs, as well as Moyer and Haywood, for defending the accused leaders, resulting in a public exchange between the two men. See Ginger, *op. cit.,* 251–253.

55. *Criminal Record of the Western Federation of Miners, from Cripple Creek to Coeur d'Alene, 1894–1904* (Colorado Springs, 1904), 3, 7, *passim; Governor Peabody to the Voters, The Colorado Situation Discussed and Misstatements Refuted* (1904), 6 (Pamphlets in the Wisconsin State Historical Society).

56. Fritz, *op. cit.,* 377; *The Worker,* XII (July 6, 1902), 1; XIII (June 24, 1903), 1; *State of Colorado, Abstract of Votes Cast* (Denver), 1901, p. 81; 1903, p. 78; 1904, p. 85.

57. *The Worker,* XIV (June 26, 1904), 1; XIV (July 3, 1904), 1; XIV (December 11, 1904); *State of Colorado, Abstract,* 1905, p. 91. Clipping from *Social Democratic Herald,* May 21, 1904 (John Mitchell Papers, Catholic University of America); Letters of acceptance from socialist candidates for governor and lieutenant-governor of Colorado (Socialist Party of America Collection, Duke University), Labor file.

58. *Miners' Magazine,* XI (February 24, 1910), 6–7; XII (May 11, 1911), 5; *Proceedings of the Eighteenth Annual Convention of the Western Federation of Miners* (Denver, 1910), 15–16.

59. Jensen, *op. cit.,* 238–243; *Proceedings, Thirtieth Annual Convention of the A.F. of L.* (St. Louis, 1910), 90–96.

60. *Solidarity,* I (July 9, 1910), 2; II (February 5, 1911), 1; II (February 25, 1911), 2; *Industrial Union Bulletin,* I (July 9, 1910), 2; *International Socialist Review,* XV (August 1914), 9.

61. *United Mine Workers' Journal,* XXII (September 24, 1911), 2.

62. Jensen, *op. cit.,* 236–237; *Proceedings, Nineteenth Annual Convention of the United Mine Workers of America* (Indianapolis, 1908), 160–162; James Kirwan to Adolph Germer, August 18, 1906 (Eugene Debs Collection, Tamiment Institute).

63. Jensen, *op. cit.,* 370–371; New York *Call,* I (July 27, 1908), 3; *International Socialist Review,* X (March 1910), 850–851; XIV (March 1914), 538; *Miners' Magazine,* XV (May 1914), 10–11.

64. *Proceedings of the Nineteenth Annual Convention of the Western Federation of Miners* (Denver, 1911), 20.

65. *Miners' Magazine,* XII (November 1912), 4–6; XIII (January 1913), 3–4; *Solidarity,* III (September 28, 1912), 3; *Proceedings of the Twentieth Annual Convention of the Western Federation of Miners* (Victor, 1912), 191–213, 221–222; *International Socialist Review,* XV (August 1914), 9.

66. Jensen, *op. cit.,* 272–288; *International Socialist Review,* XV (March 1914), 537–538; List of contributions to copper strike, January 27, 1914 (Socialist Party of America Collection, Duke University), Michigan file.

67. *Proceedings of the Twenty-second Consecutive and Second Biennial Convention of the Western Federation of Miners* (Great Falls, 1916), 40–41, 153. The statement which Moyer made to the 1916 convention was considered so striking a reversal of the wfm's former policies that Gompers later sent a copy of it to President John P. White of the umwa. Gompers described it as a "remarkable statement, . . . in which he [Moyer] points out to the Western Federation of Miners the mistaken policies which caused that organization so many disasters." See Gompers to John P. White, March 7, 1917 (Gompers' Correspondence with Affiliates, AFL-CIO Collection).

68. *Proceedings of the Twenty-first Consecutive and First Biennial Convention of the Western Federation of Miners* (Denver, 1914), 127–139.

69. See, for example, the statement of a Butte No. 1 member in the March 8, 1913, issue of *Solidarity,* an iww paper. "Butte has a miners' union in name only—the W.F.M. What we want now, and what we are going to get soon, is the One Big Union—the IWW; and we never will better our miserable conditions here without it." *Solidarity,* IV (March 8, 1913), 3.

70. *Montana Socialist,* June 21, 1914, cited in Jensen, *op. cit.,* 331. The account of the Butte miners' revolt is taken from pp. 325–353 of Jensen's book.

71. *Miners' Magazine,* XV (July 1914), 7–8.

72. Charles Moyer to Gompers, January 14, 1915; Gompers to Moyer, January 16, 1915 (Gompers' Correspondence with Affiliates, AFL-CIO Collection).

73. *Miners' Magazine,* XII (November 1912), 3–4; XIII (February 1913), 4–5; XV (March 1915), 3–4; *Proceedings of the Twenty-first Consecutive and First Biennial Convention of the Western Federation of Miners* (Denver, 1914), 13–141.

74. In 1913, for example, the wfm had been forced to borrow $25,000 from the Brewery Workers Union. At the end of 1917 it was still unable to repay ei-

ther the interest or principal on this loan. See *Proceedings of the Twenty-first Convention of the International Union of United Brewery, and Soft Drink Workers of America* (Houston, 1917), 70.

75. *Miners' Magazine,* XV (April 1915), 3; Gambs, *op. cit.,* 114–118; *Proceedings of the Twenty-second Consecutive and Second Biennial Convention of the Western Federation of Miners* (July 1916), 8, 21–22, 41–43.

76. *Miners' Magazine,* XVII (May 1917), 4; XVII (June 1917), 6; XVII (November 1917), 4–5; XVIII (April 1918), 304; Marc Karson, *American Labor Unions and Politics, 1900–1918* (Carbondale, 1958), 94; *Proceedings of the Twenty-fourth Consecutive and Fourth Biennial Convention of the Western Federation of Miners* (August 1920), 23.

77. Jensen, *op. cit.,* 430–466; *Proceedings of the Twenty-fourth Consecutive and Fourth Biennial Convention of the Western Federation of Miners* (August 1920), 18–20, 41–42.

8

Conclusion

The first chapter of this book suggested that most labor historians, in attempting to account for the failure of socialism to take root in the American labor movement, have confined themselves very largely to the opinions, tactics, and general labor policies adopted by the national leadership of the AFL and of the various socialist and Farmer-Labor parties. The intervening chapters represent one of the first attempts to look below the surface of the national leadership and to study the question in the light of evidence drawn from a sample of trade-unions representing a broad spectrum of radical opinion throughout the labor movement as a whole. Further detailed study of rank-and-file opinion will still be necessary before any final or definitive assertions can be made. In particular, attention must be paid to the ongoing regional researches of Stephan Thernstrom and others into the volatility and mobility rates of the American labor force, which is already throwing new light on some of the questions discussed in the earlier chapters of this book.[1] Nevertheless, even this limited attempt to penetrate beneath the surface suggests a number of conclusions which are sharply at variance with previously established views.

How important was the AFL's hostility toward socialism and third-party political action? Did it, as a number of radical historians have argued, prevent the emergence of a widespread, grass-roots radical movement which, had it been allowed to develop, would have transformed American labor into a revolutionary movement similar to that in most European countries? [2] Equally, what was the significance of socialist tactics? Did De-Leonism and other forms of impossibilism have a crucial effect in undermining the position of the socialists? Would it have made any difference if a gradualistic and cooperative attitude had been adopted by the socialists toward the trade-unions at an earlier point in time? [3] Or were external factors, deriving not so much from the character of the labor leadership, or from the ideological position adopted by the socialists, but from the particular characteristics of American social and industrial development, primarily responsible for the failure of socialism in the labor movement? The evidence presented in the earlier chapters suggests strongly that the second set of factors was more important than the first.

I

It is true, of course, that Gompers and the other leaders of the AFL moved from a position of tolerance and even of limited support for certain socialist doctrines in the 1870's and 1880's to one of profound hostility and mistrust in subsequent years.[4] Inside the AFL, this was evident in the failure to elect socialists to the Executive Council after 1889; [5] in the parliamentary tactics and the harsh speeches which Gompers and other AFL leaders employed against the socialists in the annual conventions of the Federation; in the treatment meted out to Thomas J. Morgan's Political Program of 1894; and in numerous other ways.[6] Among the affiliates, it was apparent from such varied incidents as the Executive Council's handling of the 1890's dispute between the International Machinists Union and the International Association of Machinists; the AFL's support for the Tobin faction in the Boot and Shoe Workers Union; or in Gompers' welcoming response to the increasing moderation of the Western Federation of Miners and other former radical organizations in the period after 1912.

Where the socialists were strong, the AFL would sometimes make exceptions to this policy, such as in Gompers' unwillingness to expel the Brewery Workers Union in 1907; in the general support which the AFL gave to the ILGWU and other socialist garment unions in the early 1900's; or in the AFL's indirect endorsement of Meyer London and other radicals in the congressional elections of 1912. But these exceptions were made for tactical reasons, or for the sake of the unity of the labor movement in general. They were not made out of any sympathy with socialism on ideological grounds. In general, Gompers' opposition to the socialists in the AFL, reinforced by the self-perpetuating character of the Executive Council and by Gompers' own personal prestige, almost certainly prevented them from being more successful in this period than they might otherwise have been. For instance, in terms of delegate support the socialists enjoyed their largest influence in the AFL in the 1890's, before the Gompers' regime had been thoroughly established, whereas their peak was not reached in the labor movement generally until the period immediately preceding and following the election of 1912.

It is also true that the dual unionist tactics of the extreme left to some extent diminished the appeal of socialism in the labor movement and were used by the conservatives as a means of deterring other trade-unionists from supporting the socialist cause. DeLeon and the SLP turned against the AFL in the 1890's just at the point when the socialists were gathering strength and when they might conceivably have been able to force the labor movement, if only temporarily, into more radical paths.[7] Similarly, the dual unionist tactics of the American Labor Union, the IWW, and the Communists undoubtedly did some harm to the cause of radicalism in the labor movement in later years. Among the affiliates, DeLeonite attacks on the Boot and Shoe Workers Union in the late 1890's were bitterly resented; and they helped to turn the Tobin administration away from its former socialist position and toward conformity with the conservative position of the labor movement as a whole. In the Western Federation of Miners, the unremitting hostility of the IWW in the post-1907 period helped to weaken it to such an extent that it had little choice but to fall back on the AFL. Fear of Communism was also used as an effective weapon against the more moderate radicals in the United Mine Workers, the IAM, and elsewhere.

But despite the attention which has been given to it by labor historians, the impact of impossibilism on the bulk of trade-unions in the labor movement was, in fact, quite small. Only in the Boot and Shoe Workers Union and the Western Federation of Miners did it have more than a marginal effect in weakening the over-all position of the socialists. In the United Mine Workers of America, fear of Communism and the efforts of extremists to exploit the discontents of the coal miners were not enough to prevent the reemergence of a strong third-party movement after World War I. Similarly, in the International Association of Machinists and the ILGWU, moderate socialist influences remained powerful despite the criticisms of the impossibilists on the extreme left and the wholesale denunciation of radicals during the period of the Red Scare.

The era of dominance by dual unionists in the socialist movement was also quite short. DeLeon maintained effective control of the SLP only between 1891 and 1896, after which the moderates revolted against his policy of opposition to the AFL. The American Labor Union and the IWW had little influence over most craft unions, and it was not until the 1920's that the Communists took up dual unionism once more. In 1901 the Socialist party adopted a policy of cooperation toward the existing trade-union movement which was maintained, save for a small minority on the extreme left of the party, throughout the entire period under review.[8] But this policy in itself had little to do with the reasons for either the growth or the decline of radical influences throughout the labor movement in general. The socialists received no spectacular increase in working-class votes because of the change in their trade-union position, nor were they able to prevent a rapid loss of influence in the labor movement after 1912.

Hence the preoccupation of various scholars with changes in the ideological position of the labor and socialist national leadership, from Philip Foner on the left to Philip Taft on the right, does not in itself provide an adequate *causal* explanation for the failure of radical influences to take root in the labor movement, unless one accepts the primacy of ideology in determining labor's political behavior—a highly questionable assumption given the generally pragmatic orientation of American social movements by and large. Foner, from the left, argues that the failure of socialism in the American labor movement was almost wholly due, on the trade-union side, to the bourgeois and "class collaborationist" character of the labor leadership. On the side of the socialists it was due, in the case of the SLP, to the "incorrect policies" of dual unionism; and in the case of the Socialist Party of America to the domination of "Center-Right" elements which Foner erroneously suggests "abandoned altogether the battle against the Federation's narrow, craft, 'pure and simple' trade unionism." [9]

If one accepts a monolithic view of American labor leadership, as radical labor historians tend to do, there is something to be said for this point of view. But without discounting the influence of Gompers and the AFL Executive Council, this is to carry the manipulative abilities of both the socialists and the trade-union leadership much too far. In practice, although in its internal structure the AFL developed the characteristics of a bureaucratic and machine-led organization quite early in its career, in its relations to the affiliates in this period it had little in the way of formal power. For example, on matters of trade autonomy, jurisdictional disputes, and strike action, which at this time were its central concerns, the AFL was primarily a collection of sovereign, independent trade-unions, with Gompers and his colleagues serving mainly as a broker between them.[10] It is extremely unlikely, in other words, that the national leadership alone could have prevented the growth of a mass revolutionary movement, had the prevailing social and economic conditions been favorable for such a development.

Another weakness of the radical position is that it tends to assume, without a great deal of evidence, that trade-union officials are by definition conservative in their outlook and that radicalism is inherent in the rank and file. This is not necessarily borne out by the evidence presented here.

In some unions the rank and file appeared to be more radical than the leadership. This was true in the early history of the International Association of Machinists or in several of the district organizations of the United Mine Workers of America. But in the ILGWU there was little difference between the political and economic outlook of the leadership and that of the local unions, while in several other trades the leaders appeared to be politically more radical than the rank and file. This was true of the Brewery Workers Union after the beginning of the decline of German influence in the union. It was also partially true of the Boot and Shoe Workers Union, and of the Western Federation of Miners during its most radical years.

Nor was there a necessary correlation between industrial unionism and political or third-party militancy, as the example of the United Mine Workers shows. Industry-wide organization sometimes went along with support for the Socialist party, as in the case of the Western Federation of Miners or the Brewery Workers Union. In the latter case, however, it is difficult to tell how far support for the socialists was determined by the German composition of the union membership, and how far by other factors. In any event, socialist tendencies appeared in craft and in semi-industrial unions as well as in industrial organizations per se, and industrial unionism was often adopted for pragmatic reasons which had little to do with the ideology of socialism as such.

II

But if radical historians err in assuming that socialism failed in the American labor movement because of the bourgeois character of the labor leadership, conservative historians tend to fall into the opposite error by assuming the innate conservatism of the rank and file. Throughout his *A.F. of L. in the Time of Gompers,* Philip Taft, like other followers of the Wisconsin school of labor history, tends to assume the essential correctness of Gompers' position on industrial unionism, third-party political action, and other radical issues without examining the needs and wishes of the affiliated membership in the trade-union movement as a whole.[11] More important, Selig Perlman, in his *Theory of the Labor Movement,* also argues the dominant role of the national leadership by suggesting that the failure of the socialists was due, among other things, to the inability of the intellectuals to secure control.[12]

This was not, of course, the only argument which Perlman used to explain the absence of a strong socialist movement in the United States. He cited numerous others, with most of which my own analysis tends to agree. But in his book it is to the anti-intellectualism of the labor leadership that he most frequently returns. On the continent of Europe, and to a lesser extent in England, Perlman argues, the intellectuals succeeded in establishing an alliance between themselves and the proletarian leaders of the labor movement, whereas in America they did not. In the absence of such an alliance, Perlman believes, there can be no successful socialist political movement: "The strongest protagonists of the idea of an American labor party are the intellectuals. The intellectuals, who . . . were the prime instigators of organization in the labor movements of Germany and Russia, have been denied a similar role in this country." [13]

If one examines the sample of trade-unions analyzed in the previous chapters, it is quite true that the intellectual, defined as an "educated non-manualist," [14] did not have any great influence in the American labor movement, save in those unions in which German, Jewish, and other central and eastern European immigrant groups played a leading role. In fact, in several unions there was evidence of the anti-intellectualism which Richard Hofstadter described in his book *Anti-Intellectualism in American Life*. In the Boot and Shoe Workers Union the argument was put forward in 1912 that the membership should not support Woodrow Wilson for the Presidency because he was a "college professor." Similarly John H. Walker of the United Mine Workers, writing to Adolf Germer on December 2, 1917, complained of "dilettante pink tea socialists [in the Socialist party] who would not associate themselves with labor in such a way as to entitle them to the right to belong to the army of labor, because they didn't mean to dirty themselves, to contaminate themselves by their associations." [15]

But although intellectuals played a minor role in the labor movement in this country compared to their role in Europe, it does not necessarily follow that American trade-unionists, in the absence of such leadership, were unwilling to espouse the cause of independent labor political action. In four of the six unions discussed, the socialist element did not consist of, nor was it led by, intellectuals, and certainly not by the type of foreign-born intellectual from the continent of Europe which American radical leaders were usually assumed to be. The socialist element in the IAM, for example, consisted entirely of workers who had come up through the ranks of the industry and were either native-born Americans or immigrants of long standing from Great Britain. The same was true of the radical element in the Western Federation of Miners and the United Mine Workers of America. All the prominent socialists in these unions—William H. Johnston, Douglas Wilson, and Peter J. Conlon in the International Association of Machinists; Edward Boyce, Charles Moyer, and William D. Haywood in the Western Federation of Miners; and John H. Walker, Frank Hayes, and Duncan McDonald in the United Mine Workers of America—had originally worked in the trade of their calling. Only

Adolph Germer was in any sense an intellectual, and even he was for some years a practicing miner. None of them conforms to the pattern of Perlman's "educated non-manualist" at all.[16]

It can be suggested, in the case of the IAM and the United Mine Workers, where Chartism and admiration for the British Labor party played an important role, that the influence of immigrants from Great Britain was also an extraneous one and conforms to the pattern of socialist influences brought in from abroad. To some extent this was true. But the radicals continued to be powerful in these unions until well after World War I, by which time major immigration from Great Britain had long since declined. It can hardly be claimed that socialism in these unions was simply the product of European influences imported from abroad, any more than it can in the case of the Boot and Shoe Workers Union. The fact that the socialists secured a following among some of the first- and second-generation Irish in this union, as well as in the International Association of Machinists (and even, to a limited extent, among the Irish ale and porter workers in the Brewery Workers Union), also suggests that the stereotype of the Irish workingman as a Democrat and a social conservative put forward by Marc Karson in his book *American Labor Unions and Politics, 1900–1918* is considerably overdrawn.[17]

Reviewing the whole issue, it is possible to suggest not only that Perlman and other social theorists have exaggerated the significance of intellectuals in the formation of radical opinion,[18] but that ethnically speaking the traditional picture of socialism in the American labor movement may have to be considerably modified. In four of the six unions considered in this sample the socialists were not German, Jewish, or eastern European immigrants who brought their radical ideology with them from the old country, but native-born Americans, or English-speaking workers who had been in this country for a considerable period of time. It has for some time been clear, as David Shannon found in his history of *The Socialist Party of America,* that the Socialist party at its height contained more native-born Americans than it did immigrants. This evidence from the trade-union movement complements Shannon's findings and should serve to dispose once and for all of the traditional assumption held by many historians that socialism was simply an extraneous movement brought over by European immigrants and intellectuals which had no real relevance to the American labor scene.

A not dissimilar kind of objection can be made to the central hypothesis presented by Daniel Bell in his essay *Marxian Socialism in the United States.* Here again excessive preoccupation with the ideological position of the national leadership has led to conclusions which the relevant evidence does not necessarily justify. Bell's argument is that the socialists in America, both in their policy formulations and in their general political behavior, were chiliastic, utopian, and otherworldly, or in other words so unpragmatic in their behavior that they never came to terms with the realities of American life. Bell argues:

> The failure of the socialist movement in the United States is rooted in its inability to resolve a basic dilemma of ethics and politics. The socialist movement, by its very statement of goal and in its rejection of the capitalist order as a whole, could not relate itself to the specific problems in the here-and-now, give-and-take political world. It was trapped by the unhappy problem of living *"in* but not *of* the world." [19]

This is similar to the position of Louis Hartz, put forward in *The Liberal Tradition*. Hartz also points to the rigidity of Marxist ideology as the major reason for the failure of attempts to adapt it to the American scene. "When the conviction of inevitable success is more significant than the number of followers," Hartz writes, "even the smallest item of doctrine becomes a crucial matter." [20]

It is again true, if we confine ourselves to the opinions of the national leaders of the socialist movement, as both Bell and Hartz do, that these leaders had an idealized blueprint of the future society which they wished to establish in the United States and an intolerant view of those who did not share it. Debs, DeLeon, and other socialist leaders tended to insist that workingmen vote socialist, and were quite likely to call them traitors to the working class if they did not. But if we examine the outlook and the behavior of socialists in the labor movement as such, the argument that they failed because they were chiliastic and unpragmatic is brought seriously into question. On the contrary, the evidence suggests that when it came to the everyday problems of practical politics, the socialists in the labor movement understood perfectly well the working of the American pluralist system and were quite prepared to use it for their own political purposes.

Perhaps the best example of this may be found in the attitude of the International Association of Machinists toward the question of railroad nationalization. As we have seen, in the early part of the period the machinists maintained that the only way of bringing the railroads under public control was to elect enough trade-unionists and socialists to Congress to bring this about. But when President Woodrow Wilson took the railroads under public control as a wartime measure in 1917, and when the Conference for Progressive Political Action sought to return the railroads to public control by lobbying and a variety of other nonpartisan political means in 1922, the machinists abandoned their insistence on third-party action over this particular issue, while on other matters continuing for some years to maintain a generally favorable attitude toward radical politics and far-reaching social change.

A similar example is provided by the response of the Brewery Workers Union, which as a German Marxist organization might have been thought to be ideologically more rigid than most socialist organizations, to the problem of Prohibition. Partly because many members of the Socialist party were ambivalent or indifferent on the issue, and partly because even at its peak the party lacked the strength to exert any decisive influence, organized brewery workers came increasingly to transfer their political support to the wets in both of the major parties. Or one can cite the behavior of John H. Walker of the UMWA in simultaneously endorsing the reelection of President Woodrow Wilson and the Republican candidate for governor of Illinois in the election of 1916. Despite this, Walker remained a political radical and ran for governor of Illinois himself on the National Farmer-Labor party ticket after World War I.

The conclusion to be drawn from this evidence is not only that Bell's assertion concerning the chiliastic and unpragmatic character of the socialists' activities is highly questionable but that, as in the case of Perlman's argument in relation to the role of intellectuals, it may need in some respects to be reversed. For it seems quite clear that when faced with the realities of the everyday political world, the socialists in the trade-union movement were realistic and pragmatic enough in their behavior, and that they failed, not so much because they were unpragmatic, but because they were too much so.[21] In each of the cases cited above, the socialists were willing to abandon their position in favor of third-party action and to exert pressure instead on one or another of the two major parties. In doing so, they followed the example of most of the trade-unions in the AFL and diminished still further the small amount of trade-union support which the Socialist party and the various minor third parties which emerged after World War I were able to secure.

These considerations tend to confirm the view, put forward by political scientists such as E. E. Schattschneider, that the failure of third parties in America has been due, not so much to ideological considerations such as the "political maturity of the Anglo-American peoples," as to the wasted vote theory and to the flexibility and endurance of the two-party system.[22] They should also prompt a more rigorous examination than is usually made of the motivation of those who customarily voted socialist. Continental immigrants were sometimes persuaded to support the Socialist party after coming to America. But generally they were German and Jewish workers who did so out of loyalty to the ideological tradition from which they came. Few of the Slavs, for example, who entered the coal mining industry after 1880 voted socialist; nor, in the garment district of New York, did many of the Italians.[23] No comparable socialist tradition existed for most of the English-speaking workers, so that an alternative explanation for their radical behavior must be found. A variety of factors determine the reasons for voting socialist, many of which, as in the case of other parties, had little to do with membership in a trade-union. But insofar as union membership is a relevant consideration, one factor, in particular, seems to have influenced most of the English-speaking workers with whom we have been concerned; namely, a relative decline in status in relation both to employment opportunities and to other ethnic groups.

English-speaking workers and northern Europeans generally, save to some extent the Irish, provided the main source of leadership and skill throughout American industry at this time. As such they usually rose fairly rapidly in the social and economic scale. But in the four industries discussed in which these workers were extensively employed—coal mining, shoemaking, metal mining, and the machinist's trade—their progress appears to have been temporarily impeded by the processes of rapid industrial change. In each of them, the relative position of the English-speaking workers was undermined by technological changes, competitive conditions, relatively static or falling wage levels, and the threat posed by the incursion of cheap immigrant labor from eastern and southern Europe, and in some cases from the Orient. In these industries, it was ex-artisans and skilled or semi-skilled workers, not the recent immigrants or the poor, who tended to become radicals. In one sense this simply serves to confirm the generally accepted hypothesis that it is from those with rising expectations, not the *Lumpenproletariat,* that we should expect radical tendencies. What is interesting, however, is that in an achievement-oriented society such as the United States the motivation for political radicalism may also have resulted partially from the frustrated aspirations of those bodies of workers whose expectations are traditionally supposed to have been high.

This conclusion suggests analogies between a relative decline in the status position of certain groups among the English-speaking workers in industry at the end of the nineteenth century and that of the Populists and Progressives which Hofstadter discusses in *The Age of Reform.*[24] It may also tend to modify the central hypothesis put forward by Seymour Lipset in *The First New Nation* concerning the lack of a class-conscious American labor movement. "The failure of the American labor movement to identify itself as a class movement," Lipset writes, "may be traced . . . to the way in which equalitarianism and achievement orientation permeated the social structure." [25] Over the long run, where these values could be substantiated in practice, or where the rags-to-riches mythology which underlay them was implemented sufficiently frequently to maintain belief in an upwardly mobile society, the emphasis on equality and achievement undoubtably undermined the central assumptions from which Marxist theory is derived.[26] But in the short run, for those English-speaking workers whose condition has been described, the inability to translate these aspirations into practice was in itself a primary cause of radical discontent.

Nevertheless—as Lipset also pointed out in attempting to reconcile the apparent contradiction between union militancy and the absence of class consciousness in America [27]—there is also a conflict between these two sets of values, which in some cases worked to the disadvantage of the socialists. On the question of wage differentials in the Brewery Workers Union, for example, of broadening membership qualifications in the International Association of Machinists, or of enrolling all the workers into a single local in the Western Federation of Miners, socialist emphasis on equality conflicted with the achievement orientation of the established workers in the industry, especially where they had been deprived of the protection formally afforded by skill.

III

The prominent role played by native-born workers in the radical minority in the labor movement reinforces the objections made earlier to the view that socialist influence in the American labor movement was weak because it derived essentially from an excessively ideological, and hence excessively European, outlook on American politics and society. By contrast, the evidence contained in the earlier chapters of this book provides strong reasons for believing that both the rise and the decline of socialist influence in the labor movement derived far more from indigenous factors arising out of the nature of American society and industry than has hitherto been supposed.

The following factors, in particular, were significant. In the labor movement, radical and in some cases socialist influence may be traced to the legacy of Knights of Labor idealism, radicalized Populism, and strong dissatisfaction with the narrow craft unionism of Gompers and the AFL. Externally, technological changes, a high degree of competition in the decades immediately after the Civil War to be followed by rapid trustification in industry in the 1880's and 1890's, and the social and economic dislocation occasioned by rapid industrialization and the destruction of traditional crafts were also extremely important.

To take the internal factors first, dissatisfaction with the AFL because of its political conservatism, its preference for craft unionism, and its voluntaristic attitude toward the state were important, if indirect, reasons for third-party activism and political militancy. Taken together, they served as catalysts for more serious ideological conflicts which the socialists were able to exploit. It is no coincidence, for example, that several of the unions considered in our sample were industrial rather than craft organizations in their structure and that at least two of them, the United Mine Workers of America and the Brewery Workers, were involved in severe jurisdictional conflicts with a number of craft unions in the AFL.

It was argued above that industrial unionism *as such* is not necessarily a sign of third-party activism. But disappointment and irritation at the failure of the AFL to recognize the broader social philosophy which lay behind demands for industrial unionism certainly helped to create sympathy for socialism and the Socialist party, as the case of the Western Federation of Miners shows. Similarly, it was not a coincidence that another socialist union, the International Association of Machinists, was intimately affected by the bureaucratic and self-perpetuating character of the AFL Executive Council. The continued presence of James O'Connell on the Council of the AFL from 1912 to 1918, even though he was no longer president of his union, created considerable bitterness among the machinists generally and served to strengthen the hand of the socialist faction as a whole.

As to Knights of Labor idealism, it has long been established that the Knights were considerably more radical than the AFL in their attitude toward industry-wide organization, third-party activity, and cooperation as a labor ideal. Less well remembered, however, is the fact that a significant proportion of the unions in the AFL had earlier been connected with the Knights of Labor and that they retained considerable sympathy for that organization and what it stood for even after they had transferred their formal allegiance to the AFL.

Four of the six unions considered in the sample maintained strong ties with the Knights of Labor and its traditions long after the Knights had passed their peak. The Brewery Workers Union retained a joint affiliation with both the Knights of Labor and the AFL until 1896. A similar dual affiliation characterized the United Mine Workers, while the Boot and Shoe Workers Union grew originally out of the Knights of St. Crispin, which had much in common with the Knights of Labor in its outlook and philosophy. Continued interest on the part of these workers in the broad social goals of the Knights of Labor, coupled with dissatisfaction at the hostility which the AFL leadership expressed toward them, helped to render the socialist message more attractive.

Care must be exercised in dealing with the third source of radical influence listed under this head; namely, radical Populism. For it is still uncertain, pending the detailed study of voting returns, just how many urban workers voted Populist in the critical elections of the early 1890's. And it is also unclear, save in the case of a few prominent men such as Debs, how many ex-Populists who were dissatisfied with the fusion of 1896 moved across into the socialist movement. Nevertheless, evidence from the International Association of Machinists, the United Mine Workers, and the

Western Federation of Miners suggests strongly that those unions which had the strongest commitment to the ideals of Populism were also those in which socialist influence turned out to be strong.

Demands for internal union democracy deriving from Populist rhetoric also helped to reinforce existing predispositions in favor of third-party political action. This was particularly true in the case of the WFM. In the United Mine Workers the need for internal democracy symbolized by opposition to John L. Lewis was extended, as in other unions, to include demands for greater democracy in the society generally which, the radicals argued, could be secured only by the election of La Follette in 1924. But it should also be added, on the general question of Populism, that it was not so much the case, as Norman Pollack argues in *The Populist Response to Industrial America,* that the Populists were more radical in their ideology than the agrarian historians have supposed.[28] It was rather that in certain limited areas and on a certain limited range of issues, such as control over the railroads, mine nationalization, and the general threat which the growing power of the trusts presented to the bargaining position of the trade-unions, there was, temporarily, sufficient common ground between the urban workers and the farmers to make possible a radical political coalition between the two.

As to the external, or second and more important, set of factors which I have listed as causes of socialist influence, in the decades after the Civil War technological changes, changes in the nature of the market—both in the labor market and in the market for goods and services—and changes also in the relationship between employers and employees were proceeding rapidly throughout American industry as a whole. Nevertheless, they had a particularly severe impact on virtually all the six trades considered in the sample. In the shoe industry the introduction of new machinery, the development of the factory system, and the effect of these developments on the earning capacity, status position, and opportunities for self-employment of the labor force were major causes of radical discontent. Similar developments occurred in the machinists' trade. In the garment industry it was not the development of the factory system, but the rapid expansion of the market and the fragmentation of employment under the contracting system, which made possible the exploitations of the sweating system.

In the coal mines and in the metal mining districts severe competition, rapid changes in the nature of the market, and repressive tactics on the part of the employers and of the state authorities were the important developments. In all these cases, severe problems resulting from the rapidity of industrialization and the turmoil which this created in social, economic, and industrial relationships were the dominant factors in producing radical discontent.

When one turns to the decline of radical influences in the American labor movement, the evidence indicates less disagreement with established opinions. Insofar as immigrant influences were responsible for the development of socialism in the German trade-unions or the needle trades, it is obviously important to emphasize the consequences of the assimilation and Americanization of these groups and their consequent acceptance of the American capitalist system and of American political values. The heightened nationalism created by America's entry into World War I obviously played an important part here, especially among the Germans.

But assimilation and Americanization also had an important meaning even for those workingmen who were not immigrants. Pressure toward conformity was generated not so much by overt coercion from the AFL as by its acceptance in the eyes of public opinion generally as the proper model for an American labor movement. This made it harder for radical opponents of AFL political and economic policies to persist with their endeavors. In a society in which a high value was placed on conformity, especially at a time when the labor movement was weak and under considerable pressure from outside, this was a matter of great importance. The response of the Irish in the Boot and Shoe Workers Union to economic success, or the results of the reentry of the Western Federation of Miners into the AFL in 1911, illustrate this point very well.

As early as 1915, Robert Michels pointed to the tendency among successful labor leaders of proletarian origins, especially in America, to modify their radical opinions when they came into contact with members of the employing class. Since then most critics of the American labor movement have taken the policy of Gompers and other national labor leaders toward the National Civic Federation as the outstanding example of this. But changes in the outlook of leaders in the individual unions were more important, since it was there that basic trade-union policy was made. From this point of view the increasing conservatism of John F. Tobin in the Boot and Shoe Workers, Charles Moyer in the Western Federation of Miners, or even of a moderate radical such as William H. Johnston in the International Association of Machinists were of great importance.[29]

More specifically, adaptation to prevailing American values had both an industrial and a political aspect. From the industrial point of view, there was an increasingly evident conflict between the logic of collective bargaining (which even the most radical trade-unionists came in the end to accept) and the demands of the socialists for separate, revolutionary action on the part of a united working class. The most dramatic example of this was in the Boot and Shoe Workers Union, where acceptance of the idea of the Union Stamp Contract helped to cause a reversal in the union's entire attitude. The adoption of time contracts by the Western Federation of Miners, the Protocol of Peace in the ILGWU, and the increasing cooperation between management and labor in the brewing industry all had similar effects. In the United Mine Workers the situation was more ambiguous, since acceptance of the principle of interstate contracts took place in 1898, *before* the most radical phase in the history of the union. But there, too, the checkoff system, the need to abide by nationally negotiated contracts, and growing cooperation between the union and the coal operators in imposing order on the anarchic coal market rapidly limited the union's potential for revolutionary change.

In societies with more traditional class barriers, such as Great Britain or Germany, there was no necessary conflict between collective bargaining and the revolutionary assumptions of socialism, at least in the short run. But in the United States, where class lines were more fluid and the pressure toward assimilation was strong, the adoption of collective bargaining techniques had profound and far-reaching implications for the relations between labor and management, especially where such cooperation (as in the garment and shoemaking industries) made a great difference to the worker's security of employment. As Paul Jacobs has pointed out, in a society dominated by the Lockian tradition, the process of bargaining *within* the system inexorably endowed the contractual relationship with primary importance.[30]

In addition, the notion of contract implies a recognition by the union of *its* responsibilities for the enforcement of the agreement, which sometimes placed even radical union leadership in the seemingly anomalous position of having to act against its own constituency when the contract was violated by members of the rank and file. Thus, the price which the union had to pay for the benefits it received was to become part of the productive system itself, able to modify but not to change in any basic way the nature of that system. The most dramatic effects of this development, again, may be seen in the case of the Boot and Shoe Workers Union. But similar consequences occurred in the coal industry, the garment industry, and the western metal mines.

From the point of view of third-party politics, most historians of the Socialist party are in agreement that it reached its peak either at or not long after the election of 1912 and that a series of subsequent events, most notably the Wilsonian reforms of 1913–1916, the refusal of the Socialist party to support American entry into World War I, the socialist-Communist split of 1919, and the whole phenomenon of the collapse of Wilsonian idealism and the return to prosperity of the 1920's were all important factors in that decline. But there is considerable disagreement as to just which of these factors was the most important and as to just when, in time, the main movement toward decline began. James Weinstein's book entitled

The Decline of Socialism in America, 1912–1925 takes the view that there was "no serious decline after 1912; the Party grew in strength and popularity during the war." "Socialist trade unionists," he argues, "played an increasingly prominent role in the Party during these years, and the Party seems to have developed greater solidarity with the labor movement. If one is to find a substantial decline of socialism in the trade unions, it must be after the United States entered the war, in April 1917." [31]

Weinstein bases this view on limited and rather fragmented evidence. When one examines carefully the change of heart which took place between 1912 and 1916 in virtually all the socialist trade-unions examined in the present book, his view is not borne out. Once Woodrow Wilson had been elected and had begun to enact the series of social reforms for which his first administration became famous (the Clayton Act, the La Follette Seaman's Act, the appointment of the first Secretary of Labor, and so on), virtually all the unions considered in this sample began immediately to turn away from their earlier political support of the Socialist party and to align themselves with the Democrats. For the socialist element in the trade-unions, American entry into World War I simply served to confirm a trend toward conservatism and conformity which had begun several years before.

The Socialist party included many other elements besides trade-unionists, and it does not follow, simply because of the loss of trade-union support, that the party as a whole went into immediate decline. But the evidence tends to confirm the view that such strength as the Socialist party was able to maintain after 1912, or more generally after the period 1912–1916, was largely composed of intellectuals, liberals, and middle-class elements who were dissatisfied with President Wilson or had some other cause for radical discontent. If one accepts the position that strong trade-union support is essential for a viable and successful independent political party of labor, the loss of trade-union support in the years after 1912 was an irremediable blow. On this point, I find myself in disagreement with Weinstein and in general agreement with earlier historians.

Last, the effect of increasing economic affluence in undermining support for revolutionary behavior must be emphasized. This has been remarked upon in general terms by a number of social scientists and historians,[32] but not in relation to specific industries and trade-unions. The years between 1873 and 1896 were, with some exceptions, a period of depression in American industry, resulting in severe difficulties for the trade-union movement and in a corresponding increase in third-party political activity.[33] In this period money wages in several of the industries examined in this sample, notably in the garment industry, coal mining, and shoemaking, were either static or actively in decline. It is true that this was not always the case with real wages, representing the purchasing power of the dollar, which in some cases rose rather than declined. But it is problematical whether a cut in money wages, which was overt and immediate in its impact, did not have a more important effect in inducing radical sentiments than a long-term, and often concealed, rise in purchasing power did in diminishing them.

At all events, it seems clear that the return to prosperity in the years after 1896, coupled with the increasing economic success of trade-unions, had a profound effect in undermining the militancy and radicalism of those who had formerly held socialist opinions.[34] This was particularly true in the case of the Boot and Shoe Workers Union, where the period of socialist influence coincided with a time of struggle and failure for the organization in the 1880's and 1890's, and the period of conservatism followed in subsequent prosperous years.

Moreover, once trade-unions had become successfully established as bargaining agents in these industries in the period after 1896, they were able to provide for their members not only a relatively high degree of economic security but also the prospect of a continuing rise in their standard of living. The economic activities of the American trade-union movement, the *Shoe Workers' Journal* wrote in January 1919, had helped to give American workers the highest standard of living in the world. "In our country not a few shoemakers working at the bench own automobiles, and this condition exists in other trades. Where else on earth can this be said of shopmen? It is not [a] labor party that we want, but more labor unionism." [35]

In those unions in which the impetus for third-party activism was partially motivated by noneconomic factors, socialist sentiment outlasted the improvements in labor's standard of living by a considerable number of years. The ILGWU obviously provides the best example of this kind of phenomenon. But even here, by the end of the period the effect of increasing economic security had begun to be shown. "It should never be forgotten," Morris Hillquit reminded the delegates to the 1924 union convention, "that the labor movement and your movement are not based solely on material struggles and material conditions. Of course, we want better material conditions; . . . but this is not the end. The labor movement is ever struggling for better and higher conditions of life, . . . for universal prosperity, and universal brotherhood, and for peace." [36] The ILGWU remained faithful to this vision of society longer than almost any other American trade-union. But until the return of radicalism to the labor movement in the 1930's it was almost the only one to do so.

IV

The evidence of this book suggests that although many of the traditional explanations for the failure of socialism in the American labor movement are valid, indigenous factors deriving directly or indirectly from the problems of industrialization in American society were more important than has hitherto been supposed. Technological innovation, the influx of cheap immigrant labor, a reduction in economic mobility occasioned by the increasing scale of production, competitive instability in industry followed by a period of rapid trustification, and the destruction of traditional crafts all helped to create discontents which were manifested, by a minority of workers at least, in demands for revolutionary change. These were no different from the causes which led to the growth of socialism in Europe.

Even in the period covered by this book, however, when the problems of industrialization were most acute, exploitation and proletarianization were clearly not the dominant factors in the American economy. To suggest this would be to fly in the face of what little we so far know in detail about the impact of industrialization on American society. New studies are now in progress which may confirm or overturn some of the generalizations attempted above. But as far as the cadre of trade-union members which we have examined here is concerned, it seems likely that it was indigenous factors, and in particular a variety of difficulties connected in one way or another with the process of rapid industrialization, which were primarily responsible for the incidence of radical beliefs. It is still unclear how far these factors affected the labor force as a whole.

Once this transition had been made, those factors which have traditionally prevented the development of a successful socialist movement in America once more became dominant. To put it another way, the intense strains created by the process of rapid industrial change, which in Europe served to accentuate profound divisions which already existed in pre-industrial society, in America found no such permanent roots in which to grow. In the end high wage levels, political pluralism, and the lack of a strong sense of class consciousness were strong enough to prevail.

Notes

1. For Thernstrom's views, see Stephan Thernstrom, *Poverty and Progress, Social Mobility in a Nineteenth Century City* (Cambridge, 1964), especially chapter 8.

2. See, for example, Frank Tannenbaum, *A Philosophy of Labor* (New York, 1952); Anthony Bimba, *The History of the American Working Class* (New York, 1927); Norman J. Ware, *Labor in Modern Industrial Society* (Boston, 1935); Philip S. Foner, *History of the Labor Movement in the United States,* 4 vols. (New York, 1947–1965), especially II, 279–300, 388–404; and III, 282–393. For a more recent discussion from the same point of view, see "The Corporate Ideology of American Labor Leaders from Gompers to Hillman," *Studies on the Left,* VI (November–December 1966), 66–96.

3. I previously subscribed to this view myself, but abandoned it as a result of further research. See John Laslett, "Reflections on the Failure of Socialism in the American Federation of Labor," *Mississippi Valley Historical Review,* L (March 1964), 635–651; Laslett, "Socialism and the American Labor Movement: Some New Reflections," *Labor History,* VIII (Spring, 1967), 136–155.

4. It tends to be assumed that Gompers himself was largely responsible for the antisocialist bias of the AFL. In fact, his views were shared by most other members of the Executive Council, including First Vice-President James Duncan, Second Vice-President John Mitchell, Treasurer John Lennon, and Secretary Frank Morrison. See *Proceedings, Twenty-fourth Annual Convention of A.F. of L.* (San Francisco, 1904), 193–202; *Proceedings, Thirty-first Annual Convention of the A.F. of L.* (Atlanta, 1911), 227–230, 255–257. See also Philip Taft, "Differences in the Executive Council of the American Federation of Labor," *Labor History,* V (Winter, 1964), 40–56.

5. The 1885 convention elected two acknowledged socialists, Henry Emrich of the Furniture Workers and Hugo Miller of the German-American Typographia, to the Executive Council. But no socialist sat on the Council after Emrich relinquished the treasurership in 1890, despite the fact that the socialists continued to poll more than one-third of the vote in convention debates for a number of years. See *Proceedings, Fifth Annual Convention of the Federation of Organized Trades and Labor Unions* (Washington, 1885), 19; Taft, "Differences in the Executive Council," *passim.*

6. In 1895 the AFL inserted into its constitution a provision that party politics of whatever kind "should have no place in the conventions of the A.F. of L." At later conventions Gompers frequently invoked this as a means of declaring socialist resolutions out of order. See, for example, *Proceedings, Twenty-fifth Annual Convention of the A.F. of L.* (Pittsburgh, 1905), 230; *Proceedings, Twenty-seventh Annual Convention of the A.F. of L.* (Norfolk, 1907), 219.

7. It must be remembered, however, that the defeat of Gompers for the

presidency and the high vote which the Morgan Program received in 1893–1894, were due as much to the depression, to the inability of some of the larger unions to be fully represented at the Denver Convention, and to general dissatisfaction with the AFL leadership as they were to socialist influence as such. Some commentators wrongly tend to attribute the socialist failure to poor leadership alone. See Foner, *op. cit.*, II, 298–299; Gerald N. Grob, *Workers and Utopia, A Study of Ideological Conflict in the American Labor Movement, 1865–1900* (Evanston, 1961), 176–182.

8. The founding convention of the party, held in July 1901, specifically repudiated the tactics of the DeLeonites and urged all socialists to "join the unions of their respective trades." "We recognize," the party declared, "that trades unions are by historical necessity organized on neutral ground, as far as political affiliation is concerned." See *Proceedings, Socialist Unity Convention* (Indianapolis, 1901), 529–530. Similar resolutions were passed at the party conventions of 1904, 1908, and 1912.

9. Foner, *op. cit.*, II, 280; III, 391.

10. Louis Lorwin, *The American Federation of Labor, History, Policies, and Prospects* (Washington, 1933), 48–50; Philip Taft, *The A.F. of L. in the Time of Gompers* (New York, 1957), xii–xiv, 163–182 ff.

11. Taft, *op. cit.*, xvi–xix, 63–83, 149–157, 225–231 ff.

12. This argument was not, of course, original to Perlman. The need for intellectuals to assume a leadership role in revolutionary movements has a long history in socialist theory, going back to Marx himself. For a useful summary of the issue, see Robert Michels, *Political Parties* (New York, 1959), 316–329.

13. Selig Perlman, *A Theory of the Labor Movement* (New York, 1928), 176. See also pages 49–65, 177–182, 280–283.

14. *Ibid.*, 182.

15. Richard Hofstadter, *Anti-Intellectualism in American Life* (New York, 1963), 282–288; *Shoe Workers' Journal*, XIII (October 1912), 5–6; John H. Walker to Adolph Germer, December 2, 1917 (John H. Walker Papers, University of Illinois Historical Survey). See also the article by Lyle Cooper, "The American Federation of Labor and the Intellectuals," *Political Science Quarterly*, XLIII (September 1928), 388–407. Writing in 1928, Cooper found some lessening of anti-intellectualism in the labor movement compared to the prewar period, a tendency which developed further in the 1930's.

16. Kenneth McNaught, of the University of Toronto, makes the interesting suggestion that radical third-party movements failed in the United States, not because American conditions were unreceptive, but because America "lacked an aristocratic tradition of eccentricity and intellectual discipline," such as helped in the formation of the British Labour party. The evidence above suggests, however, that it is possible to exaggerate the lack of potential allies in the aristocracy, just as it is possible to exaggerate the role of intellectuals. See Kenneth McNaught, "American Progressives and the Great Society," *Journal of American History*, LIII (December 1966), 504–520.

17. Marc Karson, *American Labor Unions and Politics, 1900–1918* (Carbondale, 1958), chapters 9 and 10.

18. On this, see also Adolph Sturmthal's perceptive "Comments on Selig Perlman's *A Theory of the Labor Movement*," *Industrial and Labor Relations Review*, IV (July 1951), 483–496. Sturmthal juxtaposes Perlman's view, together with that of Lenin in *What Is to Be Done?*, with the position taken by

the Marxist theoretician Georgii Plekhanoff, who argued that the revolutionary mentality of the working class develops primarily out of the conditions of capitalism itself and that intellectuals only serve to give it a scientific basis. Sturmthal adds the interesting observation that although intellectuals played an important role in the early stages of the European labor movement because of low levels of education and literacy (a factor which was, of course, far less relevant in the United States), there has been no visible decline in the political orientation of European labor because its dependence on intellectual leadership has decreased.

19. Daniel Bell, *Marxian Socialism in the United States* (Princeton, 1967), 5.

20. Louis Hartz, *The Liberal Tradition, An Interpretation of American Political Thought since the Revolution* (New York, 1955), 282. See also pages 244–248, 277–283.

21. In addition to this evidence of trade-union behavior, one can also cite the well-known pragmatism of the socialists when they won political power in Milwaukee, Butte, and Schenectady, or in various Massachusetts cities during this period. See Ira Kipnis, *The American Socialist Movement, 1897–1912* (New York, 1952), 358–364; Henry Bedford, *Socialism and the Workers in Massachusetts, 1886–1912* (Amherst, 1966), 174–180 ff. It is not suggested that the socialists would have been more successful had they been ideologically more consistent. If they insisted on third-party action, they were ignored. If they cooperated with other radicals to form a liberal coalition, as they did in 1924, or in 1968 when they joined with the liberals in the Democratic party, they lost their separate identity. Thus they were clearly on the horns of a dilemma. But it was a dilemma created by attempting to come to terms with the realities of the American political system, not by failing to do so.

22. E. E. Schattschneider, *Party Government* (New York, 1924), 67–93, 111–123. See also Norman Thomas, *Socialism Re-examined* (New York, 1963), 117–130.

23. In a recent article on the Socialist party in New York City, Melvyn Dubofsky has attempted to challenge the view, held by most historians of immigration, that recent immigrants tended to be hostile or indifferent toward movements for social and economic reform. His evidence confirms the view, however, that only the Jewish voters were drawn to the Socialist party in any numbers between 1900 and 1918; the Irish and Italian voters remained largely indifferent. See Melvyn Dubofsky, "Success and Failure of Socialism in New York City, 1900–1918: A Case Study," *Labor History*, IX (Fall, 1968), 361–375. For the more traditional view, see Oscar Handlin, *The Uprooted* (New York, 1951), 217–218 ff.

24. Richard Hofstadter, *The Age of Reform, from Bryan to F.D.R.* (New York, 1955), chapters 1–6.

25. Seymour M. Lipset, *The First New Nation, The United States in Historical and Comparative Perspective* (New York, 1963), 178.

26. For a general discussion of the role of belief in sustaining optimism about rapid upward mobility, see Seymour M. Lipset and Reinhard Bendix, *Social Mobility in Industrial Society* (Berkeley, 1960), chapter 3.

27. Lipset, *op. cit.*, 183.

28. Norman Pollack, *The Populist Response to Industrial America, Midwestern Populist Thought* (Cambridge, 1962), 1–24, 103–143 ff.

29. In many respects the career of John L. Lewis, although he was not a political radical, embodies better than that of any other American labor leader the process of *embourgeoisissement* which Michels describes. Although a brilliant trade-union organizer, Lewis was capricious, despotic, and somewhat vain; and the United Mine Workers of America under his leadership displayed in marked degree the oligarchic tendencies which it is the main purpose of Michels' book to describe. Michels, *op. cit.,* 297–315.

30. See Paul Jacobs, "What Can We Expect from the Unions?", in Irving Howe (ed.), *The Radical Papers* (New York, 1966), 262–264.

31. James Weinstein, *The Decline of Socialism in America, 1912–1925* (New York, 1967), x, 45.

32. See, for example, David M. Potter, *People of Plenty, Economic Abundance and the American Character* (Chicago, 1954), 91–127; Charles A. Gulick and Melvin K. Bers, "Insight and Illusion in Perlman's Theory of the Labor Movement," *Industrial and Labor Relations Review,* VI (July 1953), 528 ff.

33. For graphs illustrating the relationship between third-party voting and changes in the business cycle, see Murray S. and Susan W. Stedman, *Discontent at the Polls, A Study of Farmer and Labor Parties 1827–1948* (New York, 1950), 79, 81, 84, 90. Writing about the European economy in this period, where similar developments occurred, Adolph Sturmthal argues that the prolonged depression "gave the European labor organizations a long-lasting imprint. It made them susceptible to the idea that within the framework of the existing society permanent improvements in the situation of the working class were impossible." No such far-reaching consequences resulted from the American depression, partly because the class system was less rigid and the major parties were more amenable to change; partly because wage levels in the United States, although also subject to fluctuation, remained—even during a depression—in relative terms considerably higher than those in Europe; and partly, as Sturmthal himself points out, because the main manifestation of third-party activism in America, the People's Party, was anti-monopoly rather than anti-capitalist in its orientation. See Adolph Sturmthal, *Unity and Diversity in European Labor, An Introduction to Contemporary Labor Movements* (Glencoe, 1953), 35.

34. The extent to which collective bargaining was able to raise wage levels above those prevailing throughout industry generally is still somewhat unclear. The consensus seems to be by some 10 to 15 per cent. See Albert Rees, *The Economics of Trade Unions* (Chicago, 1962), 75–80; Arthur M. Ross, "The Influence of Unionism upon Earnings," *Quarterly Journal of Economics,* XXXVIII (February 1948), 241–259.

35. *Shoe Workers' Journal,* XXI (January 1919), 17.

36. *Proceedings, Seventeenth Convention of the International Ladies' Garment Workers' Union* (Boston, 1924), 115–116.

BIBLIOGRAPHY OF
UNPUBLISHED SOURCES

Printed sources provide the most extensive information concerning socialist and radical influences in the labor movement during this period, most notably trade-union journals, convention proceedings, and the labor and socialist press. Few trade-unions have preserved their records from these early years, and those that have are not always willing to grant the researcher access. The only trade-union headquarters which allowed me to consult their files were the Boot and Shoe Workers Union, the ILGWU, and the United Mine Workers of America. Some years ago the International Association of Machinists began negotiations to transfer their archives to the Wisconsin State Historical Society, but these have not yet borne fruit. Nevertheless, I am grateful to Professor Mark Perlman, of the University of Pittsburgh, who kindly allowed me to consult some of his material from their files.

The value of manuscript and document collections for the researcher in this field varies considerably. For the AFL and for the unions studied generally, the collections at the AFL-CIO headquarters and at the Wisconsin State Historical Society have already been well researched. Gompers' correspondence in the A.F. of L. Collection at Wisconsin has been largely stripped of controversial material, save for a few early letters, as Dr. Philip Foner noted in the preface to the third volume of his *History of the Labor Movement in the United States*. The Letterbooks of Samuel

Gompers in Washington are of some value, but more useful is his microfilmed Correspondence with Affiliates, which provides useful insights into the relations between individual trade-unions and the AFL. The Socialist Party of America Collection at Duke University is largely confined to post-World War I materials and contains very little on the labor movement as such. The Socialist Labor Party and Daniel DeLeon collections at Wisconsin are more useful, but they are mainly concerned with internal party matters. The Morris Hillquit Papers at Wisconsin contain almost nothing on the trade-union movement, although they are valuable for the study of socialism in general. Neither the Labadie Collection at the University of Michigan nor the I.W.W. Collection at Wayne State University contains much relevant material, save for largely complete runs of IWW newspapers such as *Solidarity* and the *Industrial Union Bulletin*.

For individual unions, the most extensive collection on the Brewery Workers Union available at the time of going to press is the collection of contracts and other official documents at the Industrial and Labor Relations School at Cornell University, few of which relate to radicalism or politics. The most valuable source for the Boot and Shoe Workers Union is the union archives in Boston, although the Thomas Phillips Papers at the Wisconsin State Historical Society contain a little material on cooperation in the early period. For the ILGWU, the Scrapbooks at union headquarters in New York are of some use, but there is very little relevant material in the Morris Hillquit collections at either Wisconsin or the Tamiment Institute. The most valuable material on the ILGWU in this period comes from the Louis D. Brandeis Collection at the University of Louisville, due to Brandeis' important role in negotiating the Protocol of Peace. No major collection is currently accessible for the International Association of Machinists, pending the time when its own archives will be publicly available.

For the United Mine Workers of America, the available material is extremely rich. The John Mitchell Papers, the John Brophy Papers, and the Mary Harris Jones (Mother Jones) Papers at the Catholic University of America are valuable for the whole period, although the Jones collection is small. These may be supplemented by the large Adolph Germer Collection at the Wisconsin State Historical Society and by the John H. Walker Papers at the University of Illinois Historical Survey. There is also a small collection of Duncan McDonald Papers at the Illinois State Historical Society in Springfield. The University of Colorado recently acquired a collection of Western Federation of Miners papers, but very little material from the early period has survived which is not already available in the *Miners' Magazine*.

In view of the detailed references to published sources in the text, unpublished sources only are listed here. A complete list of the collections consulted follows, together with a selection of unpublished theses and dissertations.

Manuscript and Document Collections

A.F. of L. Collection, Wisconsin State Historical Society
Socialist Labor Party Collection, Wisconsin State Historical Society
Thomas Phillips Papers, Wisconsin State Historical Society
Daniel DeLeon Collection, Wisconsin State Historical Society
Adolph Germer Collection, Wisconsin State Historical Society
Morris Hillquit Papers, Wisconsin State Historical Society
Letterbooks of Samuel Gompers, AFL–CIO Collection
Executive Council Vote Books, AFL–CIO Collection
Gompers' Correspondence with Affiliates, AFL–CIO Collection
Morris Hillquit Collection, Tamiment Institute
Eugene Debs Collection, Tamiment Institute
Terence V. Powderly Papers, Catholic University of America
Mary Harris Jones Papers, Catholic University of America
John Mitchell Papers, Catholic University of America
John Brophy Papers, Catholic University of America
Thomas J. Morgan Collection, University of Chicago
Western Federation of Miners Collection, University of Colorado
Louis D. Brandeis Collection, University of Louisville
Labadie Collection, University of Michigan
IWW Collection, Wayne State University
Socialist Party of America Collection, Duke University
Scrapbooks of Samuel Gompers, New York Public Library
Scrapbooks of ILGWU, ILGWU Archives
Scrapbooks of BSWU, Boot and Shoe Workers Union Archives
John H. Walker Papers, University of Illinois Historical Survey
Thomas J. Morgan Collection, University of Illinois Historical Survey
Duncan McDonald Papers, Illinois State Historical Society at Springfield

Unpublished Theses and Dissertations

Earl R. Beckner, "The Trade Union Educational League and the American Labor Movement" (M.A. Thesis, University of Chicago, 1924)
Hyman Berman, "Era of Protocol, A Chapter in the History of the International Ladies' Garment Workers' Union, 1910–1916" (Ph.D. Thesis, Columbia University, 1956)
Irving G. Cheslaw, "The National Civic Federation and Labor" (M.A. Thesis, Columbia University, 1948)
Martin A. Cohen, "Jewish Immigrants and American Trade Unions" (M.A. Thesis, University of Chicago, 1941)
Melvyn Dubofsky, "New York City Labor in the Progressive Era, 1910–1918:

A Study of Organized Labor in an Era of Reform" (Ph.D. Thesis, University of Rochester, 1960)

D. M. Feins, "Labor's Role in the Populist Movement, 1890–1896" (M.A. Thesis, Columbia University, 1939)

L. W. Fuller, "History of the People's Party in Colorado" (Ph.D. Thesis, University of Wisconsin, 1933)

Howard M. Gitelman, "Attempts to Unify the American Labor Movement, 1865–1900" (Ph.D. Thesis, University of Wisconsin, 1960)

Harold M. Groves, "The Machinist in Industry: A Study of the History and Economics of His Craft" (Ph.D. Thesis, University of Wisconsin, 1927)

Clifton H. Johnson, "The Western Federation of Miners, 1892–1906, A Study in Frontier Activism" (M.A. Thesis, University of Chicago, 1949)

William A. McConagha, "History and Progress of the United Mine Workers of America" (Ph.D. Thesis, University of Illinois, 1925)

Thomas J. McDonagh, "Some Aspects of the Roman Catholic Attitude toward the American Labor Movement, 1884–1919" (M.A. Thesis, Columbia University, 1940)

George Marshall, "The Machinists' Union; A Study in Constitutional Development" (Ph.D. Thesis, Brookings School of Economics and Government, 1930)

Edward J. Muzik, "Victor L. Berger, A Biography" (Ph.D. Thesis, Northwestern University, 1960)

Maurice S. Paprin, "American Labor and the Reform Movement" (M.A. Thesis, University of Wisconsin, 1941)

Peter Paulson, "The Western Federation of Miners, 1890–1910" (M.A. Thesis, Columbia University, 1957)

H. W. Perrigo, "Factional Strife in District No. 12, United Mine Workers of America, 1919–1933" (Ph.D. Thesis, University of Wisconsin, 1933)

Michael A. Plesher, "A Comparison of the Political and Economic Policies, and the Administration of the Socialist Party of America and the Socialist Labor Party of the United States" (Ph.D. Thesis, University of Pittsburgh, 1950)

Benjamin L. Roberts, "Jurisdiction Disputes between the Brewery Workers and Other A.F. of L. Affiliates" (M.A. Thesis, University of Chicago, 1936)

Lawrence Rogin, "Central Labor Bodies and Independent Political Action in New York City, 1918–1922" (M.A. Thesis, Columbia University, 1931)

Michael Rogin, "Voluntarism as an Organizational Ideology in the American Federation of Labor" (M.A. Thesis, University of Chicago, 1959)

Harry B. Sell, "The A.F. of L. and the Labor Party Movement of 1918–1920" (M.A. Thesis, University of Chicago, 1922)

Robert W. Smith, "The Idaho Antecedents of the Western Federation of Miners: Labor Organization and Industrial Conflict in the Coeur d'Alene Mining District of Idaho" (Ph.D. Thesis, University of California, 1937)

Alvah E. Staley, "History of the Illinois State Federation of Labor" (Ph.D. Thesis, University of Chicago, 1928)

J. B. Stalvey, "Daniel DeLeon, A Study in Marxian Orthodoxy in the United States" (Ph.D. Thesis, University of Illinois, 1946)

Edward D. Wickersham, "Opposition to the International Officers of the United Mine Workers of America" (Ph.D. Thesis, Cornell University, 1951)

Dallas M. Young, "A History of the Progressive Miners of America, 1932–1940" (Ph.D. Thesis, University of Illinois, 1940)

Alice Zipser, "The Attitude of the A.F. of L. towards Industrial Unionism" (M.A. Thesis, New York University, 1936)

INDEX